Due Process of Law
1932-1949

The Supreme Court's Use

of a

Constitutional Tool

By

VIRGINIA WOOD

LOUISIANA STATE UNIVERSITY PRESS

Baton Rouge

MANUFACTURED IN THE UNITED STATES OF AMERICA
BY THE VAIL-BALLOU PRESS, INC., BINGHAMTON, N. Y.

Due Process of Law
1932-1949

To

ROBERT S. RANKIN

Preface

Twice the Constitution spells out the guarantee that no person shall be deprived of "life, liberty, or property" by government without "due process of law." In these words found in the Fifth and Fourteenth amendments lies the Court's most prolific source of power to strike down national legislation which may be valid under the more specific clauses of the Constitution or state laws enacted to effect policies which the state deems essential for the social and economic well-being of its people. Likewise, here must be found the basis for protection under the national Constitution against state infringement of civil liberties and for the enforcement of the "rudiments of fair play" in proceedings before governmental agencies of a judicial or quasi-judicial nature.]In short, in this single phrase is included the potentialities of all the protection against government which the individual may need.

But the path of due process protection has not been straight. On the contrary, the line between what is and what is not due process has been a wavering one indeed. In 1918, Judge Charles Hough reviewed the Court's decisions under the due process clause and concluded that "The direct appeal of property to due process has failed. . . . The indirect appeal through liberty is still going on. . . . But it is dying. . . ." [1] Four years later, Professor Robert Cushman saw in the due process cases evidence that the Court was on the verge of self-abnegation so far as social and economic legislation was concerned.[2] But within three years after this prediction, the Court rendered its decision in the Gitlow case,[3] and Charles Warren bemoaned the "new liberty" ushered

[1] Charles Hough, "Due Process of Law—Today," *Harvard Law Review*, XXXII (1919), 218, 233.
[2] Robert Cushman, "Social and Economic Interpretations of the Fourteenth Amendment," *Michigan Law Review*, XX (1922), 737, 758.
[3] Gitlow *v.* New York, 268 U.S. 652 (1925).

in by it and the consequent wide extension of judicial power under the Fourteenth Amendment.[4]

In more recent years, due process has been described as "what the judges say it is" or the "approval of the Supreme Court." [5] Professor Felix Frankfurter, now Justice Frankfurter, spoke of the "blest versatility of due process" and implied that it was a cover-all phrase which could be used or not to limit any governmental action at the will of the Court.[6] Due process is no less versatile now than it was then.

Within the past two decades, twenty-one men have sat on the Supreme Court Bench. Each of these has had his private convictions of what should be protected by the due process of law clauses. Each has had some fields of activity in which he felt that the protection should be greatest. Each has, at one time or another, tried to make the weight of his convictions felt by implanting them in majority or minority opinions of the Court. Collectively these men have not been the proud possessors of any superhuman powers of insight to guide them in the decisions they made. This being true, one may expect that the meanings given to "due process of law" and to "life, liberty, or property" have been delineated within the bounds of the personal philosophies of the justices and in the light of social and economic situations within which they have been forced to make decisions.

Possibly not any term of the Court could be marked off as representing no significant interpretations of the Constitution. But certainly the records of some terms warrant a starring as landmarks in the development of our constitutional law. The decisions rendered in the 1932–33 Term places that period in the latter category. During that year the Court majorities indicated the beginning of a shift in the interpretation of the restrictive qualities of the two due process clauses. By the close of the 1947–48 term this shift had developed into a rather significant element

---

[4] Charles Warren, "The New Liberty under the Fourteenth Amendment," *Harvard Law Review,* XXXIX (1926), 431.

[5] See Edward S. Corwin, *The Constitution and What It Means Today* (Princeton, 1946), p. 186; and *Twilight of the Supreme Court, A History of Our Constitutional Theory* (New York, 1934), p. 89.

[6] Felix Frankfurter, "Social Issues Before the Supreme Court," *Yale Review,* XXII (1933), 476, 480.

in the course of constitutional law concerning the protection of individuals and their property. In more than three hundred instances the Court was called upon to weigh the conflicting interests and to determine if due process had been accorded. In such instances there was not the opportunity for the justices to avoid their difficult task by leaving the choice to other hands. The Court's awesome power entailed the duty to apply a vague legal concept to situations not faced by any previous Court. The concrete cases paraded before it under the due process banner involved some of the most significant aspects of the social and economic life of the nation and the rights of countless individuals. A review of these cases leads to the conclusion that the due process clause is not adequate to the task of protecting these rights. This will always be true, for due process is relative to other factors, which means that whatever protection is granted depends upon very subjective standards and considerations.

It is the purpose of this study to call attention to some of the attitudes expressed by justices in their attempt to apply due process requirements in actual cases. It is hoped that such a stock-taking will lead to a clearer understanding and appreciation of the difficulties of the task before the Court as well as the significance of its power to proclaim that due process of law has or has not been afforded in particular cases.

It would be impossible to mention individually all of those persons who have rendered immeasurable assistance in the preparation of this study. The following, however, deserve my special thanks: Miss Helen Oyler of the General Library and Miss Mary Covington of the Law Library of Duke University and Miss Sarah Lamar of the Lumpkin Law School, University of Georgia, for a more than generous use of their time in making available library materials; Miss Willie Weathers, Professor of English, Randolph-Macon Women's College, for reading the manuscript and suggesting revisions in style and composition; and Professor David Fellman, University of Wisconsin, for his valuable criticisms and suggestions.

V.L.W.

Table of Contents

I

Due Process of Law and
the First Amendment

In Gitlow v. New York,[1] 1925, Justice Edward Sanford, speaking for the Court, asserted: "For present purposes we may and do assume that freedom of speech and press . . . are among the fundamental personal rights and liberties protected by the due process clause of the Fourteenth Amendment."[2] Thus briefly the Supreme Court read in the due process of law guaranteed by the Fourteenth Amendment one of the rights protected by the First Amendment.

It was only assumed that the Fourteenth Amendment guaranteed freedom of speech, and Gitlow was held not to have been

[1] 268 U.S. 652 (1925).

[2] Ibid., p. 666. See Zachariah Chafee, Jr., The Inquiring Mind (New York, 1928), pp. 99–107; Chafee, Free Speech in the United States (New York, 1942), pp. 351–53; Herbert Walsh, "Is the New Judicial and Legislative Interpretation of Freedom of Speech, and of Freedom of the Press, Sound Constitutional Development?" Georgetown Law Journal, XXI (1932), 35–50, 161–91; and John Raeburn Green, "Liberty under the Fourteenth Amendment," Washington University Law Quarterly, XXVII (1942), 497, 512–20.

In Patterson v. Colorado, 205 U.S. 454, 462 (1907), the Court had "left undecided" the question of whether the prohibitions of the First Amendment were embodied in the due process of law clause of the Fourteenth Amendment. Again, in Gilbert v. Minnesota, 254 U.S. 325, 332 (1920), Justice Joseph McKenna "conceded" for the purpose of the case, "without so deciding," that freedom of speech was a natural and inherent right. Justice Louis D. Brandeis, dissenting, found it "difficult to believe" that the due process clause protected "only the right to acquire and enjoy property"; but on the record of this case, he "found no occasion" for deciding whether the law in question violated the Fourteenth Amendment. Ibid., p. 343. As late as 1922 the majority of the Court was still of the opinion that the due process guaranteed by the Fourteenth Amendment did not impose upon the states any restrictions about "freedom of speech" or the "liberty of silence." Nor was it thought to confer the "right of privacy upon either persons or corporations." Prudential Life Insurance Co. v. Cheek, 259 U.S. 530, 543 (1922).

denied any of his constitutional rights, for, said Justice Sanford: "... when the legislative body has determined generally, in the constitutional exercise of its discretion, that utterances of a certain kind involve such danger of substantive evil that they may be punished, *the question of whether a specific utterance coming within the prohibited class is likely, in and of itself, to bring about the substantive evil, is not open to consideration.* It is sufficient that the statute itself be constitutional and that the use of the language come within its prohibitions." [3] The constitutionality of the statute was considered in the light of the principle that the legislature of the state is the best judge of what measures are required for safeguarding the public welfare. The legislature had declared that the advocacy of anarchy or criminal syndicalism presented an imminent danger to the state. The Court did not question that decision. Justice Sanford said that the "clear and present danger" test did not apply in the circumstances of this case. He was of the opinion that such a test would apply only when there was a question as to whether the statements made *created or were likely to create* a danger to the state. In the present instance the state had answered that question in the affirmative for a specific class of utterances. If Gitlow's words fell within that class, they were punishable. The state had found that the accused advocated anarchy and the Court accepted that finding as conclusive.[4]

Justice Oliver Wendell Holmes, joined by Justice Brandeis, filed a dissent in which he stated his doctrine of "free trade in ideas" as follows:

> If what I think the correct test is applied, it is manifest that there was no present danger of an attempt to overthrow the government by force on the part of the admittedly small minority who shared the defendant's views. It was said that this manifesto was more than a theory, that it was an incitement. Every idea is an incitement. It offers itself for belief and if believed is acted upon unless some other belief outweighs it or some failure of energy stifles the movement at birth. The only difference between the expression of opinion

[3] Gitlow *v.* New York, 268 U.S. 652, 670 (1925). (Italics added.)
[4] *Ibid.,* pp. 670–71. See Chafee, *The Inquiring Mind,* p. 100.

and an incitement in the narrower sense is the speaker's enthusiasm for the result. Eloquence may set fire to reason. But whatever may be thought of the discourse before us it had no chance of starting a present conflagration. If in the long run the beliefs expressed in the proletarian dictatorship are destined to be accepted by the dominant forces of the community, the only meaning of free speech is that they should be given their chance to have their way.[5]

So far as freedom of speech was concerned, the only gain made by the Gitlow decision lay in the assumption that the due process clause prohibited the infringement of the right by action of the state. Had the Court taken this opportunity to determine independently whether the words complained of did actually create a danger to the welfare of the state, it would have been enabled to grant a somewhat effective protection to free speech.

Not until two years later, in Whitney v. California,[6] were the words of the Gitlow case cited as authority for the statement that the guarantee of liberty of the due process of law clause of the Fourteenth Amendment extended its protection to free speech and a free press. It is significant that in this case Justice Sanford implied that had the restrictions imposed by the state been found

[5] Gitlow v. New York, 268 U.S. 652, 673 (1925). The clear and present danger test was made by Justice Holmes in Schenck v. United States, 249 U.S. 45, 52 (1919). Of the decision in the Gitlow case, Justice Holmes wrote to his friend Pollock that "conscience and judgment are a little in doubt" as to the constitutionality of the New York law under which the conviction was made. "But the prevailing notion of free speech seems to be that you may say what you choose so long as you don't shock me." M. D. Howe (ed.), Holmes-Pollock Letters, 2 vols. (Cambridge, Mass., 1941), II, 162. Max Lerner, The Mind and Faith of Justice Holmes (Boston, 1943), pp. 289–91, says that as a philosophical concept Holmes's doctrine of free trade in ideas has a certain clear weakness. "One phase of emphasis in it tends toward the 'survival' theory of truth—the position that the idea which survives in the struggle of ideas is therefore the true one. This is a dangerous position at a time when the manipulation of symbols has become as highly organized as under the Nazi regime. . . . Another phase of Holmes' concept tends in quite a different direction—not the pragmatic view that what survives is the truth, but the idealist view that what is true will survive." (Quoted by permission of the publishers, Little, Brown & Company.)

Compare Holmes's free trade in ideas doctrine with Jefferson's statement in his First Inaugural Address: "If there be any among us who wish to dissolve this union or to change its republican form, let them stand undisturbed as monuments of the safety with which error of opinion may be tolerated where reason is left free to combat it."

[6] 274 U.S. 357 (1927).

to be arbitrary, unreasonable, or unwarrantable they would not have been upheld.[7] In the circumstances of the case, the law was said not to violate the due process clause and as applied to the appellant not to deny her the right of free speech protected by the Fourteenth Amendment. The legislature had declared that to be knowingly a member of an association which advocated the crimes described in the act in question involved so great a danger to the public peace that such membership could be punished under the police power of the state. The Court accepted this finding on the part of the state without inquiring as to whether it was justified.[8] Anita Whitney's crime consisted not of having spoken words which reasonably might have been thought dangerous to the state but in having attended an assembly at which things were said which evidenced an advocacy of criminal syndicalism on the part of the organization sponsoring the meeting. The fact that she did not leave the meeting was accepted as evidence of her support of the principles of the organization, and this was thought to be ground for her conviction.

Justice Brandeis was of the opinion that the clear and present danger test should be applied in this case. He reminded his colleagues that there could be no justification for a restriction upon an individual's freedom of speech unless the speech "would produce or [was] intended to produce a clear and present danger" which the state might lawfully seek to prevent. The Court had

---

[7] Ibid., p. 372. Chafee, Free Speech in the United States, p. 351, says that free speech profited from this decision "not only from the moral effect of the minority opinion but also from certain modifications made by Justice Sanford in the position he had taken in the Gitlow case."

[8] 274 U.S. 357, 362 (1927). Guilt by association first became a part of federal criminal law under the Alien Registration Act, 1940, 54 Stat. 670, 671. This part was found to be unconstitutional as applied to Harry Bridges in Bridges v. Wixon, 326 U.S. 120 (1945). This case involved the order for the deportation of Bridges because he was or had been a member of the Communist party. Here the Court said that "The doctrine of personal guilt is one of the most fundamental principles of our jurisprudence. It partakes of the very essence of the concept of freedom and due process." Ibid., p. 163. In Schneiderman v. United States, 320 U.S. 118, 154 (1943), the Court said, with reference to the denaturalization of William Schneiderman for allegedly having become a citizen fraudulently, in that at the time he swore allegiance to this country he was a member of the Communist party: ". . . under our traditions beliefs are personal and not a matter of mere association, and . . . a man adhering to a political party or other organization notoriously does not subscribe unqualifiedly to all of its platform or asserted principles."

committed itself to an interpretation of the Fourteenth Amendment which made "due process" applicable to "matters of substantive law as well as matters of procedure." So construed, said Justice Brandeis, due process of law extends protection against state invasion to all "fundamental rights comprised within the term liberty." Fundamental rights, it was said, surely include "the right of free speech, the right to teach, and the right of assembly." [9] Justice Brandeis' opinion is significant in the development of an extended due process protection of free speech because he urged the Court to investigate the situation in which the words were spoken and to determine independently whether within that situation the words "condoned" by Miss Whitney had created a grave danger to the state or were likely to create such a danger. But when would the danger be deemed "clear" and "present"? Justice Brandeis would answer that no danger flowing from speech can be deemed "clear" and "present" unless the "incidence of the evil apprehended is so imminent that it may befall before there is opportunity for full discussion." If, on the other hand, there is time to avert the danger or expose the fallacies through discussion and education, "the remedy to be applied is more speech, not enforced silence." [10] However, he felt compelled to concur with the majority, for the question of whether the situation existing in the state warranted such restriction was not brought before the Court.

On the same day, the Court rendered its decision in the case of Fiske v. Kansas,[11] in which, for the first time, the "assumption" of the Gitlow case became the basis of positive action. Fiske had been punished under the Criminal Syndicalism Act [12] of Kansas because he solicited membership for the Industrial Workers of the World. The only evidence presented in support of the state's finding that Fiske held and taught doctrines dangerous to the welfare of the state was a single statement taken from the preamble to the constitution of the I.W.W. It was assumed that the fact of his membership in that organization "tainted" his speech so as to bring it within the restrictive provisions of the law. The Court refused to accept this as sufficient ground for a conviction. It was

[9] 274 U.S. 357, 373 (1927).   [10] Ibid., p. 377.
[11] 274 U.S. 380 (1927).   [12] Kansas Laws, 1920, c. 37.

held that under the national Constitution utterances such as those made by Fiske were immune.[13]

This case is significant, not for the fact that it extended the scope of free speech to the content of the speech, but rather because it opened the way for the Court to go behind the findings of the state to determine if the situation actually justified the restrictive measures or the particular application of them in a given case. Only with a Court willing to make such an independent determination could there be any possibility of overthrowing a state conviction or giving any real protection to free speech.

In each of these cases, the Court had taken for granted that the due process of law clause of the Fourteenth Amendment guaranteed freedom of speech. By 1931 the Court had found that the existence of this protection was beyond doubt. In Stromberg *v.* California,[14] Chief Justice Charles Evans Hughes said that it had "been determined that the conception of liberty under the due process clause of the Fourteenth Amendment embraces the right of free speech. . . ." [15] Yetta Stromberg had been found guilty of having displayed a red flag in a communist ceremony at a summer camp. She was convicted under the California law which declared that the display of a red flag represented opposition to organized government and was, therefore, inimical to the state. The law was held by the Court to be an unconstitutional infringement of the petitioner's freedom of speech protected by the Fourteenth Amendment. The mere display of a red flag, thought the Court, did not necessarily endanger the public welfare. Since the decision in this case, the Court has held consistently that freedom of speech is a fundamental right safeguarded by due process of law.[16]

During the period 1932–48, the "speech" cases have raised issues which called for an interpretation of the term "speech" as well as the extent of the "freedom" guaranteed. The Court has taken the opportunity to expand the meaning of "speech" and "press" to include many different modes of expression and at the same time

[13] 274 U.S. 380, 387 (1927).　[14] 283 U.S. 359 (1931).　[15] *Ibid.*, p. 368.
[16] For a discussion and summary of the attitude of the Court in the speech cases of the twenties, see Herman Rosenfield and Harold Tanner, "Civil Liberties under the Roosevelt Administration," *Lawyers' Guild Review*, V (1945), 182–84; and Chafee, *Free Speech in the United States*, pp. 80–354.

to delimit the restraints that the state may constitutionally impose upon these freedoms, which have never been held to be absolute.

Previous Restraints and the Clear and Present Danger Test

In his *Commentaries* on the common law, Blackstone defines freedom of speech and press as the absence of "previous restraints" upon the content of the speech or publication.[17] This interpretation was generally accepted by the courts and was applied to protect the right to speak or publish insofar as a prior censorship was concerned. It did not withdraw from the state the power to punish speech if the written or spoken word was deemed injurious to the public welfare.[18] Thus the fear of subsequent punishment undoubtedly served as a prior restraint in many instances, especially where certain doctrines, political or social, were outlawed by the state.[19]

On the other hand, though the rights of freedom of speech and a free press are not absolute, restrictions upon their exercise are justifiable only for reasons compatible with the purposes of the guarantee itself. To avoid a rigid application of the restriction against previous restraints and at the same time to make possible the maximum degree of freedom of speech and press, the Court developed the clear and present danger test as a criterion of the validity of restrictions imposed by the states and Congress.[20] This test was a recognition on the part of the Court that there are instances when the state must be permitted to impose prior restraints and subsequent punishments upon the individual's right of free speech and press because of the nature of the information

[17] Sir William Blackstone, *Commentaries,* ed. St. George Tucker, 5 vols. (Philadelphia, 1803), IV, 151.

[18] For a discussion and criticism of the doctrine of previous restraints, see Chafee, *Free Speech in the United States,* pp. 9–30.

[19] For instance, the Court has not interpreted the "due process" or "free speech" clauses as prohibiting a state from outlawing the Communist party. See Herndon v. Lowry, 301 U.S. 242 (1937). This fact is commented upon by Charles Evans Hughes, *The Supreme Court of the United States* (New York, 1928), p. 164. See also Walton H. Hamilton, "The Jurist's Art," *Columbia Law Review,* XXXI (1931), 1073, 1084–85.

[20] For the implications of this test, see Giles W. Paterson, "A New Relation between Due Process of Law and the State Police Power," *Virginia Law Review,* XXIX (1943), 152, 166.

which may be divulged or the circumstances peculiar to a given situation. The clear and present danger standard was first enunciated by Justice Holmes in Schenck v. United States [21] in 1919. Here it was said that the test in every case is "whether the words used are used in such circumstances and are of such a nature as to create a clear and present danger that they will bring about the substantive evils that Congress has a right to prevent." [22] But whether the words complained of do create such a clear and present danger is a matter of degree and must be determined by reference to the facts and circumstances peculiar to each case.

Previous Restraints and a Free Press. In Near v. Minnesota,[23] which has been called the most important case dealing with freedom of speech and a free press since the adoption of the First Amendment,[24] the Court, for the first time, found that a state statute infringed the right of a free press guaranteed by the due process clause of the Fourteenth Amendment because it imposed a previous restraint upon a publication.[25] The Minnesota "Gag" law provided for the abatement of any publication of "malicious, scandalous, or defamatory" information. The truth of the statements published would be a defense only if they had been made with good motives.[26] In accordance with this law, the state court held the Minneapolis *Saturday Press* to be a public nuisance and issued a permanent injunction against its publication. The publisher was forbidden to publish any paper in the state except with

[21] 249 U.S. 47 (1919).

[22] *Ibid.*, p. 52. Justice Holmes had explained that ". . . the prohibition of laws abridging the freedom of speech is not confined to previous restraints. . . . But the character of every act depends upon the circumstances in which it was done." *Ibid.* Frank E. Horack, Jr., "Constitutional Liberties and Statutory Construction," *Iowa Law Review*, XXIX (1944), 448, 449, thinks that this test represents the "one constructive principle" which emerged from the tremendous amount of speech litigation during and following World War I. It was, in his estimation, the one exercise of calmness and good judgment.

[23] 283 U.S. 697 (1931). Chief Justice Hughes spoke for the Court. Justices Van Devanter, George Sutherland, James Clark McReynolds, and Pierce Butler dissented. For a discussion of the background of this case, see George Foster, Jr., "The 1931 Civil Liberties Cases," *New York University Law Quarterly Review*, IX (1931), 64-73.

[24] Chafee, *Free Speech in the United States*, p. 381; and Eberhardt P. Deutsch, "Freedom of the Press and of the Mails," *Michigan Law Review*, XXXVI (1938), 803, 849.

[25] See Chafee, *Free Speech in the United States*, p. 375.

[26] *Minnesota Laws*, 1925, c. 285, sec. I.

express permission, to be granted only on the condition that he not publish any articles which would reflect on the integrity of public officials of the state or city. When the case was brought before the Supreme Court, Chief Justice Hughes, speaking for the majority, held that the statute deprived the appellant of his right to a free press, which the Fourteenth Amendment guaranteed him.

The Chief Justice saw in the operation of the law the possibility of stamping out any publication which offered criticism of public officials,[27] and he pointed out that the purpose of the law was not punishment for past issues of the paper but rather suppression of future issues for offenses in the past.[28] In actual application, it was thought, the law puts a newspaper publisher who wishes to call attention to official misconduct at the mercy of a judge, because he, the publisher, would have to prove to that judge's satisfaction that the motives which prompted the publication were good.

The statute was defended by the state on the ground that it had been enacted to prevent scandals, breaches of the peace, and other evils which might occur as a result of such publications. But the Chief Justice explained that underlying the constitutional guaranty of a free press was the theory that an even more serious public evil would result from the state's authority to prevent publication. Consideration of the "violent reaction" of "organized defiant groups resenting exposure" could not of itself justify a previous restraint upon the individual's right to a free press. If such "legislative interference" with the "initial freedom of speech" were permitted, the constitutional guaranty of a free

[27] 283 U.S. 697, 713 (1931). Chief Justice Hughes spoke for the majority. Justice Butler, joined by Justices Sutherland, Van Devanter, and McReynolds, dissented.

[28] *Ibid.*, p. 712. The Court left open the question of the suit for libel as concerned past issues of the paper. Chief Justice Hughes said: "It has been generally, if not universally, considered that it is the chief purpose of the guaranty [of freedom of speech and of the press] to prevent previous restraints upon publications." However, "Subsequent punishments for such abuses as may exist is the appropriate remedy consistent with constitutional privileges." *Ibid.*, p. 713. Cf. Justice Frank Murphy's statement in Thornhill v. Alabama, 310 U.S. 88, 101–102 (1940), that "The freedom of speech and press guaranteed by the Constitution embraces at least the liberty to discuss publicly and truthfully all matters of public concern without previous restraint or fear of subsequent punishment."

press would, the Chief Justice thought, be reduced to a "mere form of words." The Court weighed the interests which might be served by the suppression of publications of a given category against the possible dangers of such suppression and found that the latter outweighed the former. Undoubtedly the Court took cognizance of the particular political situation existing in the state at the time and decided that this was not a bona fide attempt to protect the community against an evil which the state might legally take measures to avoid.

In the opinion of the minority the speech here proscribed was not of a kind to fall within the constitutional protection of the First Amendment. Free speech does not, says Justice Butler, cover libelous statements such as those published in the *Saturday Press*. The prohibition against previous restraints would not operate here, he thought, for the restraint is only in respect of continuing to publish something which has already been adjudged a nuisance.

Five years later the Court was called upon to consider the validity of a Louisiana tax on all newspapers of the state having a circulation of 20,000 or more copies per week and carrying advertisements. The law was challenged on the ground that it placed a previous restraint upon the publication and circulation of the papers and thereby infringed the corporations' rights of freedom of speech and a free press.[29] After a consideration of the origins and history of the prohibition against censorship, Justice Sutherland held that the previous restraint imposed by the operation of the tax was twofold. First, its effect was to curtail the amount of revenue realized from the advertising; and, second, its direct tendency was to restrict the circulation of the papers. These evils were said to be "plain enough" when one considered that if the tax were increased to a high degree, "as it might be if valid," it would destroy the advertising and the circulation.[30]

The Court found that "in the light of its history and present setting" the tax was not a revenue measure but rather a "deliber-

[29] Grosjean *v.* American Press Corp., 297 U.S. 233 (1936). Justice Sutherland spoke for a unanimous Court.

[30] *Ibid.*, pp. 245–46. Cf. Magnano Co. *v.* Hamilton, 292 U.S. 40, 47 (1934), in which the Court held that the tax was not invalid simply because it was so high that its operation would destroy the business. See J. A. Roberts, "Due Process and the Bill of Rights," *George Washington Law Review,* IV (1936), 347–50.

ate" attempt to restrain the dissemination of information.[31] In reaching this conclusion, the Court undoubtedly looked behind the scenes in the state and considered the political situation at the time the law was passed. The fact that the tax had been enacted only after a great amount of pressure had been brought to bear by the Long administration upon the state legislature, as well as the fact that only thirteen papers would be affected and that these were published by nine publishers, all of whom were actively opposed to the Long regime, were only parts of the "present setting" which possibly led the Court to invalidate the law.[32] Freedom of the press guaranteed by the First Amendment and the Fourteenth was said to "preclude the states from adopting any form of previous restraint upon printed publications or their circulation," [33] except where such publications would lead to a clear and present danger from which the states might constitutionally attempt to protect the public. No such danger was found to exist or likely to be created by the circulation of the papers, nor did the state allege that the law had been passed in an attempt to avoid such danger. Such restrictions, therefore, as the law imposed were held to be unjustified and invalid.

Here the Court recognized the corporation as the possessor of "liberty" protected by the due process of law clause of the Fourteenth Amendment.[34] In view of the fact that the Court might so easily have held this to be a deprivation of property without due process, it is significant that it chose instead to include the right to receive revenues from its advertisements as a part of the corpora-

[31] 297 U.S. 233, 250 (1936).

[32] *Ibid.*, p. 240; New York *Times*, February 11, 1936, I, 1:1 and 13:1. See Benjamin F. Wright, *The Growth of American Constitutional Law* (New York, 1942), p. 153.

[33] 297 U.S. 233, 249 (1936).

[34] *Ibid.* See Frederick Green, "Corporations as Persons, Citizens, and Possessors of Liberty," *University of Pennsylvania Law Review*, XCIV (1946), 202, 236–37; and D. J. Farage, "Non-natural Persons and the Guarantees of 'Liberty' under Due Process of Law," *Kentucky Law Review*, XXVIII (1940), 269–79. Cf. Justice Harlan F. Stone's concurring opinion in Hague *v.* C.I.O., 307 U.S. 496, 527 (1939), in which he states that the Civil Liberties Union, as a corporation, is not a possessor of liberty within the protection of the due process clause of the Fourteenth Amendment. Justice Sutherland reaffirmed the ruling that a corporation is not a "citizen" within the meaning of the "privileges and immunities" clause but held that such an organization is a "person" within the meaning of the "due process" and "equal protection" clauses. 297 U.S. 233, 244 (1936).

tion's liberty of press of which it was deprived by the operation of the law. Also, the right of circulation was held to be an essential part of the right to a free press. The prohibition against previous restraints became something more than a proscription of prior censorship of the content of the publication. It was interpreted to include any hindrance upon the circulation of the publication as well. Such restraints could be justified only by a showing that the free exercise of the right would create a clear and present danger to the community—a danger which the state might lawfully take measures to prevent.

Over a period of years, the Court has indicated that there are certain kinds of publications which may be enjoined by the state under its police power. It is said that the state may punish publications only when they create or *are likely to create* a clear and present danger to the public which the state has constitutional power to attempt to prevent.[35] In this category have been included printed matter advocating the overthrow of government by use of force or violence,[36] or endangering the possibility of a fair administration of justice in the courts of the land,[37] as well as libelous and defamatory statements.[38] In addition, the Court has said that obscene, indecent, and lewd publications were not intended to fall under the protection of the First or the Fourteenth Amendment.[39] It is observable that the first of these are punishable because they may cause widespread danger to the general public, and the state is permitted to protect its people from acts of force and violence of this nature. Libelous and defamatory statements may be proscribed and punished because they present the danger of ascertainable injury to an individual or group of

[35] See West Virginia Board of Education v. Barnette, 319 U.S. 624, 633–34 (1942).

[36] See Gitlow v. New York, 268 U.S. 652 (1925); Herndon v. Lowry, 301 U.S. 242 (1937); and Chafee, *Free Speech in the United States*, pp. 318–516.

[37] See Pennekamp v. Florida, 328 U.S. 331 (1946). The question of the existence of the danger has been so restrictively interpreted that newspapers have been substantially freed from the threat of contempt proceedings.

[38] See Near v. Minnesota, 283 U.S. 697, 712 (1931); and 19 *A.L.R.* 1470. Consult also Chafee, *The Inquiring Mind*, p. 108.

[39] See Chaplinsky v. New Hampshire, 315 U.S. 568 (1942). Here Justice Murphy added that "fighting words—those words which by their very utterance inflict injury or tend to incite an immediate breach of the peace"—are not protected from state prohibition by the due process clause of the Fourteenth Amendment. *Ibid.*, p. 572.

individuals which the injured person may not prevent. The last group—indecent or obscene publications—is not within the protection of due process of law because, said the Court, "It is well observed that such utterances are no essential part of any exposition of ideas, and are of such slight social value as a step to truth that any benefit that may be derived from them is clearly outweighed by the social interest in order and morality." [40]

But publications may be labeled "indecent" or "obscene" simply because they shock people, and the degree of their danger frequently is measured by the extent of their variance with conventional thought. Does this mean that the Court admits in effect a power of the state to prevent the publication and circulation or distribution of certain kinds of materials even though they do not create a danger to the state, only an annoyance? Some light may be shed upon the problem by the Court's opinion in the case of Winters v. People of New York,[41] in which it held unconstitutional the state law prescribing punishment for the publication or distribution of "any book, magazine, newspaper, or other printed paper devoted to the publication, and principally made up of criminal news, police reports, or accounts of criminal deeds, or pictures, or stories of deeds of bloodshed, lust or crime." [42] On its face the statute was said to be unconstitutional, for it impinges upon the area of freedom of press protected by the due process guaranty of the Fourteenth Amendment. The particular items proscribed apparently would not create any danger to the public which the legislature might seek to prevent. While heretofore the Court had implied that "freedom of press" of the First and Fourteenth amendments comprised freedom to communicate ideas and opinions—using the words to cover educative or informative ideas or opinions—Justice Stanley Reed stated specifically in the case at

[40] Chaplinsky v. New Hampshire, 315 U.S. 568, 572 (1942). See Chafee, *Free Speech in the United States,* p. 150. Justice Owen Roberts, speaking for the Court in Cantwell v. Connecticut, 310 U.S. 296, 310 (1940), declared that "Resort to personal abuse is not in any proper sense communication of information or opinion safeguarded by the Constitution, and its punishment as a criminal act would raise no question under that instrument." In Thornhill v. Alabama, 310 U.S. 88, 102 (1940), Justice Murphy spoke of the "area of free discussion guaranteed by the Constitution" which embraces all the issues about which information is needed "to enable the members of society to cope with the exigencies of their period."

[41] 333 U.S. 507 (1948).   [42] *New York Laws,* 1941, c. 925.

bar that the guaranty of a free press did not apply exclusively to the "exposition of ideas." [43] It was said that "The line between informing and entertaining is too elusive for the protection of that basic right. . . . Though we can see nothing of any possible value to society in these magazines, they are as much entitled to the protection of free speech as the best of literature." [44]

But this provision was included in the proscription of publications which are obscene and indecent, for, said the state court, "indecent and obscene" may include collections of "criminal deeds of lust and bloodshed" which are "so massed as to become vehicles for inciting violent and depraved crimes against the person." [45] The condemned publications need not urge or even suggest the commission of any crime nor need the element of conspiracy enter into the matter of the publishing or circulating. Winters, a bookdealer of New York City, was convicted under this section of the statute for having for sale a "certain obscene, lewd, lascivious, filthy, indecent and disgusting magazine entitled 'Headquarters Detective, True Cases from the Police Blotter, June, 1940.' " [46] The conviction, it will be noticed, was not based upon the possession or distribution of a paper obscene or indecent in the usual sense of the words but with one which was "obscene and indecent" because the stories included in it were "so massed" as to become vehicles of incitement to crimes against the person. Winters challenged the constitutionality of the statute as it was interpreted by the state in this instance on the ground that it was too vague and indefinite to meet the requirements of due process of law. Said Justice Reed, speaking for six members of the Court, "When the legislative body concludes that the mores of a community call for the extension of permissible limits (with regard to the punishment of acts of indecency and obscenity injurious to the public morals) an enactment aimed at the evil is plainly within its power, if it does not transgress the boundaries fixed by the Constitution for freedom of expression." But, he added, "The standard of certainty in statutes punishing for offenses is higher than those depending primarily upon civil sanction for enforcement." [47] Also, it appears that the Court will hold the state to more

[43] Winters v. People of New York, 333 U.S. 507, 510 (1948).
[44] Ibid.   [45] Ibid., p. 513.   [46] Ibid., p. 511, n. 2.   [47] Ibid., p. 515.

rigid standards of certainty when the vagueness complained of deals with free speech and a free press than when it concerns other types of action difficult to define. The ordinary individual must be able to look at the statute and ascertain its meaning and the boundaries of the action prohibited as well as the persons to whom it is applicable.[48] And so the Court must determine whether the proscription embodies an indefiniteness of such character that "men of common intelligence must necessarily guess at its meaning." [49] If the prohibition falls within that class, it does not measure up to the prerequisites of the guarantee comprehended by the due process of law clause of the Fourteenth Amendment. In the present case the statute was said to be of that nature and therefore in violation of due process, for, explained Justice Reed: "Even though all detective tales and treatises on criminology are not forbidden, and though publications made up of criminal deeds not characterized by bloodshed or lust are omitted from the interpretation of the Court of Appeals, we think fair use of collections of pictures and stories would be interdicted because of the utter impossibility of the actor or the trier to know where this new standard of guilt would draw the line between the allowable and the forbidden publications." [50] This is necessarily true, thought the majority, for the statute does not require that conspiracy to commit a crime be shown but only the printing or circulating of publications "that courts or juries may think influence generally persons to commit crimes of violence against the person." The phrase "so massed as to incite to crime" has no technical or common-law meaning, said Justice Reed, for this is not the usual connotation of the words "indecent or obscene." [51] Since no crime is defined in such way as to give fair notice to the individual and no definite bounds are fixed beyond which the state may not go, the section of the statute cannot stand.

Justice Frankfurter, voicing dissent for Justices Harold Burton, Robert H. Jackson, and himself, was of the opinion that just as the Fourteenth Amendment does not enact Herbert Spencer's *Social Statics*, it does not "enact the psychological dogmas of the

---

[48] *Ibid*. See the note entitled "Due Process Requirements of Definiteness in Statutes," *Harvard Law Review*, LXII (1948), 77-79.
[49] 333 U.S. 507, 518 (1948).   [50] *Ibid.*, p. 519.
[51] *Ibid*.

Spencerian era." But the dissenters are judging the statute as one intended to prevent crime, while the majority scrutinized the particular section in question as one embodying a definite restriction upon freedom of the press. To the dissenting members, the "uncertainty derives not from the terms of the condemnation, but from the application of a standard of conduct to the varying circumstances of different cases." [52] This leaves the courts of the land with the duty to see that in the application of the law to specific cases violation be established as precisely as possible before penalty is imposed. This is on the assumption that the statute, on its face, was not an unconstitutional restriction upon freedom of the press but that the violation might arise from the Court's interpretation of the statute. It would follow, it seems, that in this particular instance the Court of Appeals of New York has so interpreted the statute as to make it a violation of the guaranty of free press as embodied in the due process of law clause. But the minority in this case would say that the state has the authority to proscribe certain types of publications and that the legislature could not describe the particular kind of thing encompassed in the proscription in the more exact terms and therefore it should not be required to do so.

The Court and the legislatures are here faced with a problem much more difficult than that entailed in restrictions upon other kinds of printed matter. To describe a book or paper as indecent or obscene may produce an emotional effect which possibly makes more conventional persons acquiesce in the prohibition of such a publication without much regard to the aptness of the adjective used or the threat engendered. But it has been said, by Justice Frankfurter, one of the dissenters in the present case, that restrictions upon freedom of speech and press "are tolerated by our constitution only when the expression presents a clear and present danger of action of a kind which the state is empowered to prevent and punish." [53] At that time, he felt that the state legislature did have authority within the Constitution to attain its purposes of unity by the method deemed preferable by the legislative body.[54]

[52] *Ibid.*, p. 535.
[53] Justice Jackson pronounced this as the ruling of the Court, Justice Frankfurter dissenting, in Board of Education *v.* Barnette, 319 U.S. 624, 633-34 (1942).
[54] *Ibid.*, p. 649. See the note entitled "The Supreme Court During the October

Again, as in the Pennekamp case, he objected vigorously to the application of the clear and present danger test "to express a technical legal doctrine or to convey a formula for adjudicating cases." [55] But it would be impossible to prove that the publications of the nature described in the section of the statute under which this conviction was made fall within the bounds of permissible restrictions. Crime is rarely just a matter of cause and result which can be drawn out in words but rather the result of an accumulation of factors which baffle even the experts. On the other hand, it is difficult to conceive of a reasonable person's assuming that certain types of stories, or even stories told in certain ways, do not influence some persons to commit crimes, given an attitude of mind susceptible to the suggestions. But this knowledge does not of itself bring the publication under the ban of a permissible previous restraint. Only one alternative remains to the legislature, namely, consider such publications "indecent" and "obscene," for those of that type have never found protection under the First and Fourteenth amendments.[56] When this course is followed, however, the question becomes whether the bookdealer is able to predict with a fair degree of assurance when the materials are so massed as to fall within the proscription. This takes us back to the original complaint—the vagueness of the terms of the statute as interpreted by the state courts. Certainly there are great possibilities of extending the prohibitions of such a law to comprehend almost any type of printed matter which does not meet with the approval of the Court.

Perhaps it would be less confusing, for purposes of future use, if the Court would cease to use the term "ideas" with the implication that it comprises only statements of a "knowledge imparting"

Term, 1942," *Columbia Law Review*, XLIII (1943), 837, 936–37; and Charles P. Curtis, "Due and Democratic Process of Law," *Wisconsin Law Review*, 1943, pp. 39–52.

[55] Pennekamp v. Florida, 328 U.S. 331, 369 (1946). See Thornhill v. Alabama, 310 U.S. 88, 98; and American Federation of Labor v. Swing, 312 U.S. 321, 326 (1941), where the benefits to society were said to "outweigh the private injury to the employers." Cf. Justice Frankfurter's approach to the same problem in Milk Wagon Drivers Union v. Meadowmoor Dairies, 312 U.S. 287, 293 (1941), in which it was said that the guaranty of freedom of speech was intended to protect "rational modes" of communications.

[56] See Chaplinsky v. New Hampshire, 315 U.S. 568, 572 (1942); and Chafee, *Free Speech in the United States*, p. 150.

nature. Though this seems to be the meaning of the word as used by the Court in many instances, in exceedingly few instances have the states made it the line of demarcation between permissible and forbidden publications. In the present case, freedom of press has been expressly extended to publications having no educative value for society. By so ruling, the Court has further delimited the restrictive power of the state and has once again required that a crime be defined accurately and precisely when it involves a penalty upon the exercise of freedom of speech or press. While the present case involves a publication which is said to have no value for society and one which perhaps would not even be missed if enjoined by the state, the principle entailed indicates more clearly than many of the speech and press cases the importance of a more defined boundary within which alone the state's restrictive power may operate.

The Right of Peaceful Assembly. In the case of De Jonge *v.* Oregon [57] the Court reiterated the clear and present danger test as the only justification for the state's interference with the right of free speech, a free press, and the right to assemble peacefully. De Jonge had been convicted under the Criminal Syndicalism Act,[58] which defined as criminal the teaching or advocating of criminal syndicalism in the state. The accused had not been found to have taught or advocated any of the things included in the state's definition of criminal syndicalism; rather he was accused only of having assisted in a meeting held under the auspices of the Communist party. Thus the only offense with which the appellant was charged was that of assisting in a meeting lawful except that it had been called by an organization which had as one of its doctrines the overthrow of the government by use of force. The party itself had not been outlawed by the state.

Chief Justice Hughes said that the Court might have disposed of the case on the ground that "Conviction upon a charge not made would be sheer denial of due process." He took this opportunity, however, to give an exposition of the right of freedom of peaceful assembly under the due process of law guaranteed by

[57] 299 U.S. 353 (1937).
[58] *Laws of Oregon*, 1933, c. 459, sec. 14, par. 3110–12.

the Fourteenth Amendment. He explained: "Freedom of speech and of the press are fundamental rights which are safeguarded by the due process clause of the Fourteenth Amendment of the Federal Constitution. The right of peaceful assembly is a right cognate to those of free speech and free press and is equally fundamental." [59] He went further, saying that the "holding of meetings for peaceful purposes" could not be proscribed. Nor might the state, consistently with due process, make mere participation in a "peaceful assembly" the basis of criminal charge.[60] The Court, however, recognized that the rights of free speech, press, and assembly might be abused and that the people, through legislative action, had the power to protect themselves against such abuse. But the legislative interference must strike at the abuse rather than at the right itself. The statute was said to be valid, but the application of it in this instance was held to be violative of the individual's right to participate in a peaceful assembly.

This decision did not indicate any great tolerance on the part of the Court for the Communist organization or for the doctrines of communism. The state did not show that De Jonge had discussed the principles of communism or that he had in any way advocated the use of violence at the meeting. The Court did not decide that mere membership in the Communist party could not be punished by the state, only that in this instance the statute applied had not sought to punish such membership.[61] It did hold, however, that if the state sought to punish "advocacy" of criminal syndicalism it must prove that the accused did advocate the proscribed doctrines. The mere fact of membership in an organization which advocates the use of violence and the overthrow of organized government could not be accepted as evidence against the individual unless such membership had been made criminal by law. In any trial on a charge such as the one made in this case, there is likely to be introduced evidence as to the seditious nature of the "communist" or "radical" principles generally. With the present attitude toward these principles, such evidence, if con-

---

[59] 299 U.S. 353, 364 (1937).   [60] *Ibid.*, p. 365.

[61] *Ibid.*, p. 362. Impliedly the state might have punished a member of the party "for participating in its organization or for joining it, or for soliciting members, or for distributing its literature," if membership had been outlawed by the state.

sidered by a jury, condemns the accused before he has an opportunity to prove his innocence. It was this kind of evidence to which the Court objected and which it declared invalid in the present case.[62] The state's determination that criminal syndicalism presented a danger to its welfare and was therefore punishable was left intact.[63]

Three months after the De Jonge case a Georgia statute prohibiting the teaching of, or inciting to the use of, violence for making political changes in the government was challenged in Herndon v. Lowry.[64] Here a Negro Communist had been arrested and convicted under the law because he conducted a meeting under the auspices of the Communist party. At the gathering, he discussed the living conditions among the Negro population. The Court declared the statute invalid on the ground that its provisions were too vague and indefinite to afford any ascertainable standard of guilt. The state had not proved that Herndon did advocate violence or did intend to incite to violence at the meeting. It had reached its decision and based the conviction upon a consideration of the "bad tendency" of the literature which was found in Herndon's possession at the time of his arrest.[65] Justice Roberts, expressing the views of the majority, said that the appellant's right to "address meetings" and to "organize parties" was

[62] See "The Supreme Court as Protector of Minorities," *Yale Law Journal*, XLVI (1937), 862–66.

[63] Edwin M. Borchard, "The Supreme Court and Private Rights," *Yale Law Journal*, XLVII (1938), 1051, 1072–73.

[64] 301 U.S. 242 (1937). Herndon had sought to have his case heard by the Supreme Court on two previous occasions. On the first, 295 U.S. 441 (1935), Justice Sutherland dismissed the case on the ground that no federal question had been raised in the state court. Justices Cardozo, Stone, and Brandeis dissented, holding that the Court should have decided the case on its merits. A second attempt was made, but the Court, without opinion, refused a rehearing, 296 U.S. 661 (1935). Herndon was then granted a writ of certiorari to the court of Fulton County on the ground that the constitutionality of the statute was never passed upon. Thus he had been given the opportunity to bring his case once more to the Supreme Court.
See Julian P. Boyd, "Subversive of What?" *Atlantic Monthly*, CLXXXII (1948), pp. 19–23.

[65] 301 U.S. 242, 260, 263 (1937). Justice Roberts, speaking of the rule followed in the Gitlow case, said: "It is evident that the decision sustaining the New York statute furnished no warrant for appellee's contention that under a law general in its description of the mischief to be remedied and equally general in respect of the intent of the actor, the standard of guilt may be made the 'dangerous tendency' of his words." *Ibid.*, p. 258.

protected by the due process of law guaranteed by the Fourteenth Amendment. That right, he said, could not be restricted *unless in exercising it Herndon violated some prohibition of a valid statute.* But the statute which appellant was held to have violated made "incitement" or "attempted incitement" to insurrection unlawful. Before the state could convict him on the charge of having violated the statute, it must prove that he "did so incite" to violence.[66] The majority held that since it was not proved that Herndon actually "urged violence" by speech at any meeting, his intent "to incite insurrection, if it is to be found," must rest upon his procuring members for the Communist party and his possession of that party's literature when he was arrested.[67] But the state had not defined membership in the party as criminal, and it had not shown that Herndon distributed any of the party's literature. Therefore, the conviction could not stand even if the statute had been valid.

Justice Roberts recognized the power of the state to place restrictions on one's freedom of speech; but, he said, the restriction "is the exception rather than the rule," and the imposition of a penalty "even for utterances of a defined character" is justifiable only because of a reasonable apprehension of danger to organized government or the welfare of the state. The Court reiterated its ruling of the De Jonge case, saying: "If . . . a state statute penalize innocent participation in a meeting held with an innocent purpose merely because the meeting was held under the auspices of an organization membership in which, or advocacy of whose principles, is also denounced as criminal, the law, so construed and applied, goes beyond the power to restrict abuses of freedom of speech and arbitrarily denies that freedom." [68] The majority did not find that Herndon's words resulted in, or were intended to result in, a public danger which alone would justify the restrictions imposed by the statute. On the other hand, Justices Van Devanter, Butler, McReynolds, and Sutherland thought that there was sufficient proof of an intent to incite violence to warrant a

[66] *Ibid.* Chafee, *Free Speech in the United States*, p. 392, says that the chief concern of the state was the fact that Herndon urged equality for whites and blacks.

[67] 301 U.S. 252, 259 (1937).

[68] *Ibid.*, p. 258.

conviction under the law. Herndon's intent to incite violence was said to create a clear and present danger to the state. Justice Van Devanter, as spokesman for the dissenters, urged that the Court examine the "words" in a case of this nature "with appropriate regard" to the "capacity and circumstances" of the listeners. Herndon's listeners, it was said, were all Negroes who because of their social and economic position would be easily swayed by his words. This, Justice Van Devanter thought, was a factor which the state had a right to consider in determining whether a clear and present danger had been created or was likely to result from the words spoken.[69]

This decision, though it overthrew the criminal-syndicalism law of the state, cannot be taken as indication that the Court has changed its policy of upholding such statutes. Had the provisions of the statute not been couched in such general terms that no crime was actually defined, the Court might not have invalidated it. While it is significant that the clear and present danger test was here expressly reaffirmed, the decision did not add to the right of "radical" political groups to preach their doctrines, for the ruling rested in large part on the failure of the state to prove that Herndon did preach the doctrines of the Communist party or distribute its literature. It did, however, narrow the interpretation of "intent." The fact that Herndon had party literature which undoubtedly he did intend to distribute was held not to be sufficient evidence that he "intended" to "incite" in such a manner as to endanger the state. The Court specifically stated that it did not pass on the question of the state's right to make membership in the party per se criminal.[70]

The Court made a significant restriction upon the state's power in Thomas v. Collins [71] by holding that "As a matter of principle a requirement of registration of labor organizers would seem generally incompatible with an exercise of the rights of free speech and assembly." [72] A Texas statute required labor organizers to

[69] *Ibid.*, pp. 276–77.
[70] *Ibid.*, p. 260. It must be remembered that Georgia had not made membership in the Communist party a crime by reason of the "bad tendency" of its doctrines. See Borchard, "The Supreme Court and Private Rights," *loc. cit.*, pp. 1051, 1073.
[71] 323 U.S. 516 (1944).   [72] *Ibid.*, p. 539.

register and to receive an identification card before soliciting membership for a labor organization in the state. The Court held that to justify such a restriction on the freedom of speech and the right of assembly, the public interest must be threatened by a clear and present danger, not by a danger "still remote" or "doubtful." The "rational connection" between the remedy and the evil to be corrected, which in many spheres of activity would satisfy the requirements of due process of law, does not suffice when the issue involved is the right of free speech and press. Justice Wiley Rutledge interpreted the clear and present danger test to mean that "Only the gravest abuses, endangering paramount interests, give occasion for permissible limitation." [73]

The state based its contention that Thomas incited others to violence on the fact that he solicited membership for the union. But since, under federal law, the workers had a right to organize, solicitation without actual incitement was not punishable by the state. Moreover, Justice Rutledge said that any speech other than a "philosophical discussion" of the subject would, under the state law, be solicitation; for the very fact that a man spoke in favor of a union was of itself solicitation—or might be so interpreted by his hearers.[74] But, it was said, the "free speech" guaranteed by the due process clause of the Fourteenth Amendment is speech "persuading to action." [75] The labor organizer, said Justice Rutledge, was not to be given a greater freedom than other speakers, only an opportunity to present his side of the issue. If the Texas statute were enforced, he would be put at a disadvantage in relation to other speakers, for the regulation applied specifically to labor organizers. Once again the Court emphasized the fact that those rights guaranteed by the First and Fourteenth amendments were to be guarded more carefully than other rights protected by due process of law, for the former "are great and indispensable democratic freedoms." They may be restricted only when there

[73] *Ibid.,* p. 530. See Prince *v.* Massachusetts, 321 U.S. 158, 161 (1944), *supra,* p. 69. This represents the opinion of only four members of the Court, for Justice Jackson agreed with the opinion of Justice Rutledge only to the extent of admitting that the action here involved fell in the category of "speech" rather than of practicing a vocation as a solicitor.
[74] 323 U.S. 516, 535 (1944).
[75] *Ibid.,* p. 537. See Cantwell *v.* Connecticut, 310 U.S. 296, 310 (1940).

is evident a clear and present danger to the community, while the latter may be limited when there is a "rational basis" for the state's action.[76]

That the Court, along with other thinking citizens, needs to reconsider and redefine the free-speech guarantee is forcefully demonstrated by the Terminiello case in 1949.[77] Terminiello, falsely represented as a Catholic priest in good standing, was brought from Birmingham, Alabama, to address an assembly called by Gerald L. K. Smith, a well-known advocate of racial discrimination. The meeting hall was crowded with people who for one reason or another wanted to hear the speaker, and the streets outside were seething with persons who wanted to prevent the speaking. Terminiello's speech, if one might grace what he had to say with that term, was at most a vicious, unreasoning attack upon Jews, Negroes, Roosevelts, Wallaces, and anything else which seemed to oppose him. The speaker's words aroused those who heard to anger but not to action against the crowds outside. His very presence infuriated the people outside to such an extent that rocks were hurled, windows broken, and seventeen persons arrested. Later Terminiello was arrested and charged with violation of the Chicago ordinance which read: "All persons who shall make, aid, countenance, or assist in making any improper noise, disturbance, breach of the peace, or diversion tending to a breach of peace, within the limits of the city . . . shall be deemed guilty of disorderly conduct." [78] The speaker was found guilty and fined $100.

Terminiello appealed to the Supreme Court on the ground that

[76] *Ibid.*, p. 530. Justice Rutledge explained that it was "the character of the right, not the limitation, which determines what standard will be used" in testing the validity of the restriction. In his concurring opinion in the present case, Justice Jackson said that the decision guarantees the labor organizer far greater freedom than has been allowed to the employer. See Hill *v.* Florida, 325 U.S. 538 (1945), in which the Court held that a statute requiring each union to file a copy of its constitution, bylaws, and membership in any international union with the state secretary of labor imposed an unlawful previous restraint upon the union's activities and unconstitutionally infringed its rights of free speech and assembly.

[77] Terminiello *v.* City of Chicago, 337 U.S. 1 (1949). Justice William O. Douglas wrote the Court's opinion. Chief Justice Fred Vinson and Justice Frankfurter dissented primarily on the technicality by which the Court disposed of the case. Justice Jackson, joined by Justice Burton, dissented on grounds of the technical point as well as the Court's interpretation of free speech.

[78] *Rev. Code*, City of Chicago, 1939, c. 193.

the ordinance as applied to him was a violation of the due process clause of the Fourteenth Amendment. He insisted that his speech was constitutionally protected and that the imposition of the fine infringed upon that protection. The arguments of the state court rested upon the contention that petitioner's speech consisted of "derisive, fighting words, which carried it outside the scope of the constitutional guarantees." Justice Douglas, apparently speaking for Justices Hugo Black, Reed, Murphy, Rutledge, and himself, chose not to dispose of the case on that issue. It was, in his opinion, not necessary to determine whether actually the words of the speaker were within the protection of the First Amendment and due process clause because he found an infirmity in the ordinance, as construed by the municipal court, which made it unconstitutional as applied to Terminiello, regardless of the speech he made. The municipal court had construed the ordinance as touching speech which "stirs the public to anger, invites disputes, brings about a condition of unrest, or creates a disturbance. . . " Justice Douglas thought that such a broad interpretation of the law would certainly take in speech which was constitutionally guaranteed against infringement and that since he could not be sure that Terminiello's speech had not been punished, for instance, as "inviting dispute" he held the proscription invalid.

The majority's respect for freedom of speech meets with the approval even of the dissenters. But Justice Douglas perpetuates one of the uncertainties of the constitutional guaranty of freedom of speech. The Constitution, he says, protects speech "unless shown *likely* to produce a clear and present danger of a serious substantive evil"—an evil more serious than mere public inconvenience, annoyance, and unrest; and, he adds, "There is no room under our Constitution for a more restrictive view." [79] Any other view of the constitutional guarantee would, he explains, permit the standardization of ideas by legislators, judges, or other political groups. Actually it seems that the clear and present danger doctrine has permitted a large degree of such standardization. It is important, however, that in this case no such doctrine was applied to the speech complained of. The ordinance, it was found, could be applied to speech which merely invited dispute or

[79] 337 U.S. 1, 4 (1949).

stirred the people; and since that was true, it could not stand. The city was forbidden authority to punish Terminiello's speech.[80]

Chief Justice Vinson dissented because the Court had erroneously rested its case upon a technicality rather than upon the issue of the constitutional protection of free speech. Justice Frankfurter, in dissent, is as favorably inclined toward the protection of freedom of speech as the majority. What is "free speech" to Justice Frankfurter? "Freedom of speech," he explains, "undoubtedly means freedom to express views that challenge deepseated, sacred beliefs and to utter sentiments that may provoke resentment." [81] But he objected to the Court's disposition of the case on a technical point not before the state court or the Supreme Court.[82]

Justice Jackson's dissenting opinion hinges upon the principle that "liberty" and "order" are equally essential to democratic society. Apparently, if either is to give ground, he would place the preference with order. Therefore, the disorder among those outside the hall who could not possibly have heard the words of Terminiello are made the grounds for permissible punishment of the speech. To him, freedom of speech means: "Every person may freely speak, write, publish on all subjects, *being responsible for the abuse of that liberty.*" [83] But the effects of the speech frequently depend as much upon the listeners as upon the words spoken. In the case at bar the disorder aroused was among large numbers of people who did not hear the speech but who had been aroused before the speaker appeared at the meeting hall. True, they, or some of them, probably imagined correctly the general tenor of any speech made under the auspices of Gerald L. K. Smith. However, it seems unusual and even dangerous to make that the test of the permissible bounds of free speech.

But Justice Jackson would go so far as to say that it is the right of any American citizen to "advocate peaceful adoption of fascism

---

[80] See Thomas *v.* Collins, 323 U.S. 516, 530, 535 (1944), where it was said that "speech persuading to action" is protected by the Constitution.

[81] 337 U.S. 1, 11 (1949).

[82] Since Terminiello had not objected to the municipal court's construction of the ordinance and had not included mention of it in his petition to the Court, Chief Justice Vinson and Justice Frankfurter thought that it should not have been considered by the Court in the final disposition of the case.

[83] 337 U.S. 1, 29 (1949), citing Illinois Constitution, Art. II, par. 4.

or communism, socialism or capitalism." [84] His argument reaches rather dangerous proportions, however, when he implies that public intolerance may be the determining factor in whether or not the speech is constitutionally protected. Under this test, many speeches, such as Terminiello's, may be legally permissible but may nevertheless in some surroundings be a menace to peace and order because the words spoken are distasteful to some of those who hear. Justice Jackson explains, "When conditions show the speaker that this is the case, as it did here, there certainly comes a point beyond which he cannot indulge in provocations to violence without being answerable to society." [85]

Neither of the opinions written in this case serves to clarify the issue of constitutional protection for freedom of speech. In each opinion there are expostulations in praise of such freedom. In this respect there is nothing new here. The justices might do well to reread the First Amendment and see for themselves that it says there shall be "no law" which abridges freedom of speech. Further, they might consider that historically only a few kinds of speech were excluded from this protection, namely, libelous or slanderous words and lewd and obscene speech.[86] Terminiello's speech would not fall within either of these categories. It would seem that the solution of the problem here presented must lie in the willingness of the public to tolerate even obnoxious speech. Suppose no one had gathered outside the hall in Chicago? If no opposition had been offered, would not most of the force of the speech have been dissipated without any disorder? In spite of the fact that just such demonstrations of disorder have afforded Smith and his followers most of their sensational publicity, neither opinion in this case touches upon the possibility of permitting the local police to quell the riotous conduct outside rather than the speech inside.

Constructive Contempt of Court. The extent of one's freedom of speech and press with regard to the disposition of cases pending

---

[84] *Ibid.*, p. 32.   [85] *Ibid.*, p. 33.

[86] See Alexander Meikeljohn, *Free Speech and Its Relation to Self-Government* (Ithaca, N.Y., 1948); as well as James Lawrence Fly, "Freedom of Speech and Press," in Francis Biddle and others, *Safeguarding Our Civil Liberties Today* (New York, 1945); and Robert Cushman, "Civil Liberty and Public Opinion," *ibid.*

before the courts presents more difficult problems than most free-speech cases. It is recognized that the courts must have some protection against outside influences which may interfere with the administration of justice. But here there is the further difficulty of maintaining an impartial tribunal in order to afford justice to an accused, and at the same time of preventing infringement upon the right of freedom of speech and press without which the rights of the accused might easily become mere symbols. A fundamental right of the individual and the interest of society are involved on either side of the controversy. The courts have, for the most part, accepted and built upon the doctrine of "constructive contempt" as set forth in Blackstone's *Commentaries*. According to this doctrine, one may be punished for contempt for making remarks outside the court which will reflect upon the character of the judge or affect the manner in which he carries out his duty.[87] The method of summary punishment for contempt has been severely criticized because it allows the judge to be prosecutor, judge, and jury in his own case.[88]

Only once prior to 1941 had the Court had occasion to pass judgment upon the power of the courts of a state to protect themselves by the use of this summary procedure.[89] The facts of the second constructive contempt case, Bridges *v.* California,[90] may be stated briefly. Harry Bridges, labor leader on the West Coast, had been very much interested in the state court's decision that the American Federation of Labor rather than the Committee of Industrial Organization was the legal representative of the longshoremen. After the case was decided, but before the expiration of the time for moving for a new trial, Bridges sent a telegram to

[87] John C. Fox, *The History of Contempt of Court* (Oxford, 1927), pp. 5–15, indicates that Blackstone based his doctrine on the opinion written by a friend in the case of Almon but never rendered in court. See Eberhardt P. Deutsch, "Liberty of Expression and Contempt of Court," *Minnesota Law Review*, XXVII (1943), 296, 297–98.

[88] See James A. Doyle, "Free Speech and Fair Trials," *Nebraska Law Review*, XXII (1943), 1, 15; and Frank Swancara, "The Los Angeles Times Contempt Decision: A Reply," *Rocky Mountain Law Review*, XII (1942), 315–23.

[89] Bridges *v.* California, 314 U.S. 252, 267, n. 13 (1941), names Patterson *v.* Colorado, 205 U.S. 454 (1907), as the only previous case. Justice Black said that this case could not be taken as decisive on the point here involved, for the Court in the Patterson case "left undecided" the question of due process protection for freedom of speech.

[90] 314 U.S. 252 (1941).

the United States Secretary of Labor saying that if the ruling of
the court should be enforced there would be a strike and all of the
ports on the West Coast would be tied up. A copy of the telegram
was sent to the California papers. The California court held
Bridges in contempt for having published the telegram.[91] Along
with this case the Supreme Court heard that of the Los Angeles
Times-Mirror, which had been held in contempt of court for the
publication of editorials concerning two persons who had been
tried for attacking a nonunion man. The verdict had been given
by the jury, but the case was pending the judge's action upon a
request to release on probation as first offenders. The paper, at this
stage of the proceedings, published several articles telling the
judge that it would be "a big mistake" to release the "thugs." [92]
Surely no one would seriously doubt that both Bridges and the
Times-Mirror intended to influence the action of the judge. Both
alleged offenders challenged the right of the court to punish these
publications as contempts.[93]

The Court had to decide whether, consistently with the due
process of law guaranteed by the Fourteenth Amendment, the
state court could punish these out-of-court publications as contempts.[94] Justice Black, in rendering the decision of the Court,
declared that the clear and present danger test would be applied
here as in other speech cases. In his words: "History affords no
support for the contention that the criteria applicable under the

[91] Bridges v. Superior Court, 94 P. (2d) 983, 995 (1940).
[92] *Times-Mirror v.* Superior Court, 98 P. (2d) 1029 (1940).
[93] Interpreting the phrase in the federal statute limiting contempts to acts
"so near thereto," in Nye v. United States, 313 U.S. 33, 40 (1941), the Court said:
"If the phrase be not restricted to acts in the vicinity of the court but be allowed
to embrace acts which have a 'reasonable tendency' to 'obstruct the administration of justice' . . . then the conditions which Congress sought to alleviate in
1831 have already been restored." There was no statute in California authorizing
the court to punish for contempt. The proceedings were under the common-
law rule instead.
[94] Bridges v. California, 314 U.S. 252 (1941). See Leon Yankwich, "Freedom
of Speech in Prospect and Retrospect," *Southern California Law Review*, XV
(1942), 322–39; Ralph L. Crosman, "The Los Angeles Times Contempt Decisions: A Dangerous Holding," *Rocky Mountain Law Review*, XIV (1942),
193–202; Swancara, "The Los Angeles Contempt Decision: A Reply," *loc. cit.*,
pp. 315–16; Taoul Berger, "Constructive Contempt: A Post Mortem," *University of Chicago Law Review*, IX (1942), 602–42; and Max Radin, "Freedom
of Speech and Contempt of Court," *Illinois Law Review*, XXXVI (1942), 599–
620.

Constitution to other types of utterances are not applicable, in contempt cases, to out-of-court publications pertaining to pending cases." [95] He recognized the importance of protecting individuals in their right to criticize the administration of justice in the courts of the states. As a practical matter, he found that if courts were allowed to exercise an unlimited power to punish comments and publications as contempts, they could withdraw from the area of public discussion many topics of the greatest public interest. To the contention that had the comments been made after the final disposition of the cases, they would not have constituted contempts, Justice Black replied that he could find in the Constitution no suggestion that the freedom of speech and press guaranteed "bears an inverse ratio to the timeliness and importance of the ideas seeking expression." [96] Here it appears that Justice Black was not being exactly realistic in the light of the actual intent of the speech in this case.

In applying the clear and present danger test, Justice Black stated that "the likelihood, however great," that evil will result from the publication could not of itself justify a restriction. The evil must actually be "serious" and "substantial." Mere "legislative preferences," he said, will not transform a trivial matter of public convenience or annoyance into an evil of sufficient seriousness to justify a restriction of freedom of speech and press. He concluded, with regard to the test applied:

> What finally emerges from the "clear and present danger" cases is a working principle that *the substantive evil must be extremely serious and the degree of imminence extremely high before utterances can be punished.* Those cases do not purport to mark the furthermost constitutional boundaries of protected expression nor do we here. They do no more than recognize a minimum compulsion of the Bill of Rights. For the First Amendment does not speak equivocally. It prohibits any law "abridging freedom of speech or of the press." It must be taken as a command of the broadest scope that explicit language, read in the context of a liberty-loving society, will allow.[97]

[95] 314 U.S. 252, 268 (1941).
[96] *Ibid.*, pp. 268–69.
[97] *Ibid.*, p. 263. (Italics added.) Said Justice Black: "The same meaning attaches to the Fourteenth Amendment." *Ibid.*, n. 6.

Neither the telegram nor the editorials were found to have created a danger sufficiently serious and substantial as to fall within the ban of the court under such an interpretation of due process of law. Justice Black was of the opinion that the sending of the telegram was no more than the exercise of the constitutional right to petition the government. He did not consider the real complaint of the court. The judge had not found Bridges guilty of contempt because the telegram had been sent to the Secretary of Labor but because it had been published in the local papers.[98] The majority of the Court held that the proper function of the trial court had not been impaired by the telegram, for the judge must have known all along the attitude which Bridges would take toward an adverse ruling. As for the editorials, the Court said that the particular paper's position on the labor problem was well known throughout the state. The publications did not convey any theretofore unknown information or any unsuspected attitude. Since the paper only confirmed that which was undoubtedly known to the judge, Justice Black held that it did not necessarily have any effect upon the decision he would render. Therefore, the contempt proceedings were said to have denied the corporation due process of law by infringing upon its freedom of speech and press.[99]

Justice Frankfurter dissented, declaring that the public's interest in a fair and impartial administration of justice is of equal importance to its interest in the protection of free speech and press. He would not ban all criticism of court proceedings, but he would penalize an individual for any threatening or intimidating remarks intended to influence the court or which reasonably might be expected to influence the judge in the disposition of a case.[100] To

[98] *Ibid.*, p. 267.

[99] *Ibid.*, p. 273. In holding that the proceedings denied the paper due process of law, the Court, in effect, extended "liberty" of the due process clause to this corporation. Cf. the opinion of Justice Black in Connecticut General Life Insurance Co. *v.* Johnson, 303 U.S. 77, 88, 89 (1938), in which he urged that the due process clause did not extend its protection to corporations. Among commentators there is considerable dispute as to whether the decision in the present case can be viewed as admitting that an "artificial" person may be denied liberty within the meaning of the due process clause of the Fourteenth Amendment. The Court said, in deciding the two cases as one, that the constitutional issue was the same. It made no distinction as to the clause of the Amendment it applied in the two cases. See Grosjean *v.* American Press Corp., 297 U.S. 233 (1936). See p. 10, *supra*.

[100] 314 U.S. 252, 297 (1941).

him the difference between "reasonable tendency" and "clear
and present danger" as a criterion appeared too slight to have any
effect in this case.[101] Speech which has a reasonable tendency to
effect a given decision in a case pending before the court does
create a clear and present danger to the administration of justice.[102]

Once again Justice Frankfurter held that the Court should uphold the legislative policy of the state, which in this case, he
thought, favored leaving the challenged power vested in the
courts. Justice Black reminded his dissenting colleague that the
power to punish for constructive contempt of court which existed
in California rested not on legislative policy but on a common-law
basis. Neither the constitution of the state nor any statute vested
this power in the courts. To the contrary, the legislature had tried
to abolish the power, but the statute enacted for that purpose had
been declared unconstitutional.[103]

The Court's ruling that summary punishment for constructive
contempt could be justified only when the utterances or publications actually presented a substantial danger of immediate evil to
the state which it had the constitutional power to prevent is not
out of line with other decisions extending due process protection
to speech, press, and assembly. If the purpose in extending protection under the due process clause is to keep open the channels
of public opinion and the sources of information, surely the right
to comment upon court proceedings should be protected. As
was suggested by Justice Douglas in Nye v. United States,[104] if
the publisher libels the judge, he should be given a hearing before
a duly constituted court and punished according to the law. If
the criticisms are true, the judge should not expect to conceal
incompetencies and injustices by instituting summary contempt
proceedings against his critic. In view of the number of criminal
cases which have come to the Supreme Court because of alleged

[101] The reasonable-tendency test had been enunciated by Chief Justice White
in the case of Toledo Newspaper Co. v. United States, 247 U.S. 402, 421 (1918).
If the publication had a reasonable tendency to intimidate or influence the judge
in the disposition of a case, it could be punished as contempt.

[102] 314 U.S. 252, 299 (1941). Justice Frankfurter thought that the publications would most certainly have an effect upon the judge, since within the year
he must stand for re-election. For this reason the state was justified, he said,
in protecting the courts from this particular attempt to coerce the judge.

[103] Ibid., p. 261, n. 1.   [104] 313 U.S. 33, 53 (1941).

unfair proceedings in the state courts, it would seem that this right to criticize might well serve a useful purpose. On the other hand, the utterances of Bridges and the *Times-Mirror* were not of the usual critical nature. They were not designed to urge a more careful administration of justice but rather to insist upon a decision in keeping with the personal attitudes of the critics. Certainly it does not require great skill in the law to discern that the intent here was to sway the judge to render a given decision. In this respect the principle of a clear and present danger as the sole justification for a restriction upon the right to comment on cases pending before the court was dangerously interpreted and applied.

In the recent case of Pennekamp *v.* State of Florida,[105] Justice Reed, for the Court, said that in borderline cases where it is difficult to determine whether the publication did create a danger to a fair administration of justice "the specific freedom of public comment should weigh heavily against a possible tendency to influence pending cases." [106] Here the editor and publisher of a Florida paper had commented upon a judge's attitude toward the accused in several rape cases which were then pending in his court. The editor was especially critical of the court's willingness to dismiss such cases. Justice Reed said that such criticism would have only a remote effect, if any, upon the jury which eventually might hear the cases. The personal comments about the judge would or would not influence him according to his own personality and integrity. Whatever the influence exerted by the criticisms complained of, it was not of a nature to interfere with the fair disposition of the cases before the court. Here again the reason behind the Court's solicitude in the cause of free speech is stated in the words of Justice Reed: "When the door [of public comment] is closed, it closes all doors behind it." [107]

Justice Frankfurter, concurring with the majority, said that the real test in such cases is whether the comments did actually influence, or were likely to influence, a judge to render a decision or take an action in a pending case which he would not have made or taken had the comments not been made. "Forbidden comment is such as will or may throw psychological weight into the scales which the court is immediately balancing." [108] This is the test

---

[105] 328 U.S. 331 (1946).
[106] *Ibid.*, p. 347.
[107] *Ibid.*, p. 348.
[108] *Ibid.*, p. 369.

which Justice Frankfurter applied in the Bridges case. There he found it reasonable to conclude that the comments did, and were intended to, coerce the court into taking an action which at least the "commentators" thought it would not take otherwise.

From this decision emerges the rule that out-of-court publications may be punished only when they create an immediate and serious threat to a fair administration of justice. Such danger will be created if the comments concern cases actually pending before the court and if they are of a nature which would effect a given disposition of the case or a given action on any part of the proceedings which have not become final. Mere personal criticism of a judge does not create such a danger to the state as to bring the critic within the contempt power of the court. Nor will a state court's finding that a particular phase of a proceeding was pending at the time the comments were made preclude review by the Supreme Court. The Court reserves the right to determine independently, not only whether the litigation was pending, but also whether the criticism offered was of a nature to create a real threat to the fair administration of justice.

But the standards by which due process protection against constructive contempt will be judged was not settled by this decision, and the agreement apparently reached in it proved transitory. The issue was again before the Court in Craig v. Harney.[109] The question for determination by the trial court was merely which of two persons was entitled to a lease on a cafe building. The answer depended upon whether nonpayment of rent entailed a forfeiture of the lease held by Mayes. The judge refused to consider Mayes's offer of a postdated check actual payment, and upon the request of both parties he instructed the jury to find in favor of Jackson, the other party to the suit. The jury refused to follow his instruction and returned with a verdict in favor of Mayes. The judge rejected the jury's decision and instructed the jurors to reconsider the matter and find in favor of Jackson. After some bickering the jury complied with the instructions, stating that it did so under coercion. These activities were commented upon in three papers having a monopoly on news circulation in the community, at the time the judge was considering the case for rehear-

[109] Craig v. Harney, 331 U.S. 367 (1947).

ing. However, in reporting the court proceedings, the editors failed to mention the legal point upon which the case turned—a postdated check is not legally a tender of payment. Public opinion was aroused at least enough to cause some threat of action to bring the judge into line. The judge found the editors in contempt of court for having interfered with the fair administration of justice.

The editors appealed to the Court on the ground that the contempt finding of the trial court denied them the freedom of speech and press guaranteed by the Fourteenth Amendment. Justice Douglas spoke for the Court majority, upholding the contention of the editors. This opinion was based on the rather unreasonable assumption that an accurate reporting of the court proceedings and the basic facts of the case made no difference so far as criticism of the trial court was concerned.[110] The judge was said to have acted in a "high handed" manner and the result of the trial was described as a "travesty on justice." But, said Justice Douglas, "The vehemence of the language used is not alone the measure of the power to punish for contempt. The fires which it kindles must constitute an *imminent, not merely a likely, threat* to the administration of justice. The *danger must not be remote or even probable; it must immediately imperil.*" [111] Previously the Court had implied that the clear and present danger test should be reworded to mean that to be proscribed the publication must "create a danger" rather than "create or [be] *likely* to create" a danger to the public. This, however, is the most direct statement of the amendment.[112]

Justice Murphy concurred, declaring again that "A free press lies at the heart of our democracy and its preservation is essential to the survival of liberty." [113] Even the slightest inroad upon that freedom "tends to undermine the freedom of all men to print and read the truth." Justice Murphy expressed the opinion that the Constitution forbids a judge to punish summarily a newspaper editor for printing an unjust attack upon him or his method of

[110] *Ibid.*, p. 375. Justice Douglas declared that "it takes more imagination than we possess to find in this . . . report of a case any imminent or serious threat to a judge of reasonable fortitude."

[111] *Ibid.*, p. 376.

[112] See for instances Thomas *v.* Collins, 323 U.S. 516 (1945); and Radin, "Freedom of Speech and Contempt of Court," *loc. cit.*, pp. 599–620.

[113] 331 U.S. 367, 383 (1947).

dispensing justice. Such a threat of suppression was, he thought, outlawed by the provisions of the First Amendment.[114] Here again is the suggestion that if the editors have committed a crime they should be tried by regular court proceedings.[115]

Dissent was sounded by Justice Frankfurter, joined by Chief Justice Vinson. The dissenting opinion is significant for its statements concerning the method or scope of the Court's function as well as for its attitude toward the particular issue involved.[116] ". . . it would be a novel doctrine . . . ," said Justice Frankfurter, "to say that we must consider the record as it comes before us from a State court as though it were our duty or right to ascertain the facts in the first instance." [117] While the state court's findings would not preclude the Court's scrutiny of the facts upon which an appraisal of a constitutional right depends, the Court cannot "find a violation of a constitutional right by denying to a State its right to a fair appraisal of the facts and circumstances peculiarly its concern." [118] So far as Justice Frankfurter is concerned, if the Court bases its right or duty to make an independent finding of facts on the fundamental nature of the right in question, it might make such finding with regard to any right claimed under the Constitution, for "Every right claimed under the Constitution is a fundamental right." [119] This, in his judgment, the Court has no authority to do. The dissenters are opposed to the Court's maintaining that in principle there are instances where constructive contempt is within the power of the states and at the same time denying the state the right to exercise such power. "If it be deemed that the Due Process Clause put an end to the historic

[114] *Ibid.* Apparently Justice Murphy would read the Constitution to outlaw all summary contempt proceedings. "Any summary suppression of unjust criticism carries with it an ominous threat of summary suppression of all criticism. It is to avoid that threat that the First Amendment, as I view it, outlaws the summary contempt methods of suppression." *Ibid.,* p. 383.

[115] See Nye *v.* United States, 313 U.S. 33, 53 (1941); and Bridges *v.* California, 314 U.S. 252 (1941).

[116] Justice Frankfurter finds the question to be whether the Court would declare unconstitutional an act of the legislature of Texas if that representative body should pass a law saying that publications such as the ones in issue constitute contempt of court. If it would not so find, then why, he would ask, does it find the pronouncement of "Texas, speaking through its authoritative judicial voice," unconstitutional? Craig *v.* Harney, 331 U.S. 367, 385 (1947).

[117] *Ibid.,* pp. 390–91.   [118] *Ibid.,* p. 391.

[119] *Ibid.,* pp. 394–95.

power of States to allow summary proceedings for contempt by
interference with an actually pending controversy, or even if it
be deemed offensive to due process for the judge whose conduct
is called in question to sit in judgment upon the contemnor because self-interest is too great . . . such break with the past had
best be completely candid." [120]

Justice Jackson, recognizing that "the reasons we give for our
decisions are more important in the development of the law than
the decision itself," wrote a separate dissent. The basis of his opinion in this instance seems to rest upon the realization that "The
right of the people to have a free press is a vital one, but so is the
right to have a calm and fair trial free from outside pressures and
influences." He believed that the publishers in this case went
beyond a legitimate use of their freedom of press and impinged
upon the citizens' right to a fair trial. He questioned the assumption of the majority that "judges are made of sterner stuff" than
persons in other walks of life and are immune to public criticism
or popular acclaim.

Once again there becomes apparent the divergent points of
view from which the members of the Court look upon regulations
and actions which are alleged to impinge upon the freedom of
speech and press protected by the First and Fourteenth amendments. Yet the point of view may make the very significant difference between permitted and proscribed speech. An almost im-
perceptible line has been drawn to separate the allowable from the
forbidden uses of speech and press, but that line may also be the
point of demarcation between a society with the channels through
which it may be informed open and one which may have many of
the avenues of communication and expression closed. If, as at least
some individuals must have thought, the action of the judge in
the present case was unfair and unjust, what possible objection
to saying so in the papers could be raised? If the judge was so much
concerned about his position in the minds of the people in the
community, he should not act in such manner as to give rise to
adverse comment. One should bear in mind that the basis of the
editorials was an alleged unfairness in the trial.

[120] *Ibid.*, p. 394. Justice Frankfurter was of the opinion that a clear interference
with the administration of justice need not be demonstrated. *Ibid.*, p. 392.

From the three constructive contempt cases which have been before the Court since 1941, there does not emerge any very clear rule to be followed. Apparently publications must constitute an actual threat to the fairness of the trial before the publisher can be punished for contempt. "Reasonable tendency" or "likeliness" to impinge upon the discretion and judgment of the court is not enough to warrant proscription. The Court will determine when such actual threat has been created, and so long as the present majority remains, that determination will be made with a presumption in favor of freedom of speech and press.

PICKETING AS FREE SPEECH

Prior to 1937 the Fourteenth Amendment had been invoked successfully to prohibit anti-injunction statutes, for the employer was thought to have a kind of property right in the labor of his employees as well as in carrying on his business without their interference. To deny him the protection of the injunction in the event of picketing during a labor dispute was said to deprive him of property without due process of law.[121] Due process and freedom of contract had been applied in the defense of the employer with little or no consideration for the rights of the employees, who were left helpless so far as constitutional protection was concerned.

In 1937, Justice Brandeis found that "due process of law" afforded protection for the employees against injunctions insofar

---

[121] In Truax v. Corrigan, 257 U.S. 312 (1921), the Court held unconstitutional the Arizona statute which had attempted to legalize mass picketing. And in American Steel Foundries Co. v. Tri-City Trades Council, 257 U.S. 184 (1921), the Court unanimously held all picketing illegal. This opinion, however, must be read in the light of the stated purpose of a restriction upon this activity: "to prevent the inevitable intimidation of the presence of groups of pickets, but to allow missionaries." Felix Frankfurter, *Law and Politics* (New York, 1939), pp. 44–45, questioned the basis of the holding that "denial in labor cases of the extraordinary relief by injunction" deprived the employer of property without due process of law. Rather than finding that the Constitution protects fundamental rights, he was of the opinion that the Court should consider whether the "injunction relief" is actually a fundamental right. The injunction, first issued in a labor dispute in 1888, had by 1928 become "an immutable principle of liberty and justice." Frankfurter thought that this erroneous concept resulted from "abstract reasoning and canonizing the familiar into the eternal," and thus stereotyping the judge's limitations into constitutional limitations. *Ibid.*, p. 47.

as the right to picket was concerned. In Senn *v.* Tile Layers Protective Union,[122] he announced: "Clearly the means which the statute authorizes—picketing and publicity—are not prohibited by the Fourteenth Amendment. *Members of a union might, without special statutory authorization by a state, make known the facts of a labor dispute, for freedom of speech is guaranteed by the Federal Constitution.*" [123] In this case plaintiff challenged the validity of that section of the Wisconsin Labor Code [124] which permitted picketing. Under the provisions of the code, members of the Tile Layers Protective Union were allowed to picket Senn's premises to induce him to sign a union contract which would prevent his participation in the manual labor of his business.[125] Senn contended that he could not maintain his business under such conditions. Therefore, he contended that the statute deprived him, without due process of law, of his right to engage in an ordinary occupation.[126]

Justice Brandeis, for the Court, upheld the statute. He described the activities of the pickets as a kind of advertising comparable to the practice of merchants seeking customers by means of news ads or circulars. The state, it was said, had simply "put this kind of publicity on a par with advertisements in the press." He went further, saying that "Because Senn's action was harmful to the union in that it took work from union members, the union acted and had a right to act as they did, to protect the interests of their members against the harmful effects upon them of Senn's ac-

---

[122] 301 U.S. 468 (1937).

[123] *Ibid.*, p. 478. (Italics added.) For a discussion of the disadvantages of identifying picketing with free speech, see Charles O. Gregory, "Picketing and Free Speech," *American Bar Association Journal*, XXVI (1940), 709-15; Ludwig Teller, "Picketing and Free Speech," *Harvard Law Review*, LVI (1942), 180-218; and Eugene Kinder, "Peaceful Picketing Guaranteed by the Due Process Clause of the Fourteenth Amendment," *Michigan Law Review*, XXXIX (1940), 110-18. See also Louis Jaffe, "In Defense of the Supreme Court's Picketing Doctrine," *ibid.*, XLI (1943), 1037-59.

[124] *Wisconsin Laws*, 1935, c. 376, par. 5.

[125] 301 U.S. 468, 481 (1937). Senn was not eligible for membership in the union even if he did not contract, because he had not served the required apprenticeship. He did much of the work on his jobs, usually hiring only two or three helpers.

[126] Justice Butler, dissenting, said that the statute was a violation of due process in that it deprived appellant of his right to work. *Ibid.*, pp. 490, 491. Justices Van Devanter, Sutherland, and McReynolds joined in this dissent.

tion." [127] The fact that Senn's employees were not union members was thought to be immaterial. Here it appears that the right of the individual or the right of the group, the union, had to go. Justice Brandeis decided that the right of the group should stand. In so doing he came dangerously near the position that it was unlawful for the individual to compete with the union. The majority of the Court found that the Constitution did not forbid "unions to compete with non-union concerns for customers by means of pickets—as freely as one merchant competes with another by advertisements or window displays." [128]

The Court seems to have disregarded entirely the nature of picketing and to have assumed that free competition and picketing can go on at one and the same time, that pickets and picketed are equally situated insofar as such competition is concerned. It was said that Senn had a right to declare the facts of the labor dispute in such manner and in such detail as he deemed desirable and "on the strength of the facts to seek the patronage of the public." If the end sought by the union—to force Senn to cease working with his tools in the industry—is lawful, then, said Justice Brandeis, there are no constitutional grounds for saying that the picketing is not lawful. As to the lawfulness of the ends, he found "no basis for a suggestion that the union's request that Senn refrain from working with his own hands, or their employment of picketing and publicity, was malicious; or that there was a desire to injure Senn. The sole purpose of the picketing was to acquaint the public with the facts, and by gaining its support, to induce Senn to unionize his shop." [129] Thus the Court assumes that picketing is a legitimate kind of peaceful persuasion. The fact

[127] *Ibid.*, p. 481. Cf. National Labor Relations Board *v.* Virginia Electric Co., 314 U.S. 469 (1941), in which the Court indicated that under some circumstances the employer's freedom of speech might be taken away completely. See the note "Permissible Curtailment of Employer's Speech under the N.L.R.A.," *Columbia Law Review*, XLII (1942), 862–67.

[128] 301 U.S. 460, 478, 481 (1937). Gregory, "Picketing and Free Speech," *loc. cit.*, p. 714, says that "True liberals of this country no longer look askance at economic compulsion. But to call such coercion constitutionally guaranteed freedom of speech, thereby placing it beyond the reach of regulatory legislation deemed practicable by the majority, seems ridiculous policy and sheer misunderstanding of the concept under discussion." See Thomas McDermott, "Peaceful Picketing and Unfair Labor Practices," *Marquette Law Review*, XXVII (1943), 145, 152.

[129] 301 U.S. 460, 480 (1937). In effect the union was demanding a "closed shop."

that it inevitably involves a certain amount of economic pressure and coercion is not considered significant. Also, the Court ignored the fact that incidentally Senn would be deprived of a means of livelihood.[130] The identification of picketing with free speech in this case had the far-reaching effect of extending due process of law protection to picketing, even stranger-picketing. Thus the opinion indicates that that form of economic coercion is to be taken out of the category of a prima-facie tort in which the burden of proof of the lawfulness of the activities of the pickets falls on those participating. Rather there is to be a presumption in favor of the validity of the activities of the pickets, the burden of proof to the contrary being placed upon the employer concerned.[131]

Nor does the state have the right to prohibit an unincorporated labor union from picketing the premises of an employer to induce him to require his employees to join the union.[132] The employees had been asked to join and had refused. The Court did not discuss the legality of the purpose of the picketing, but it may be assumed that it was "lawful" picketing, since the state was not allowed to enjoin it.[133]

Following the lead in the Senn case, the Court held in Thornhill v. Alabama that "The freedom of speech and of the press guaranteed by the Constitution embraces at least the liberty to discuss publicly and truthfully all matters of public concern without previous restraint *or fear of subsequent punishment*." [134] The

[130] See J. R. Leffler, "Freedom of Speech—Right of the Employer," *Nebraska Law Review*, XX (1942), 65.

[131] This implication of the decision is commented upon at length by Ludwig Teller, *Labor Disputes and Collective Bargaining*, 3 vols. (New York, 1940), 1943 Supplement to Vol. I, 47–48; and Ira Schlusselberg, "The Free Speech Safeguard for Labor Picketing," *Kentucky Law Journal*, XXXIV (1945), 5–33.

[132] Lauf v. Shinner, 303 U.S. 323, 328 (1938). See T. Richard Witner, "Civil Liberties and the Trade Union," *Yale Law Journal*, L (1941), 621–35.

[133] Justice Butler dissented in this case on the ground that to allow a union to use coercive methods against other employees gave one group of workers too much power over the activities and rights of another. Cf. the action upheld in this case with the action of the city in the handbill cases, in which the Court held that to allow a majority to decide for a minority deprived the latter of due process of law.

[134] 310 U.S. 88, 101 (1940). (Italics added.) Justice Murphy explained: "Where regulations of the liberty of free discussion are concerned, there are special reasons for observing the rule that it is the statute, not the accusation or the evidence under it, which prescribes the limits of permissible conduct and warns against transgression."

Court declared that a labor dispute could no longer be looked upon as a private quarrel between worker and employer; it had actually become a matter of general public concern. Free discussion of the dispute by the employees was said to be *"within the area of free discussion* guaranteed by the Constitution," which embraces all issues about which information is needed "to enable the members of society to cope with the exigencies of their period." [135]

The statute in question was adjudged invalid on its face without particular reference to the activities or purposes of the pickets. Justice Murphy declared that such a law, *by its very nature*, would "lend" itself to harsh and discriminatory enforcement. For that reason there was said to be a "pervasive threat" inherent in the very existence of such a statute, which would result in a restraint on all freedom of discussion that might reasonably be regarded as within its purview.[136]

In neither the Senn case nor the present case did the Court withdraw from the state all authority to restrict or regulate picketing. Justice Brandeis had said that the state might "regulate the methods and the means of publicity, as well as the use of the streets." [137] He assumed that the Wisconsin statute authorized only peaceful picketing; and he interpreted "peaceful picketing" to mean "not only the absence of violence but the absence of any unlawful act." [138] In the Thornhill case Justice Murphy said that the Court, when determining whether free discussion had been infringed, should "weigh the circumstances" and "appraise the substantiality of the reasons advanced to support the challenged regulation." The limitation of the right would be

[135] *Ibid.*, pp. 101–102. (Italics added.) The Court cites Hague *v.* C.I.O., 307 U.S. 496 (1937); Schneider *v.* State, 308 U.S. 147, 155, 162–63 (1939); and Senn *v.* Tile Layers Protective Union, 301 U.S. 468, 478 (1937), as authorities for this holding. The statement of the Senn case is made the basis of the rule in the Thornhill case. William Murish, "Freedom of Speech in Labor Disputes," *California Law Review*, XXIX (1941), 366, 368, n. 5, thinks that the subject matter has become the thing protected rather than the act of speaking or the method.

[136] 310 U.S. 88, 97–98 (1940). John Raeburn Green, "Liberty Under the Fourteenth Amendment, 1943–1944," *Michigan Law Review*, XLIII (1944), 427, 456–57, thinks that this attitude on the part of the Court is very dangerous in view of the fact that picketing has been used to curb the free dissemination of information.

[137] Senn *v.* Tile Layers Protective Union, 310 U.S. 468, 478 (1937).

[138] *Ibid.*, p. 479.

justifiable, it was said, if it met the requirements of the clear and present danger test laid down in previous speech and press cases.[139]

In each of these cases the Court was called upon to balance the right of the pickets under the National Labor Relations Act and the due process clause of the Fourteenth Amendment against the property rights of the employer. In each instance it was found that the rights of the former outweighed those of the latter, and Justice Murphy was certain that "the danger of injury to an industrial concern is neither so serious nor so imminent as to justify the sweeping proscription of freedom of discussion." [140] Picketing, as free speech, was thus brought within the rule of Near *v.* Minnesota [141] and Herndon *v.* Lowry.[142]

On the same day, the Court handed down its decision in Carlson *v.* California.[143] Appellant challenged a municipal ordinance which made it unlawful for any person to carry or display any sign, banner, or badge in the vicinity of any place of business for the purpose of inducing or attempting to induce any person to refrain from purchasing merchandise or performing the services of labor. Here the Court, speaking through Justice Murphy, held that the ordinance violated the due process clause of the Fourteenth Amendment in that it placed a prior restraint on the exercise of the right of freedom of speech. It was said that the inexact words of the law "disclosed a threat to freedom of speech in-

[139] 310 U.S. 88, 96 (1940). Justice Murphy did not see that destruction of property or violence was inherent "in the activities of every person who approaches the premises of an employer and publicizes the facts of a labor dispute involving the latter." The criterion to be applied must be whether "the danger of substantive evils arises under circumstances affording no opportunity to test the merits of ideas by competition in the market of public opinion." *Ibid.*, p. 105.

[140] *Ibid.* But the Court did not find that the action of the state was arbitrary; rather it was said to be contrary to the policy of Congress set forth in the National Labor Relations Act. Thus the Court implies at least that Congress has the right to extend the speech protection with regard to one group, at the same time restricting it with regard to another. In Hill *v.* Florida, 325 U.S. 538 (1945), the Court held that the state law requiring labor unions to register and file certain papers with the state's secretary of labor was invalid in that it was contrary to the policy set forth in the National Labor Relations Act. See Joseph C. Owens, "A Study of Recent Labor Legislation," *Illinois Law Review,* XXXVIII (1944), 309, 316–17, for general remarks about this type of restriction.

[141] 283 U.S. 697 (1931). See the comment by Murish, "Freedom of Speech in Labor Disputes," *loc. cit.*, pp. 368–74.

[142] 301 U.S. 242 (1937).

[143] 310 U.S. 106 (1940).

herent in its existence." [144] Any doubt that the Court, in the Thornhill case, had intended to extend free-speech protection to picketing was dispelled in the present case by the statement that the carrying of banners was a "natural and appropriate" manner of disseminating information of public concern. It was said that the pickets were merely "publicizing the facts of a labor dispute in a peaceful way through appropriate means." [145] Such publicizing, "Whether by pamphlets, by word of mouth, or by banner must now be regarded as within that liberty of communication which is secured to every person by the Fourteenth Amendment." [146]

Probably the peak of immunity for labor in the exercise of the right to picket, insofar as the Court's decisions are concerned, is to be found in the ruling in American Federation of Labor v. Swing.[147] In this case the Court had to decide whether the state's common-law policy which forbade resort to peaceful picketing unless the employer's own employees were in controversy with him violated the free speech guaranteed by due process of law. Justice Frankfurter, for the majority of the Court, ruled that "Such a ban of free communication [is] inconsistent with the guarantee of free speech." [148] In effect the Court held that it would be unconstitutional as violative of due process of law for a state to forbid picketing in any situation except where the activity has been related to violence, libel, or threats thereof. The usual employer-employee relationship was held not to be a prerequisite for the exercise of the right to picket.[149] In this connection Justice Frankfurter said that "communication by such em-

[144] *Ibid.*, p. 112.
[145] *Ibid.* See William J. Bernhard, "Peaceful Picketing—Free Speech or Economic Weapon?" *Georgetown Law Journal,* XXXI (1942), 70–79.
[146] *Ibid.*, pp. 112–13.
[147] 312 U.S. 321 (1941).
[148] *Ibid.*, pp. 325–26. In Cantwell v. Connecticut, 310 U.S. 296 (1940), the Court for the first time held that the common-law policy or other nonstatutory action of the state might violate the guarantee of free speech embodied in the Fourteenth Amendment due process clause.
[149] *Ibid.*, p. 326. Justice Frankfurter said that the state could not exclude workingmen "from peacefully exercising the right of free communication by drawing the circle of economic competition between employers and workers so small as to contain only an employer and those directly employed by him." *Ibid.* See M. G. Ratner and N. J. Come, "The Norris-LaGuardia Act in the Constitution," *George Washington Law Review,* XI (1943), 428, 455–57.

ployees [not in the employ of the person whose premises are picketed] of the facts of a dispute deemed by them relevant to their interests, can no more be barred because of the economic interests against which they are seeking to enlist public opinion than could the utterances in the Thornhill case." [150] Picketing as a form of free speech was said to be basic to our society and the public benefit produced by it to outweigh the private injury to the employers.[151]

Those who read this decision and rejoiced that the struggle for constitutional protection of the right to picket had been won must have been confused as well as disappointed by the Court's pronouncement in the case of Milk Wagon Drivers Union v. Meadowmoor Dairies,[152] handed down on the same day. Here the Court, speaking again through Justice Frankfurter, placed limitations upon the rule of the Thornhill, Carlson, and Swing cases. In the first two of these cases it was implied, at least, that the states were left free to enjoin picketing under some circumstances, which circumstances were not defined. In the Swing case the Court had said that picketing closely related to violence and destruction was enjoinable by the state. In the present case, Justice Frankfurter reaffirmed the identification of picketing with free speech, but declared that it was enjoinable by the state in the interest of public welfare.

The power of the state to enjoin picketing was said to be derived from the power to prevent future coercion.[153] Justice Frankfurter traced the concept of free speech to the eighteenth-century belief in the efficiency of an appeal to reason. He found that freedom of speech was given wide scope to protect "rational modes" of communication. But he held that "utterances in a context of violence can lose their significance as an appeal to reason and become a part of an instrument of force. Such utter-

---

[150] 312 U.S. 321, 326 (1941). There was said to exist an economic interdependence of all employees engaged in the same industry, whether or not they worked for the same employer.

[151] See McDermott, "Peaceful Picketing and Unfair Labor Practices," *loc. cit.*, p. 152; and the remarks by Teller, *Labor Disputes and Collective Bargaining*, I, Supp., 1943, p. 56.

[152] 312 U.S. 287 (1941).

[153] *Ibid.*, p. 296. But Justice Frankfurter said that the ". . . right of free speech cannot be forfeited because of disassociated acts of violence. Nor may a state enjoin peaceful picketing merely because it may provoke violence in others."

ances were not intended to be sheltered by the Constitution." [154]

It is of significance that Justice Frankfurter did not withdraw all picketing from the scope of free-speech protection under the due process of law clause of the Fourteenth Amendment, but only that picketing which had ceased to be an exercise of the right of free speech and therefore had become something other than the kind of speech heretofore held to be protected by the constitutional guaranty. Such a general and indefinable standard, however, serves no really useful purpose other than that of justifying or rationalizing a particular decision. For the first time since 1937 the Court recognized a distinction between picketing and other modes of free speech. Picketing remained an exercise of the right of free speech but had become an even less absolute right than other forms of speech. Here a new criterion was set up for determining whether the right of free speech to the extent that it is embodied in the right to picket may be restricted by the state. The context within which the activity is placed will in large part indicate whether the picketing is simply another kind of "appeal to reason" protected by due process of law or an "instrument of force" falling outside that protection. In this case the due process of law concept was held to allow the state a discretionary power to enjoin even peaceful picketing when it would be justified in assuming that the past fear caused by the violence would survive. Justice Frankfurter held that the state might through its legislature withdraw the injunction from labor controversies "but that no less certainly the Fourteenth Amendment does not make unconstitutional the use of the injunction as a means of restricting violence." [155]

Here, the Court modified the status it had previously given picketing as free speech, or it failed to apply the rule against previous restraints as set forth in Near v. Minnesota.[156] In that case the Court had refused to permit the state to restrict future issues of a paper or the future exercise of the right of free speech and press because of the nature of past issues. In the Meadowmoor

[154] *Ibid.*, p. 293.
[155] *Ibid.*, p. 297. See Ratner and Come, "The Norris-LaGuardia Act in the Constitution," *loc. cit.*, p. 457.
[156] 283 U.S. 697 (1931).

case the state had not based its decision upholding the restriction on the existence of violence or the likeliness of violence in the future.[157] However, it was said that the state had not violated the due process clause in restricting the employees' freedom of speech because past violence had created an atmosphere of fear and danger of future violence. This case was distinguished from the Swing case on the ground that the ban invalidated in the latter was general, prohibiting "all free discussion by means of picketing, while in the present case the restriction was limited to the very narrow scope within which violence had actually existed." [158]

On March 30, 1942, the Court handed down its decisions in three picketing cases involving the power of the state to restrict the right of union members to picket.[159] The first of these—Bakery, Pastry Drivers and Helpers Union v. Wohl [160]—concerned the picketing of the premises of an employer not a party to the labor dispute. Members of the union of drivers engaged in the distribution of baked goods, in an attempt to induce the peddlers to work only six days a week and hire a union unemployed man at union wages on the seventh, picketed bakeries from which the peddlers obtained their goods and also the shops to which they delivered goods. The New York court had ruled that the picketing was enjoinable because there was no labor dispute within the meaning of the state labor statute. Justice Jackson, following the ruling of the Swing case, held that it was not necessary for one to be engaged in a labor dispute "as defined by state law" to have a right under due process of law "to express a grievance in

---

[157] See Justice Black's dissent, 312 U.S. 287, 300–301 (1941). See also the note in *Harvard Law Review*, LIV (1941), 1064–66.

[158] 312 U.S. 287, 297–98 (1941). For a discussion of the thesis that this part of the decision necessitates a modification of the status of picketing as free speech, see Teller, *Labor Disputes and Collective Bargaining*, I, Supp., 1943, p. 50. Logically, past violence is the chief evidence that a given kind of speech is "likely to create" a danger to the state.

[159] Two of these involved "due process of law." In the third, Allen Bradley, Local 1111 v. Wisconsin Employment Relations Board, 315 U.S. 740 (1942), Justice Douglas, speaking for the Court, held that the state's enjoining the picketing of the homes of nonstriking employees did not violate the National Labor Relations Act.

[160] 315 U.S. 769 (1942). See Ratner and Come, "The Norris-LaGuardia Act in the Constitution," *loc. cit.*, p. 472.

a labor matter by publications unattended by violence, coercion, or conduct otherwise unlawful or oppressive." [161] Applying the clear and present danger test, he could "perceive no substantial evil of such magnitude as to mark a limit to the right of free speech which the petitioners sought to exercise." [162]

Justice Jackson intimated that the Court would have upheld the injunction had the circumstances warranted a belief that danger to the general public would result from the activities of the pickets. For, said the Court, "The state is not required to tolerate in all places and all circumstances even peaceful picketing." [163] Also, it was implied that picketing might be enjoined if the Court did not consider its purposes valid and in the interest of the community. But upon an examination of the record, Justice Jackson found not "the slightest suggestion of embarrassment in the task of governance." Nor did he find any circumstances from which he could draw an inference that "the publication was attended or was likely to be attended by violence, force or coercion, or conduct otherwise unlawful or oppressive." Neither did he find any reason to believe that there had been any "actual" or "threatened" abuse of the right to disseminate information through this form of speech.[164] While the implication here is that had the state found that the picketing was for an unlawful purpose, it would have been permitted to enjoin it, Justice Jackson seems to have overlooked the fact that according to the law of the state the picketing in this instance was for an unlawful purpose. The result of the decision is that the Court, not the state, will determine in each instance whether the activities of the pickets are directed toward a lawful end, and if so, whether they entail any danger to the community.

[161] 315 U.S. 769, 777 (1942). Here the Court said that " 'since the dissemination of information concerning the facts of a labor dispute' is constitutionally protected, a state is not free to define 'labor dispute' so narrowly as to accomplish indirectly what it may not accomplish directly."
[162] *Ibid.*, p. 775. ". . . so far as we can tell, respondent's mobility and their insulation from the public as middlemen made it practically impossible for petitioners to make known their legitimate grievances to the public whose patronage was sustaining the peddling system except by means here employed and contemplated; and those means are such as to have slight, if any, repercussions upon the interests of strangers to the issue."   [163] *Ibid.*
[164] *Ibid.* See the note "Freedom of Speech and Secondary Picketing," *Yale Law Journal*, LI (1942), 1209.

In his concurring opinion in the Wohl case, Justice Douglas called attention to the fact that picketing was something quite different from other forms of free speech. Even peaceful picketing, he said, inevitably involves essentially coercive elements. Therefore, the exercise of the right to picket should be subject to restrictive regulations.[165] This opinion was followed by Justice Frankfurter in the second of the trio of picketing cases, Carpenters' and Joiners' Union v. Ritter's Cafe.[166] In brief, the facts of the case were these: Ritter owned a cafe in which he did not employ any union members. In another section of town and in no way related to his business he employed a contractor to supervise the construction of a building for him. The contractor hired non-union men to do the work. To induce Ritter to force the contractor to employ members of their union, the Carpenters and Joiners picketed his restaurant. Justice Frankfurter, speaking for the Court, said picketing is one of the "familiar weapons of industrial warfare," [167] and that while it is an exercise of the right of free speech, this ". . . does not imply that the *states must be without power to confine the sphere of communication to that directly related to the dispute.* . . . To deny to the states the power to draw that line is to write into the Constitution the notion that every instance of picketing . . . is necessarily a phase of the controversy which provoked the picketing. Such a view of the Due Process Clause would compel the states to allow the disputants in a particular industrial episode to conscript neutrals having no relation to either the dispute or the industry in which it arose." [168]

---

[165] 315 U.S. 769, 776–77 (1942). Justice Douglas said that "Picketing by an organized group is more than free speech, since it involves patrol of a particular locality and since the very presence of a picket line may induce action of one kind or another quite irrespective of the nature of the ideas which are being disseminated. Hence, those aspects of picketing make it the subject of restrictive regulation." Here, for the first time since the statement of Justice Brandeis in the Senn case, the Court recognized that picketing as an exercise of free speech may create difficulties not involved in other methods of communication.

[166] 315 U.S. 722 (1942).

[167] *Ibid.*, p. 725.

[168] *Ibid.*, pp. 727–28. (Italics added.) Justice Reed, in his dissent in this case, declared: "The philosophy behind the conclusion of the Court in this case gives to the state the right to bar from the picket lines workers who are not a part of the industry picketed. . . . The decision withdraws from the Federal Constitutional protection the freedom of workers outside an industry to state their side

The pickets had no dispute with Ritter, nor were they eligible to contract with him. Therefore, the Court held that the necessary "interdependence of economic interest" of picket and picketed was lacking.[169] When the right to picket as a phase of free speech was balanced against the duty and the right of the state to impose "reasonable regulations for the protection of the community as a whole" the former had to give way.[170] The mere fact that a labor dispute was involved in the exercise of the right of free communication was said neither to enhance nor lessen the scope of the free-speech guarantee.[171]

Both the Wohl and the Ritter cases involved secondary picketing. In the former the parties were a part of the same industry and the "unfair product" was being sold at a profit by the employer whose premises were picketed. The activity directed against a third party in that case was upheld because it seemed to the Court to be the only means afforded the union members to make known their grievances to the public. In order for the union to attain what the majority of the Court believed to be legitimate ends, it had to be allowed to solicit the support of the general public. Thus the right of the union, under the free speech protected by the due process of law clause, was said to extend to an attempt to force an independent bakery owner to sell only to union drivers. In the latter case there was no such close relation between the union and the cafe owner; but the issue of the existence of a labor dispute was the same in the two cases. The distinction which the Court made could not account for the difference in the results reached. The majority here again modified the status of picketing as an exercise of the constitutionally protected free speech, or it applied

---

of a labor controversy by picketing. So long as civil government is able to function normally for the protection of its citizens, such a limitation upon free speech is unwarranted." *Ibid.*, p. 739.

[169] *Ibid.*, p. 727. E. Merrick Dodd, "Picketing and Free Speech: A Dissent," *Harvard Law Review*, LVI (1943), 513, 528–30, sees in this ruling only a "geographic" limitation rather than an actual restraint on the activities of the pickets. See Ratner and Come, "The Norris-LaGuardia Act in the Constitution," *loc. cit.*, pp. 470–72.

[170] *Ibid.*, pp. 725–26. It was said that "While the right of free speech is embodied in the liberty safeguarded by the Due Process Clause, that clause postulated the authority of the states to translate into local law policies 'to promote the health, safety, and morals, and general welfare of the people.'"

[171] *Ibid.*, p. 725.

the clear and present danger test in a manner different from the application made of it in the previous case.[172]

For seven years the Court's decision in the Wohl case remained the law of the land. However, it did not offer a solution to the question of whether a state might, without running afoul of the due process clause of the Fourteenth Amendment, prohibit peaceful picketing which it finds to be an integral part of a conspiracy or combination illegal under state law. The implication of Justice Jackson's opinion in the Wohl case was that picketing for an unlawful purpose might be enjoined by the state. In the case of Giboney v. Empire Storage and Ice Company,[173] Justice Black, speaking for a unanimous Court, clarified the Court's present position on the issue. The facts of the case may be stated briefly. In Kansas City, Missouri, a truck-drivers' union controlled all except a small number of the ice peddlers. Also, they had agreements with all ice manufacturers, except Empire, whereby these agreed to sell ice only to union members. Union members picketed the premises of Empire in an attempt to force the owners to enter a similar agreement. Their picketing was enjoined by the court on the ground that the activities of the union constituted an attempt to force an agreement or conspiracy in restraint of trade and in violation of the state's law against the restraint of trade.[174] In this instance Justice Black approached the issue in a manner different from the approach followed in other speech cases. Heretofore, when the issue of freedom of speech was involved, the Court tended to scrutinize the law as though the mere

---

[172] Schlusselberg, "The Free Speech Safeguard for Labor Picketing," *loc. cit.*, pp. 18–19, is of the opinion that the former alternative furnishes the explanation of the decision. See Ratner and Come, "The Norris-LaGuardia Act in the Constitution," *loc. cit.*, pp. 470–71. Compare the statement in this case that other modes of communication were open to the employees with that of Schneider v. State, 308 U.S. 147, 163 (1939), to the effect that the freedom of speech cannot be prohibited at one legitimate place on the ground that it might be exercised elsewhere.

[173] 336 U.S. 490 (1949).

[174] *Missouri Rev. Stat.*, par. 8301: "Any person who shall create, enter into, become a member of or participate in any pool, trust, agreement, combination, confederation or understanding with any person or persons in restraint of trade or competition in the importation, transportation, manufacture, purchase or sale of any product or commodity in this state, or any article or thing bought or sold whatsoever, shall be deemed and adjudged guilty of a conspiracy in restraint of trade, and shall be punished as provided by this article."

question implied an invalid statute embodying a "pervasive" threat to the exercise of the right. But the statute involved in this case simply did not lend itself to that kind of approach. Such trade restraints as agreements or combinations not to buy or sell goods from particular persons or to attempt to dictate the terms upon which trade would be permitted have long been recognized as within the regulatory power of the state and national government. Hence, the statute is a valid exercise of legislative power. If there is any violation of the due process clause of the Fourteenth Amendment, it must be found in the specific application of the statute in this instance.

The issue, then, must turn upon whether or not the type of organization involved and the particular kind of activity engaged in would draw the cloak of immunity about it. Justice Black held, as he had in many cases not involving the speech issue, that labor unions were not *ipso facto* immune to the application of anti-trade-restraint laws; [175] that if such immunity exists, it depends upon specific legislative enactment.[176] The union was not allowed to defend itself by the plea that its actions were in behalf of better wages and working conditions for its members, for, said Justice Black, the Court is "without Constitutional authority to modify or upset Missouri's determination that it is in the public interest to make combinations of workers subject to laws designed to keep the channels of trade wholly free and open." [177] The union supported its argument by pointing to previous Court decisions upholding the right to picket as just one of the means of publicizing the facts of a labor dispute, which right is guaranteed by the due process clause of the Fourteenth Amendment. In this instance,

[175] 336 U.S. 490, 494 (1949). See Justice Black's opinion in Fashion Originators' Guild of America v. Federal Trade Commission, 312 U.S. 668 (1941), and the opinion, again by Justice Black, in Watson v. Buck, 313 U.S. 387 (1941).

[176] To support this statement, he cites Allen Bradley Co. v. Local Union, No. 3, International Brotherhood of Electrical Workers, 325 U.S. 797 (1945), which did not involve picketing; and United States v. Hutcheson, 312 U.S. 219 (1941). In the Senn case Justice Brandeis said that the right to picket peacefully was guaranteed by the Fourteenth Amendment, regardless of state law. 301 U.S. 468, 478 (1937). In American Federation of Labor v. Swing, Justice Frankfurter ruled that the due process clause of the Fourteenth Amendment forbade the state to ban picketing in instances where there is not a labor dispute between the pickets and the employer picketed. 312 U.S. 321, 325-26 (1941).

[177] 336 U.S. 490, 497 (1949).

found the Court, the evidence shows that the use of the placards and posters, while displaying truthful information, was an "essential and inseparable part of a grave offense against an important public law." The mere fact that there was information of a specific kind being disseminated cannot withdraw the action, picketing in this case, from the application of the law which makes the purpose of the picketing unlawful.[178] Picketing for an unlawful purpose, held the Court, may be enjoined by the state without any violation of the guarantee of free speech to the extent that it is protected by the due process clause of the Fourteenth Amendment. The Carlson [179] and Thornhill [180] cases were distinguished on the ground that the statutes involved in each instance sought to ban all picketing, regardless of the purpose toward which it was directed. Justice Black makes a feeble attempt to reconcile the decision in the present case with that in the Wohl case.[181] In spite of the final ruling in that case, Justice Black finds that the Court specifically states that the "State is not required to tolerate even peaceful picketing in all places. . . ." [182] And in that case, the Court did not find any unlawful acts. This in spite of the fact that under the law of the state the picketing was not for a lawful purpose.

As is pointed out in the Court's opinion, the holding in this case is not out of line with the actual words of many previous opinions. It is, however, not within the spirit of most of those decisions. It must be noticed that the statute held to apply to the union activity in this case makes unlawful actions directed toward a rather narrow type of agreement—specifically one that would lead to a monopoly over certain articles of commerce. At least the Court here took a more realistic view of picketing as a kind of economic coercion than it had since 1937, when Justice Brandeis announced the Court's decision in the Senn case. For the first time since that decision the Court has recognized the fact that "free speech" and even "peaceful" picketing are quite different. One aspect of the speech-picketing issue is made less clear by this decision: If picketing is a kind of speech guaranteed by the Fourteenth Amendment,

---

[178] *Ibid.*, pp. 501–502. [179] 310 U.S. 106 (1940).
[180] 310 U.S. 88 (1940).
[181] Bakery, Pastry Drivers and Helpers Local *v.* Wohl, 315 U.S. 769 (1942).
[182] *Ibid.*, pp. 776–77.

how is it that the state may by statute make that guarantee ineffective? Picketing, in this opinion, does not fall under the ban
of the clear and present danger test.

These decisions permitting restrictions upon the exercise of
the right to picket cannot be taken as indicative of the Court's
willingness to recognize the essential coercive nature of picketing
or of its intention greatly to limit the activities of pickets. This
is evidenced by the ruling in Cafeteria Employees Union v.
Angelos,[183] in which the state was not allowed to enjoin members
of the union from picketing a cafeteria in order to induce the
owner, who did not hire any help, to organize according to union
rules. This decision had brought the status of picketing back to
the Senn, Thornhill, Carlson, and Swing holdings.[184] The Empire
Storage and Ice Company case is the first inroad upon that trend.

UNION SECURITY AGREEMENTS AND FREE SPEECH

Under the New Deal labor legislation, both state and national,
not only did union membership increase, but the use of such
security devices as the closed shop, union shop, maintenance of
membership, and checkoff also increased tremendously. By 1946
nearly seven and one-half million workers were covered by agreements containing some union security provisos.[185] The percentage
of workers covered by union membership or hiring requirements
increased from 65 per cent in 1942 to 75 per cent in 1944 and 78
per cent in 1946. The number of those covered by closed- or
union-shop clauses with preferential hiring provisions was four
and one-fourth million in 1945 as compared with four and four-
fifths million in 1946. Union-shop provisions without preferential
hiring provisos were specified for approximately two and three-
fifths million workers in 1946, whereas such provisions had been
specified for two million in 1945. On the other hand, maintenance

[183] 320 U.S. 293 (1943). See Green, "Liberty Under the Fourteenth Amendment, 1943–1944," loc. cit., p. 459, for a criticism of the Supreme Court's ruling in
these cases. The chief basis of the criticism here is that the Court's decisions came
too late, that by 1940 picketing had lost whatever elements of free speech it might
have had, and that by then it had become a weapon to curb freedom of speech.

[184] See Schlusselberg, "The Free Speech Safeguard for Labor Picketing," loc.
cit., p. 32.

[185] Monthly Labor Review, LXIX (1949), p. 143.

of membership clauses decreased from three and nine-tenths million in 1945 to three and three-fifths million in 1946.[186]

It is in the field of union security agreements that are found some of the most significant restrictions upon labor-union objectives in recent state labor-relations laws. Some states have limited the restrictions upon a closed shop to the use of violence or intimidation of employees or employers in order to obtain such an agreement. These have not proscribed the making of voluntary agreements of this kind.[187] Others have conditioned the legality of closed-shop contracts upon the affirmative vote, by secret ballot, of a given percentage of the workers involved.[188] Other statutes prohibit unconditionally the making of contracts obligating the employer to hire only union persons or the making of any contract which would make the obtaining of, or continuing in, employment conditional upon union membership.[189]

In April of 1942 the Court refused certiorari in the case of Milk and Ice Cream Drivers and Dairy Employees Union v. Wisconsin Employment Relations Board,[190] in which the union challenged the Wisconsin requirement of a three-fourths vote of the em-

[186] C. E. Warne (ed.), *Labor in Postwar America* (New York, 1949), p. 31, citing United States Department of Labor, Bureau of Labor Statistics, *Extent of Collective Bargaining and Union Recognition in the United States in 1946*, Bulletin No. 909 (Washington, D.C., 1947).

[187] *Alabama Laws*, 1943, No. 298; and *Maine Laws*, 1947, c. 395, are of this type. The term "closed shop" is used with reference to a plant which hires only union members, usually recommended by the union. A "union shop" usually designates one in which a new employee is required to join the union within a given period of time after being hired. See E. E. Cummins and Frank T. De-Vyver, *The Labor Problem in the United States* (New York, 1947), Chap. IX; Charles C. Killingsworth, *State Labor Relations Acts* (Chicago, 1948), pp. 77–88; and David Ziskind, "Countermarch in Labor Legislation," *Labor in Postwar America*, Chap. XIII.

[188] *New Hampshire Laws*, 1947, c. 195, requires that the employer with whom an agreement is sought must employ more than five persons and that at least two thirds of the employees cast secret ballots in favor of a closed shop. Any such contract must include a clause prohibiting discrimination in union membership on the basis of race, creed, religion, or sex. The Wisconsin law requires a two-thirds vote and the Colorado, a three-fourths vote.

[189] *Arizona Laws*, 1947, c. 81; *Arkansas*, constitutional amendment, 1944; *Florida*, constitutional amendment, 1944; *Georgia Laws*, 1947, No. 140; *Iowa Laws*, 1947, No. 109; *Nebraska*, constitutional amendment, 1946, and *Nebraska Laws*, 1947, No. 344; *North Carolina Laws*, 1947, c. 328; *South Dakota Laws*, 1945, c. 80; *Tennessee Laws*, 1947, c. 36; *Virginia Laws*, 1947, c. 2.

[190] 316 U.S. 668 (1942). See McDermott, "Peaceful Picketing and Unfair Labor Practices," *loc. cit.*, pp. 151–52.

ployees before the union could demand a closed-shop contract with its employers. In this instance the union was enjoined from picketing to force a closed-shop agreement because it had not complied with the law. Apparently, then, as early as 1942 the Court recognized its untenable position in the Senn,[191] Swing,[192] and Wohl [193] cases. At least it was not anxious to take this opportunity to strike down a state law which seems to have taken into account the fact that picketing is something more than free speech and that to permit a minority to force a closed-shop agreement upon an employer would lead to too great a monopoly for the unions. Such an issue did not come to the Court for decision for another five years. In January of 1949 the antiunion security provisions of the laws of three states were challenged before the Court on the ground that such restrictions infringed upon the rights of freedom of speech, press, assembly, and petition constitutionally guaranteed to labor organizations more extensively than to other groups. In Lincoln Federal Labor Union v. Northwestern Iron and Metal Company [194] and American Federation of Labor v. American Sash and Door Co.[195] the Court upheld the authority of the state to impose such a regulation. Each of these states provided, in effect, that no person in the state shall be denied an opportunity to obtain or retain employment because he is or is not a member of a labor union. Employers were forbidden to enter agreements obligating themselves to exclude persons because they are or are not union members. In each instance the violation of due process of law was said to lie in the fact that the state by its law was proscribing an element of security indispensable to the existence of organized labor on a large enough scale to put labor and employer on a basis of equality for collective bargaining. The plaintiff unions insist that there is no constitutionally protected right to work as a nonunionist, but that the right to maintain employment without discrimination because of union membership is constitutionally guaranteed.

[191] 301 U.S. 468 (1937).   [192] 312 U.S. 321 (1941).   [193] 315 U.S. 769 (1942).
[194] 335 U.S. 525 (1949). Justice Black announced the opinion of the Court. Justices Frankfurter and Rutledge each offered concurring opinions, and Justice Murphy concurred with Justice Rutledge.
[195] 335 U.S. 538 (1949). Justice Black spoke for the Court. Justices Frankfurter and Rutledge concurred with opinion; Justice Murphy dissented without opinion. This case involved an issue of equal protection not touched upon here.

But the Court declared that the right to work and to assemble for the purpose of discussing improvements in their working conditions does not extend to labor organizations the right to drive nonunionists from remunerative employment.[196] Said Justice Black: ". . . where conduct affects the interests of other individuals and the general public, the legality of that conduct must be measured by whether the conduct conforms to valid law, even though the conduct is engaged in pursuant plans of an assembly."[197] And so the significant question becomes: Does the due process of law clause bar the state from legislating to protect the opportunity of nonunionists to get and hold jobs, free from discrimination against them because they do not belong to a union? The Court, says Justice Black, has completely rejected the constitutional doctrine of the Allgeyer,[198] Lochner,[199] Adair,[200] and Coppage[201] cases. It has returned, he thinks, to the earlier constitutional principle that "states have power to legislate against what are found to be injurious practices in their internal commercial and business affairs, so long as their laws do not run afoul of some specific federal constitutional prohibition" or some valid federal law.[202] Such an interpretation of the Fourteenth Amendment relieves the states of the strait jackets in which they had been encased by the due process clause when they attempted to legislate "to suppress business and industrial conditions which they regard as offensive to the public welfare."[203] The Court is beginning to recognize that the same due process of law clause which formerly was used to protect employers under the guise of not violating employees' or employers' freedom of contract and was later used to protect union members against the competition of nonunion

[196] 335 U.S. 525, 530 (1949).   [197] *Ibid.*, p. 531.
[198] Allgeyer *v.* Louisiana, 165 U.S. 578 (1897), in which the right to make contracts was said to be a part of the liberty guaranteed by the due process clause of the Fourteenth Amendment.
[199] Lochner *v.* New York, 198 U.S. 45 (1905), in which the due process of law clause was said to have been violated by a state law regulating the hours for workers in bakery shops.
[200] Adair *v.* United States, 208 U.S. 161 (1908). Here the Court held unconstitutional a law forbidding discrimination by employers against employees because of union membership. Relations between an interstate carrier and its workers bears no relation to interstate commerce, it was said.
[201] Coppage *v.* Kansas, 236 U.S. 1 (1915). Here the Court held unconstitutional a state law prohibiting the making of "yellow-dog" contracts.
[202] 335 U.S. 525, 536 (1949).   [203] *Ibid.*, p. 537.

members actually offers the same protection to nonunion members that it extends to labor organizations. Therefore the state legislation prohibiting the making of contracts which would make the obtaining of, or continuation in, employment conditional upon union membership was said not to violate the due process clause of the Fourteenth Amendment.

Regardless of one's evaluation of the ultimate decisions in these cases, the reasoning by which they were reached is somewhat unconvincing. Justice Black, speaking for the Court, says in effect, "Sorry, we've changed our minds and there isn't much you can do about it." The underlying attitude of the majority is much more explicitly stated by Justice Frankfurter in his concurring opinion. The Constitution has nothing to say on the matter. If the people, through their elected representatives, determine that legislation of this nature is desirable, the Court has no authority to overrule that decision. To quote Justice Frankfurter: "Even where the social undesirability of a law may be convincingly urged, invalidation of the law by a court debilitates popular democratic government. . . . If the proponents of union-security agreements have confidence in the arguments addressed to the Court in their 'economic brief,' they should address those arguments to the electorate."

Justice Rutledge concurred with the majority with one significant reservation. If the issue should arise where this decision might be construed to permit a state to proscribe the concerted refusal of union members to work with nonunion workers or to permit a state to enjoin a strike for such purpose, he would have the case reargued.

CIRCULATION AND DISTRIBUTION

Once the Court had brought freedom of speech, press, and assembly within the protection of the due process clause of the Fourteenth Amendment, it was not a long step to the extension of "free press" to include the "distribution" of handbills, pamphlets, and leaflets.[204] The right to distribute handbills and leaflets, as well as newspapers and periodicals, was upheld as a phase of the

[204] For a general discussion of the handbill cases, see Green, "Liberty Under the Fourteenth Amendment, 1943–1944," *loc. cit.*, pp. 441–50.

constitutionally guaranteed freedom of speech and press in Lovell
v. Griffin.[205] Chief Justice Hughes interpreted "speech" and
"press" to comprehend "every sort of publication which affords
a vehicle of information and opinion," and a "free" press to include the freedom to distribute or circulate as well as freedom
to publish.[206] Hence, he held that a city ordinance which forbade
persons to distribute handbills on the streets except with a permit
from the city manager infringed the petitioner's freedom guaranteed by the due process clause of the Fourteenth Amendment.
Regardless of the motive which prompted the adoption of such
ruling, "its character," said the Chief Justice, "is such that it strikes
at the very foundation of the freedom of press by subjecting it
to licensers and censorship." [207] It was not thought legally significant that petitioner had not sought a permit and met with refusal
before bringing her case before the Court. The ordinance was to
be judged on its face. Inherent in its existence was said to lurk a
restriction upon the right of free speech and press.[208] In this
method of judging laws restraining the rights of speech and press
lies one of the most significant features of this and others of the
speech cases. But this was only the beginning of extensive litigation over "handbill ordinances." Justice Roberts wrote a single
opinion in Schneider v. State of New Jersey,[209] adjudging invalid
several city ordinances which imposed various types of restrictions upon the distribution of leaflets, pamphlets, and handbills.
One such restrictive measure was that passed prohibiting the
distribution of leaflets and handbills on the streets of Irvington,
New Jersey, except with a permit obtained from the police. The
city contended that the ruling had been passed to keep the streets
of the town free of litter and trash; therefore, it represented a valid

[205] 303 U.S. 444 (1938).

[206] Ibid., p. 452. See James K. Lindsay, "Council and Court: The Handbill
Ordinances, 1889–1939," Michigan Law Review, XXXIX (1941), 561–96.

[207] 303 U.S. 444, 451–52 (1938). See p. 66, infra.

[208] 303 U.S. 444, 452–53 (1938). Cf. Thornhill v. Alabama, 310 U.S. 88 (1940).
See p. 41, supra.

[209] 308 U.S. 147 (1939). Justice McReynolds dissented. The activities interfered with by these ordinances included the distribution of leaflets announcing
a meeting under the auspices of the "Friends of Lincoln Brigade" to discuss the
Civil War in Spain, a picket standing in front of a meat store, the distribution of
leaflets announcing a protest meeting in connection with the administration of
the state unemployment insurance, and a member of Jehovah's Witnesses who
was distributing leaflets and soliciting funds.

exercise of the police power. But "public convenience with respect to the cleanliness of the streets does not justify an exertion of the police power which invades free communication of information and opinion secured by the Constitution" was the Court's reply.[210] Justice Roberts suggested that if the city was interested in keeping the streets clean, it should penalize those who threw down the papers rather than those who peacefully handed them out; for the restriction must strike at the abuse of the right, not the right itself.[211] The right here restrained was said to occupy a "preferred" status and therefore not to be limitable because of mere legislative preferences respecting matters of public convenience. While such preferences may support restrictions on the exercise of other rights, they are insufficient to justify limitation of the exercise of those rights "vital to the maintenance of democratic institutions." [212]

A second ordinance prohibited the distribution of handbills on the streets and in the alleys of the town. It was contended by city officials that unlike other limitations held invalid, this one did not ban all distribution of handbills. It was thought to be enough that persons were free to hand out leaflets in other public places. Justice Roberts replied, "The streets are natural places for the dissemination of information and opinion; and one is not to have the exercise of his liberty of expression in appropriate places abridged on the plea that it may be exercised elsewhere." [213]

A third ordinance passed upon in this case prohibited the knocking on doors for the purpose of handing out leaflets or soliciting except with the permission of the chief of police. The city was held to have no power, within the limitations of the free-speech guarantee, to subject to the discretion of an administrative officer the right of petitioner to communicate with the inhabitants of the town. It was specifically stated, however, that commercial canvassing or soliciting was not held to have this immunity from

---

[210] *Ibid.*, pp. 160, 161.   [211] *Ibid.*, p. 162.

[212] *Ibid.*, p. 161. See Louis Lusky, "Minority Rights and Public Interest," *Yale Law Journal*, LII (1942), 1, 13–15. The author is of the opinion that the Court's anxiety to protect freedom of speech because of its value in a democratic society stems from the general international situation and the contrast between our government and those of Europe.

[213] 308 U.S. 147, 163 (1939).

restriction.[214] In neither of these cases is there any mention of the clear and present danger test, for the city had not defended the regulations as attempts to guard against a danger to the public. The Court decided only that the police power of the town could not be exercised in such a manner as to infringe upon the rights of freedom of speech and press, which include the right to distribute the leaflets and handbills.

A statute of Connecticut which prohibited any person from soliciting funds for a religious or charitable cause except with a permit from the secretary of public welfare was challenged before the Court in Cantwell v. Connecticut.[215] According to the law the secretary of public welfare would grant a permit if he found that the cause for which the applicant wished to solicit was actually a religious or charitable one. The Court, again through Justice Roberts, held this to be an invalid censorship of religion in that it allowed an administrative officer to determine whether the cause for which an applicant wished to solicit was a religious or charitable one and on the basis of that determination to grant or refuse a permit.[216] Petitioners did not show that they had sought a permit or that they had any reason to think one would be refused if they applied. This fact was not considered a bar to the right of would-be solicitors to challenge the law before the Court. In effect Justice Roberts said that the mere possibility of an infringement inherent in the existence of such a statute on the books was of itself a denial of due process protection of free speech, press, and religion.[217] It was not denied that the state had a right to protect its citizens from fraudulent solicitation by requiring that strangers before soliciting in the community obtain a permit identifying themselves as authorized to act for the cause they purported to represent. But the state was held not to have the right to make such a regulation involving a religious test as a prerequisite for the permit.

Cantwell also challenged the action of the judge in convicting him for breach of peace under the common-law definition of

[214] Ibid., p. 165. See "The Supreme Court During the October Term, 1942," loc. cit., pp. 932–33.
[215] 310 U.S. 296 (1940).   [216] Ibid., p. 305.
[217] Ibid. Cf. Thornhill v. Alabama, 310 U.S. 88 (1940). See p. 42, supra.

"breach of peace." In reaffirming the clear and present danger test in respect to the judicial action here complained of, Justice Roberts concluded that the restraint was unjustified. The fact that one of Jehovah's Witnesses stood on the street in a Catholic community and denounced the Pope, the Saints, and the organized Church was immaterial. In the appraisal of the Court this tirade was nothing more than could be expected of a person of strong convictions who was anxious to win others to his cause. For the first time freedom of speech was said to be guaranteed against the application of common-law rules and other nonstatutory action of the states,[218] as well as state statutes and municipal ordinances. When the rule applied is that of a common-law concept, the decision of the Court will rest apparently on an independent finding of the nature of the speech involved and a determination of whether violence or danger actually followed rather than whether the speech was "likely" to result in such breach of peace. Said Justice Roberts: ". . . the people of this nation have ordained in the light of history, that, in spite of the probability of excesses and abuses, these liberties are, in the long view, essential to enlightened opinion and right conduct on the part of the citizens of a democracy." [219]

In the handbill cases the Court had gone a long way in invalidating local regulations which might infringe the exercise of freedom of speech, press, and assembly. But its decision in Cox v. New Hampshire [220] indicated that some restrictions are permissible under the due process protection of these rights. Members of Jehovah's Witnesses were arrested for violating a municipal ordinance prohibiting the use of the streets for processions and parades except with a permit. They challenged the validity of the regulation on the ground that it placed an unlawful prior restraint upon their rights of freedom of speech and press. Chief Justice Hughes, in upholding the ordinance, said that the constitutional guarantee of free speech, press, and assembly implies "the existence of an organized society maintaining public order without which liberty itself would be lost in the excesses of unrestrained

[218] 310 U.S. 296, 311 (1940). Cf. Justice Frankfurter's statement in the Gobitis case that the guarantee does not extend to general laws and restrictions. See Dodd, "Picketing and Free Speech: A Dissent," *loc. cit.*, p. 521.

[219] 310 U.S. 296, 310 (1940).   [220] 312 U.S. 569 (1941).

abuses." [221] Regulation of the use of public thoroughfares was said to be a traditional exercise of control by local government. The city, therefore, did not deny due process by restricting the time and manner of parades and processions on the streets.[222]

To this limitation upon the protection afforded by due process the Court added specifically that the clause did not protect obscene, libelous, or slanderous speech.[223] This holding was reiterated in Chaplinsky v. New Hampshire,[224] in which appellant contended that the application of the ordinance prohibiting offensive language on the streets deprived him of freedom of speech, press, and the exercise of his religion. Justice Murphy explained that there are kinds of speech which have never been held to fall within the constitutional guarantee; among these were obscene, profane, libelous, or "fighting" words. It was observed that ". . . such utterances are no essential part of any exposition of ideas, and are of such slight social value as a step to truth that any benefit that may be derived from them is clearly outweighed by the social interest in order and morality." [225] The fact that Chaplinsky had been distributing his literature and speaking to a crowd on matters of his religion at the time of his arrest did not bring the application of the ordinance into conflict with the due process guarantee of freedom of speech or religion. His manner of speaking had created restlessness in the crowd and thus had threatened order on the city streets. His actions, therefore, were brought within the police power of the city.[226]

The distribution of handbills or leaflets of a commercial nature is not protected by the due process guarantee of freedom of speech and press embodied in the Fourteenth Amendment. This was specifically decided in Valentine v. Chrestensen.[227] The Sanitary Code of New York forbidding the distribution on the streets of leaflets bearing commercial or business advertising matter was challenged as a violation of the right of freedom of speech and

[221] *Ibid.*, p. 574.   [222] *Ibid.*
[223] Near *v.* Minnesota, 283 U.S. 697, 712 (1931).
[224] 315 U.S. 568 (1942).   [225] *Ibid.*, p. 572.
[226] *Ibid.*, p. 574. The Court found that the "epithets" used by Chaplinsky were of a kind "likely to provoke the average person to retaliation and thereby cause a breach of peace."
[227] 316 U.S. 52 (1942). See Schneider *v.* State of New Jersey, 308 U.S. 147, 165 (1939).

press. In this case petitioner handed out leaflets inviting persons to visit his submarine. The amount of the fee to be charged was included on the advertisement, and on the other side of the leaflet was a notice of a "public protest" meeting. Petitioner contended that the matter distributed was of public interest and could not be prohibited. Justice Roberts, speaking for a unanimous Court, replied: "This court has unequivocally held that the streets are proper places for the exercise of the freedom of communicating information and disseminating opinions and that, though the states and municipalities may appropriately regulate the privilege in public interest, they may not unduly burden or proscribe its employment in these public thoroughfares. *We are equally clear that the Constitution imposes no such restraint on government as respects purely commercial advertising.*"[228] The regulation in question was said not to infringe upon the freedom of speech and press protected by the Constitution. Here again it appears that the Court is using the due process concept as a means of protecting a given subject matter rather than a mode of expression or method of disseminating information. There seems to be no logical reason why the particular information here imparted should not have constitutional protection along with other kinds of "advertising," since the method of distributing it is the same and the difference in ideas expressed made no more likely a danger to the public.

Following the ruling of the Chrestensen case, Justice Reed, expressing the views of the majority in Jones *v.* Opelika,[229] held that a nondiscriminatory tax for the privilege of selling printed material within the city did not infringe any right of free speech, press, or the free exercise of religion. Members of Jehovah's Witnesses challenged the validity of such a tax on the ground that it deprived them of their liberty of speech, press, and religion guaranteed by the due process of law clause. But the Court found that the sales taxed by the city partook more of commercial than of

---

[228] 316 U.S. 52, 54 (1942). (Italics added.) John Raeburn Green, "Liberty Under the Fourteenth Amendment, 1942–1943," *Washington University Law Quarterly,* XXVIII (1943), 254, thinks this is unjustified in view of the Court's effort to include the right to hear as well as the right to speak in the due process guarantee.

[229] 316 U.S. 584 (1943). See Irving Dilliard, "About Face to Freedom," *New Republic,* CVIII (1943), p. 693.

religious or educational transactions.[230] Justice Reed summarized the Court's views on this type of regulation thus: "When proponents of religious or social theories use the ordinary commercial methods of sales of articles to raise propaganda funds, it is a natural and proper exercise of the power of the state to charge reasonable fees for the privilege of canvassing. . . . it is difficult to see in such enactments a shadow of prohibition of the exercise of religion or of abridgement of freedom of speech or of the press." [231] It was said that since the tax did not weigh heavier upon the petitioner than upon others who wished to sell books and pamphlets and since the officer issuing the permits had no discretionary authority to refuse a permit to those who applied for one and paid the fees, there was no cause to find the statute invalid.[232] The discretionary power of revocation could not be invoked to void the law, for the petitioner had not sought a permit and therefore had not had his license revoked.[233]

Chief Justice Stone, with whom Justices Black, Douglas, and Murphy joined, filed a dissent in this case. To him, the due process of law clause of the Fourteenth Amendment guaranteed the same protection to freedom of speech, press, and religion as the First Amendment.[234] So far as a previous restraint was concerned, the Chief Justice could see no difference between the power to revoke the license allowed in this case and the discretionary power to refuse such permit which had been held invalid in the Lovell case.[235] Moreover, the sheer amount of the tax made it prohibitive as applied to the petitioner.[236] He commented: "No one could doubt that taxation which may be freely laid upon activities not within the protection of the Bill of Rights, could—when applied to the

[230] 316 U.S. 584, 594 (1943). Cf. the ruling here and in the Chrestensen case with that in Grosjean v. American Press Corp., 297 U.S. 233 (1936).

[231] 316 U.S. 584, 597 (1943).   [232] Ibid., pp. 598–99.

[233] Ibid., pp. 599–600. Cf. the statement in Thornhill v. Alabama, 310 U.S. 88, 97 (1940), to the effect that inherent in the existence of the restriction was an unlawful threat to freedom of speech.

[234] 316 U.S. 584, 600 (1943).

[235] Ibid., p. 604. Chief Justice Stone explained that "To say that he who is free to withhold at will the privilege of publication exercises a power of censorship prohibited by the Constitution, but that he who has the power to withdraw the privilege does not, would be to ignore history and to deny the teachings of experience, as well as to perpetuate the evils at which the First Amendment was aimed."

[236] Ibid., p. 605. Cf. Magnano Co. v. Hamilton, 292 U.S. 40, 44 (1934).

dissemination of ideas—be made the ready instrument for destruction of that right. Few would deny that a license tax laid specifically on the privilege of disseminating ideas would infringe the right of free speech. For one reason among others, if the state may tax the privilege, it may fix the rate of the tax and, through the tax, control or suppress the activity which it taxes." [237] That the tax was nondiscriminatory was thought to be no defense, because the lack of discrimination was with reference to other activities which were thought to have no connection with the constitutional rights of free speech, press, or religion. The minority held that the First and the Fourteenth amendments safeguarded these rights from every form of taxation imposed as a condition to their exercise, because such taxation was capable of being used to suppress the right.[238] As a potential restriction on the exercise of the rights here involved, the flat tax was said to fall just short of actual censorship and suppression.[239]

Justice Murphy also filed a dissent, which he began with a statement in reverse of the position he had taken in the recent Gobitis case. In his words: "When a statute is challenged as impinging on freedom of speech, freedom of press, and freedom of worship, . . . it is the duty of this Court to subject such legislation to examination, in the light of the evidence adduced, to determine whether it is so drawn as not to impair the substance of those cherished freedoms in reaching its objective." [240] Considering the fact that in none of the towns involved in this case was the challenged tax enforced against ministers "functioning in a more orthodox manner," it was reasonable, thought Justice Murphy, to conclude that the ordinances were intended as measures of suppression.[241] In reaching such a conclusion Justice Murphy did not consider the fact that the "more orthodox" ministers of whom he spoke had not, by their actions, come into conflict with the law. However, Justice Murphy thought it was better for the Court to err on the side of overprotectiveness than otherwise.

Justices Murphy, Black, and Douglas were ready to admit

[237] 316 U.S. 584, 607 (1943).   [238] Ibid., p. 608.
[239] Ibid., p. 611. The Chief Justice would protect the right to hear as well as the right to speak.
[240] Ibid. Cf. Grosjean v. American Press Corp., 297 U.S. 233 (1936).
[241] 316 U.S. 584, 617 (1943).

that, in their opinion, the Gobitis case had been wrongly decided. "Our democratic form of government" was said to have a responsibility to "accommodate itself" to religious views of minority groups, "however unpopular and unorthodox" those views might be. The three recanting justices now realized that, contrary to the purpose of the First Amendment, the Gobitis decision placed freedom of religion in a subordinate position. Therefore, by express statement they repudiated their former decision as to the validity of a nondiscriminatory tax imposed upon the sale or distribution of religious literature.[242]

The Court, in Jamison v. Texas [243] and Largent v. Texas,[244] continued to hold invalid, as an infringement of the rights of free speech, press, and religion, city ordinances prohibiting the distribution of handbills and leaflets or making the distribution conditional on obtaining a permit to be granted at the discretion of an administrative officer.[245] But the ruling that a nondiscriminatory tax on the privilege of canvassing or selling did not violate the Fourteenth Amendment remained the law of the land until the case of Murdock v. Pennsylvania,[246] in which a reversal was handed down on a set of facts similar to that of the Opelika case. Justice Douglas spoke for the majority in the present case. He restated the rule of previous cases that a city ". . . may not prohibit the distribution of handbills in the pursuit of a clearly religious activity merely because the handbills invite the purchase of books for the improved understanding of the religion or because the handbills seek in a lawful fashion to promote the raising

[242] *Ibid.*, pp. 623–624.   [243] 318 U.S. 413 (1943).
[244] 318 U.S. 418 (1943).
[245] 318 U.S. 413, 417 (1943). However, the Court, through Justice Black, reaffirmed the rule that the distribution of purely commercial handbills, even though they contained a civic appeal, was not protected by the due process clause. But in Jamison v. Texas, 318 U.S. 413, 417 (1943), Justice Black held that an ordinance making the distribution of leaflets or pamphlets dependent upon a permit from an administrative officer authorized administrative censorship of the publication or speech and was therefore invalid. He thought it unnecessary to determine whether the distributions were sales or contributions. See Largent v. Texas, 318 U.S. 418, 422 (1943).
[246] 319 U.S. 105 (1943). On the basis of the decision here, the Court in a *per curiam* opinion specifically overruled the Opelika decision, 319 U.S. 103 (1943). Thus the law on this particular subject was changed, not because any justice who had voted in the Opelika case had changed his mind as to the meaning of the constitutional right involved, but because Justice Rutledge, who had replaced Justice Byrnes, voted with the minority of the former case.

of funds for religious purposes.[247] Though the activities for which
petitioners were penalized here were the same as those of the
Opelika case, the Court, following the minority of that case,
found that "On this record it plainly cannot be said that petitioners were engaged in a commercial rather than a religious venture." [248] The rights of those engaged in religious activities, even
though they are similar in many respects to commercial ventures,
are not to be gauged by the standards controlling the activities
of retailers and wholesalers. Thus the Court, as it had in the labor
speech cases, committed itself to the principle that the Constitution affords a greater amount of protection to some subjects of
lawful speech than to others.[249] Here, for the first time, speech
concerning a religious subject was set apart for a treatment more
favorable than that secured by the due process clause to other
equally lawful subjects of speech and press. The tax here complained of was said to bear no relation to any benefit accorded by
the state, for the right of free speech and press were granted by
the federal Constitution.[250] Such rights, it was said, may not be
taxed by the state. It was thought to be no defense that the tax
was nondiscriminatory. Justice Douglas declared: "The protection afforded by the First Amendment is not so restricted. A
license tax does not acquire validity because it classifies the privileges protected by the First Amendment along with the wares
and merchandise of hucksters and peddlers and treats them all
alike. . . . Freedom of press, freedom of speech, and freedom
of religion are in a preferred position." [251]

The Court did not find that the tax could be called a valid exercise of the police power. Its provisions were thought not to be
of a nature to protect the community against fraud or to promote
the general safety or convenience of the public in the use of the
streets. Rather, the law authorized, in the words of Justice Douglas, "a flat tax levied and collected as a condition to the pursuit of
activities whose enjoyment is guaranteed by the First Amend-

[247] 319 U.S. 105, 111 (1943). Citing Jamison v. Texas, 318 U.S. 413, 417 (1943).
[248] 319 U.S. 105, 111 (1943).
[249] Justice Jackson dissented from this particular principle, for, said he: "I had
not supposed that the rights of secular and non-religious communications were
more narrow or in any way inferior to those of avowed religious groups."
Douglas v. Jeannette, 319 U.S. 157, 179 (1943).
[250] 319 U.S. 105, 115 (1943).   [251] *Ibid.*

ment. Accordingly it restrains in advance those constitutional liberties of press and religion and inevitably tends to suppress their exercise." [252] To the emphasis placed by the city on the provocative nature of the literature distributed, Justice Douglas answered: "But those considerations are no justification for the license tax which the ordinance imposes. Plainly a community may not suppress, or the state tax, the dissemination of views because they are unpopular, annoying, or distasteful." [253] In his opinion the upholding of such a tax would "forge" a ready instrument for the suppression of the rights of the minority to express views which were not at the time in favor. This was said to be the "inherent vice and evil" of such a tax. It was not thought necessary for the Witnesses to prove that their activities had been restricted by the operation of the law. The ordinance was held invalid on its face, for there was the possibility that its application would restrain appellants in their religious activities.[254]

Justice Jackson, in his dissent, expressed concern lest the Court go so far in its interpretation of religious liberty as to destroy the very thing it sought to protect.[255] Justices Reed and Frankfurter dissented on the ground that "free" in the First Amendment did not refer to freedom from a nondiscriminatory tax but "freedom to print or pray without permission and without accounting to authority for one's action." [256]

If the Court itself was clear as to the status to be accorded to the activities of members of the Jehovah's Witnesses sect, it was not very successful in making that status plain in Prince v. Massachusetts.[257] In that case the child-labor laws of Massachusetts, as applied to the activities of young members of the Witnesses, were challenged as a violation of the religious freedom guaranteed by due process of law. The views of the majority were expressed by Justice Rutledge. He did not think that any question of the nature, commercial or religious, of the child's activities was before the Court. That issue had been foreclosed by the state in its decision that the child was engaged in a commercial enterprise. Without

---

[252] *Ibid.*, p. 114. [253] *Ibid.*, p. 116. [254] *Ibid.*, p. 114.

[255] Douglas v. Jeannette, 319 U.S. 157, 181–82 (1943). Here Justice Jackson wrote a single dissent to cover the majority decisions in the Murdock, Struthers, and Douglas cases.

[256] 319 U.S. 105, 122 (1943). [257] 321 U.S. 158 (1944).

comment upon that determination, Justice Rutledge reasoned that the state's authority over the activities of children was somewhat greater than over adults. The application of the labor laws in this case was held to be a valid exercise of the police power in that the state was protecting such children from the hazards of the streets and from difficulties which might arise from their activities and with which they would not be able to cope.[258] Apparently Justice Rutledge made a novel application of the clear and present danger criterion. It was found that the likelihood of danger to the children, and hence to society at large, was sufficient to bring this activity within the regulatory power of the state.[259]

Justice Murphy dissented on the ground that the activities of the children did not create any clear and present danger to the state and therefore could not validly be regulated. He went further, to say that "the fact that the zealous exercise of the right to propagandize the community may result in violent or disorderly situations difficult for children to face is no excuse for prohibiting the exercise of that right."[260]

Justice Jackson dissented on the ground that the line should have been drawn according to the nature of the activity performed. The Court, he thought, should determine which of the activities of this group were constitutionally immune to regulation as religious practices and which were capable of restriction as nonreligious.[261]

In the case of Martin v. Struthers[262] the Court held invalid a municipal ordinance which prohibited persons from knocking on doors or in any way summoning occupants to the door for the purpose of handing out handbills or other printed materials. Here Justice Black expressed the view that "Freedom to distribute information to every citizen wherever he desires to receive it is so clearly vital to the preservation of a free society that, putting aside reasonable police and health regulations of the time and manner of distribution, it must be fully preserved."[263] The Court did not

---

[258] Ibid., pp. 169–70.   [259] Ibid., p. 174.   [260] Ibid., p. 175.

[261] Ibid., p. 178. Justices Frankfurter and Roberts joined in this dissent.

[262] 319 U.S. 141 (1943).

[263] Ibid., pp. 146–47. See also, Douglas v. Jeannette, 319 U.S. 157 (1943). Chafee, Free Speech in the United States, p. 406, thinks that of all the methods of disseminating information, that protected by this decision is the least entitled to constitutional guarantee. Lusky, "Minority Rights and Public Interest," loc. cit.,

base its decision in this case on the religious nature of handbills but rather on the right of freedom of speech and press, and, as a corollary, on the right to hear. To Justice Black the right to distribute literature "necessarily projects the right to receive it." [264] But the city had substituted the "judgment of the community that the literature was not wanted for the possible judgment of the householder that it was." He would leave "the decision as to whether distributors of literature may call at a home where it belongs—with the home owner himself." [265]

Possibly one of the most significant of the handbill cases concerning the due process clause of the Fourteenth Amendment to come before the Court is that of Marsh v. Alabama,[266] in which members of Jehovah's Witnesses challenged the application of the state trespass law to their activities. Here one of the Witnesses was arrested for distributing religious literature within a company-owned town in spite of warnings against such distribution on the premises. The Court went farther in this case than it had in any of the previous cases. Speaking through Justice Black, it held that persons could not be prevented from distributing religious literature on the company's premises even though "no trespass" warnings had been posted.[267] It was said: "Whether a corporation or a municipality owns or possesses the town the public in either case has identical interest in the functioning of the community in such a manner that the channels of communication remain free . . . the town of Chickasaw does not function differently from any other town. . . . The managers appointed by the corporation cannot curtail the liberty of press and religion of these people consistently with the purposes of the Constitutional guarantees, and a state statute . . . which enforces such action by criminally punishing those who attempt to distribute religious literature clearly violates the First and Fourteenth Amendment. . . ." [268]

---

p. 37, fears that unless the Court sees fit to draw a line soon, civil liberties of free speech and press may defeat themselves.

[264] 319 U.S. 141, 143–44 (1943).   [265] Ibid., p. 148.

[266] 326 U.S. 501 (1946).

[267] For a description of the status of civil liberties in company-owned towns in the United States, see Chafee, The Inquiring Mind, pp. 172–82.

[268] 326 U.S. 501, 507–508 (1946). Tucker v. Texas, 326 U.S. 517 (1946), ex-

Immunity based on the private ownership of the property was abandoned. The property here concerned is "property affected with a public interest," hence subject to state regulation and constitutional restrictions. Justice Black could see little difference between the rights of these citizens and other citizens of the state. Were their liberties to be taken away because of the location of their homes? He thought not, for "Just as all citizens they must make decisions which affect the welfare of the community and nation. To act as good citizens they must be informed. In order to enable them to be properly informed, their information must be uncensored." [269] Justice Black reminds appellee that when the constitutional rights of property owners are balanced against the right of the people to enjoy freedom of the press and religion, the latter "occupies a preferred position." Therefore the Court concluded: "In our view the circumstance that the property rights to the premises where the deprivation of liberty, here involved, took place, were held by others than the public, is not sufficient to justify the State's permitting a corporation to govern a community of citizens so as to restrict their fundamental liberties and the enforcement of such a restraint by the application of a state statute." [270]

As in the Struthers case the Court emphasized the right of the people of the town to hear as well as the right of the Witnesses to speak. Thus the rights of persons not parties to the litigation were made, in part, the bases of the decision. This may be explained by the increasing recognition of the Court of the importance of the right to hear as fundamental to a democratic society.

Dissent was voiced by Justice Reed, with whom the Chief Justice and Justice Burton joined. Justice Reed would concede that the state has a moral duty to furnish the opportunity for its

---

tended this rule to property owned by the federal government. Justice Black spoke for the Court, Justice Frankfurter concurred, and Chief Justice Stone, Justices Reed and Burton dissented.

[269] 326 U.S. 501, 509 (1946).

[270] *Ibid.* See footnote 4 of the Marsh opinion. Justice Frankfurter concurred with the majority because the Court had definitely accorded "purveyors of ideas" a preferred position, and their decisions expressed the law on the subject. He could attach no significance to the fact that the property was company owned rather than publicly owned. *Ibid.*, pp. 510–11.

citizens to obtain information, religious or otherwise, but, he said, "it has not heretofore been adjudged that it must commandeer, without compensation, the private property of other citizens to carry out that obligation." [271] In the opinion of the dissenters, the Constitution protects certain rights of the property owner which are not outweighed by the interests of the trespasser "even though he trespass in behalf of religion or free speech." [272] Justice Reed said the result of the Court's decision was to give Jehovah's Witnesses a preferred place under constitutional protection so that they would be able with impunity to invade, for religious activities, the private property of others even though that property had been opened to the general public for limited purposes only. The minority concluded: "Even though we have reached the point where this Court is required to force private owners to open their property for the practice of religious activities or propaganda distasteful to the owner, because of the interest of the public in freedom of speech and religion, there is no need for the application of such a doctrine here." [273]

The majority expressly recognized the private aspects of the ownership of the property involved. In spite of the fact that the property is open to the public for limited purposes, it is essentially private. Chickasaw, a shipbuilding community in which almost all the property is owned by the corporation, is not an incorporated town and does not have a charter or a set of bylaws under which to operate. Thus the warning posted by the manager was that of a private owner warning against trespassing. To declare that owners of such property may not invoke the aid of a state statute to protect them against trespassers has taken the Court away from its consistently held rule that the individual owner may forbid any person to enter or remain on the premises. It may, however, evidence a growing recognition on the part of the Court that many of the most potentially dangerous violations of freedom of speech and press result from "private" action rather than action by the state.

Thus, under the Court's decisions since 1938, one who wishes to distribute handbills and leaflets bearing on religion may invoke the due process of law clause to protect him against a city ordi-

[271] *Ibid.*, p. 515.   [272] *Ibid.*, p. 516.   [273] *Ibid.*, pp. 516–17.

nance prohibiting distribution of such handbills on the streets, even though other information in the same form may not be disseminated in like manner. He may claim exemption from the payment of a tax for the privilege of distributing his literature. Even though he sells his books and pamphlets at a profit, his work may not be classed as a commercial enterprise so as to bring him within the restrictions imposed upon the peddlers and salesmen of other articles. The city may not forbid him to ring doorbells or in other ways to summon the occupants to the door in order to hand them leaflets or to sell a book. At least in the Marsh case, the Court has allowed a minority group to invade an individual company's private rights which are equally as valuable to its existence as the right to distribute handbills is to that of the Jehovah's Witnesses. The Court did not indicate whether this limitation on the right of the owner to be protected against trespassers would apply also to corporations and companies organized in a different manner.

On the other hand, the handbill cases have extended due process protection of the right to distribute information in the form of handbills and leaflets to groups other than religious ones. Many of the decisions were not based on the particular subject matter involved nor the group distributing it. As yet, however, information found by the Court to be "purely commercial" cannot claim immunity from city or state regulation under the due process of law clause.

THE USE OF SOUND AMPLIFIERS

A city ordinance of Lockport, New York, prohibited the use of loud-speakers or sound amplifiers except with permission obtained from the chief of police. In Saia *v.* New York City,[274] appellant, a member of Jehovah's Witnesses, challenged the validity of the ordinance as a violation of his rights under the due process clause. He had obtained one permit and had used an amplifier for lecturing in a public park on Sunday afternoons. His permit expired, and when he applied for a second, he was refused on the ground that there had been complaints from users of the park. In spite of this he used his equipment on four occasions to amplify speeches made in the public park. Justice Douglas, speaking for

[274] 334 U.S. 558 (1948).

the Court, found in this ordinance all the vices of those invalidated in Cantwell *v.* Connecticut,[275] Lovell *v.* Griffin,[276] and Hague *v.* C.I.O.[277] An administrative officer was given wide discretionary power to determine whether a permit would be granted or refused. No standards for the use of this discretionary authority were prescribed. The ordinance, moreover, did not seek to regulate specifically the times and places for using sound amplifiers or the volume of the sound amplification permitted. But, said Justice Douglas, "Loudspeakers are today indispensable instruments of effective public speech. The sound truck has become an accepted method of political campaigning. It is the way people are reached. . . . The present ordinance would be a dangerous weapon if it were allowed to get a hold on our public life." [278] He was willing to have the city enact a narrowly drawn law to prevent abuse of the use of sound equipment by regulating the decibels. "In this case," he found, "a permit was denied because some persons were said to have found the sound annoying. In the next one, a permit may be denied because some people find the ideas annoying. Annoyance at ideas can be cloaked as annoyance at sound." [279]

Four justices disagreed with the majority in this case. Justice Frankfurter dissented because he thought that the ordinance permitted a valid regulation of the use of sound equipment so that the privacy of those who did not choose to listen would not be infringed. There was no evidence of discrimination in the use of the discretion vested in the public official. Justices Burton and Reed concurred with this opinion. Justice Jackson dissented, for in his opinion this case did not involve an issue of free speech but that of the use of sound amplifiers in public parks. He believed that the issue had been decided in Davis *v.* Massachusetts, where the Court upheld a Boston ordinance prohibiting anyone from speaking, discharging firearms, selling goods, or maintaining a booth for public amusement on any of the public grounds of the city except under a permit from the Mayor.[280] The fact that Hague *v.* C.I.O. was the opinion of two, possibly three, of the justices "fatally impairs" that case as authority in this instance, or at least Jus-

---

[275] 310 U.S. 296 (1940).   [276] 303 U.S. 444 (1938).   [277] 307 U.S. 496 (1939).
[278] 334 U.S. 558, 561 (1948).
[279] *Ibid.*, p. 562.
[280] *Ibid.*, p. 586. See Davis *v.* Massachusetts, 167 U.S. 43 (1897).

tice Jackson thought so.[281] ". . . society has the right to control as to times, places, and volume the use of loudspeaking devices for any purposes, provided the regulations are not unduly arbitrary, capricious, or discriminatory." [282] Justice Jackson could not agree with the majority's statement that the Court must weigh the various community interests in passing on the constitutionality of local regulations of the kind in question here. If this was, as he thought, a civil liberties case, he believed that the regulation was a valid one made in the interest of organized society and the maintenance of public order.[283]

The decision and the three opinions expressed in the Saia case [284] did not clarify current constitutional law on the subject of municipal power to regulate the use of sound amplifiers. In October of 1948 the Court was once again faced with the issue when a labor organizer named Kovacs challenged the Trenton, New Jersey, ordinance making unlawful the use of any sound-amplifying device which "emits loud and raucous noises" on the streets or thoroughfares of the city. Kovacs used a loud-speaker to make known to the public passing by the municipal building the facts of a labor dispute then in process in the city. He was arrested for violating the ordinance mentioned above and was convicted, though neither police nor court charged or found that he had made any "loud and raucous" noise in the streets. The only charge brought against him was that he used a loud-speaker. Kovacs appealed to the Supreme Court on the ground that the ordinance violated the due process clause of the Fourteenth Amendment for its provisions were too vague and indefinite to meet due process requirements and that as applied to him the ordinance infringed upon his right to freedom of speech guaranteed by the Fourteenth Amendment.[285]

[281] 334 U.S. 558, 568, n. 1 (1948). Hague v. C.I.O., 307 U.S. 496 (1939), called forth several opinions. Justice Roberts, joined by Justice Black, read the "judgment of the Court." Justice Stone was joined by Justice Reed in an opinion concurring with Justice Roberts. Chief Justice Hughes concurred with Justice Roberts on the affirmance of the judgment, but with Justice Stone on the basis of jurisdiction. Justices Butler and McReynolds each wrote a brief dissent.

[282] 307 U.S. 496 (1939).

[283] 334 U.S. 558, 569 (1948). He finds the decision incompatible with that of the McCollum case, 333 U.S. 203 (1948), in which the Court held that tax-supported property could not be used for the furtherance of a religious doctrine.

[284] 334 U.S. 558 (1948).   [285] Kovacs v. Cooper, 336 U.S. 77 (1949).

Justice Reed pronounced the judgment of the Court, though his opinion had the approval of Justice Burton and Chief Justice Vinson only. Justice Frankfurter wrote a concurring opinion which as a whole was approved by himself alone. Justice Jackson rendered an opinion concurring with Justice Reed's final decision but with Justice Black's conclusion that the present decision repudiated that of the Saia case. Justice Black, joined by Justices Rutledge and Douglas, wrote a dissenting opinion. Justice Rutledge also offered a special dissent, adding a specific dissent from the opinion expressed by Justice Frankfurter. Justice Murphy dissented without opinion. The particular alignment of the Court in this case is significant, for it indicates the terrific conflicts with which even the final court is faced in deciding such an issue. Neither group can be certain that it is right, for this is not a question of a "yes" or "no" answer. There are involved conflicts of interests which cannot be resolved except through an adjustment or balancing of powers and interests which are difficult to define.

So far as the "indefiniteness" issue was concerned, Justice Reed felt that only a passing comment was needed. Apparently everyone is so familiar with the current legal usage of the term "loud and raucous" noise that there could be no doubt as to what is forbidden under the ordinance. It is said that the provisions of the present law meet the standards of the Winters case.[286] One glance at the Court's opinion in that case shows how very vague indeed the standard is. Certainly the terms such as "obscene," "lewd," "lascivious," "filthy," "indecent," or "disgusting" applied to the printed word and "loud and raucous" used to describe a noise are equally indefinite and obscure in a specific instance. They are definite enough to meet the requisites of due process only because the Court has said so. But in the Winters case the Court implied that a more rigid standard of certainty is required when the ordinance deals with the rights stated in the First Amendment than when it restricts other activities. "Men of common intelligence" must be able to know, not guess, at its meaning.

The two justices who joined in this opinion found, here as in many instances before, that any regulation of the subject at hand requires a skillful balancing of social interests. On the one side,

[286] 333 U.S. 507 (1948).

the three had to concern themselves with the interests of those whose social or business activities would be disturbed by the use of the sound amplifier. Opposing were the interests of those who feel that they must use such sound devices in order to reach the ears of the public with the information which they wish to disseminate. This attempt to balance the interests of the two groups was distinguished from that involved in the Lockport, New York, case, for here no administrative agent has discretionary authority over the granting or refusal to grant a permit to use the sound trucks. It seems that the three justices overlook the fact that an absolute prohibition is as burdensome as a conditioned permission regardless of the agency giving the permission. But the present ordinance, they found, does not apply even to all uses of sound amplifiers. Rather it is applicable only (1) to loud-speakers attached to vehicles operated or standing on the streets, alleys, or thoroughfares of the city; (2) when such sound devices emit loud and raucous noises.[287] Apparently the restriction would not apply to sound amplifiers if in the opinion of the Court they were so toned as not to make loud or raucous noises. The Court does not indicate why this is any more compatible with the exercise of the right of free speech than the Lockport rule that a police officer should determine when loud-speakers should be used. They found in favor of the ordinance one other element, namely, the use of loud-speakers was not banned from the parks or open spaces off the streets. Justice Reed does not attempt to reconcile this holding with the ruling of the Schneider case [288] that "one is not to have the exercise of his liberty of expression in appropriate places abridged on the plea that it may be exercised elsewhere." The mere fact that the would-be speakers were permitted to use other property in the town did not make the ordinance forbidding the use of the streets more valid, for the streets are customary places for such activities.

But regardless of the conclusion reached on the issue of regulation or prohibition, Justice Reed seems to make the issue turn upon whether there remains, along with the freedom of speech, freedom not to listen for those who do not choose to hear. This recognition of the comparable right of those who do not wish to

[287] 336 U.S. 77, 88 (1949).   [288] 308 U.S. 147, 163 (1939).

participate in the specific freedom involved has become rather prominent in the opinions of the Court recently.

Argued the three: "The unwilling listener is not like the passer-by who may be offered a pamphlet in the street but cannot be made to take it." [289] Freedom of speech is the right of every person to "reach the minds of willing listeners," and to exercise such a freedom there must be an opportunity to win the attention of a prospective audience. The freedom, however, does not entail the right to force one's thoughts upon those who are not interested, and so, in the opinion of the three justices, the ordinance is justified as a reasonable protection of persons in their homes and business houses against distracting noises of vehicles equipped with sound-amplifying mechanisms. The opinion of these would seem to restrict the free-speech guarantee to discussion by the unaided human voice and the printed word. Neither of these can be thrust upon the public against the will of the individuals involved, and "The preferred position of freedom of speech in a society that cherishes liberty for all does not require legislators to be insensible to claims by citizens to comfort and convenience." [290]

But in the opinion of Justice Frankfurter freedom of thought is as important as freedom of speech. An uncontrolled freedom of speech may decrease the opportunities for "reflection and serenity" and thus infringe upon one's freedom to think. The notion of a preferred position for those rights named in the First Amendment does not meet with the approval of Justice Frankfurter. In his opinion such a notion has never met with the approval of a majority of the Court.[291] As in other instances, Justice

[289] 336 U.S. 77, 86–87 (1949).   [290] *Ibid.*, p. 88.
[291] Only Justice McReynolds dissented from the expression of this opinion in Schneider v. State of New Jersey, 308 U.S. 147, 161, 163 (1939). In Jones v. Opelika, 316 U.S. 584, 608 (1942), Chief Justice Stone, joined by Justices Black, Douglas, and Murphy, expressed the same opinion in dissent from the Court's ruling. Only Justices Reed, Frankfurter, and Jackson dissented from a like opinion in Murdock v. Pennsylvania, 319 U.S. 105, 115 (1943). Justice Frankfurter concurred with Justice Black in Marsh v. Alabama, 326 U.S. 501 (1946), because these rights had been given preferred status by previous Court decisions. See his concurring opinion in American Federation of Labor v. American Sash and Door Co., 335 U.S. 538, 550 (1949), to the effect that: "The very limited function of this Court is discharged when we recognize that these issues are not so unrelated to the experience and the feelings of the community as to render legislation addressing itself to them willfully destructive of cherished rights. For these are not matters like censorship of the press or separation of Church and

Frankfurter would leave to the legislature a wide area of discretion as to the kinds and degree of restrictions to be imposed. The determination of whether, and if so on what terms, sound trucks will be allowed to operate is for the legislature and not for the Court.

Justice Jackson, concurring, finds that the use of any mechanical sound-amplifying device is a proper subject for legislative regulation. The due process clause of the Fourteenth Amendment will not be violated unless such regulation is an attempt to "censor the contents" of the speech. He would not extend this ruling to methods of speech other than the sound truck. The Court's decision in this case he believed to have repudiated that in the Saia case,[292] for he could see no reason for making the requirement of a loud and raucous noise the basis for distinction.

Three justices offered dissenting opinions in this case. They could see no reason for the talk about the standard of loud and raucous noise, for Kovacs was not charged with, or convicted of, having caused such noise but only for having used a sound truck on the street. But, said Justice Black: "The basic premise of the First Amendment is that all present instruments of communication, as well as others that inventive genius may bring into being, shall be free from governmental censorship or prohibition." He concluded that the decision of the Court, in effect, favored competing channels of communication, thus discriminating against those who were forced or chose to use the nonfavored channels. He expressed concern lest the main sources of public information dwindle to those controlled by small groups of persons. Justice Black would agree that an ordinance which reasonably restricts the volume, place, and time for the use of sound amplifiers would not unconstitutionally infringe upon one's freedom of speech. On the other hand, any ordinance banning all use of such trucks on the streets does violate the due process clause of the Fourteenth Amendment.

Justice Rutledge also offered an explanation of his opposition to the ordinance in question. If the speech issue were not involved, the ordinance would still be unconstitutional, for its provisions

State, on which history, through the Constitution, speaks so decisively as to forbid legislative experimentation,"
[292] 334 U.S. 558 (1948).

are so indefinite that even the members of the Court have not been able to agree upon the reach of its restrictions. So far as the question of speech is concerned, Justice Rutledge is of the opinion that the municipality has the power to regulate the time, place, and volume of the sound trucks; it does not have the power to ban all use of them on the streets of the town.

SEPARATION OF CHURCH AND STATE

Between 1932 and 1948 the Court encountered many problems concerned with the free exercise of religion. Until 1947, however, it had not been called upon to decide specifically the delicate issue of where to draw the line between church and state in accordance with the First Amendment, made applicable to the states by the due process clause of the Fourteenth Amendment.[293] The question arose when the town of Ewing, New Jersey, acting under state statute, authorized the reimbursement of parents of money expended by them for the transportation of their children on regular buses operated by the public-transportation system if the children attended public or parochial schools. This action was challenged as a violation of the due process clause of the Four-

[293] For interpretations of state constitutional provisions touching upon this point, see Terrett v. Taylor, 9 Cranch 43 (1815), Va. Const.; Watson v. Jones, 13 Wall. 679 (1871), involving status of Ecclesiastical courts in Kentucky; and Davis v. Beason, 133 U.S. 333 (1889). Cochran v. Louisiana State Board of Education, 281 U.S. 370 (1930), is actually the only decision concerned with a problem comparable to the one presented in this instance. A Louisiana law providing for free textbooks to children in private schools, including parochial schools, as well as to those attending the public schools, was upheld in an opinion written by Chief Justice Hughes, who relied upon the social welfare of the children rather than any support to the religious institutions as justifying the statute. But the contention was that the law allowed the taking of property for a private use.

The New York law providing free transportation to school children regardless of the nature of the school attended was invalidated by the State Court of Appeals in Judd v. Board of Education, 278 N.Y. 200-21, ISN.E. (2d) 576 (1938). The facilities of transportation were made available to all children in private or parochial schools by constitutional amendment. See New York Constitution, Art. XI, sec. 4. Both the "transportation" and "free textbook" provisions were endorsed by the President's Advisory Committee on Education. See Report of the President's Advisory Committee on Education (Washington, D.C., 1938), pp. 53–54. Evarts B. Greene, Religion and the State: The Making and Testing of an American Tradition (New York, 1941), p. 131, thinks the Cochran decision covered the point at issue in the Everson case, 330 U.S. 1 (1947). For other educational practices of a similar nature, see W. G. Torpey, Judicial Doctrines of Religious Rights in America (Chapel Hill, 1948), Chap. IX.

teenth Amendment, which had imposed upon the states the prohibition, embodied in the First Amendment, against "laws respecting an establishment of religion." A taxpayer contended that the spending of tax funds for the transportation of children to Catholic schools violated due process because it amounted to the use of public monies for a private purpose. Secondly, he contended that the statute permitting such payment was a "law respecting an establishment of religion" in that it provided at public expense a means of children attending the church schools.[294]

Justice Black spoke for the Court in saying that there were no reasonable grounds for holding that legislation intended to aid children to obtain a secular education served no public purpose. Briefly thus the first contention was discarded. He then reviewed the circumstances which had given rise to the demand for a separation of church and state and concluded that as a minimum, the prohibition of the First Amendment meant:

> Neither a State nor the Federal Government can set up a church. Neither can pass laws which aid one religion, aid all religions, or prefer one religion over another. Neither can force nor influence a person to go to or remain away from church against his will or force him to profess a belief or disbelief in any religion. No person can be punished for entertaining or professing religious beliefs, for church attendance, or non-attendance. No tax in any amount, large or small, can be levied to support any religious activities or institutions, whatever they may be called, or whatever form they may adopt to teach or practice religion. Neither a State nor the Federal Government can, openly or secretly, participate in the affairs of any religious organizations or groups and vice versa.[295]

He possibly found that the state was on the verge of overstepping the bounds of the permissible here, and likewise that rationalization of the action would be difficult under his own conception of the degree of the proscription. To meet the challenge, however,

[294] Everson v. Board of Education of Ewing, New Jersey, 330 U.S. 1 (1947). See Reynolds v. United States, 98 U.S. 145 (1878), in which use of tax money was said to be one reason for the insistence of this provision of the First Amendment.

[295] Everson v. Board of Education of Ewing, 330 U.S. 1, 15 (1947).

he called attention to another prohibition embodied in the First Amendment, namely, that the state cannot abridge the free exercise of religion. If the state cannot aid any religion to propagate its doctrines, neither can it "hamper its citizens in the free exercise of their own religion." [296] Therefore, argued he, "it cannot exclude individual Catholics, Lutherans, Mohammedans, Baptists, Jews, Methodists, Nonbelievers, Presbyterians, or members of any other faith *because of their faith or lack of it*, from receiving the benefits of public welfare legislation." [297] On the basis of such reasoning he found that no fissure had been made in the "wall" erected between church and state by the First and Fourteenth amendments.[298] But the majority, unfortunately it seems, looked upon the New Jersey statute and the Ewing resolution as only a piece of social legislation and overlooked its most vital feature, namely, the aid afforded to parochial schools. Justice Black's own definition in this very case precludes the state's lending such aid, for it forbids a state to levy any tax "to support any religious activities or institutions, whatever they may be called, or whatever form they may adopt to teach or practice religion." [299] If the First Amendment means less than that, it is inadequate to the high purpose which called it into existence. If it means that much, it proscribes the action challenged in the case at bar. Such interpretation must not be construed to embody any thrust against the Catholic church school. The danger in the decision rendered by the Court lies in the impossibility to find reasonable and logical grounds for preventing other and less desirable types of aid so that gradually the line of demarcation between church and state may be dimmed to the detriment of both.

Heretofore statutes or ordinances restricting one of the freedoms protected by the First and Fourteenth amendments have been presumed invalid unless they can be justified under the clear and present danger test. In this instance, involving aid to rather than restriction upon religion, the same mode of decision was not

---

[296] *Ibid.,* p. 16. [297] *Ibid.* (Italics added.)
[298] *Ibid.,* p. 18.
[299] See Quick Bear *v.* Leupp, 210 U.S. 50 (1907). Where free transportation to and from parochial schools has been upheld in state courts, the basis of the decisions usually has been that attendance at such schools constituted compliance with the state compulsory-attendance law. See Board of Education *v.* Wheat, 174 Md. 314, 199 Atl. 628 (1938).

followed. Surely the Court would not permit the state to override a standard so adamantly defended as the clear and present danger test by indicating that general welfare required it to do so.

Justice Black, however, did not have the support of all of his colleagues. Two dissenting opinions were written, one by Justice Jackson, joined in by Justice Frankfurter; and the other by Justice Rutledge, in which Justices Frankfurter, Burton, and Jackson joined. Justice Jackson looked upon the discrimination in the application of the statute as indicating that the state made "the character of the school, not the needs of the children" the determining factor in its reimbursement program.[300] Since much of the cohesion and unity among Catholics has resulted from the Catholic schools, "to render tax aid to its church school is indistinguishable . . . from rendering the same aid to the Church itself." [301] Justice Jackson was of the opinion that "The prohibition against establishment of religion cannot be circumvented by a subsidy, bonus, or reimbursement of expense to individuals for receiving religious instruction and indoctrination." [302]

Justice Rutledge saw in the Court's opinion the second step toward the obliteration of the barrier between church and state. He interpreted the prohibition against laws concerning "an establishment of religion" to mean "the complete and permanent separation of the spheres of religious activity and civil authority by comprehensively forbidding every form of public aid of support for religion." [303] In the judgment of Justice Rutledge, if the test is to remain that pronounced by Jefferson and Madison, the state cannot afford any support, financial or other, to religion in any guise. Said he, the First Amendment made applicable to the states by the due process clause of the Fourteenth Amendment "forbids the state to use the taxing power to support religion, religious establishments, or establishments having a religious foundation whatever their form or special religious function." [304] He did

[300] Everson v. Board of Education of Ewing, 330 U.S. 1, 20 (1947). See A. W. Johnson, *The Legal Status of Church-State Relations in the United States* (Minneapolis, 1934).

[301] 330 U.S. 1, 24 (1947).   [302] *Ibid.*

[303] *Ibid.*, pp. 31–32. He believed that the first step toward the breakdown of the barrier was in Cochran v. Louisiana State Board of Education, 281 U.S. 370 (1931).

[304] 330 U.S. 1, 44 (1947).

not believe that the argument of "social welfare" should be permitted to override the constitutional prohibition against legislation "respecting an establishment of religion." [305] Since transportation costs amount to a considerable portion of the total expense of sending these children to school, state defrayment of that cost in reality does support religious education. Said Justice Rutledge, the "public function argument, by casting the issue in terms of promoting the general cause of education and the welfare of the individual, ignores the religious factor and its essential connection with the transportation, thereby leaving out the vital element of the case." [306] If this infringement of the prohibition is permitted to stand, there could not be, in his judgment, any valid objection to other types of state support to religious education.

In March of 1948 the Court was faced with a situation which called for a sharper delineation of permissible and prohibited relations between the church and the state. The case concerned the power of the state to use "its tax-supported public school system in aid of religious instruction insofar as that power may be restricted by the First and Fourteenth Amendment." [307] This statement of the issue, which incidently seems to be the only reasonable one, indicates that some members of the Court have made a mental shift since the Everson case in February of 1947.[308] There is no hint that this use of the state's power might be rationalized into an attempt to promote education or culture, though possibly that purpose was actually the basic one in permitting the instruction program in the schools. The state was only making available to children a kind of education which they deemed desirable and which possibly they could not have obtained otherwise. In Champaign, Illinois, school children who presented a written-permission card signed by their parents were released by school authorities from their secular school work for one period a week of religious training. Children whose parents failed to sign the cards remained

---

[305] Ibid.   [306] Ibid., p. 50.

[307] McCollum v. Board of Education of School District No. 71, Champaign, Illinois, 333 U.S. 203 (1948). For an excellent discussion of some of the problems involved in the issue and the decision in this case, see Arthur E. Sutherland, "Due Process and Disestablishment," Harvard Law Review, LXII (1949), 1306–44.

[308] In the Everson case Justice Black appeared to add the idea that to deny the parochial-school children the benefits of the free transportation would have infringed upon their right to free exercise of their religion.

in their rooms for a study period. The program of religious instruction became a part of the regular school week for those wishing to attend the classes. Teachers were selected and paid by the religious organizations participating in the program, though they had to be approved by the school superintendent. Classes were conducted in the school building during school hours, and attendance records were kept just as for regular secular classes.

Justice Black, rendering the Court's opinion,[309] held: "This is beyond all question a utilization of the tax-established and tax-supported public school system to aid religious groups to spread their faith. And it falls squarely under the ban of the First Amendment (made applicable to the States by the Fourteenth) as we interpreted it in Everson v. Board of Education." [310] But the complaint made by a mother who did not want her son to be taught anything about God or the Scriptures requested the Court to ban all teaching which suggests the evidence of a God. In rendering the decision of the Court, Justice Black did not qualify the ruling, which in effect meant that the complaint should be complied with. He did suggest that the Court's holding "does not . . . manifest a governmental hostility to religion or religious teaching." It merely operates on the premise that "both religion and government can best work to achieve their lofty aims if each is left free from the other within its respective sphere." [311] There was no attempt to distinguish between the aid given to sectarian groups by the Ewing resolution and that afforded by the Champaign religious-education program. Justice Black stated categorically that "The State affords sectarian groups an invaluable aid in that it helps to provide pupils for their religious classes through the state's compulsory public school machinery."

Justice Frankfurter, concurring, expanded the Court's opinion by placing the "released time" religious-education program in its historical setting. He called attention to the fact that "Separation in the field of education . . . was not imposed upon unwilling

---

[309] Four opinions were written. Justice Frankfurter wrote a separate concurring opinion in which Justices Jackson, Rutledge, and Burton joined (Justices Rutledge and Burton expressly concurred in the Court's opinion). Justice Jackson wrote a separate concurring opinion, and Justice Reed delivered a dissenting opinion.
[310] 333 U.S. 203, 210 (1948).   [311] Ibid., p. 212.

States by force of superior law. In this respect, the Fourteenth Amendment merely reflected a principle then dominant in our national life." [312] The program challenged in this case was not discriminatory, but that did not weigh in its favor when there was an attempt to square it with the provision of the First and Fourteenth amendments.[313] "Separation," said Justice Frankfurter, "is a requirement to abstain from fusing functions of government and of religious sects, not merely to treat them all equally." [314]

Justice Jackson, concurring with the opinion of Justice Frankfurter as well as that of the Court, was persuaded that some limits should have been placed upon the sweeping opinion given in this case. Somehow the Court should have based jurisdiction upon definite grounds, but it appears that Justice Jackson could not decide what those grounds might have been. Jurisdiction, he said, could not be based on the injury to a child whose parents would not permit him to attend the religious-education classes, for though the Constitution protects a right to dissent, there is doubt whether it protects from the "embarrassment that always attends non-conformity." [315] Nor should the Court have taken jurisdiction on the ground that an individual had been taxed for an unconstitutional purpose. The cost to the taxpayer was so slight, if it existed at all, as to be indefinable, and further, the plaintiff had not made this ground for complaint. But apparently Justice Black had deemed it sufficient to base jurisdiction on an alleged violation of the respecting an establishment of religion clause of the First Amendment, and Justice Jackson thought something more concrete and in keeping with previous decisions was necessary. He was willing to admit that in this particular instance, where "formal and explicit" religious instruction was challenged, the Court could proscribe it under the First and Fourteenth amendments. However, the plaintiff did not ask this and no more. She requested that "every form of teaching which suggests or

[312] *Ibid.*, p. 215.
[313] *Ibid.*, p. 227. See State *v.* Frazier, 102 Wash. 369, 173 Pac. 35 (1918).
[314] 333 U.S. 203, 227 (1948).
[315] *Ibid.*, p. 233. See Herold *v.* Parish Board of School Directors, 136 La. 1034, 68 So. 116 (1915), where the state court held that excusing children from attendance at classrooms in which the Bible is to be read places a religious stigma on the children so excused.

recognizes the existence of God" be prohibited. In the opinion of Justice Jackson the Court, in complying with this request, grounded its decision on statements too broad to serve any useful purpose in the development of a concept of "separation of church and state." Thought he, it would be impossible to teach many subjects of a cultural and broadening nature without recognizing the role of the religious element, and "One could hardly respect a system of education that would leave the student wholly ignorant of the currents of religious thought that move the world society for a part in which he is being prepared." [316] Unfortunately, Justice Jackson failed to say just what bounds he would put upon the use of religious materials in the public schools.

Justice Reed could not agree with his brethren on the Court, for he was persuaded that "the history of American education is against such an interpretation of the First Amendment." [317] He continued: "The phrase 'an establishment of religion' may have been intended by Congress to be aimed only at a state church." [318] This meaning is supported by Madison's statement that "Congress should not establish a religion, and enforce the legal observance of it by law, nor compel men to worship God in any manner contrary to their conscience," [319] and Jefferson's statements concerning religious education at the University of Virginia. Jefferson invited religious sects to "establish within, or adjacent to, the precincts of the University" schools for instruction in the religion of their sect. Justice Reed believed that these defenders of the idea of separation of church and state had in mind something different from the rule imposed by the Court in the case at bar. To him, the Court had made a "rule of law" from a "figure of speech." [320] Likewise, he could not see that Madison's *Memorial and Remonstrance Against Religious Assessments* had anything to do with the subject at hand. Said the lone dissenter:

[316] 333 U.S. 203, 236 (1948).   [317] *Ibid.*, p. 241.   [318] *Ibid.*, p. 244.

[319] Citing James Madison's argument in Congress when the proposal of the First Amendment was under discussion. Joseph Gales (comp.), *Annals of Congress*, 42 vols. (Washington, D.C., 1834), I, 730.

[320] 333 U.S. 203, 246 (1948), citing Andrew H. Lipscomb (ed.), *The Writings of Thomas Jefferson*, 22 vols. (Washington, D.C., 1904), XIX, 449. In reply to an address to him by a committee of the Danbury Baptist Association of Connecticut, Jefferson said he believed the people, in adopting the First Amendment, had "erected a wall of separation between church and state." *Ibid.*, XVI, 281.

I agree as there stated that none of our governmental en-
tities can "set up a church." I agree that they cannot "aid"
all or any religion or prefer "one over another." But "aid"
must be understood as a purposeful assistance directly to the
church or to some religious organization doing religious work
of such character that it may be fairly said to be performing
ecclesiastical functions. . . . I agree that pupils cannot "be
released in part from their legal duty" of school attendance
upon condition that they attend religious classes. But as Illinois has held that it is within the discretion of the School
Board to permit absence from school for religious instruction no legal duty of school attendance is violated.[321]

Whatever aid is afforded by the Illinois plan, Justice Reed thought
it might have been classed as "incidental advantages that religious
bodies, with other groups similarly situated obtain as by-products
of organized society." [322]

With these two somewhat conflicting decisions there has been
opened a whole new field for judicial review in the realm of civil
liberties. Probably to most laymen separation of church and state
had two chief purposes, namely, to prevent the clergy from
dominating politics and to prevent persecution or infringement of
religious freedom by a state which supported with its money and
its authority any one or all religious organizations. The particular
actions and situations which aroused the members of the first
Congress to propose an amendment prohibiting laws respecting
an establishment of religion were quite different from those in
question in the two recent cases discussed. The church and state
have been virtually separated for so long a time that their separate-
ness is taken for granted. Possibly few individuals other than those
directly involved give the issue much consideration until some
action is questioned. Many parents want their children to have
some religious instruction such as that offered in the Champaign
schools. They feel that the public-school atmosphere tends to give
the instruction less of an optional nature and thus to make it more

[321] 333 U.S. 203, 248–49 (1948).
[322] Ibid., p. 249. Other such advantages, says Justice Reed, are freedom from
taxation, transportation as upheld in the Everson case, free lunches under the
federally supported free-lunch program, and free textbooks as upheld in
Cochran v. Louisiana State Board of Education, 281 U.S. 370 (1931).

impressionable upon children who would rather be playing than
having religious instruction. To say that these same parents would
condone state interference with religious freedom would be unwarranted. In the very casualness of the acceptance of such a program, however, lies one of the real dangers. Infringement of
ecclesiastical authority upon civil affairs or of the civil authority
upon the church may develop gradually from small, seemingly
unimportant beginnings. To protect both church and state the
prohibition of even small encroachments must be guarded against.
In this particular instance it seems the Court unfortunately has
placed the weight of legal authority on the side of no religion
rather than on that of freedom of religion.

THE FLAG SALUTE AND THE RIGHT TO REMAIN SILENT

In the case of Minersville v. Gobitis,[323] Justice Frankfurter, for
the Court, upheld a compulsory flag-salute rule of the Minersville
School District.[324] Two children of the Jehovah's Witnesses sect
refused to salute the flag and to repeat the pledge of allegiance

[323] 310 U.S. 586 (1940). Curtis, "Due and Democratic Process of Law," loc. cit.,
pp. 39–52, writes in approval of the position taken by Justice Frankfurter in the
case. For briefer comments approving the decision, see the notes in George
Washington Law Review, VIII (1940), 1094, 1097; Michigan Law Review,
XXXVI (1940), 485; St. Johns Law Review, XIII (1940), 144. Among the more
disapproving critics of the decision are William G. Fennell, "The Reconstructed
Court and Religious Freedom: The Gobitis Case in Retrospect," New York Law
Quarterly Review, XIX (1941), 31–48; Green, "Liberty Under the Fourteenth
Amendment," loc. cit., pp. 497, 521; and William F. Anderson, "Compulsory
Flag Salute," Michigan Law Review, XXXVIII (1940), 149, 152. Lerner,
The Mind and Faith of Justice Holmes, p. 320, n. 4, disapproves of the result
reached but thinks that Justice Frankfurter's approach, in an attempt to balance
social and legal values and his refusal to make religious freedom an absolute con-
trolling consideration, is sound.

[324] The question had been before the Court on several previous occasions, but
no opinion had been rendered. Coale v. Pearson, 165 Md. 224, 167 Atl. 54 (1935),
was dismissed for lack of a federal question, 290 U.S. 597 (1934); Hering v.
Board of Education, 117 N.J.L. 455, 189 Atl. 629 (1937), because no federal question was found to be involved, 303 U.S. 624 (1937); likewise Leoles v. Landers,
302 U.S. 656 (1937), and Gabrielli v. Knickerbocker, 306 U.S. 621 (1939), cited
by Justice Frankfurter in his dissent in the Barnette case, 319 U.S. 624, 664 (1942).
In 1939 the Court affirmed the lower court's decision in the Massachusetts case
Johnson v. Deerfield, 25 F. Supp. 918, 306 U.S. 621 (1939), and denied a rehearing,
307 U.S. 650 (1939). Although no opinion was written in the last case, the fact
that the Court assumed jurisdiction was indication that the question of compulsory flag salute had become a federal problem and was recognized as involving a constitutional right.

because to do so would violate their religious principles. When they were expelled from school, the ruling under which they had been punished was challenged on the ground that it denied them the freedom of religion guaranteed by the Constitution. The Court recognized that the practice of religion was protected from infringement by state action. "Certainly the affirmative pursuit of one's convictions about the ultimate mystery of the universe and man's relation to it is placed beyond the reach of law," [325] said Justice Frankfurter. But the state contended that the purpose of the regulation was to secure national cohesion and unity. The ends sought were thought to be admirable, and so far as Justice Frankfurter was concerned, the selection of the means to be used in attaining those ends was a matter for the legislature to decide. He refused to "stigmatize" the legislature's judgment as a "lawless inroad" on freedom of religion, for to do so would be "no less than the pronouncement of pedagogical and psychological dogma in a field where the courts possess no marked and certain competency." [326] The majority, consisting of all the members of the Court except Justice Stone, agreed that the proper remedy for the situation at hand lay in a change of state legislative policy rather than judicial invalidation of the regulation.[327]

Justice Stone alone filed a dissent in this case. His position on the responsibility of the Court to defend those liberties through which the democratic processes might be kept intact had been embodied in a note in the case of United States v. Carolene Products Co.[328] In that case he had indicated that a presumption of validity attached to state regulations of the kind challenged by

[325] 310 U.S. 586, 593 (1940). Cf. Hamilton v. Regents, 293 U.S. 245, 265 (1934), in which the Court held that the requirement of military training as a condition of attending the state university did not infringe any constitutional rights of the students who objected to such training on religious grounds. Edward S. Corwin, Constitutional Revolution, Ltd. (Claremont, Calif., 1941), p. 112, finds this "smug assumption that the Court is the happy possessor of a patent formula which enables it in cases like this to dispense with expressing its own judgment" more distasteful than the ruling of the Court that the regulation was valid.

[326] 310 U.S. 586, 597–98 (1940). Only six weeks previously Justice Frankfurter had concurred in the Thornhill decision, 310 U.S. 88 (1940), in which no particular deference for the legislative judgment had been shown. Cf. Prince v. Massachusetts, 321 U.S. 158 (1944), in which Justice Frankfurter is of the opinion that the Court should draw the line between the religious and nonreligious activities of this group.

[327] 310 U.S. 586, 600 (1940).   [328] 304 U.S. 144, 152, n. 4 (1938).

Carolene Products Company but not to statutes or state regulations alleged to restrict civil liberties. He stated:

> There may be narrower scope for the operation of the pre-
> sumption of constitutionality when legislation appears on
> its face to be within a specific prohibition of the Constitu-
> tion such as those of the first ten amendments, which are
> deemed equally specific when held to be embraced within the
> Fourteenth Amendment.
>   It is unnecessary to consider now whether legislation which
> restricts those political processes which can ordinarily be
> expected to bring about repeal of undesirable legislation, is
> to be subjected to more exacting scrutiny under the general
> prohibitions of the Fourteenth Amendment than are most
> other types of legislation. . . . Nor need we inquire whether
> similar considerations enter into the review of statutes di-
> rected at particular religions, . . . or national, . . . or
> racial minorities, . . . whether prejudice against discrete
> and insular minorities may be a special condition, which tends
> seriously to curtail the operation of those political processes
> ordinarily to be relied upon to protect minorities, and which
> may call for correspondingly more searching judicial in-
> quiry.[329]

This was his position in the present case. The regulation was said
to do "more than suppress freedom of speech and more than prohibit the free exercise of religion which are concededly forbidden
by the First Amendment and are violations of the liberty guaranteed by the Fourteenth Amendment." [330] He was willing to admit
that the state might restrict the free exercise of religion or free
speech in the interests of public welfare and safety.[331] He was
not willing to go so far as to allow the state to compel public
affirmation of a belief which violated the religious principles of
the individuals involved.

Under the ruling in this case some twenty thousand children

---

[329] *Ibid.*, p. 152, n. 4. See Lusky, "Minority Rights and Public Interest," *loc. cit.*,
p. 20. See Justice Frankfurter's comment on this statement in Kovacs *v.* Cooper,
336 U.S. 77, 91 (1949).

[330] 310 U.S. 586, 601 (1940).

[331] Samuel Konefsky, *Chief Justice Stone and the Supreme Court* (New York,
1945), p. 222, interprets this to mean that Justice Stone was telling his colleagues
that wisdom and justice must be the test in civil-liberties cases.

were expelled from public schools throughout the country.[332] Attacks upon members of Jehovah's Witnesses became more numerous and unreasonable,[333] and severe criticism was heaped upon the Court.[334] The Court was called upon to reconsider its position on the flag-salute issue in Board of Education v. Barnette,[335] a case involving the validity of a flag-salute ruling similar to that upheld in the Gobitis case. By the time this case came before the Court, Justices Murphy, Black, and Douglas had recanted their position in the previous case.[336] With the concurrence of Justice Jackson, the dissent of Justice Stone in that case became the opinion of the Court in the Barnette case. The majority views were announced by Justice Jackson, who said: "There is no doubt that, in connection with the pledges, the flag salute is a form of utterance. Symbolism is a primitive but effective way of communicating ideas. . . . Here it is a state that employs a flag as a symbol of adherence to government as presently organized. It requires the individual to communicate by word and sign his acceptance of the political ideas it thus bespeaks. Objection to this form of communication when coerced is an old one, well known to the framers of the Bill of Rights." [337]

The Bill of Rights, which protected the individual in the right to speak his own mind, could not be said to have left the way open for the state to compel him to utter words which were not in his mind and which were offensive to him.[338] Though the ruling of

---

[332] See *United States Law Week*, XI (1943), 3279.

[333] See Victor Rotnem and F. G. Folson, Jr., "Recent Restrictions upon Religious Liberty," *American Political Science Review*, XXXVI (1942), 1053–63; H. R. Southworth, "Jehovah's 50,000 Witnesses," *The Nation*, CLI (1940), 110–12; and Francis Heller, "A Turning Point in Religious Liberty," *Virginia Law Review*, XXIX (1943), 440–58.

[334] Some of the most rabid criticisms of the Court's decision and approach in the case were made by Heller, "A Turning Point in Religious Liberty," *loc. cit.*, p. 455, who thinks that the Court's announced opinion is a doctrine of "majority absolutism"; Fennell, "The Reconstructed Court and Religious Freedom: The Gobitis Case in Retrospect," *loc. cit.*, p. 33, who thinks that the Court, in effect, said that the will of the majority was per se constitutional; and Anderson, "Compulsory Flag Salute," *loc. cit.*, p. 152, in whose opinion the decision subordinated a fundamental liberty to a legislative policy of very questionable worth. For citations to other criticisms, see C. H. Richards, "Jehovah's Witnesses: A Study in Religious Freedom" (unpublished dissertation, Duke University, 1945), p. 97, n. 92.　　　　　　　　　　　　　　[335] 319 U.S. 624 (1943).

[336] Jones v. Opelika, 316 U.S. 584, 623–24 (1942).

[337] 319 U.S. 624, 632–33 (1942).　　　　　　[338] *Ibid.*, p. 634.

the school board had been challenged by the Witnesses as an infringement of their religious liberty, the majority introduced the free-speech issue and made their decision turn, not on religious beliefs, but on a fundamental right to be silent as a part of freedom of speech.[339] The majority felt that if the state were said to have the power to coerce one into the acceptance of a political creed, it could not be doubted that the state would hold the power to determine the contents of that creed.

The clear and present danger test was made the standard of validity of the restriction imposed by the regulation. The Court said that it had become commonplace that censorship or restraint of expression ". . . is tolerated by our constitution only when the expression presents a clear and present danger of action of a kind which the state is empowered to prevent and punish. It would seem that involuntary affirmation could be commanded only when on even more immediate and urgent grounds than silence."[340] Justice Jackson's position was that the right to act positively might be infringed under some circumstances, but the right not to act at all could be restricted, if ever, only in the most serious situations.

Once again the Court declared that those rights protected by the First and Fourteenth amendments were to be guarded with greater care than those protected by the due process of law clause alone. In this connection, it was said:

> The test of legislation which collides with the Fourteenth Amendment, because it also collides with the principles of the First, is much more definite than the test when only the Fourteenth Amendment is involved. Much of the vagueness of the due process clause disappears when the specific prohibitions of the First Amendment become its standard. . . . [The rights of freedom of speech and press] are susceptible of restrictions only to prevent grave and immediate danger to interests which the State may lawfully protect. It is important to note that while it is the Fourteenth Amendment which bears directly upon the State, it is the more specific limiting principles of the First which finally govern this case.[341]

[339] *Ibid.*   [340] *Ibid.*, pp. 633–34.
[341] *Ibid.*, p. 639. Justice Sutherland, dissenting in the case of Associated Press *v.* National Labor Relations Board, 301 U.S. 103, 135 (1937), virtually designated

To the contention in the Gobitis case that the remedy for such legislation lay in a change of legislative policy, Justice Jackson answered that the purpose of the Bill of Rights was specifically to withdraw from the scope of legislative authority certain subjects. Among these were the rights of freedom of speech, press, and religion. The exercise of these rights may not be determined by a vote, for they do not depend on the outcome of an election but rather on an express provision of the federal Constitution.[342] In the words of Justice Jackson: "If there is any fixed star in our constitutional constellation, it is that no official, high or petty, can prescribe what shall be orthodox in politics, nationalism, religion, or other matters of opinion or force citizens to confess by word or act their faith therein. If there are any circumstances which permit an exception, they do not now occur to us." [343]

Justice Frankfurter dissented, declaring that the Court did not have authority to deny the state the right to attain its purposes of unity and cohesion by means of the flag salute if the legislative authorities deemed that the preferable method. He was of the opinion that unless the statute was "plainly contrary" to the Constitution, the Court should assume that it was in conformity with the constitutional guarantees. Responsibility for legislation was said to lie with the state legislatures, "answerable as they are directly to the people." [344]

The latest flag-salute case involved the validity of a Mississippi statute making it unlawful to teach disloyalty or to encourage others to be disloyal to the state or national government. The statute was interpreted by the state to include the encouragement of "stubborn refusal" to salute the flag. Members of Jehovah's Witnesses challenged the law as a violation of their freedom of

---

the freedoms of the First Amendment as absolute rights. He said that "The difference between the two amendments [the First and Fifth] is an emphatic one and readily apparent. Deprivation of liberty not embraced by the First Amendment, as for example, freedom of contract, is qualified by the phrase 'without due process of law,' but those liberties enumerated in the First Amendment are guaranteed without qualification, the object and effect of which is to put them in a category apart and make them incapable of abridgment by any process of law."

[342] 319 U.S. 624, 638 (1942).
[343] Ibid., p. 642.
[344] Ibid., p. 649. See "The Supreme Court During the October Term, 1942," loc. cit., pp. 837, 926, 937; and Curtis, "Due and Democratic Process of Law," loc. cit., pp. 39–52.

religion and speech. In Taylor *v.* Mississippi [345] the Court declared that if the state could not compel one to salute the flag in violation of his religious principles, the state could not punish him for conveying to others his beliefs on the subject.

Thus the flag salute has become a kind of utterance which the state is not at liberty to force from an individual. The right to remain silent is an essential part of the rights of freedom of speech and religion. To what extent the rulings in these three cases were dictated by the circumstances or the personal beliefs of the justices cannot be known. The position taken by Justice Frankfurter, if carried to its logical conclusion, would lead to a complete defeat of the purposes of the constitutional guarantees of free speech, press, and religion as now read into due process of law.

It is significant that the ruling in the Barnette case was based on freedom of speech rather than freedom of religion. Aside from the importance of this fact insofar as the scope of the First Amendment is concerned, such a basis of decision saved the Court from the criticism that it was interpreting the Constitution so as to protect minority groups only.

THE FIVE FREEDOMS

Beginning with the "assumption" that freedom of speech was protected by the due process of law clause of the Fourteenth Amendment,[346] the Court has brought within the protection of that clause all of the guarantees of the First Amendment. Thus the exercise of these rights, which are of the greatest significance in the maintenance of a democratic state, cannot be restricted by the state without due process of law. Generally speaking "due process," for this purpose, has been interpreted to mean that any restriction of these rights must find its justification in the existence of a clear and present danger to the public which the state constitutionally may attempt to prevent.

In the light of the foregoing cases it may be said, however, that the clear and present danger test has not been developed into a reliable criterion by which the Court may judge the validity of

[345] 319 U.S. 543, 589 (1942).
[346] Gitlow *v.* New York, 268 U.S. 652 (1925).

previous restraints on the exercise of freedom of speech, press, or assembly. While it is much less subjective than any criterion in which the "bad tendency" of the speech is made the basis of conviction, "bad tendency" remains an important factor for consideration so long as the test permits the previous restraint of speech "likely" to create a danger to the state. In applying the test the Court must answer two questions, namely, did there exist a situation which would justify the enactment of any restriction in the particular field of speech sought to be limited by the state and, if so, did the speech complained of in the case at bar create such a clear and present danger or was it so likely to create such a danger as to bring the speech action within the scope of the restriction. To meet the requirements of the test the danger must be one which the state has constitutional authority to prevent; it must be clear and likely to befall the community immediately rather than in the remote future. The Court has reserved the right to determine in each instance whether the requirements have been met.

There are some kinds of speech to which the constitutional rights of freedom of speech and press do not attach. The right of free speech does not protect the use of obscene or libelous words or statements. Nor does it extend to the teaching or advocacy of communism or other "radical" doctrines which adhere to the principle of the use of violence to make political changes, for these are said to create a danger to the state. So far the Court has not invalidated a state criminal syndicalism act because it punished a particular kind of speech. It has gone no farther than to hold the application of the law invalid in that the speech punished did not fall within the proscribed classes of speech or that the statute did not provide any definite standard by which to judge whether the speech complained of did actually fall within that sought to be proscribed by the state. If the statute declares that the advocacy of violence and force is unlawful, to convict under that statute the state must prove that there was actual advocacy of the particular thing made unlawful. The Court has held consistently that it did not pass on the right of a state to make membership in the Communist party or other radical organizations criminal per se. On the other hand, there is no indication that if the issue were before the Court it would or would not uphold such a statute.

But the state may not introduce as evidence statements of the dangerous principles of the organization unless it can show that the accused did teach or encourage others to accept such principles. Herein lies the greatest significance of the decisions in the criminal syndicalist cases. It would be almost impossible to prevent all prejudice in a jury hearing which involved an avowed Communist, because of public opinion as to the dangerous tendencies of communism. However, the biased feeling of the court may be reduced somewhat by prohibiting a consideration of the evils of the party and its doctrines as evidence against the accused. Without such a prohibition the person held would be tried, not for the act he had committed, but for ideas which he may or may not have advocated or believed. The principle involved here will surely be put to a crucial test now that the government has arrested and convicted the leaders of the Communist party.

The Supreme Court has used the due process clause to extend protection to some groups because of the subject matter involved. Information concerning labor disputes has received greater protection within the last decade than ever before. Not only do the workers and unions have at their disposal the usual facilities of press, speech, and radio for the dissemination of their views; they also have the right to acquaint the public with the facts of a dispute by means of a picket line. The extension of due process protection to picketing as free speech has brought within the scope of freedom of speech a somewhat irreconcilable element. The fact that the parties to one side of the dispute may employ a kind of speech which inevitably involves economic coercion while the parties to the other side may not makes it too obvious that the Court is throwing the weight of legal sanction on one side of the issue. Such a position would have been more understandable had the right to picket been restricted to the area of the dispute in which the employer might otherwise use his economic position to coerce his employees. The state may restrict the right to picket only when there is a clear and present danger to the interests of the community, not when the danger is to the interests of the employer alone. However, picketing for an unlawful purpose may be enjoined by the state without violation of due process of law.

The Court has held that the state or city may regulate the dissemination of information as to the proper time, place, and manner. However, from the possible regulations as to place it has with one exception withdrawn streets and other public places, private homes, at least to the extent of a prohibition against summoning occupants to the door in order to hand them printed matter, and property situated within a company-owned town. In the case of picketing, the regulation as to place may go only so far as to keep the activities of the pickets within an area where there is some economic interdependence; and thus far that regulation has been interpreted to mean that the pickets and the picketed must be in the same industry, though not necessarily employee and employer. As to the manner: The state may not impose previous restraints or subsequent punishments in the form of contempt proceedings upon publication in a daily paper unless such publication causes a clear and present danger which the state constitutionally may prevent. Playing of phonographs for the purpose of disseminating religious information may not be prohibited nor punished unless there is created some substantive evil which would justify a restriction. But the use of loud-speakers, regardless of the information to be disseminated, may be prohibited on the streets, alleys, and parks of the town. Picketing as a manner of disseminating information may be restricted by the state only when there is a real danger of violence which may be the result of actual violence by the pickets in a given situation or of past violence which justifies the state in thinking there will be more.

From the speech and press cases decided by the Court since 1925 several rather definite principles may be drawn. The Supreme Court has found that the protection of free speech and press, the right of peaceable assembly, and the right to petition the government are matters of public interest. The success of the democratic process depends to a large extent on a free access to information. It was only when the right of free speech was viewed in this light that it weighed heavily enough to gain protection when balanced against a right such as that of the nation to wage war successfully. It is possible that the European situation, a contrast of our system of government with the system of states in which the democratic element found scant recognition, helped to bring about the realization that freedom of speech and press and assembly are fundamental to our political system. From legislative history over a period of years, it may be seen that the exercise of those rights guaranteed by the First Amendment had as much to fear from restrictive state laws as from federal statutes. In order to lend any real protection to the exercise of these rights the Court had to extend constitutional protection to them against infringement by the states by extending the meaning of "liberty" and "due process."

The Court has become minority conscious. Neither the city nor the state may decide for individual householders that persons canvassing for the sale or distribution of literature may not enter their property. The decision in the Marsh case may be accounted for as the result of a conscious protection of the minority group to disseminate its religious literature as well as the right of the citizens of the company-owned town, who are in a sense a minority group, to hear or receive the literature. The corporation was not allowed to decide for these would-be listeners that they should not have access to this particular information. The principle underlying this decision seems to have been that there will be a few who will want to receive the information or literature and that these few have a right to do so. There is no indication whether the same protection would be extended to groups distributing materials on subjects other than religion.

The notion that the state must or will be allowed to protect property rights against the possible inconvenience or annoyance created by the exercise of the rights of freedom of speech and press was discarded in the thirties. Until recently the position of the Court with reference to that matter seems to have been quite the opposite—a law was held invalid if in its application there was possibility that it could be interpreted so as to infringe the individual's rights of free speech and press. The rights guaranteed against federal infringement by the First Amendment and against state action by the Fourteenth are of a nature different from that of the other rights protected by due process of law. Property rights, private annoyances, or public inconveniences weigh very lightly when balanced against the rights safeguarded by the First and Fourteenth amendments. The recent loud-speaker case may possibly be the beginning of a trend in the other direction.

The states may pass legislation defining certain acts as unlawful because they would create a danger to the state. But if the enforcement of the law is challenged as a violation of the rights of free speech, press, religion, or assembly, the Court will not accept the state's finding that the law was itself justified or that the particular application of it was valid. Rather it will make an independent finding to determine whether the speech created or is sufficiently likely to create a danger to the public to justify the restriction.

On the other hand, an expressed legislative policy will be given greater consideration by the Supreme Court than a common-law concept. This may be because the latter is not necessarily the expression of the will of the people to the extent that a statute would be. Moreover, the common-law concept is less concrete and definite, therefore allowing for much greater discretion on the part of the enforcement agent.

The Court has at times applied the due process clause of the Fifth Amendment to restrict the authority of Congress in the exercise of its enumerated powers in such a way as to impose a prior restraint upon free speech and press. For instance, in the Schneidermann case [347] the Court held that due process was denied by an act of Congress which was construed as permitting the denaturalization of a naturalized citizen because it is shown that he was, at the time he became a citizen, or has since become, a member of an organization advocating the change of political systems by use of violence. At other times the due process clause of the Fifth Amendment has not been so applied, although a restraint was imposed by act of Congress. Due process was said not to be denied by an interpretation of the National Labor Relations Act which makes it an unfair labor practice for an employer to speak in such a manner as to discourage his employees in their efforts to organize. The employer may not discharge his employees because of union activities, for to do so would violate the National Labor Relations Act. But the employees, in accordance with the

[347] 320 U.S. 118 (1943).

construction of that same statute, may picket the premises of an employer and by their activities deprive him of the right to work.

It seems that in the protection of these rights of speech, press, assembly, religion, and petition the Court must balance the benefits which will accrue to each of two groups having widely divergent interests. To allow too much scope to the exercise of these rights by either group is to allow for the infringement of the exercise of the same rights of the other group. The desirable solution would be one suited to the best interests of the community as a whole. It does not seem likely that the Court will be able to arrive at such a solution soon.

II

Due Process of Law and
Socioeconomic Legislation

The period 1932–49 is marked by an increasing participation of government in the social and economic life of the nation.[1] During the early years of this period the chief problem was that of marshaling the full capacity of government for the promotion of the welfare of the nation. The "natural" laws of supply and demand, which Justice Sutherland had once classed with the "multiplication tables, the Sermon on the Mount, and the American Constitution,"[2] failed to resolve the economic and social disruptions precipitated by the upheaval of December, 1929. The onslaught of the depression wrought a revolutionary change of attitude on the part of the people toward their government. As prices fell and the number of unemployed mounted to the millions, the idea that somehow the American system of laissez-faire individualism must give way to the larger interests of social groups and of the nation at large became at least partially compatible with the thinking of businessmen, industrialists, and workers as well as the man on the street.[3] Professor Edward S. Corwin, sage of

---

[1] Wright, *The Growth of American Constitutional Law*, p. 110, finds that this is the "central problem involved in the constitutional adjudication of the last half century. . . ."

[2] George Sutherland, "Principle or Expedient," *Report of the New York Bar Association*, XLIV (1921), 263–81.

[3] Charles A. Beard, *America Faces the Future* (New York, 1932), pp. 1–10, says that there was in 1932 a strong conviction in the United States that such disasters were dangerous to the entire social order. He found that ". . . the challenge to capitalism and the effort to meet the challenge by a combination of individual liberty and initiative with collective bargaining, control, and action seem to mark a new phase in the intellectual climate" of the nation. Eleven years later Justice Jackson said that the laissez-faire concept, or the principle of non-

American constitutional law, addressing the American Political Science Association in 1932, tendered the suggestion that a "measure of social planning, and in the long run, a considerable measure of it" would have to take the place of individualism and free enterprise. Otherwise, he said, the nation would experience "social dissolution" or a "social order based on rather obvious force." [4]

Under existing conditions legislation to regulate competition and to alleviate the lot of the unemployed was looked upon as inevitable at least, if not altogether desirable. But in spite of the widespread recognition of the need for government intervention, much of the legislation enacted by Congress and the state legislatures in an attempt to remedy the situation was challenged before the Supreme Court as violative of due process of law of the Fifth and Fourteenth amendments. The effectiveness of such legislation was further endangered because it was brought before a Court unprepared to meet realistically many of the social and economic issues of the day. But much economic legislation in no way related to the depression was also called into issue before the Court, on the due process question. The greater number of these cases fell roughly under the headings of (1) price regulation, (2) bankruptcy legislation alleged to impair the obligations of contracts, (3) labor legislation, (4) regulation of production.

STATE POWER TO FIX PRICES

For many years the states had been permitted, within the requirements of due process of law, to regulate prices only in businesses affected with a public interest.[5] By an application of that

---

interference, had withered, at least as to economic affairs. West Virginia Board of Education v. Barnette, 319 U.S. 624–40 (1932). See Dixon Wecter, *The Age of the Great Depression, 1929–1941* (New York, 1948).

[4] Edward S. Corwin, "Social Planning and the Constitution: A Study in Perspectives," *American Political Science Review*, XXVI (1932), 26. Professor Corwin expressed the opinion that the social planners would not be confronted with constitutional obstacles, for constitutional law was more flexible and more free from autonomous concepts than it had been in forty years.

[5] See Sutherland, "Principle or Expedient," *loc. cit.*, p. 277; Maurice Merrill, "The New Judicial Approach to Due Process and Price Fixing," *Kentucky Law Journal*, XVIII (1929), 1–17; and the dissent in O'Gorman Insurance Co. v. Young, 282 U.S. 251 (1931).

doctrine the Court, in 1914, upheld a Kansas statute regulating fire-insurance rates because of the importance of the business in the rural economy of the state.[6] But during the twenties the doctrine was applied to invalidate a New York law forbidding the resale of theater tickets at a profit of more than fifty cents per ticket,[7] a New Jersey statute regulating the rates to be charged by private employment agencies,[8] and a Tennessee statute fixing a maximum price for gasoline.[9] However, in 1931 the Court upheld the power of the state to fix the rates of compensation to be paid to insurance agents.[10] In each of the cases invalidating the price-fixing regulation, the views of the Court were expressed through Justice Sutherland; Justices Stone, Holmes, and Brandeis dissented. In the latter case, Justice Brandeis spoke for the majority; Justices Sutherland, Butler, McReynolds, and Van Devanter dissented. The fixing of commodity prices was frowned upon by the Court.

Minimum Commodity Prices. By 1932 the "free and open market" in the New York milk industry had long since given way to a system of private regulation within the industry. Producers and distributors had for many years determined the price of milk through a system of so-called "collective bargaining." But, by the very nature of the commodity and of the market, the distributors had a singular control over the price at which they would buy and sell, and the producer was under constant pressure to sell at whatever price he could.[11] In the early thirties, when milk sold to the consumer in New York for twelve and one-half cents

[6] German Alliance Insurance Co. *v.* Kansas, 233 U.S. 389 (1914).

[7] Tyson and Bros. United Theatre Ticket Office, Inc. *v.* Banton, 273 U.S. 418 (1927). Here the Court held that ". . . the right of the owner to fix a price at which his property shall be sold or used is an inherent attribute of the property itself . . . and, as such, within the protection of the due process clauses of the Fifth and Fourteenth Amendment." *Ibid.,* p. 429.

[8] Ribnik *v.* McBride, 277 U.S. 350 (1928).

[9] Williams *v.* Standard Oil Co., 278 U.S. 235 (1929).

[10] O'Gorman Insurance Co. *v.* Young, 282 U.S. 251 (1931). See "Price-Fixing by Legislative Fiat—New Alignment of the Members of the Supreme Court," *University of Cincinnati Law Review,* V (1931), 218-20.

[11] Irene Till, "Milk—The Politics of an Industry," Walton H. Hamilton and Associates, *Prices and Price Policies* (New York, 1938), pp. 431, 495-500.

per quart, the producer was receiving approximately five cents per quart.[12] These prices were fixed by distributor groups within the industry, over which the producer had little if any control. The New York legislature found that the price war of the early depression years had left the farmer with an income so far below the costs of production that the milk supply of the state was jeopardized. Further, price cutting by retail stores, which the legislature found could buy at a lower price than the larger distributors, was said to be one of the chief evils of the industry. By creating the Milk Control Board and endowing it with authority to fix maximum and minimum prices, the legislature was exercising the right to review the private control of the market in order to correct it in the public interest. A member of the Cabinet Committee on Price Policy of 1934 found that the real question was not whether the state might interfere with the "natural operation of the competitive system," but whether it might "regulate and amend the arrangements which were the products of individual agreement." [13]

The Milk Control Board issued an order establishing a minimum price of nine cents per quart to be charged by stores for milk sold for consumption off the premises and ten cents per quart to be charged by other distributors of milk. The purpose of the scheme was to prevent the retail stores from selling at a price low enough to impair the business of the house-to-house distributor. Leo Nebbia, a retail grocer, sold two quarts of milk for eighteen cents and gave the customer a five-cent loaf of bread. The Milk Control Board held that the "gratuity" was the equivalent of a price reduction below that fixed for such dealers. Nebbia thereupon challenged the validity of the statute giving the board authority to fix minimum prices for the milk industry. He alleged that the law deprived him of property without due process and denied him the equal protection of the laws. The Supreme Court, speaking through Justice Roberts, declared that the state's right to regulate private property for the common interest was equally as fundamental as the individual's private right of property or freedom

[12] Federal Trade Commission, *Agriculture Income Inquiry* (Washington, D.C., 1938), pt. I, p. 114.
[13] Till, "Milk—The Politics of an Industry," *loc. cit.*, p. 500.

to contract.[14] Only the action of the state was involved in this case, but Justice Roberts went beyond this to assert that neither the Fifth Amendment nor the Fourteenth Amendment prohibits the respective governments from regulating for general welfare. The guaranty of due process was said to require only that the legislation not be "unreasonable, arbitrary, or capricious," and that the remedy selected bear a "substantial relation" to the ends sought. Justice Roberts explained that since the reasonableness of the regulation must depend upon the relevant facts, what is due process in one situation for a given business may not be for another business in the same situation or for the same business in another situation.[15] The ultimate determination in each instance must await the decision of the Court.

As late as 1932, Justice Sutherland had said specifically that the dairy industry was private and not subject to state control.[16] By 1934, five of the nine justices were convinced that it was imperative for New York to regulate prices for the milk industry. Therefore, something had to be done about Justice Sutherland's classification. To this end, Justice Roberts announced that the phrase "affected with a public interest" meant only that the industry, "for adequate reason," was subject to governmental control for "public good." It had been admitted, he said, that the words "clothed with a public use" and "affected with a public interest" were not "susceptible to definition," and that, therefore, they would not serve as adequate criteria of the constitutionality of legislation directed at business prices or practices. The Court's decisions in which regulations were invalidated by an application of either of these tests rested, he said, not on the mere fact of the regulation, but on the Court's finding that the laws were "arbitrary in their operation or results." And so the matter of classification was dispensed with by the explanation that

[14] 291 U.S. 502, 523 (1934). See Robert Hale, "The Constitution and the Price System: Some Reflections on Nebbia v. New York," *Columbia Law Review*, XXXIV (1934), 401–25. For some of the implications of the decision, see Irving B. Goldsmith and Gordon W. Winks, "Price Fixing from Nebbia to Guffey," *Illinois Law Review*, XXXI (1936), 179–201. See also Emmet W. Wilson, "Property Affected with a Public Interest," *Southern California Law Review*, IX (1935), 1–13.

[15] 291 U.S. 502, 525 (1934).

[16] New State Ice Co. v. Liebmann, 285 U.S. 262, 277 (1932).

it had become clear that there existed "no closed category of business affected with a public interest." The Court must determine in each case whether the "circumstances vindicate the challenged regulation as a reasonable exertion of governmental authority or condemn it as arbitrary or discriminatory," in order to decide if the law violates the Fifth or the Fourteenth Amendment.[17] Thus with slight ceremony the Court laid to rest, for the time, the restrictive concept of "a business affected with a public interest" as a test of the "due process" of the regulation. "Upon proper occasion" and "by appropriate measures" the state was said to have the power to regulate industry in *any of its aspects, including the prices to be charged for the products or commodities it sells.*" [18] Price regulation, held Justice Roberts, is not different from any other kind of restriction.[19] After nearly a half a century the Court discovered that the due process clause made "no mention of sales or prices any more than it speaks of business or contracts or buildings or other incidents of property." [20]

The Court did not rely upon the emergency occasioned by the depression to support this decision.[21] Clearly the legislation was not intended as a temporary measure, although the law did contain a time limit. The situation which called it into existence was neither recent nor temporary, and the Court did not attempt to interpret it as such. The legislation represented the state's policy of economic control over a particular field of industry. The critical situation during which it was enacted may have been a factor considered by the Court, but it was not made essential to

[17] 291 U.S. 502, 536 (1934). It was said that the statement that an individual had dedicated his business to a public use meant only that "if one embarks in a business which public interest demands shall be regulated, he must know that regulation will follow." Not since 1934 has the Court held invalid an attempt to regulate prices. The provision of price fixing under the Guffey Coal Act was "disposed of without coming to the question of [its] constitutionality." See p. 115, *infra.*

[18] 291 U.S. 502, 537 (1934). (Italics added.)

[19] *Ibid.*, p. 539. Only seven years before, the Court, in Tyson and Bros. *v.* Banton, 273 U.S. 418, 431 (1927), had held that price fixing not only was a "more definite and serious invasion of the rights of property" but also that its exercise could not always be justified by circumstances which have been found to justify regulations of the manner of carrying on a business.

[20] 291 U.S. 502, 531-32 (1934).

[21] Harry Polikoff, "Commodity Price Fixing and the Supreme Court," *University of Pennsylvania Law Review,* LXXXVIII (1940), 934, 945, comments on the implications of this fact.

the decision that the regulation was valid. Justice Roberts declared that so far as due process of law is concerned, "The State is free to adopt whatever economic policy may reasonably be deemed to promote the public welfare. . . ." When such policy is declared by the legislature, he said, the Court is without authority to override it. Justice Roberts would go so far as to say that "Whether the free operation of the normal laws of competition is a wise and wholesome rule of trade and commerce is an economic question which this court need not consider or determine." If the legislature finds that unrestricted competition is an inadequate safeguard of the interests of the consumer or that it portends the destruction of the industry itself, "appropriate statutes passed in an honest effort to correct the threatened consequences may not be set aside because the regulation adopted fixed prices *reasonably deemed by the legislature* to be fair to those engaged in the industry. . . ." Justice Roberts was of the opinion that the Constitution did not give anyone the right to conduct his business in such a manner as to injure the "public at large, or any substantial group of the people." [22]

Justice McReynolds served as spokesman for the minority, which consisted of Justices Sutherland, Van Devanter, and himself. These held that *any price regulation* was violative of due process of law. Forgetting that the producers of the milk industry did not engage in unhampered action and that the prices were not the result of "free and open competition," the minority found that price fixing by the state constituted "management, control, and dictation," which had no part in the free-enterprise system.[23] Even in times of emergency, price fixing was thought to be beyond the pale of legitimate regulation.[24]

Once again there is indication of the Court's partial withdrawal as reviewing agent of economic legislation. Without the support

[22] 291 U.S. 502, 537–38 (1934). (Italics added.)

[23] *Ibid.*, p. 554.

[24] *Ibid.*, p. 546. The dissenting justices had expressed a similar opinion in their dissent in the Blaisdell case, 290 U.S. 398 (1933). In the present case Justice McReynolds feared that "hereafter every right must yield to the voice of an impatient majority when stirred by distressful exigency." 291 U.S. 502, 545 (1934). For comments by some who follow the work of the Court, see Corwin, *The Twilight of the Supreme Court*, p. 99; Morris Duane, *The New Deal in Court* (Philadelphia, 1935), p. 87; and Alpheus T. Mason, "Has the Supreme Court Abdicated?" *North American Review*, CCXXXVIII (1934), 353, 360.

of an emergency situation, it upheld price regulation in an industry in which the public had long been recognized as having an equity, but one which had not been held by the Court to be "public." The basis of the decision was said to be the finding by the legislature that such regulation was necessary to save the industry and to protect the producer and the consumer.

Soon after the Nebbia decision a second order of the Milk Control Board fixing minimum prices to be charged by distributor and minimum prices to be paid the producer was challenged before the Court as a deprivation of property without due process.[25] The minimum price for Grade B milk to be paid to producers had been fixed at five cents per quart, and the minimum to be charged by the wholesaler, at nine cents per quart. The board found that Hegeman Farms owed to 400 farmers a sum of $23,000 for underpayments on milk purchases. Hegeman's license was revoked and he was ordered by the board to repay the farmers. Thereupon he challenged, not the power of the board to fix a minimum price, but rather the reasonableness of the prices established. He complained that the spread between the two minimum prices fixed by the board was too slight to allow him to operate at a profit. Though the price to be charged by the distributor was a minimum, the strong competition in the industry made it, in effect, the maximum that could be obtained for the milk. But to allow a higher minimum price for distributors in order to permit marginal dealers to earn a profit would make the price to the consumer exorbitant and therefore decrease the demand, which, in turn, would ruin the farmer.[26]

Here, then, the issue was not the validity of a retail price but of a minimum price established primarily for the protection of the farmer. Justice Benjamin N. Cardozo, speaking for the Court, was faced with the problem of price fixing for a phase of industry where the laws of supply and demand, because of the surplus supply and the relatively decreased demand, could not operate to protect the producer and the middleman at the same time. His answer: "If the designation of a minimum price is within the scope

[25] Hegeman Farms Corp. v. Baldwin, 293 U.S. 163 (1934).
[26] The author of the note "The Right of the Milk Dealer to a Fair Return," Columbia Law Review, XXXIV (1934), 1551, sees in the decision only the application of the rule that due process of law does not protect a dealer against the hazards of competition.

of the police power, expenses and losses made necessary thereby must be borne as an incident, unless the order goes so far beyond the needs of the occasion as to be turned into an act of tyranny." [27] Justice Cardozo found nothing in the due process of law concept to prevent the legislature from fostering the producer, by placing a minimum price on the products he has to sell, and the house-to-house distributor, by establishing a minimum price at which his competitor, the retail grocer, must sell. Nor was there anything in that phrase to guarantee that the wholesale dealer would be able to sell at a profit.

In Highland Dairy Farms, Inc. *v.* Agnew [28] the Court refused to invalidate the Virginia Milk and Cream Act,[29] which authorized a Milk Commission to designate natural market areas and to fix maximum and minimum prices for various grades of milk. Dealers were required to obtain a license from the commission. Prices already established would be canceled by the commission upon the request of a majority of the producers and distributors of a given area. The Highland Farms Dairy, a processing company located in Washington, D.C., sold all of its fluid milk to a single operator of retail stores in Virginia. The appellant company was charged with having sold milk at prices much lower than those fixed by the commission. It challenged the validity of the law on two grounds: first, that the provision which in effect allowed a majority of the producers and distributors to establish prices was a denial of due process; secondly, that the provision which gave the commission authority to refuse a license to an applicant was arbitrary and a denial of due process of law.

The Court dismissed the complaint without passing on the constitutionality of the statute. Appellant did not show that the power of cancellation had been exercised by the commission. Until he could make such a showing, he could not complain of the validity of that provision of the law. Mere possibility that such a power might be exercised was not enough to cause the Court to invalidate the statute.[30] Nor had appellant applied for a license. Therefore, he could not complain that the commission would

---

[27] 293 U.S. 163, 170 (1934).   [28] 300 U.S. 608 (1937).

[29] *The Virginia Code of 1936*, pars. 1211x–1211z.

[30] 300 U.S. 608, 613 (1937). Cf. the Court's views on this as a method of arriving at the regulation of wages and hours in Carter *v.* Carter Coal Co., 298 U.S. 238 (1936).

arbitrarily use its power to refuse a license to any applicant.[31]

The rulings as to price fixing were not confined to the milk industry. The Court's recognition that the state is the best judge of the policies which will most adequately serve its interests was carried into other fields. Justice Roberts, speaking for the Court, in Mayo *v.* Lakeland Canning Co.[32] upheld the validity of the Florida statute regulating the price and distribution of canned citrus fruit in that state. The allegation that the price-fixing provision was a denial of due process was held not to raise a substantial federal question. Justice Roberts said that the presumption of validity attaching to the act would preclude appellant's obtaining injunctive relief "except in extraordinary situations." To support a decision invalidating the law, appellant would need findings which were "unequivocal." [33] The legislature had found that price stability in the citrus-fruit industry was essential to the economy of the state. That finding was said to outweigh any complaint on the part of a canner that the regulation was contrary to the due process of law guaranteed by the Fourteenth Amendment.

The appropriateness of the regulations made in the citrus-fruit industry was left entirely to the state legislature, "in whose keeping is the shaping of that State's social and economic plan." Justice Frankfurter, joined by Justices Black and Douglas, disclaimed all power to judge of the wisdom of the policy or of its effectiveness in achieving the ends for which the regulation was made.[34]

Price Fixing by Private Contract under the Fair-Trade Laws. In 1911 the Court handed down its decision in Dr. Miles Medical Co. *v.* Park,[35] in which it held invalid minimum-price contracts

---

[31] 300 U.S. 608, 613 (1937). See Bourjois, Inc. *v.* Chapman, 301 U.S. 183 (1937); and Premier-Pabst Sales Co. *v.* Grosscup, 298 U.S. 226, 227 (1936), in which the Court held that the complaint of a denial of due process of law was without merit unless the appellant could show that he was refused a license. In United States *v.* Jefferson Electric Co., 291 U.S. 386 (1934), the Court upheld a statute requiring that one applying for a refund of taxes on the ground that the tax had been paid on property not within the tax law must show that he had borne the tax and had not passed on to his customers any part of it.

[32] 309 U.S. 310 (1940). See Polikoff, "Commodity Price Fixing and the Supreme Court," *loc. cit.,* p. 944. The author interprets the fact that the Court cited the Nebbia and the Rock Royal cases in support of its decision here to mean that the price-fixing power of the state and federal government is the same.

[33] 309 U.S. 310, 318 (1940).   [34] *Ibid.,* pp. 319, 320.

[35] 220 U.S. 373 (1911). Justice Hughes said that "The complainant having sold its products at prices satisfactory to itself, the public is entitled to whatever ad-

between producers and distributors. Prior to this decision, producers had looked upon the practice of resale-price maintenance as a right.[36] The Capper-Kelly Fair Trade Bill [37] permitting resale price maintenance was passed in the House in 1931 but was defeated in the Senate. Meanwhile, California in 1931 enacted a fair-trade law legalizing resale-price contracts on all trade-marked or branded goods.[38] In 1933 this law was amended to make the prices fixed by such agreements binding on all dealers who sold the products, whether or not they were parties to the contract.[39]

Immediately other states followed California's lead, and by 1936, thirty-two states had enacted some kind of fair-trade law, paralleling, in most cases, the California law as amended in 1932.[40] The purpose of these laws is to permit a producer or a distributor authorized by the producer to enter private contracts fixing the minimum resale price of his commodity. Resale prices may be established in this manner only for commodities which bear a trade-mark or other distinctive brand or name of the producer and which are in fair and open competition with other commodities of the same general class produced by others.[41] The prices so fixed are, under most state fair-trade laws, applicable to any dealer selling the article, whether or not he was a party to the price-fixing contract.

The Illinois Fair Trade Law of 1935,[42] challenged as violative of the due process clause in Old Dearborn Distributing Co. *v.*

---

vantage may be devised from competition in the subsequent traffic." *Ibid.*, p. 409. Louis D. Brandeis, as attorney for the public interest, later Associate Justice on the Supreme Court, appeared before the House Committee on Interstate and Foreign Commerce when this decision was under discussion and "respectfully" submitted that the Court had made an error which the legislature should correct. 72 Cong., 1 Sess., H.R. 441, Ser. 9487.

[36] Burton A. Zorn and George Feldman, *Business under the New Price Laws* (New York, 1937), pp. 278–81.

[37] 72 Cong., 2 Sess., S.R. 441, Ser. 9487.

[38] *General Laws of California*, III, Act 8782.

[39] *California Laws*, 1933, Act 8782, pars. 1–1/2.

[40] Theodore Beckman and Herman C. Nolen, *The Chain Store Problem: A Critical Analysis* (New York, 1938), pp. 283–84. The number had increased to forty-three in 1938. John W. Norwood, *Trade Practice and Price Law: Federal* (New York, 1938), p. 136.

[41] Norwood, *Trade Practice and Price Law*, pp. 139–49. See also, Zorn and Feldman, *Business under the New Price Laws*, p. 301.

[42] *Laws of Illinois*, 1935, p. 1436.

Seagram Distillers Corp.,[43] was of this general type. The legislature of Illinois found that retailers, especially in cut-rate stores, were using well-known products as "loss leaders" to attract customers and that this practice had a tendency to lead the general public to believe that it paid an additional price for the trade-mark or label of a given producer. Apparently the legislature felt that such an enlightening of the public constituted a kind of unfair competition and loss of market against which the producer of such goods could claim constitutional protection. It was also discovered that in some instances a non-cut-rate dealer refused to handle the product which had been used as a loss leader because its worth had been lowered in the eyes of prospective buyers. Thus as soon as a particular product was abandoned as a loss leader, the producer's market might be seriously affected.[44] On the basis of such findings the legislature enacted a fair-trade law on the theory that a producer had a right to protect his good will, evidenced by his trade-mark, by the maintenance of a minimum resale price.

The Court found that the law was actually a measure to protect the good will represented by the trade name. The producer was said to have a vested right in the reputation and additional sale price of his product under the specified name. The dealer might sell the commodity at a reduced price if he removed the label and if the producer's mark or brand did not enter into the bargain. Thus the regulation was thought not to be arbitrary or unreasonable in any way.[45]

Here the due process of law clause was interpreted as permitting the legislature to guarantee the producer of a commodity a resale price in excess of the actual value of his article, which price he had the right to fix by means of contracts with dealers.[46] Once the

[43] 299 U.S. 183 (1936). For a discussion of this particular kind of price fixing see "Symposium on Unfair Competition," *Iowa Law Review*, XXI (1936), 175–254; and Hugo E. Weisberger, "The Supreme Court Decisions on the Fair Trade Acts," *Journal of the Patent Office Society*, XIX (1937), 136–45.

[44] Weisberger, "The Supreme Court Decisions on the Fair Trade Acts," *loc. cit.*, pp. 136–40.   [45] 299 U.S. 183, 186 (1936).

[46] Cf. the statement in the Carter case to the effect that the delegation to producers and employees of the power to determine wages and hours which would be binding on persons not parties to the agreements was "so clearly arbitrary and so clearly a denial of the rights safeguarded by the due process clause of the Fifth Amendment" that the Court found it necessary to do no more than cite former decisions to foreclose the question. 298 U.S. 238, 310–11 (1936).

price was established in a contract, it became binding on other dealers who purchased the product from a wholesale dealer, even though they were not parties to the price-fixing contract. The price fixing did not rest on any emergency nor was it confined to a business affected with a public interest. The price was to be fixed by the producers to protect themselves. It was not shown that any particular benefit would accrue to the consumers or to the public in general. That the legislature found such a regulation advisable was thought to be sufficient to sustain the law in the face of the due process challenge.

CONGRESSIONAL PRICE FIXING

Minimum Prices. In 1935, Congress enacted the Bituminous Coal Conservation Act,[47] which provided for federal control of wages and hours in the bituminous-coal industry and for the regulation of prices in the sale and distribution of bituminous coal. The validity of the law was challenged in Carter v. Carter Coal Co.,[48] and the Court, for the first time, was called upon to consider the power of Congress to regulate commodity prices in time of peace.[49] In spite of the express provision that the two parts of the act should be considered separately and that a finding that one part was unconstitutional should not affect the validity of the other, the Court held that the two were inseparable and declared the wages-and-hours provisions unconstitutional. The fall of the wages-and-hours provisions entailed the fall of the price regulations. Justice Sutherland found "The conclusion unavoidable" that the price-fixing provisions were so closely related to the wages-and-hours provisions that had the latter failed to pass in the legislature, the former, in all probability, would have failed also. On the basis of that conclusion "The price-fixing provisions were disposed of without coming to the question of their constitutionality. . . ."[50] Justice Sutherland, however, explained that

[47] 49 *Stat.* 991.
[48] 298 U.S. 238 (1936). See Goldsmith and Winks, "Price Fixing from Nebbia to Guffey," *loc. cit.*, pp. 179–201.
[49] See Goldsmith and Winks, "Price Fixing from Nebbia to Guffey," *loc. cit.*, p. 199.
[50] 298 U.S. 238, 316 (1936).

neither the Court's disposition of the matter nor anything said in the opinion should be taken to mean that the price provisions, if enacted separately, would be sustained.

Chief Justice Hughes and Justices Cardozo, Stone, and Brandeis dissented from the majority's ruling on the price-fixing provisions of the law. Each of them felt that the price regulations should have been upheld. Justice Cardozo insisted that "Congress was not condemned to inaction in the face of price and wage wars so pregnant with disaster." To him, liberty protected by the Fifth Amendment did not include the "right to persist in this anarchic riot." [51]

Not until nearly three years after this decision was the power of the federal government to regulate commodity prices and distribution upheld.[52] Under the Marketing Agreements Act of 1937 [53] the secretary of agriculture issued an order relating to the sale of milk in the metropolitan area of New York. Milk producers in the New York milkshed had long complained of the difference in prices received for milk sold for fluid use and that sold for dairy processing. The order challenged in the present case was enacted in an attempt to stabilize the marketing conditions by equalizing the burden of the surplus milk. It provided for a uniform price to the producer for his milk irrespective of the use to be made of it. The order fixed a minimum price for each class of milk. If the handler paid less to the producer than the minimum price fixed for the class of milk he bought, he was required to pay the difference between the uniform price and the minimum price into a producers' settlement fund. If, on the other hand, the uniform price was greater than the minimum for that class of milk, the handler would be reimbursed from the settlement fund. In either case the handler would pay no more than the minimum

---

[51] *Ibid.*, p. 331.

[52] United States *v.* Rock Royal Cooperatives, 307 U.S. 533 (1939). For comments on the various aspects of the decision, see George S. Feldman, "Legal Aspects of Federal and State Price Control," *Boston University Law Review*, XVI (1936), 570–94; Henry Rottschaefer, "The Constitution and a 'Planned Economy,'" *Michigan Law Review*, XXXVIII (1940), 1133–64; and Polikoff, "Commodity Price Fixing and the Supreme Court," *loc. cit.*, pp. 934–56. For a more comprehensive study of the whole problem of price fixing in the milk industry, see W. P. Mortenson, *Milk Distribution as a Public Utility* (Chicago, 1940), pp. 3–12.

[53] 50 *Stat.* 246, 247.

price as fixed by the secretary of agriculture, and the producers would be assured a uniform price irrespective of the use to be made of their milk, thus spreading the loss on milk over the entire market.

It was contended that these regulations were contrary to the due process guaranteed by the Fifth Amendment in that price fixing was beyond the scope of Congress' commerce power.[54] The Court asserted that most of the milk used in the metropolitan area came from outside the state and that much of the milk bought there was for use beyond the state lines. Therefore, the sale was held to be an essential part of the interstate transaction and within the regulatory power of Congress. As to the power to regulate prices as a part of the commerce power, it was explained that Congress' power over interstate commerce, "when it exists, is complete and perfect," and that the authority of the federal government over interstate commerce "does not differ in extent from that retained by the states over intrastate commerce. . . ."[55]

It was alleged that the "pool" system was a denial of due process, for it resulted in the taking of one person's property for the benefit of another. The Court replied that "common funds for equalizing risks are not unknown and have not been considered as violative of due process." Here, for the first time, the pooling device was recognized by the Court as appropriate for agricultural products.

Though the Court did not specifically find that the milk industry was one within the class formerly called "affected with a public interest," undoubtedly it did consider the conditions existing in the industry and that they did involve the public interest. On the other hand, the milk industry was not designated as a completely private business by the Court. Justice Roberts declared that if the legislature found that the public interests could be

[54] Unfair discrimination was charged on the grounds that the producer cooperatives were exempt from payment of the minimum price required of the proprietary handlers, that the minimum prices applied only to milk sold within the marketing area or passing through a plant in the marketing area, and that the order made price differentials between territories located favorably or unfavorably to the market area.

[55] 307 U.S. 533, 569 (1939). Cf. the Court's opinion with reference to pooling for a pension fund in Railroad Retirement Board v. Alton, 295 U.S. 330 (1935). This device had been approved by the Court, however, in the Social Security cases. See pp. 373–74, infra.

served by fixing the prices in the milk industry, it could make regulations for that purpose and the Court would not interfere. It was necessary only for Congress to find that the industry was interstate and that there was a rational basis for the regulation.

Shortly after the decision in the Carter case, Congress had enacted a second Bituminous Coal Conservation Act,[56] which embodied only the price-fixing provisions of the first act. In Sunshine Anthracite Coal Co. v. Adkins [57] the Court took cognizance of the fact that Congress had found price fixing and the elimination of unfair competitive practices to be "appropriate methods of prevention of the financial ruin, low wages, poor working conditions, strikes, and disruption of the channels of trade which followed the wake of the demoralized price structures in this industry." [58] Without further explanation it was said that price control was one of the means available to Congress for the protection and promotion of the welfare of the economy.[59] Therefore, there was no violation of due process involved in the operation of the law. The lapse of three years and the appointment of four new justices to the Supreme Court had worked a change in the constitutional law on the subject of price regulation.[60] In 1939 the Court found that due process did not prohibit Congress from fixing prices for the milk industry. Moreover, it was said that the price-fixing power of Congress was no more limited by the Fifth Amendment than was the states' power to regulate prices restricted by the due process clause of the Fourteenth Amendment.[61] On the basis of this decision the power of Congress to fix prices for the bituminous-coal industry was sustained in 1940.[62] In 1941 it was said that the congressional power to regulate prices paid for the service of mining the coal and for the consideration of the mining rights was beyond dispute.[63]

[56] 50 Stat. 72.
[57] 310 U.S. 381 (1940).
[58] Ibid., p. 395.
[59] Ibid., p. 394.
[60] Between October, 1937, and April, 1939, Justices Van Devanter, Sutherland, Brandeis, and Butler left the Court and their places were filled by Justices Black, Reed, Frankfurter, and Douglas.
[61] United States v. Rock Royal Cooperatives, 307 U.S. 533 (1939). See Federal Power Commission v. Natural Gas Pipeline Co., 315 U.S. 575, 582 (1941). See Justice Black's dissent in the latter case, in which he argues that price fixing is no different, so far as due process is concerned, from any other type of regulation.
[62] Sunshine Anthracite Coal Co. v. Adkins, 310 U.S. 381 (1940).
[63] Gray v. Powell, 314 U.S. 402, 417 (1941).

Price Ceilings and the War Power. In United States *v.* Mac-Intosh,[64] Justice Sutherland explained:

> From its very nature, the war power, when necessity calls for its exercise, tolerates no qualifications or limitations, unless found in the Constitution or in the applicable principles of international law. In the words of John Quincy Adams— "This power is tremendous; it is strictly constitutional, but it breaks down every barrier so anxiously erected for the protection of liberty, property and of life." To the end that war may not result in defeat, freedom of speech may by act of Congress, be curtailed or denied so that the morale of the people and the spirit of the army may not be broken by seditious utterances, freedom of the press curtailed to preserve our military plans and movements from the knowledge of our enemy; deserters and spies put to death without indictment or trial by jury; ships and supplies requisitioned, property of alien enemies, theretofore under the protection of the Constitution, seized without process and converted to the public use without compensation and without due process of law in the ordinary sense of that term; prices of food and other necessities of life fixed or regulated; railways taken over and operated by the government; and other drastic powers, wholly inadmissible in time of peace, exercised to meet the emergencies of war.[65]

Certainly such an interpretation of the war power of Congress would not admit of doubt as to the power of the legislature to prescribe ceiling prices for foods and other necessaries in time of a war emergency. The Emergency Price Control Act of 1942 [66] was not challenged primarily on the ground that Congress did not have the power to fix maximum prices in such a situation in order to protect the consumer public from soaring prices. The greatest objection was that the procedures prescribed for challenging the prices fixed by the Emergency Price Control Board violated due process of law. This aspect of due process will not be considered here. In Yakus *v.* United States [67] appellant contended that the

[64] 283 U.S. 605 (1931).   [65] *Ibid.,* p. 622.   [66] 56 *Stat.* 23.
[67] 321 U.S. 414 (1944). Some constitutional aspects of the act are discussed by Donald Holdoegel, "The War Power and the Emergency Price Control Act of 1942," *Iowa Law Review,* XXIX (1944), 454–62.

choice allowed by the provisions of the statute lay only between selling at a loss or going out of business. The Court replied that in the light of the circumstances which called forth the regulation, it could not be said that the law was arbitrary or unreasonable.[68] The law, it was said, did not represent an exercise of the power of Congress over interstate commerce; it was an exercise of the war power under which regulations are not limited to interstate commerce.

A second provision of the statute delegated to the price-control administrator the authority to fix ceilings on rents in order to protect the public from exorbitant charges during the critical housing shortage. The rent-controls orders were challenged as a deprivation of property without due process of law in Bowles v. Willingham.[69] With little discussion the power of Congress to provide rent controls in time of emergency was upheld as not violative of due process of law.[70] Justice Rutledge, concurring, stated: "Since in these cases the right of property, not of personal liberty or life as in criminal proceedings, the consequences, though serious, are not of the same moment under our system, as appears from the fact that they are not secured by the same procedural protections in trials. It is in this respect perhaps that our basic law, following the common law, most clearly places the rights to life and to liberty above those of property." [71] These regulations were

[68] 321 U.S. 414, 423-24 (1944).   [69] 321 U.S. 503 (1944).
[70] Ibid., p. 512.
[71] Ibid., p. 525. But it would appear from the treatment accorded the Japanese on the West Coast that the war emergency power may be exercised without any greater solicitude for the rights and liberty of individuals than for the rights of property. In Hirabayashi v. United States, 320 U.S. 81, 103-104 (1944), the military order forbidding persons of Japanese ancestry residing within the military zone to leave their places of residence between 8:00 P.M. and 6:00 A.M. was upheld. The Court said that "The circumstances were such" that the restriction did not violate due process of law. That the Japanese were discriminated against was not a denial of due process, for, the Court held, the due process guaranteed by the Fifth Amendment does not include equal protection of the laws. The validity of the Japanese evacuation order was challenged in Korematsu v. United States, 323 U.S. 214 (1944). In that case, the Court held that "pressing public necessity may sometimes justify the existence" of restrictions which curtail the civil rights of a single racial group. Korematsu was said not to have been deprived of his liberty without due process of law, because of the time element which made selection impracticable and the impending danger of invasion which justified such restrictions. However, in Ex parte Endo, 323 U.S. 283, 302 (1944), it was held that admittedly loyal American citizens of Japanese ancestry could not be held indefinitely in evacuation centers. Cf. Chief Justice Hughes's statement in St.

held to be a valid exercise of the war-emergency power of Congress. There was no indication that similar measures would be upheld under other circumstances.

Price fixing has come to be regarded as a legitimate regulatory measure. The determination that prices or rates charged by a particular industry are of sufficient public interest to bring them within the police power of the state is a matter left almost entirely to the legislature. Congress has a comparable power in the field of interstate commerce.

FEDERAL REGULATION OF AGRICULTURAL PRODUCTION

The Supreme Court has had only a few occasions to pass upon the due process of federal attempts to regulate agricultural production. Until the initiation of the New Deal policies it had been generally thought that agriculture, insofar as production and distribution within the state were concerned, lay within the exclusive domain of the state. But the farm depression which had been precipitated in the early twenties by the postwar deflation had become increasingly worse after 1930. As the depression continued to affect business, domestic demand for agricultural products dropped sharply. The states were not able to remedy the situation because of the interstate aspects of any effective agricultural-control program. Therefore, the federal government asserted its power to legislate in behalf of the farmer group by virtue of its power to regulate interstate commerce. To effect a remedy for the plight of the farmer, Congress enacted the Agricultural Adjustment Act of 1933,[72] which was declared invalid in 1936 as an unconstitutional exercise of the congressional power to tax.[73] Two years later a second Agricultural Adjustment Act [74] was passed to accomplish the same purposes which had prompted the first, namely, to keep surpluses off the market and thus to bring about a rise in agricultural prices. This time Congress took

---

Joseph Stock Yards Co. *v.* United States, 298 U.S. 38, 52 (1936); and Justice Stone's remark in United States *v.* Carolene Products Co., 304 U.S. 144, 152 n. 4 (1938).

[72] 48 *Stat.* 31.
[73] United States *v.* Butler, 297 U.S. 1 (1936).
[74] 49 *Stat.* 31, 38, 39.

a slightly different approach to reach the same ends. For surplus production control it substituted control of marketing in interstate commerce. The United States secretary of agriculture was empowered to establish quotas for farmers in a given area if there was a favorable referendum vote on the matter. Once quotas were fixed, any farmer who produced more than his share was subject to a penalty.

The Tobacco Inspection provision of this statute [75] was challenged by North Carolina tobacco warehousemen operating markets which had been designated as inspection centers. They complained that many of the growers took their tobacco to other markets in order to escape the provisions of the law, thus decreasing the volume of business for those operating inspection-center markets. Further, it was said that due process was violated by the provision which allowed producers to take a referendum vote to determine whether quotas would be imposed.[76] The Court found that Congress had not abdicated its power to enact regulatory measures dealing with the subject of the volume of produce to go into interstate commerce. It had only "placed a restriction on its own regulation by withholding its operation as to a given market 'unless two-thirds of the growers vote for it.' " [77] This was said to involve no denial of due process. Thus an entirely novel due process question—that of a restriction of the marketing of agricultural crops as a part of a federal price-control program—was disposed of in favor of the legislature.[78]

Tobacco growers also challenged the application of quotas to the 1938 crops. A statement of the quota for the 1938 market had

[75] *Ibid.*, p. 45.
[76] Currin v. Wallace, 306 U.S. 1 (1939).
[77] *Ibid.*, pp. 15, 18. The act provided that quotas would be prescribed when excessive supplies piled up in the tobacco industry and two thirds of the producers of a given marketing area approved the imposition of quotas. After quotas were fixed, any grower who marketed in excess of his quota became subject to a penalty, to be paid by the warehouseman to the government and to be deducted by him from the amount owing to the producer.
[78] See Thomas Reed Powell, "Changing Constitutional Phases," *Boston University Law Review*, XIX (1939), 509, 520. Powell thinks it is significant that the majority neither cites the earlier decisions so as to make a distinction on the basis of facts nor overrules those decisions in which the Court had held a different view of congressional attempts to regulate agriculture. He is of the opinion that the issue was of sufficient importance to deserve more than summary treatment at the hands of the Court.

been sent to the individual farmers just before the opening of the market in August of that year. The growers contended that since the crops to be marketed at that time had been planted and harvested at great expense prior to the notification of quotas, the application of the regulation was retroactive and therefore violative of due process of law. The Court, in upholding the provision and its application, in this instance insisted that the arguments of the growers overlooked the circumstance that the statute "operates not on the farm production," but upon the "marketing" of the tobacco in interstate commerce. It was said that the growers might hold over their excess tobacco and put it on the market another year. The fact that growers in Georgia and Florida were not adequately equipped to process and store the surplus tobacco for a later market was said to be of "no legal consequence." [79]

In Wickard v. Filburn [80] the wheat quotas established under the Marketing Agreements Act of 1937 [81] were challenged as resulting in a deprivation of property without due process of law. In this case the Court held that the government had given the farmer a choice—he might limit his crop to the quota fixed for his farm or he might pay a penalty of fifty cents per bushel for all wheat threshed in excess of the quota. No penalties attached to the farmer's growing as much wheat as he wished. If he harvested an excess, he might sell it to the government to be stored for later use or he might use it as hay. If, on the other hand, he chose to thresh it, he must pay the penalty. This was said to impose no restriction on the production of wheat and to involve no taking of property without due process of law. Without regard for the fact that the farmer had been given no choice as to the government subsidy, Justice Jackson said that "it is hardly a lack of due process for the government to regulate that which it subsidizes." [82] The Court could "hardly find a denial of due process" in the operation of the law, "since it is doubtful that appellee's burden under the program outweighs his benefits."

As to the complaint that the statute was retroactive in effect,

[79] Mulford v. Smith, 307 U.S. 38, 50–51 (1939). Justice Butler, with whom Justice McReynolds concurred, wrote a dissent.
[80] 317 U.S. 111 (1942). Justice Jackson spoke for a unanimous Court.
[81] 50 Stat. 246.
[82] 317 U.S. 111, 131 (1942).

Justice Jackson said that the penalty was contingent upon the act of threshing an excess amount of wheat which the appellee had not committed prior to the passage of the law. The farmer might have chosen to feed his wheat as hay and no penalty would have been exacted. In view of these alternatives which were open to the wheat grower, the Court held that he had not been denied due process by the operation of the law.[83]

But appellee contended that he was not engaged in interstate commerce and therefore did not fall within the provisions of the law. But, read the Court's opinion, "Control of the total supply, upon which the whole statutory plan is based, depends upon control of individual supply." The Fifth Amendment was said *not to have guaranteed the individual farmer the right to plant as much as he likes or the right to dispose of his crop as he sees fit.*[84]

Thus it is established, at least for the present, that Congress may, consistently with due process of law, control production of certain farm products. There is no indication in the Court's decision on this subject as to the limitations which may be placed upon the exercise of that power. Though the laws under which the regulation of production has taken place were passed at a time of great surpluses of the particular products restricted, they were passed upon by the Court when that condition no longer existed. The regulations were not upheld as emergency measures but as a valid exercise of the power of Congress to control interstate commerce. The fact that farmers whose products did not go into interstate commerce were restricted made no material difference, for the prices on the interstate market depended upon the amount of wheat available to the individual farmer. If he could not raise enough for his own use, he would have to buy on the market; that, in turn, would boost the price on the entire market. Benefits to an individual farmer did not appear to be the concern of Congress

[83] *Ibid.*, p. 133.

[84] *Ibid.* Professor Carl B. Swisher thinks that the decision in this case went so far in justifying federal regulation of agricultural production "as to shatter almost all previous conceptions of limitations of such power." *The Development of American Constitutional Law* (New York, 1943), pp. 964-65. In United States *v.* Rock Royal Cooperatives, 307 U.S. 533, 568 (1939), it was said that the power to establish quotas for the milk which would be left in the state of production was an essential part of the right to regulate the amount to go into interstate commerce. No denial of due process was involved in such an order.

in enacting these regulations; rather the program was to benefit a large segment of the population. Legislation enacted for such a purpose is now due process.

EMERGENCIES AND THE OBLIGATIONS OF CONTRACTS

In 1930 the farm-mortgage debt of the United States had reached ninety-two billions, or 16 per cent of the total value of the farm property reported in the census of that year.[85] Over half of this was accounted for by the farm debts in Illinois, Nebraska, Minnesota, Wisconsin, Texas, Iowa, and California.[86] Over 61 per cent of the farms in South Dakota were mortgaged. The ratio of forced sales to all the farm-property transfers increased from 34 per cent in 1929 to 42 per cent in 1931, to 54 per cent in 1932, and to 58 per cent in 1933.[87] In 1933 the mortgage foreclosures reached the highest peak in more than fifty years.[88]

It was in such a setting that twenty-five states adopted some form of mortgage-moratory legislation.[89] Many of the statutes were found unconstitutional by the state courts. The Minnesota and New York laws came before the Supreme Court as violations of the due process and contracts clauses.

Minnesota Moratorium Act, 1933. At the close of 1932 over one half of the farm lands of Minnesota were subject to mortgages.[90] Many of these debts had been incurred at a time when the general price level was much higher, and the farm price level was nearly four times higher than in 1932.[91] Under the law of

[85] "Farm Debt Problem," 73 Cong., 1 Sess., *House Document*, No. 9 (Ser. 9751), p. 5.

[86] Robert F. Martin, *Income in Agriculture, 1929–1935* (New York, 1936), p. 55.

[87] *Ibid.*, p. 58. See B. R. Stauber, "The Farm Real Estate Situation, 1923–1933," *U.S. Department of Agriculture*, Cir. No. 309, December, 1933, pp. 42, 57.

[88] *New York Legislative Documents*, 1942, No. 45, p. 16.

[89] Alabama, Colorado, Connecticut, Florida, Georgia, Indiana, Kentucky, Maine, Massachusetts, Missouri, Nevada, New Jersey, New Mexico, North Carolina, Oregon, Pennsylvania, Rhode Island, Tennessee, Utah, Virginia, West Virginia, Washington, and Wyoming never passed moratory legislation. *New York Legislative Document*, 1942, No. 45, p. 13.

[90] William L. Prosser, "The Minnesota Moratorium," *Southern California Law Review*, VII (1933), 353, 354, citing the Minnesota *Department of Agriculture Technical Bulletin*, No. 888, on Farm Mortgage Credit, 1932.

[91] Prosser, "The Minnesota Moratorium," *loc. cit.*, p. 354. The author describes

Minnesota in 1932, the mortgagee could force a public sale of the property. Due to the large number of sales under this law the land prices dropped to such an extent that land virtually could not be sold in many parts of the state. Therefore, mortgagees were able to bid in the land at a nominal price and obtain from the court a deficiency judgment for the remainder of the debt.[92] In such circumstances it could hardly be said that Minnesota destroyed arbitrarily and unreasonably the contract rights of creditors in declaring a mortgage moratorium for the duration of the emergency.

The Moratorium Act[93] provided that the mortgagor should remain in possession of the land and should pay the mortgagee a "reasonable" rental to be determined by the Court. The mortgage-redemption period was to be extended for two years or until, in the discretion of the court, the emergency which had given rise to the legislation had ceased to exist. The constitutionality of the law was challenged on the ground that the creditor had been deprived of his property rights, created by the mortgage contract, without due process of law, and on the ground that the state had impaired the obligations of a contract contrary to the contracts clause of the Constitution. The Supreme Court upheld the legislation by a five to four decision in Home Building and Loan Ass'n v. Blaisdell,[94] which has been described as the Court's most important decision on the capacity of the government to act in a protective function for the common good and its own preservation.[95] In upholding the law the Court gave considerable weight to the fact that the creditor was not being deprived of all remedy. He

---

the social and economic situation which had resulted from the large number of foreclosures in the state. The extent of the unrest may be seen from the fact that to quiet the "farmer" march to the capital, the governor of the state promised to declare martial law and force the creditors to afford the debtors relief. *Ibid.*, pp. 355-56.

[92] *Ibid.*, p. 355.   [93] *Minnesota Laws*, 1933, c. 339.

[94] 290 U.S. 398 (1934). For a discussion of the decision see Edward S. Corwin, "Moratorium over Minnesota," *University of Pennsylvania Law Review*, LXXXII (1934), 311-16; Benjamin F. Wright, *The Contract Clause of the Constitution* (Cambridge, Mass., 1938), Chap. V; C. C. Hynning, "Constitutionality of Moratory Legislation," *Chicago-Kent Law Review*, XII (1934), 182-212; Joseph V. Heffernan, "The Minnesota Moratorium Case," *Indiana Law Journal*, IX (1934), 337-56; and Prosser, "The Minnesota Moratorium," *loc. cit.*, pp. 353-71.

[95] James Barclay Smith, "Constitutional Limitation on Sovereign Competition," *Temple University Law Review*, XIII (1934), 415, 416.

was to receive a rental thought by the court to be reasonable.[96]

This was admittedly an emergency situation, but, explained the Court, "emergency does not create power. . . ." It may give rise to an occasion for the exercise of an existent power only. "The constitutional question presented in the light of an emergency is whether the power possessed embraces the particular exercise of it in response to the particular conditions." [97] As a practical matter, the Court was unwilling to assume responsibility for using its power to disrupt further the economy of the state and thereby to deprive thousands of farmers of homes and livelihoods. The legislation of Minnesota, and similar enactments in nearly half the other states, was involved. But the Court apparently ignored the fact that under the Constitution, the state had no power to impair the obligations of the contracts. Regardless of the name given the process by which it was made possible, a new power was exercised by the state and was sanctioned by the Court, sanctioned because any other action on the part of the Court would have

[96] "The Minnesota Moratorium Case," *Brooklyn Law Review*, III (1934), 313–29. The author of this note is of the opinion that the legislation in question is not a departure from precedent and that the Court "grasped" the provision for the payment of rental because it realized the justice and the necessity of such a measure. Wright, *The Growth of American Constitutional Law*, p. 171, finds the decision "surprising" and "out of line with precedents."

On several occasions the Court has held that an individual had no ground for complaint, either under the contracts clause or the due process clause, merely because legislation substituted one kind of remedy for that provided in the contract. ". . . all he is guaranteed by the Fourteenth Amendment is the preservation of his substantial right to redress by some effective procedure." Gibbs *v.* Zimmerman, 290 U.S. 326, 332 (1933). See Doty *v.* Love, 295 U.S. 64, 70 (1935); and Treigle *v.* Acme Homestead Association, 297 U.S. 189, 191 (1936), in which the Court held invalid a state law which altered the method of withdrawal from a building-and-loan association in such a way as to leave the time and manner of paying the withdrawing member's share to the discretion of the directors.

[97] 290 U.S. 398, 426 (1934). Samuel Zelkowick, "Mortgage Moratorium," *Illinois Law Review*, XXVIII (1934), 830, 835, says of this: "If, then, precedent, history, and logic are true guide posts of the law, the Minnesota statute was unconstitutional, unless *Ex parte* Milligan [4 Wall. 2 (1866)] and Wilson *v.* New [243 U.S. 322 (1917)] to the contrary notwithstanding, and emergency operates to generate new governmental powers. This possibility would, of course, have been an anathema to the authors of Art. I, sec. 10, who fatuously, as it at present appears, supposed that they had forever banned stay laws from the legislative repertoire. Yet the only deduction which can be drawn from the instant case is that an emergency does have that effect." See Jane Perry Clark, "Emergencies and the Law," *Political Science Quarterly*, XLIX (1934), 268–83. The Court, in the early years of its existence, had held that "the rights of necessity form a part of our law." 1 Dal. 357, 362 (1798).

been disastrous. Here, the Court was faced with an economic problem which had demanded a ready answer of the state legislature. Whether one calls it "rationalizing" [98] or merely "discovering" [99] that the Constitution admitted of an interpretation which would cover this situation, the opinion of the majority indicates that the Court read the constitutional limitations in the light of an economic and social crisis which a majority of the justices believed could best be resolved by the state. Neither the contracts clause nor due process of law was found to tip the scales in favor of the creditors. The Court declared: "Not only is the constitutional provision qualified by the measure of control which the State retains over remedial processes, but the State also continues to possess authority to safeguard the vital interests of its people." It does not matter that legislation appropriate to that end "has the result of modifying or abrogating contracts already in existence." [100] Existing laws are read into contracts in order to fix obligations between the parties, but "the reservation of essential attributes of sovereign power is also read into contracts as a postulate of the legal order." [101] The prohibition against the impairment of contracts was said to presuppose the maintenance of a government with authority adequate to secure the peace and order of society.[102]

The opinion of the Court did not condone the destruction of contractual rights. Such action on the part of the state was said to be beyond the pale of due process. But "it does not follow that conditions may not arise in which a temporary restraint of enforcement may be *consistent with the spirit and purpose of the constitutional provision* and thus be found to be within the range

[98] "Constitutionality of Mortgage Relief Legislation," *Harvard Law Review*, XLVII (1934), 660, 668. The author of the note thinks that to justify the decision in this case "the majority is really 'rationalizing' a constitutional limitation to subserve what it deems the requirements of an increasingly complex economic structure."

[99] Howard L. McBain, "Some Aspects of Judicial Review," *Boston University: The Gasper Bacon Lectures on the Constitution of the United States* (Boston, 1939), pp. 375, 378–81.

[100] 290 U.S. 398, 434 (1934), citing Stephenson *v*. Binford, 287 U.S. 251 (1932).

[101] 290 U.S. 398, 435 (1934).

[102] *Ibid*. The Court found that the question was "no longer merely that of one party to a contract as against another, but of the use of reasonable means to safeguard the economic structure on which all good depends." *Ibid.*, p. 438.

of the reserved power of the State to protect the vital interests of the community." [103]

The legislation here challenged was a temporary measure. It applied to already existing mortgages only and would come to an end whenever the court of the county found that the emergency no longer existed in that locality. The Court implied that if the provisions extended beyond the emergency it might be interpreted as virtually destroying the contracts and would be invalid. But no criterion was established for determining the existence of an emergency. In this particular instance few persons would be so unreasonable as to say that there was no emergency. The more difficult problem—that of determining the moment at which the emergency comes to an end—did not come before the Court until eleven years later.

The Existence of an Emergency a Matter for Legislative Determination. In 1933, New York enacted a mortgage-moratorium law similar to that of Minnesota. The law was upheld by the state court as an emergency measure and supposedly was to become ineffective when the emergency ceased to exist. Year after year the legislature found that the emergency situation in the state made the moratorium law necessary and so extended its provisions. In 1942 the Legislative Committee on Mortgages investigated the debt situation in the state and the number of mortgages which would be callable as soon as the moratorium was lifted. On the basis of the facts found, the committee concluded that the emergency which existed in 1933 and which had called forth the moratory legislation still existed in New York. Further, a new emergency, probably more serious than the first, would be precipitated if the ban on foreclosures were lifted.[104] In 1943 the moratorium was extended to July, 1944,[105] and when the law was applied to a mortgage which had been due in 1924, the mortgagee challenged

---

[103] *Ibid.,* p. 439. (Italics added.)

[104] *New York Legislative Documents,* 1942, No. 45. See Robert H. Skilton, "Mortgage Moratoria since 1933," *University of Pennsylvania Law Review,* XCII (1943), 53–90, for a discussion of the undesirable aspects of the states' extension of this type of legislation over a period of high wages and full employment. See also *New York Legislative Documents,* 1938, No. 58, p. 38.

[105] *Thompson's Laws of New York, Supp. 1943, Uncon. Laws,* par. 1807.

the extension of the moratorium as a deprivation of property without due process.[106]

Justice Frankfurter, for the Court, found that the challenge as a denial of due process of law was too feeble to merit consideration.[107] However, he made several observations which leave no doubt as to the attitude of the majority of the Court on the matter. Justice Frankfurter said that since the Court's decision in the Blaisdell case there were no open spaces for controversy as to the constitutionality of moratory legislation referable to the depression.[108] He considered that the action of the legislature was based on the findings of an "expert" commission which had concluded that "the sudden termination of the legislation which has dammed up normal liquidation of these mortgages for more than eight years might well result in an emergency more acute than that which the original legislation was intended to alleviate." [109] In view of this expert information Justice Frankfurter thought that it would be very strange indeed if the federal Constitution would operate to prevent the state legislature from protecting the people of the state against such dangers. He concluded that the Constitution did not so restrict the states.[110]

It was said that when a "widely diffused public interest" has become enmeshed in a "network of multitudinous private arrangements," the state's authority to protect the vital interests of its people cannot be hindered by "abstracting one such private arrangement from its general public context and treating it as though it were a private contract constitutionally immune." Thus,

[106] East New York Savings Bank *v.* Haln, 326 U.S. 230 (1945).
[107] *Ibid.*, p. 231.
[108] *Ibid.*
[109] *Ibid.*, p. 235. Judge Lewis, dissenting from the decision of the Federal Circuit Court upholding the legislation, concluded that there existed in the state no emergency which would justify the extension of the moratorium. He found that the 1933 legislation had been upheld chiefly because of the unemployment situation. Between 1933 and 1943 the number of employed persons had increased from 323,071 to 735,265, or over 91 per cent, and the weekly payrolls had increased approximately 266 per cent. He found that in 1943 time and demand bank deposits in New York banks had reached an all-time maximum of 25.7 billions. East New York Savings Bank *v.* Haln, 59 N.E. (2d) 625, 629 (1944).
[110] 326 U.S. 230, 235 (1945). In July, 1944, the legislature declared that on the basis of information gathered by the Committee on Mortgages, it found that the emergency "still continues and that it may reasonably be expected to continue to and including July 1, 1945." *Thompson's Laws of New York, Supp. 1944, Uncon. Laws,* par. 1807.

the Court, without inquiring into the situation existing in the state, accepted the legislative finding that an emergency situation comparable to that of the early thirties continued to plague the state. On the basis of that finding the state was permitted to extend legislation which in effect impaired the obligations of a private contract. Apparently neither the contracts clause nor the due process of law clause is at present a bar to enactments of this nature. Justice Frankfurter reminded the appellant that the place to determine how much weight should be given to the elements which were considered in extending the moratorium was in the legislature, not in the courts.[111]

The Court has frequently said that emergencies do not create power, but only give rise to new occasions for the exercise of already existent powers. Little distinction can be seen between the two in these cases involving the impairment of the obligations of contracts. The state is expressly forbidden by the Constitution to impair contract obligations or to take property without due process of law. Yet under some emergency conditions such impairment is held not to be a violation of the Constitution. Logically, it would seem that since the moratory legislation is upheld as an emergency measure, the state in enacting it exercised a power which it did not possess under other circumstances. As the decisions now stand, not only will such measures be upheld as emergency legislation but also, the state's declaration of the existence of an emergency will be accepted by the Court.

Rehabilitation Through Bankruptcy Proceedings. Though other states followed Minnesota's lead and enacted moratory legislation, the problem of the mortgagor became of national import as the depression continued. The Frazier-Lemke Act of 1934, which became Section 75 (s) of the federal bankruptcy law,[112] was intended to afford relief to farmer-debtors by providing a moratorium for all mortgage debts. Under this section the debtor was afforded the alternative of making a composition of his debts

[111] 326 U.S. 230, 232–33 (1945). Cf. Sterling v. Constantine, 287 U.S. 378 (1932), where the governor's proclamation of an emergency in the oil fields did not save his action under a declaration of martial law from the Court's condemnation as a violation of due process of law.

[112] 48 *Stat.* 1289.

in agreement with the mortgagee, or failing that, being adjudged a bankrupt under 75 (s). As a bankrupt, he acquired alternative options as regards the mortgaged property. Under paragraph 3 of 75 (s) all proceedings against the farmer would be stayed. He could then buy all or any part of the mortgaged property, free from the claims of his creditors, by paying the value at which such property was appraised by the court. Payment of the appraised value, plus a nominal interest, would be made on the installment plan to extend over a period of six years. During this period the farmer would remain in possession of the land.

If the mortgagee refused to assent to this plan, the debtor could demand that the bankruptcy court stay all proceedings for five years, during which the property would be under the control of the court but the farmer would remain in actual possession. He would be required to pay a reasonable rental determined by the court, to be distributed among the secured and unsecured creditors as their interests appeared. At the end of the five-year period the debtor could pay into the court the full amount of the appraised value, or the reappraised value if the creditor asked for a reappraisal, and obtain full possession of, and title to, the property. The provisions of the statute were to be applied only to already existing mortgage debts, so as not to destroy the farmers' credit.

The validity of Section 75 (s) was challenged as a violation of due process of law in Louisville Joint Stock Land Corp. v. Radford.[113] Justice Brandeis, speaking for a unanimous Court, held the law invalid as operating to deprive the creditor of its property without due process of law. It was said that the power of Congress to enact uniform bankruptcy laws must be exercised with regard for the requirements of the due process of law guaranteed by the Fifth Amendment.[114] By the operation of the law, the mortgagee

[113] 295 U.S. 555 (1935). See comments on this case by Z. M. Diamond and Alfred Letzler, "The New Frazier-Lemke Act: A Study," *Columbia Law Review*, XXXVII (1937), 1092–1135.

[114] 295 U.S. 555, 589 (1935). But under the bankruptcy power, Congress may discharge the debtor's personal obligations, because neither the Fifth Amendment nor any other clause in the Constitution contains a prohibition against the impairment of the obligations of a contract applicable to the national government. *Ibid.*, p. 589. In Continental Illinois National Bank and Trust Co. of Chicago v. Chicago, Rock Island and Pacific Ry. Co., 294 U.S. 648, 680 (1935), speaking of Section 77 of the bankruptcy law, the Court said that "The Constitution, as has many times been pointed out, does not in terms prohibit Congress from impairing

was said to have been deprived without due process of law of at least five specific property rights of substantial value. Justice Brandeis enumerated these rights as: (a) the right to retain the lien until the indebtedness is paid; (b) the right to realize upon the security by a judicial public sale; (c) the right to determine when such sale will take place; (d) the right to protect its interests in the property by bidding at such sale whenever held, and thus to be assured that the mortgaged property will be devoted primarily to the satisfaction of the debt, either through the receipt of the proceeds of fair competitive sale or by taking the property itself; (e) the right to control the property during the period of default, subject only to the discretion of the court, and to have the rents and profits collected by a receiver for the satisfaction of the debt.[115] Justice Brandeis rejected the idea that the same emergency which had given occasion for the Minnesota moratory legislation would support the law now challenged. There was little weighing of the social interests involved. The creditor had been deprived of certain rights acquired by the terms of the mortgage contract, and that was sufficient to invalidate the law. "The province of the Court," it was said, "is limited to deciding whether the Frazier-Lemke Act as applied has taken from the bank without compensation, and given to Radford rights in specific property of substantial value. . . . As we concluded that the Act, as applied, has done so, we must hold it void. For the Fifth Amendment commands that however great the Nation's needs, private property shall not thus be taken even for a wholly public use without just compensation." [116]

---

the obligation of contracts as it does the states. . . . Speaking generally, it may be said that Congress, while without power to impair the obligation of contracts by law acting directly and independently to that end, has authority to pass legislation pertinent to any of the powers conferred by the Constitution, however it may operate collaterally or incidently to impair or destroy the obligation of private contracts." See Norman v. Baltimore & Ohio Ry. Co., 294 U.S. 240, 307 (1935), where the Court held that the due process clause of the Fifth Amendment did not forbid Congress to impair the obligations of contracts and that whatever deprivation of property resulted from the abrogation of the "gold clause" was merely incidental to the exercise of a dominant constitutional power to regulate the currency. Justices McReynolds, Van Devanter, Butler, and Sutherland dissented in this case.

[115] 295 U.S. 555, 594 (1935).

[116] Ibid., pp. 601–602. (Italics added.) The author of "Invalidity of the Frazier-Lemke Amendment to the Bankruptcy Act," Columbia Law Review, XXXV

In 1937 an amended Frazier-Lemke Act [117] was passed, again for the purpose of relieving the debtor-farmers whose property otherwise would be lost through foreclosure sales. The constitutionality of the statute, as amended, was upheld in Wright v. Vinton Branch of the Mountain Trust Bank of Roanoke,[118] with Justice Brandeis again writing the opinion of the Court. There was said to be no doubt as to the power of Congress to offer to distressed farmers a means of rehabilitation under the bankruptcy power.[119] The bank contended that it had been deprived of property without due process of law. Further, it was alleged that the three-year stay provided by the act was absolute and therefore per se a denial of due process.

The opinion of the Court in this case evidences a much less exacting scrutiny of the provisions of the act with regard to the requirements of due process than had been shown in the Radford case. The Court found that three of the rights of which the creditor was said to have been deprived without due process by the operation of the original act were definitely secured to him by the amended section. In the Radford case the Court had said that the creditor had a substantial right in being permitted to bid on the property at a public sale. This defect was not specifically

---

(1935), 1136–37, felt that there was an exaggeration of the deprivation suffered by the creditor and a summary treatment of the agricultural situation adduced to justify the measure. This might, it was said, be interpreted to mean that the Court has rejected the criteria of reasonableness set up in previous decisions.

[117] 49 *Stat.* 943–45.

[118] 300 U.S. 440 (1937). For a discussion of the act and the decision in the present case see Alfred Letzler, "Bankruptcy Reorganization for Farmers," *Columbia Law Review,* XL (1940), 1133–73.

[119] 300 U.S. 440, 456 (1937). In Kuehner v. Irving Trust Co., 299 U.S. 445, 451–52 (1937), the Court said that there is ". . . as respects the exertion of the bankruptcy power, a significant difference between a property interest and a contract, since the Constitution does not forbid the impairment of the obligations of the latter. . . . While, therefore, the Fifth Amendment forbids the destruction of a contract, it does not prohibit bankruptcy legislation affecting the creditor's remedy for its enforcement against the debtor's assets, or the measure of the creditor's participation therein, if the statutory provisions are consonant with a fair, reasonable, and equitable distribution of those assets." In determining whether the remedy had been arbitrarily or unreasonably circumscribed, the Court considered that in the judgment of Congress the limitations appeared necessary and advantageous to a successful reorganization of the bankrupt. Justice Roberts said that ". . . its judgment is conclusive upon us, if the enactment is within its power." See Continental Illinois National Bank and Trust Co. of Chicago v. Chicago, Rock Island and Pacific Ry. Co., 294 U.S. 648, 674 (1935).

remedied by the terms of the new section, but Justice Brandeis thought that the law, as amended, should be construed as protecting that right, for that seemed to have been the intent of Congress. In view of the fact that the new law was passed expressly to remedy the defects of the first, which had been invalidated in the Radford case, and in the light of the reports and explanations given in Congress when the amendment was under discussion, he did not think it unreasonable to assume that Congress intended to protect this particular right. The creditor's right to retain the lien until the indebtedness was paid was said to be secured by the provision that the debtor's possession of the land under the supervision of the bankruptcy court was to remain "subject to all existing mortgages, liens, pledges, and encumbrances." His right to realize the security by a public sale was said to be secured by the provision that "Upon request in writing by any secured creditor or creditors, the court shall order the property upon which secured creditors have a lien to be sold at public auction." [120] If this provision had been applied, as the Court implied that it would be, it would seem that the primary purpose of the act would have been defeated.[121]

The Court did not specifically answer the creditor's contention that an absolute stay of three years denied due process. Justice Brandeis merely explained away the basis of the complaint by interpreting the law to mean that the stay was not absolute. In the first place, he found that the bankruptcy court could order the property to be sold if the debtor defaulted on the payment of the rent. Secondly, if after a reasonable time it became evident that the debtor had no hope of rehabilitating himself financially within the three-year period, the court might order the property to be sold.[122] Lastly, if the court found that the emergency which had

[120] 300 U.S. 440, 460–62 (1937). Cf. United States v. Shreveport, 287 U.S. 77, 83 (1932), where the Court declared that punctuation was no part of an act of Congress. If necessary to arrive at the natural meaning of the words, the Court said that it would repunctuate the measure. In this case, it was said that congressional-committee reports were not determining factors in the construction of an act.

[121] That this provision was not to be applied so as to protect the creditor's right to demand a public sale became evident in the case of Wright v. Union Central Life Insurance Co., 304 U.S. 502, 514 (1938).

[122] 300 U.S. 440, 462, n. 6 (1937). Justice Brandeis said that this construction was in harmony with the requirement that the proceedings be initiated in good

prompted the passage of the act no longer existed in the locality, it might shorten the stay and proceed to liquidate the estate.[123] In reply to the mortgagee's contention that he had been denied due process of law by not being allowed to control the property during the period of default, the Court declared that it was not true that possession by the mortgagor during this period was less favorable to the creditor than possession by a receiver.[124]

In the Radford case Justice Brandeis had seen the issue to be simply "Did the application of the act take away valuable property rights without compensation?" The answer was in the affirmative, and therefore it was held that due process had been denied. In the present case he found that "The question which the objections raise is not whether the act does more than modify remedial rights. It is whether the legislation modifies the secured creditor's rights, remedial and substantive, *to such an extent as to deny the due process of law guaranteed by the Fifth Amendment.*"[125] The answer was simply: ". . . we are of the opinion that the provisions of section 75 (s) make no *unreasonable modification* of the mortgagee's rights; and hence are valid."[126]

The Court did not deny that some of the creditor's rights under the mortgage contract were infringed by the operation of the new bankruptcy law. It held, in effect, that the discharge of a valid contract obligation by an approved section of the bankruptcy law was itself due process of law. The social and economic interests of the state in protecting the individual debtor were found to outweigh interests involved in the creditor's loss of con-

---

faith. Relief under Section 75 (s), he said, was available only to those who had made a bona fide attempt to effect a composition under Section 75 (a)–(r) and had failed. If the debtor is beyond all reasonable hope of financial rehabilitation, he said, and the proceeding under the general provision of Section 75 cannot be expected to have any effect other than to postpone the inevitable liquidation, the proceedings would not have been in good faith and might be halted at the outset. See Adair *v.* Bank of America National Trust and Savings Ass'n, 303 U.S. 350 (1938), in which the Court held that the stay provisions under judicial discretion in Section O did not deprive the mortgagee of property without due process.

[123] 300 U.S. 440, 462–63 (1937).   [124] *Ibid.*, p. 466.
[125] *Ibid.*, p. 470. (Italics added.)
[126] *Ibid.* (Italics added.) In United States *v.* Bekins, 304 U.S. 27, 54 (1938), the Court sustained the second municipal bankruptcy law, saying that since the bankruptcy power could be extended to effect a composition, there was no merit to the objection under due process.

tract rights. The Court did not hold that the due process clause
had ceased to protect a creditor in his right to have a valid contract
fulfilled. Rather, it held that this was not an absolute right and
that under some circumstances it is not unreasonable, therefore
not a denial of due process, for Congress to infringe this right.[127]

In Wright v. Union Central Life Insurance Co.[128] the Court
upheld Section 75 (n) of the bankruptcy law, which extended
the period of redemption from a foreclosure sale allowed the
mortgagor by the state law. In Wright v. Vinton Branch [129] the
Court had based its finding that the stay was not absolute on that
part of the law which provided that the bankruptcy court might
order a public sale if it appeared that the debtor would not be able
to rehabilitate himself within the three-year period. In the present
case, immediately after the debtor-farmer was adjudicated a bankrupt, the mortgagee petitioned the court for a sale of the property
on the ground that the mortgagor had failed to comply with the
orders of the court and that he had no hope of financial rehabilitation. In pursuance of this petition the court conducted a sale, and
the property was purchased by the mortgagee. On cross-petition
the debtor had sought to obtain possession of the land by paying the appraised value. He appealed from the sale, alleging that
under the law he must be given an opportunity to redeem the property.

The Court in this case was faced with the inevitable conflict of
the provision of the law allowing the debtor a three-year extension and a right to redeem the land with the provision that the
secured creditor might demand a public sale of his security. To
resolve the conflict Justice Brandeis explained that "The debtor
has a right of redemption of which the purchaser is advised, and
until that right of redemption expires the rights of the purchaser
are subject to the power of the Congress over the relationship of
debtor and creditor and its power to legislate for the rehabilitation of the debtor." [130] That such an opportunity for redemption
and a moratorium did not violate the due process of law guaran-

---

[127] 300 U.S. 440, 470 (1937). See Treigle v. Acme Homestead Association,
297 U.S. 189, 197 (1936), where the Court said that the obligations of contracts
must sometimes yield to the proper exercise of the police power of the state.
[128] 304 U.S. 502 (1938).   [129] 300 U.S. 440 (1937).
[130] 304 U.S. 502, 514 (1938).

teed the creditor by the Fifth Amendment was thought to be evident from the decision in the Blaisdell case.[131] The purchaser was said to have no reason to complain so long as he retained the right to have the court terminate the stay upon the debtor's violation of its orders, or so long as he was protected to the present value of the property.[132] The debtor had asked to redeem the property in accordance with the federal law. Unless such request, said Justice Brandeis, took precedence over the creditor's petition for a public sale, the purpose of the law, namely, to protect the farmer-debtor victims of the depression, would be defeated. Therefore, the creditor's right to demand a sale must be contingent upon the debtor's failure to exercise his power to redeem the property before a foreclosure sale. The property must be appraised by the court, and if the mortgagor is able to redeem it at the value fixed, the creditor loses his right to demand a sale and bid the amount of the debt. In effect the decision in this case seems to rest on the theory that the mortgagor's debt decreases with the decreased value of the property. Certainly this would indicate a substantial change, since the Court's decision in the Radford case, in the extent of the due process protection afforded the mortgagee.

In the case of John Hancock Mutual Life Insurance Co. v. Bartels [133] the Court was faced squarely with the issue of whether the stay could be terminated when it appeared that the debtor could not become financially rehabilitated within the three-year period. Here the petitioner asked that Bartel's adjudication as bankrupt be set aside and his petition dismissed. Petitioner alleged that the debtor was not entitled to relief under Section 75 (s) because his petition had not been filed in good faith or with any hope of working out a composition of his debts. A unanimous Court, through Chief Justice Hughes, declared: "The subsections of Section 75 which regulated the procedure in relation to the efforts of a farmer-debtor to obtain a composition or extension contains no provision for a dismissal because of the absence of a reasonable

---

[131] *Ibid.*, p. 515.
[132] Cf. Borchard v. California, 310 U.S. 311, 317 (1940). See Wright v. Union Central Life Insurance Co., 311 U.S. 273, 278 (1940), where it was said that the creditor had no constitutional claim to more than the present value of the property.
[133] 308 U.S. 180 (1939).

probability of the financial rehabilitation of the debtor." [134] In a footnote the Chief Justice explains that "What was said upon this point in Note 6 in Wright v. Vinton Branch, 300 U.S. 440, 462, was not essential to the decision in that case and is not supported by the terms of the statute." [135]

REGULATION OF EXTRASTATE ACTIVITIES

The general rule has been that a state may not extend the operation of its laws beyond its own boundaries. Jurisdiction, under such a rule, was thought to be coincident with the state line, and any regulation which took effect beyond the jurisdiction resulted in a denial of due process of law. In the case of New York Insurance Co. v. Dodge,[136] Justice Brandeis, in a dissenting opinion, proffered a different rule. He was of the opinion that the test of a state's legislative jurisdiction over a contract should be whether the state had a substantial interest in the substance of the contract obligation. The rule was expressly applied, in the matter of due process, for the first time in Hartford Insurance Co. v. Delta Pine Land Co.[137] This case arose as a result of a contract for bond entered into in Tennessee, where both parties to the contract had offices. The bond was to guarantee the integrity and faithfulness of any person in the employ of the insured. Though made in Tennessee, the contract contained no stipulation as to payment if one or all parties involved were in other states at the time of loss on which a claim could be made. According to the law of Tennessee the statute of limitations would act to bar the right of action if the claim were not presented within fifteen months after the loss. The employee, the obligor, and the obligee were in Mississippi at the date of the defalcation. The surety company was notified of the loss but it made no payment. The formal claim was not presented until nearly two years later. Under the laws of Mississippi there was no statute of limitations, and the application of the fifteen-month limitation to invalidate this claim would

---

[134] *Ibid.*, p. 184. [135] *Ibid.*, p. 184, n. 3.

[136] 246 U.S. 357, 383, 386 (1918).

[137] 292 U.S. 143 (1934). See G. W. C. Ross, "Has the Conflict of Laws Become a Branch of Constitutional Law?" *Minnesota Law Review*, XV (1931), 161–81, for a discussion of earlier cases which led to the ruling in the Dodge case.

constitute a violation of the constitution of the state. According to the laws of Mississippi, as construed by the courts of that state, this was a Mississippi contract by virtue of the fact that the parties were in the state at the time the obligation matured.

Justice Roberts, speaking for the Court, held that Mississippi had deprived appellant of due process of law by extending its statute so as to impair the contract obligation. The law of Tennessee, under which the contract had been made, was said to be binding, and the rights which had become vested under the Tennessee statute of limitations were said to be protected by the due process of law clause of the Fourteenth Amendment.[138] Here the court of the forum applied its own law to a subject matter in which a second state with a different law was thought to have a superior interest. Such application was held to be a denial of due process because it gave an unwarranted extraterritorial effect to the legislative authority of the state.[139] Under the ruling of this case the state of the forum, if it has a substantial interest in the substance of the contract obligation, will be permitted to extend its laws beyond its borders to reach such contract.

The "governmental interest" rule was given further application in Alaska Packers Ass'n v. Industrial Accident Commission of California.[140] In this case the Court held that the due process clause did not require the state of the forum to apply the compensation law of the state in which the injury occurred when the law of the latter conflicted with its public policy or a "substantial governmental interest." Briefly, these were the facts of the case. Palma, a Mexican worker in California, contracted for employment in Alaska during the salmon season. Under the terms of the contract the employer was to pay Palma upon his return to San Francisco. Both agreed to be bound by the compensation laws of Alaska, which, as construed by Alaska, were exclusive of all other remedies in the case of a claim arising from injury in that territory. Palma was injured during his employment in Alaska, but upon his return to California he entered a claim and was granted a reward by the Industrial Accident Commission of that

138 292 U.S. 143, 149–50 (1934).
139 E. Merrick Dodd, "The Power of the Supreme Court to Review Decisions in the Field of Conflicts of Laws," *Harvard Law Review*, XXXIX (1926), 533–62.
140 294 U.S. 532 (1935).

state in accordance with the compensation law of California. The employer assailed this action on the part of the commission as void, on the ground that it deprived him of property without due process of law. He contended that California should have applied the law of Alaska as had been agreed upon in the contract of employment.

The Court reaffirmed its former ruling that due process of law denies the state the power to extend its control to contracts executed and to be performed outside its bounds. But California, it was found, did not purport to give extraterritorial effect to its laws. The statute provided a remedy "for injuries received in the course of employment entered into within the State, wherever they may occur." [141] The fact that the contract was made within the state gave the legislature control over its terms.[142] Therefore, the legislature did not deprive the employer of due process of law by specifying that its remedy was exclusive of all others.

In the light of the extent to which the state could control the terms of the contract, the Court found that the only question which might arise under the due process of law clause was whether the manner in which the state had exercised its power was so arbitrary and unreasonable as to amount to a denial of due process. In reaching an answer the Court considered that the employee was two thousand miles from home and three thousand miles from Alaska. Under such conditions it would be unlikely that he ever would return to Alaska to make his claim. Any judgment which he might have obtained under the laws of Alaska in a California court would have been enforcible only in Alaska. Meanwhile he might have become a burden on the state. For these reasons the Court agreed that unless he were afforded a remedy in California under the laws of that state, he most likely would be without relief. This was a matter of grave concern to the state.[143] On these considerations the Court held that there was a rational basis for the legislation under which the action of the commission was taken and that therefore the action was not unreasonable or arbitrary. Hence, there was no denial of due process.[144] The Court

[141] *Ibid.*, p. 540.
[143] *Ibid.*, p. 542.
[142] *Ibid.*, pp. 540–41.
[144] *Ibid.*, pp. 542–43.

went further, to say that the due process clause does not impose upon the state any obligation to apply the remedy of another state rather than its own. It was said that only the "full faith and credit" clause imposed upon the courts of one state the duty to enforce the laws of another state.[145] The refusal on the part of California to grant full faith and credit to the laws of Alaska, however, was said not to deny appellant due process of law, for the state of the forum had a substantial interest in seeing that the obligations of the contract were fulfilled.[146]

Probably of greater significance than the application of the governmental-interest rule in either of the foregoing cases is its application to state regulation of business activities which cut across the state line. The rule was first applied to the regulation of the insurance business in the case of Osborn *v.* Ozlin,[147] in which the Court upheld a Virginia statute fixing the part of the insurance agent's commission which could be shared with an out-of-state broker. The Court found that Virginia had not sought to prevent the making of insurance contracts beyond its borders. Rather, it was said that "She merely claims that her interests in the risks which these contracts are designed to prevent warrant the kind of control she has here imposed." [148] In view of the numerous regulations already imposed by the states upon the insurance business, the Court concluded that the state might itself go into the business. If the state could pre-empt the field of insurance, it was not unreasonable, the Court held, to say that it might "stay its intervention short of such drastic step by insisting that its own residents shall have a share in devising and safeguarding protection against its local hazards." [149]

Upon a review of the difficulties involved in protecting its citizens against fraud and inefficiency, the Court held that the

[145] *Ibid.,* p. 543. Cf. Justice Stone's dissent in Yarborough *v.* Yarborough, 290 U.S. 202, 214 (1933). In this case the Court held that a Georgia decree of alimony for the support of a minor child must be given full faith and credit by South Carolina and that therefore, in accordance with due process, South Carolina was precluded from imposing other obligations upon the father, even though the child was a resident of that state and the father owned property there. Justice Stone did not find this relation between "due process" and "full faith and credit."

[146] 294 U.S. 532, 549–50 (1935).

[147] 310 U.S. 53 (1940). See Holmes *v.* Springfield Fire and Marine Insurance Co., 311 U.S. 606 (1941), 32 F. Supp. 964.

[148] 310 U.S. 53, 63–64 (1940).   [149] *Ibid.,* p. 66.

state has a "definable interest in the contract she seeks to regulate." [150] Whether the regulations imposed would remedy effectively the evils said to exist or whether any social advantage would
accrue to the state as a result of such regulations was said to be
without the province of the Court.

The appellant contended that the provision requiring the local
agent to retain at least one half of the commission forced the
company to pay for services not rendered, since the local agent
did little more than solicit and transmit the applications to the
office in Illinois. To this Justice Frankfurter replied that if the
local agent performed his functions adequately, the people of
the state might benefit. Or, said he, "At least Virginia may have
believed so. And she may have concluded that an agency system,
such as this legislation was designed to promote, is better calculated to further these desirable ends than other modes of 'production.' When these beliefs are emphasized by legislation embodying similar notions of policy in a dozen states, it would savor
of intolerance for us to suggest that a legislature could not constitutionally entertain the views which the legislation adopts." [151]

In answer to the contention that the legislation in question
denied due process by extending the state's regulatory measures
to contracts outside the state, Justice Frankfurter replied that the
question was not whether the Virginia regulation would restrict
appellant's freedom of action outside the state by subjecting that
freedom of action to financial burdens. So long as the restrictions
imposed by the state were "not within that domain which the
Constitution forbids," the mere fact that they may have reper-

[150] *Ibid.*, p. 65. In the Federal Circuit Court several facts concerning the economic interests which led Virginia to enact this law were pointed out. In 1937
the plaintiff companies received premiums of $410,967.62 on policies of Virginia
coverage produced outside the state. These twelve companies paid $70,860.90 in
commissions to nonresidents for the production of these policies. In 1938 the
companies received as premiums $183,727.38, and ten of the companies paid as
commissions to nonresidents $31,635.53. It was estimated that resident agents lost
$185,161.00 in commissions to out-of-state agents during 1938. Foreign insurance
companies wrote from 10 to 20 per cent of the coverage for Virginia during
the years of 1937–38. Virginia companies could not compete for this part of the
insurance business because they were not able to offer the reduced rates offered
by the larger foreign companies. Osborn *v.* Ozlin, 29 F. Supp. 71, 75 (1939).

[151] 310 U.S. 53, 64–65 (1940). Cf. the slight weight accorded the fact that in
1936 twenty-three states had wage and hour laws similar to the New York statute
invalidated in Morehead *v.* New York ex rel. Tipaldo, 298 U.S. 587 (1936).

cussions beyond the state bounds is of no judicial significance. Apparently the Constitution does not forbid the extension of the state's legislative jurisdiction to extrastate insurance activities if the state has a substantial governmental interest in the transaction.[152]

In 1939, New York amended its insurance law so as to provide a detailed plan for the regulation of all types of insurance companies doing business in the state. The regulations were made applicable to reciprocal insurance companies, associations, and corporations. In Hoopeston Canning Co. *v.* Cullen [153] appellants challenged the validity of the law as applied to them in that their business was carried on by the attorney, in fact, through the main offices located in Illinois. Of significance in this case is the Court's distinction between the bases upon which such cases have been decided in the past and the more recent approach of the Court. Justice Brandeis explained that "In determining the power of the State to apply its own regulatory laws to insurance business activities, the question in earlier cases became involved by conceptualistic discussion of theories of the place of contracting or performance. More recently it has been recognized that the State may have substantial interests in the business of insurance of its people or property regardless of these isolated factors. This interest may be measured by highly realistic considerations such as the protection of the citizen insured or the State from the incidents of loss." [154] New York was said to have a right to protect the property interests of the state, and, Justice Brandeis added, "There is no more reason to bar the State from authority over the insurance of the property within it than to exclude it from control over other property interests mentioned." [155]

The company alleged that the only activity carried on by the local agent was the solicitation and transmission of applications

---

[152] *Ibid.* For a discussion of the relation of "due process" to "conflicts of laws" in the regulation of the life-insurance business, see Charles W. Carnahan, *Conflicts of Laws in Life Insurance Contracts* (Chicago, 1942), pp. 63–84; and Joseph O'Meara, "Constitutional Aspects of the Conflicts of Laws: Recent Developments," *Minnesota Law Review,* XXVII (1942), 500–18.

[153] 318 U.S. 313 (1943). See "Annotation: Reciprocal Insurance," 145 *A.L.R.,* 1121, and "Annotation: Reciprocal or Inter-Insurance," 94 *A.L.R.,* 836.

[154] 318 U.S. 313, 316 (1943). Cf. Allgeyer *v.* Louisiana, 165 U.S. 578, 587 (1897).

[155] 318 U.S. 313, 318 (1943).

to the Illinois office. For this reason it was complained that the present law would regulate contracts wholly outside the state. But the Court countered with the answer that the determining factor is not where the formalities of contract are carried out but rather whether the insurance enterprise as a whole so affects New York interests as to give that state the power to impose the regulations.[156]

The case of State Farm Mutual Automobile Insurance Co. v. Duel [157] involved the validity of a Wisconsin statute requiring foreign insurance companies to set aside a reserve fund computed on the basis of 50 per cent of the premium and 50 per cent of the membership fees collected by the company in all the states in which it operates. The company, an Illinois corporation doing business in Wisconsin, alleged that its property had been taken without due process of law because the amount of the reserve fund was determined by reference to out-of-state income. The Court held that "The mere fact that the state action may have repercussions beyond state lines is of no judicial significance so long as the action is not within the domain which the Constitution forbids." [158] Unfortunately the Court did not indicate the bounds of the domain constitutionally withdrawn from regulation by the states. However, the law in question was held not to violate the due process clause. It was held that the state might embark upon a policy of regulation which to be effective must extend to activities beyond its borders if these activities have any actual bearing upon the public interests of the regulating state. Such regulation of extrastate matters does not deny the due process guaranteed by the Fourteenth Amendment.

The most recent, and in some respects the most extreme, application of this doctrine of governmental interest may be seen in the case of Connecticut Mutual Life Insurance Co. v. Moore.[159] Under New York's Abandoned Property Law three classes of insurance policies issued on the lives of persons resident of the state are deemed abandoned and will escheat to the state, namely, matured endowment policies which have been unclaimed for seven years; policies payable on death where the insured, if living,

156 Ibid., p. 319. 157 324 U.S. 154 (1945).
158 Ibid., pp. 157–58. 159 333 U.S. 541 (1948).

would have attained the limiting age under the mortality tables on which reserves are based, as to which no transactions have occurred for seven years; and policies payable on death in which the insured has died and no claim by persons entitled thereto has been made within a seven-year period from the date of the insured's death. Connecticut Mutual contended that the statute, applied to policies issued by it to New York residents, deprives the company of property without due process because it permits New York to take over unclaimed moneys issued by nonresident insurers for delivery in New York upon the lives of persons resident in New York at the time of issuance but not resident in that state at the time of maturity of the claim. Justice Reed spoke for the majority and found that the issue turns upon the question "Does the state have sufficient contacts with the transactions here in question to justify the exertion of the power to seize abandoned moneys due to its residents?" The question is answered affirmatively and the statute upheld by a recitation of the reasoning of the New York Court of Appeals to the effect that "the core of the debtor obligations of the plaintiff companies was created through acts done in this State under the protection of its laws, and the ties thereby established between the companies and the State were, without more, sufficient to validate the jurisdiction here asserted by the Legislature." [160]

Justice Jackson, joined by Justice Douglas, dissented. He could not agree with the Court's application of the vague "sufficient contacts" doctrine as supplying the prerequisites for jurisdiction in this instance. He was not in favor of expressing any opinion as to the validity of the declaratory judgment of the New York court now before the Court. Such decision should await concrete cases in which the Court will be able to see more clearly the results of the application of the law. Justice Frankfurter, agreeing with Justices Jackson and Douglas, would have the Court decline jurisdiction.

It appears that the Court has borrowed a great amount of trouble for itself as well as for states and individuals by this decision. Perhaps there are numerous contacts any one of which would logically meet the requirements of substantial interest so as

[160] *Ibid.*, p. 551.

to give jurisdiction over such abandoned funds. Obviously, an insurance company owes just one beneficiary the amount of the policy and therefore could not be called upon to pay more than one state. Necessarily, when such an issue arises, the Court will have to climb down to concrete cases and make a determination. This it will not be able to do as long as it attempts to apply anything so general and without meaning as the sufficient-contacts standard as expounded in this opinion.

LABOR LEGISLATION

Regulation of Hours and Wages. On June 16, 1933, Congress enacted into law the National Industrial Recovery Act,[161] in which it was asserted that the "wide-spread unemployment and disorganization of industry" burdened interstate commerce and was detrimental to the public welfare. To remedy the situation, Congress embodied in this law a provision for fixing minimum wages and maximum hours in industry. By the Court's decision in the Schechter case,[162] the labor regulations of the statute were voided, along with its other provisions, on the ground that there was an unconstitutional delegation of legislative power and that the subject regulated was not interstate commerce. The due process aspects of the statute were not considered by the Court, though the Schechters had contended that the regulations violated the due process clause. The second attempt by Congress to legislate on the subject of hours and wages on a less grandiose scale was included in the Bituminous Coal Conservation Act [163] of 1935 and was confined to the coal industry.

The statute provided that regulations of hours and wages should be accepted by the entire bituminous coal industry whenever the producers of two thirds of the annual national tonnage of production and representatives of one half the mine workers agreed upon such regulations. When the law was challenged as a denial of due process in Carter *v.* Carter Coal Co.,[164] the Court, speaking

[161] 48 *Stat.* 195.
[162] Schechter Poultry Co. *v.* United States, 295 U.S. 495 (1935).
[163] 49 *Stat.* 991.
[164] 298 U.S. 238 (1936). This decision called forth numerous criticisms, for the most part unfavorable to the Court's position. See Corwin, *Constitutional*

through Justice Sutherland, found that the labor provisions were
"so clearly arbitrary and so clearly a denial of the rights safeguarded by the due process clause" that a reference to previous decisions of the Court would "foreclose" the question.[165] The Chief
Justice concurred with the majority as to the labor provisions of
the statute. To permit a group of employees and producers to make
wage and hour regulations which would be binding on other employees and producers was plainly outside the commerce power of
Congress as restricted by the due process clause of the Fifth
Amendment. The wishes of the majority of workers and producers could not be allowed to override the due process guaranteed to
the minority by that amendment. "Due process" was read to place
a definite restriction upon congressional power to regulate commerce.[166]

Soon after the Carter decision the issue of the state's power to
legislate minimum wages for women without running afoul of the
due process requirements of the Fourteenth Amendment was
before the Court in Morehead v. New York ex rel. Tipaldo.[167]
Justice Butler, for the Court, held that the state in enacting such
a law infringed the employee's as well as the employer's freedom
of contract guaranteed to each by the due process clause.[168] He
did not rest his decision upon the standard of fixing the amount
of the wage but rather on the principle that the legislature had
no power to legislate wage minimums in a business not affected
with a public interest. This was inevitable, given his major premise
that the issue was only "Can this law be distinguished from that
held void in the Adkins case?" and the misconstruction of the
statute by the New York court. He explained that "If the State
had the power to single out for regulation the amount of the wage

---

Revolution, Ltd., p. 89; Osmond Fraenkel, "What Can Be Done About the Constitution and the Supreme Court?" Columbia Law Review, XXXVII (1937), 212–
27; and Kenneth Carr, Democracy and the Supreme Court (Oklahoma City,
1936), Chap. VIII.

[165] 298 U.S. 238, 311 (1936).   [166] Ibid., pp. 318–19.

[167] 298 U.S. 587 (1936). See Robert Hale, "Minimum Wages and the Constitution," Columbia Law Review, XXXVI (1936), 629–33; and Leroy Broun, "Minimum Wage Cases in the Supreme Court," Southern California Law Review,
XI (1938), 256–64.

[168] 298 U.S. 587, 610–11 (1936). The Court had, in Adkins v. Children's Hospital, 261 U.S. 525 (1923), held the minimum-wage law of the District of Columbia
invalid as a violation of due process also.

to be paid women, the value of their services would be a material consideration. But that fact has no relevancy upon the question of whether the State has such power. . . . The dominant issue in the Adkins case was whether Congress had power to establish minimum wages for adult women workers. . . . The ruling that defects in the prescribed standard stamped that act as arbitrary and invalid was an additional ground and of subordinate consequence." [169] This is a much broader view than Justice Sutherland had expressed in the Adkins case. In that case the majority implied at least, that with a proper standard for determining the minimum wage, the legislation would have been held valid.[170]

Nor was the majority in 1936 prevailed upon to change its mind as to the validity of the New York law because of the changes in economic and social conditions since 1923. To the contention that state policies should be considered in the light of the times, Justice Butler said that the statute did not set forth a remedy to meet the emergency situation but rather embodied a permanent policy of the state. The majority views in this case must have come as quite a shock to those who thought that two years previously Justice Roberts had performed the last rites for the affected with a public interest concept. Strangely, he who said in that case that "So far as due process of law is concerned, the States are free to adopt whatever economic policy they deem best suited to their needs" [171] voted with the majority in the instant case to invalidate the New York wage law.

Chief Justice Hughes spoke for Justices Stone, Brandeis, Cardozo, and himself in a dissenting opinion, in which he urged that the Court should have considered the law on its merits, since obviously it was not similar to the act of Congress invalidated in the Adkins case. Furthermore, he thought that since the Adkins case was decided by so close a margin, it should not have been accepted as the ruling law in the present case. To the Chief Justice

[169] 298 U.S. 587, 613–14 (1936).

[170] 261 U.S. 525, 555–57 (1923). There Justice Sutherland conceded that "A statute to pay the value of the services rendered, even to pay with fair relation to the extent of the benefit obtained would be understandable." Thomas Reed Powell, "The Judiciality of Minimum Wage Legislation," *Harvard Law Review,* XXXVII (1924), 545, 552, says one may attribute the Adkins decision to the "malfeasance of the Calendar" rather than to any legal principle.

[171] Nebbia v. New York, 291 U.S. 502, 537–38 (1934).

the issue was clearly that of freedom of contract and the state's power to restrict that freedom. In his judgment due process did not guarantee absolute freedom of contract. Hence, the test of a valid restriction was "whether the limitation upon the freedom of contract is arbitrary and capricious or one reasonably required in order appropriately to serve the public interest in the light of the particular conditions to which the power is addressed." [172] The dissenters could see no logic in the reasoning which would permit the state, within the requirements of due process, to regulate the hours of an employee but forbid it, by an application of that same phrase, to regulate wages.

Justice Stone filed a separate dissenting opinion in which Justices Brandeis and Cardozo concurred. He disagreed with the Chief Justice in basing his dissent solely on the distinction between the law voided in the present case and that held valid in the Adkins case. The "vague and general pronouncement" of the Fourteenth Amendment which forbade a state to deprive one of his liberty without due process was a "limitation of legislative power," he admitted, but not a "formula for its exercise." [173] He explained that

> the liberty which the Amendment protects is not freedom from restraint of all law or any law which reasonable men may think an appropriate means for dealing with any of those matters of public concern with which it is the business of government to deal. There is grim irony in speaking of the freedom of contract of those who, because of their economic necessities, give their services for less than is needful to keep body and soul together. But if this is freedom of contract no one has ever denied that it is freedom which may be restrained, notwithstanding the Fourteenth Amendment, by a statute passed in the public interest. [174]

Justice Stone felt that only the personal "economic predilections" of the members of the Court could explain the opinion that the contract of employment was less a subject for legislative regulation than scores of other subjects already regulated. But "It is not

[172] 298 U.S. 587, 629–30 (1936).   [173] *Ibid.*, p. 636.
[174] *Ibid.*, p. 632. (Italics added.)

for the Courts to resolve doubts whether the remedy by wage regulation is as efficacious as many believe, or is better than some other, or is better even than the blind operation of uncontrolled economic forces." He was of the opinion that the ruling in the Nebbia case should be controlling in this instance. The three dissenters for whom Justice Stone spoke felt that the Court had deliberately avoided passing on the New York statute on its merits and that the issue before the Court specifically called for such consideration.[175] Even if the issue had not been expressly stated in the application for certiorari, they thought the Court should have given it due consideration.

Thus in the face of the Nebbia decision, which had been heralded as the beginning of a new era in the Court's attitude toward its role in the review of economic and social legislation of the states, the due process clause was found to forestall New York in its efforts to provide a living wage to women employed in industry. The fact that due process of law might have been found to protect the employee as well as the employer and that in this instance as in most cases involving that phrase, the interests of the one were actually weighed against the interests of the other seems to have been ignored completely. Apparently it was the considered opinion of the majority of the Court that the subject of a minimum wage was not to be regulated by state or federal government. Any attempt at such regulation would be stricken down as contrary to the due process of law guaranteed the employer and the employee by the Fifth and Fourteenth amendments.

Just what happened to effect the conversion of Justice Roberts on the subject of minimum-wage laws must remain a matter of conjecture. Many answers have been offered. Some of them may be partially correct, for certainly the trends of the times must influence the thinking of a justice on the Supreme Court just as they do the thinking of many other persons. This year was to hold many opportunities for expression of opinions indicative of such trends. It was a presidential-election year as well as a gubernatorial-election year in many states. Both major parties had com-

[175] Ibid., p. 636.

mitted themselves to support state regulation of hours and wages for women and children.[176] Living costs had soared above those of any year since 1931.[177] With these things in mind, as well as with a knowledge of the Court's action upon previous wage and hour regulation, large numbers of people went to the polls. Slightly more than a majority of these people cast their vote for a man who had openly criticized the action of the Court. On February 5, 1937, the President made his "Court Reform" program public and officially announced it to the Congress. Certainly one would have to assume that a justice, per se, is unaware of such events to assume that his thinking would in no way be changed by them. But perhaps it would be equally correct to assume that the Court's vote on the Washington law was taken before the Reform plan reached the Congress,[178] that Justice Roberts, being an open-minded individual, alert to changes in the social and economic situation, considered well the former ruling of the Court and found it not so good. For whatever reason one may ascribe, when the Washington minimum-wage law was challenged before the Court less than a year after the Morehead decision, Justice Roberts voted with the four dissenters of that case and made it possible for the Court to uphold the Washington law.[179] Chief Justice Hughes spoke for the Court; Justices Sutherland, Butler, Van Devanter, and McReynolds dissented.

The majority thought that the action of the state court on the minimum-wage issue demanded a re-examination of the holding in the Adkins case. Here again the majority noted that the once-

[176] See the *Proceedings of the Democratic National Convention* (Washington, D.C., 1936), pp. 44–47, 90–92, where two of the chief speakers announced against the Morehead decision. See also Landon's acceptance address, August 23, 1936, quoted in the *Text Book of the Republican Party*, Republican National Committee (Washington, D.C., 1936), pp. 33, 121.
[177] See United States Department of Labor, Bureau of Labor Statistics, *Report* (Washington, D.C., 1937).
[178] The case was argued December 16–17, 1936. See Charles P. Curtis, *Lions under the Throne* (Boston, 1947), p. 161.
[179] West Coast Hotel Co. v. Parrish, 300 U.S. 379 (1937). Hugh E. Willis, "Constitution Making by the Supreme Court Since 1937," *Indiana Law Journal*, XV (1940), 179–201, concludes that the period from this decision does not mark a new approach by the Court, but only a return to that of the judge-made law of the period of Marshall, Story, and Taney. See Hugh E. Willis, "Growth in the Constitution and Constitutional Law Since the Decision in the Case of West Coast Hotel Co. v. Parrish," *Tulane Law Review*, XX (1945), 22–55.

reverenced freedom of contract was nowhere guaranteed—or even mentioned—in the Constitution.

> No, the Constitution *speaks of liberty and prohibits the deprivation of liberty without due process of law*. In prohibiting that deprivation, the Constitution does not recognize an *absolute and uncontrollable liberty*. Liberty in each of its phases has its history and its connotations. But *the liberty safeguarded is liberty in a social organization which requires the protection of law against the evils which menace the health, safety, morals, and welfare of the people. Liberty, under the Constitution, is thus necessarily subject to the restraints of due process, and regulation which is reasonable in relation to its subject and is adapted in the interests of the community* is due process of law.[180]

The majority did not attempt to distinguish the Washington wage law from that held void in the Morehead case. Instead, the provisions of the two were admitted to be similar. But the Chief Justice described the views expressed in the Adkins case, on which the Morehead decision had rested, as a "departure from the application of the principles governing the regulation by the State of the relation between employer and employee." [181] He concluded that the Adkins case should be overruled and the Washington law sustained as consistent with due process of law.[182] In arriving at this conclusion he reasoned that "The legislature had the right to consider that its minimum wage requirements would be an important aid in carrying out its policy of protection. The adoption

---

[180] 300 U.S. 379, 391 (1937). (Italics added.) See Treigle v. Acme Homestead Association, 297 U.S. 189, 197 (1936), on the police power. See B. H. Levy, *Our Constitution: Tool or Testament* (New York, 1941), 168–69, where the author concludes that " 'Police power' is no longer on the defensive. 'Freedom of contract' is no longer the rule. 'Liberty' is recognized to be a relative matter." See Hartford Accident and Indemnity Co. v. Nelson Co., 291 U.S. 352 (1934), sustaining a Mississippi statute enacted to protect the subcontractor's equity in amounts due from a builder to the contractor under which the materialmen or subcontractor works, or Life and Casualty Co. of Tennessee v. McCray, 291 U.S. 566 (1934), sustaining the award of an attorney's fee when the payment of an insurance policy has been wrongfully refused. A year later Justice Roberts clarified the status of "freedom of contract." In National Labor Relations Board v. Mackay Radio and Tel. Co., 304 U.S. 333, 348 (1938), he declared that "except for the mandate of the statute [N.L.R.A.]" the board's reinstatement order would be a violation of the employer's liberty of contract.

[181] 300 U.S. 379, 397 (1937).   [182] *Ibid.*, p. 400.

of a similar requirement by many states evidences a deep-seated conviction both as to the presence of the evil and as to the means adapted to check it. Legislative response to that conviction cannot be regarded as arbitrary or capricious, and that is all we have to decide. Even if the wisdom of the policy and its effects are debatable and uncertain, *still the legislature is entitled to its judgment.*" [183]

The fact that one justice changed his mind in the matter of the constitutional protection of freedom of contract meant that the minimum-wage laws in operation in more than half of the states remained valid as not violative of due process of law. Considered along with the Morehead decision, the action of the Court here serves to emphasize how slender the thread on which the development of our constitutional law as well as the validity of much of the present social legislation hangs. Once again the significance of Court personnel looms large.

The Fair Labor Standards Act,[184] passed by Congress in 1938, provided minimum-wage regulations for men and women engaged in interstate commerce. The validity of the statute, challenged primarily as a violation of the Tenth Amendment, was upheld in United States *v.* Darby.[185] Justice Stone, speaking for a unanimous Court, declared that in view of the decision in the Parrish case the power of the legislature to prescribe minimum wages was "no longer open to question" under the due process of law clause.

Pensions, Unemployment Compensation, and Social Security. The Railroad Retirement Act of 1926, as amended in 1934,[186] required all railway companies, considered as a single transportation unit, to establish a pension system for railway employees. The pension fund was to be created from contributions by employers and employees and was to be administered by a governmental agency, the Railroad Retirement Board. All railway employees and persons who had been in the employ of a railroad company within the year preceding the passage of the law were eligible to

---

[183] *Ibid.*, p. 399. (Italics added.) See Cohen *v.* Beneficial Industrial Loan Corporation, 337 U.S. 541, 550–51 (1949).

[184] 52 *Stat.* 1060.   [185] 312 U.S. 100 (1941).

[186] 48 *Stat.* 1283.

receive benefits under the statute. Re-employed persons were to be permitted to count former years of railway service in computing annuities at the age of sixty-five or in computing years of service necessary for retirement. The statute was held unconstitutional in Railroad Retirement Board *v.* Alton,[187] as beyond the commerce power of Congress as well as violative of the due process clause. According to Congress this statute represented an attempt to promote the efficiency of the railway transportation system by making room for younger men in the service. But Justice Roberts, as spokesman for the Court, investigated the evidence which had been available to the legislature when the retirement measure was considered and concluded that the remedy suggested would not lead to the ends sought. The "fostering of a contented mind" was said to be in no "just sense" a regulation of interstate commerce. Further, Justice Roberts thought that even if a pension system could reasonably be said to promote efficiency in the service, the bounty should not come from Congress. If, he said, Congress rather than the employers made the pensions available to the employees, the workers would transfer their loyalty and gratitude from the employer to the legislature which had been responsible for their aid.[188]

In addition to the fact that the solution provided was found to be inappropriate as a remedy for the evils said to exist, Justice Roberts discovered in the measure other flaws which made it "arbitrary in the last degree." By virtue of the provision which made the pension benefits available to persons who had been in the service within the year preceding the enactment of the law, there was imposed on the railroad companies the burden of gratuities to persons who had been discharged for cause or who had elected to leave the railway for more lucrative employment. Justice Roberts, for the majority, held that the provision was "clearly" a denial of due process. The law was said to be retroactive in that it "resurrects for new burdens transactions long since past and

[187] 295 U.S. 330 (1935). For criticisms of the decision, see Carr, *Democracy and the Supreme Court*, Chap. IV; Osmond Fraenkel, "Constitutional Issues Before the Supreme Court; 1934 Term," *University of Pennsylvania Law Review*, LXXXIV (1936), 345–88.

[188] 295 U.S. 330, 351 (1935). See United States *v.* Lowden, 308 U.S. 225, 239 (1939), in which the Railroad Retirement Plan was upheld.

closed." Further, in the case of some railroads it was said to constitute an appropriation of private property on the basis of transactions to which the employers were never parties. The operation of
the law was found to take the property of one group and bestow
it upon another, thus violating due process of law.[189]

Nor would due process of law permit Congress to treat the railroad companies as a single unit. The statute had provided for a
pool of the contributions of all companies and for the distribution
of pension allowances without regard to the employer's financial
status at the time the pension came due. Only by such a plan could
the pension system be made effective. In this system of pooled
contributions, the Court envisioned the solvent companies which
had maintained their financial status unimpaired penalized by
being forced to contribute to a fund to meet the demands upon
the insolvent carriers. To Justice Roberts this appeared as much
a taking of private property in contravention of due process as
the arbitrary transfer of ownership of equipment from one company to another because the latter needed equipment and could
not afford to purchase it.[190] In this connection it was said that "the
provision of the Act which disregards the private and separate
ownership of the several respondents, that treats them as a single
employer, and pools all their assets regardless of their individual
obligations and the varying conditions found in their respective
enterprises, cannot be justified as consistent with due process." [191]
Even the dissenter, Chief Justice Hughes, agreed that the provisions of this particular pension system clearly denied due process
of law. The Chief Justice, however, could not see why it was
beyond the commerce power of Congress to treat the railway
companies as a single transportation system and thus to establish
a single system of retirement allowances to be paid from a common fund.[192] It was this part of the majority ruling which gave
him the greatest concern.

[189] 295 U.S. 330, 349-50 (1935). Cf. Grange Lumber Co. v. Rowley and Department of Labor of the State of Washington, 326 U.S. 295 (1945); Paramino
Lumber Co. v. Marshall, 309 U.S. 370 (1940); and Mattson v. Department of
Labor, 293 U.S. 151 (1934), in which retroactive legislation concerning workmen's compensation was sustained as not violative of due process of law guaranteed by the Fourteenth Amendment.

[190] 295 U.S. 330, 357 (1935).   [191] Ibid., p. 360.
[192] Ibid., p. 387.

The Court would have been looked upon as less of a menace had it stopped with its expression of disapproval of the statute on the ground that the specific system established violated due process. Such a defect could be remedied by a more carefully drawn statute. But at a time when the unemployed in the country still numbered in the millions, a decision which prohibited Congress, under its commerce power, from legislating on the subject of pensions was thought to be very critical indeed. On the other hand, the Court's invalidation of the law on the ground of its inappropriateness represented a serious setback in the development of a concept of due process of law which would leave place for adequate police regulations.[193]

In 1937 the issue of setting up a pooling system in order to establish a pension and unemployment compensation fund was again before the Court in Carmichael v. Southern Coal and Coke Co.[194] In this case the validity of the workmen's-compensation law of Alabama, passed in pursuance of the federal social security law, was at stake. In accordance with the federal law, Alabama had enacted an unemployment-compensation statute providing for a tax upon the payroll of all persons employing eight or more persons for a designated number of weeks during the year. The contributions were to go into a single fund to be administered through a governmental agency. Compensation was to be paid without regard to the financial status of the employee, the employment record of the employer, or the amount he contributed to the fund. In sustaining the law, the majority apparently rejected the holding of the Butler and Alton cases that money cannot be taken from one group for the benefit of another. Such an idea was said to have been based on the "outmoded" benefit theory of taxation. Here the Court gave a new interpretation of its role in the application of the due process of law clause to state social and economic legislation. In this interpretation is seen one of the most

[193] Carr, *Democracy and the Supreme Court*, p. 54, thinks that judicial review, as exercised in this case, "assumes a new significance, one that would appear fraught with danger for the continued welfare of our American democracy."

[194] 301 U.S. 495 (1937). Here, for the first time, the Court definitely sustained a state unemployment-compensation law. By a four to four decision without opinion the New York compensation law had been allowed to stand in Chamberlain, Inc. v. Andrews, 299 U.S. 515 (1936).

significant changes in the Court's attitude during the momentous two months which closed with the social security decisions. Justice Stone expressed the views of the majority, saying:

> This restriction upon the judicial function, in passing on the constitutionality of statutes, is not artificial or irrational. A state legislature, in the enactment of laws, has the widest possible latitude within the limits of the Constitution. *In the nature of the case it cannot record a complete catalogue of the considerations which move its members to enact laws. In the absence of such record, courts cannot assume that its action is capricious, or that, with its informed acquaintance with local conditions to which the legislation is to be applied, it was not aware of facts which would afford a reasonable basis for its action.* Only by faithful adherence to this guiding principle of judicial review of legislation is it possible to preserve to the legislative branch its rightful independence and its ability to function.[195]

He recognized that the Fourteenth Amendment does place a restriction upon the state's exercise of the taxing power. The rule that the state can exercise that power only to effect a public purpose was left intact. But, said Justice Stone, that is not a valid objection to the present tax, conforming in other respects to the Fourteenth Amendment and "devoted to a public purpose." Nor was there room for valid objection on the ground that the amount of the benefits or the people to whom they would be paid bears no relation to the amount of the tax or the persons who pay it. In short, said Justice Stone, "that those who pay the tax have not contributed to the unemployment situation and may not be benefited by the expenditures" is immaterial.[196]

The federal Social Security Act [197] was challenged as a violation of the Tenth Amendment, the due process clause, and the taxing power. The chief complaint under the due process of law clause was that the system of exemptions denied appellant equal

---

[195] 301 U.S. 495, 510 (1937). (Italics added.)

[196] *Ibid.,* p. 511. Cf. the statement at the close of the Radford opinion: "If the public requires, and permits, the taking of property of individual mortgages in order to relieve the necessities of individual mortgagors, resort must be had to proceedings through eminent domain; so that through taxation, the burden of the relief afforded in the public interest may be borne by the public." 295 U.S. 555, 602 (1935).

[197] 49 *Stat.* 620.

protection of the laws.[198] But the due process clause of the Fifth Amendment was held not to contain an equal protection clause and not to purport to protect an individual against discriminatory legislation unless the discrimination is "so gross" as to amount to confiscation.[199] The "grossness" must be determined in each instance by the Court. This decision did not make the test of discriminatory legislation more or less subjective than it was before. As a practical matter any judgment upon discriminatory legislation is almost inevitably a subjective one. The arguments which may be offered in behalf of the genuine desirability of a regulation may also be given in behalf of the reasonableness of the same regulation. And if a regulation is reasonable it is not so discriminatory as to violate the due process of law guaranty. When the Court then looks with favor upon a given piece of legislation which has been challenged as discriminatory, it finds, as in the present case, that the discrimination is not equivalent to confiscation. On the other hand, when it has pleased the Court to invalidate a piece of legislation challenged on this ground, even a slight discrimination has been found too gross to pass the due process test.[200]

The Right to Bargain Collectively. In Virginian Railway Co. *v.* Federation 40,[201] the validity of the Railway Labor Act of 1926, as amended in 1934,[202] was challenged as a violation of due process insofar as it imposed upon the railroad any obligation to negotiate with a labor union. The Court expressly considered that the power of Congress over interstate commerce was limited by the requirements of due process of law. But in Justice Stone's opinion, which expressed the views of the majority, there is little

[198] Steward Machine Co. *v.* Davis, 301 U.S. 548 (1937). See Vincent B. Nicholson, "Recent Decisions on the Power to Spend for the General Welfare," *Temple Law Quarterly,* XII (1938), 435–61.

[199] 301 U.S. 548, 584 (1937). See Detroit Bank *v.* United States, 317 U.S. 329, 337 (1943), for a comparable ruling.

[200] Cf. the ruling in the present case with that in Heiner *v.* Donnan, 285 U.S. 312 (1932). Levy, *Our Constitution: Tool or Testament,* pp. 280–85, concludes that this should show the American people that the Constitution once thought of as a "testament" must now be recognized as a "tool" of government.

[201] 300 U.S. 515 (1937). Seven years earlier the original statute had been upheld in the face of the due process challenge. At that time the law was said to prevent the company from fostering a company union. Texas and N.O. Ry. Co. *v.* Brotherhood of Ry. and S.S. Clerks, 281 U.S. 548 (1930).

[202] 48 *Stat.* 1185.

room for the operation of the due process clause when the means of regulation are appropriate to the permissible end, namely, the regulation of interstate commerce.[203] In other words, Justice Stone would look first to the statute as a regulation of interstate commerce. If he found it to be a valid exercise of the commerce power, by virtue of that fact he would hold it to be valid under the due process clause of the Fifth Amendment. To the majority in this instance neither the Fifth nor the Fourteenth Amendment could guarantee "untrammeled freedom of action and of con-tract. In the exercise of its power to regulate commerce, Congress can subject both to restraints not shown to be unreasonable." [204] The Court found among its decisions one upholding the state's requirement of compulsory settlement by arbitration of the amount of fire-insurance liability.[205] It was held that if such a re-quirement was not contrary to due process of law, there could be no good reason for holding that a statutory command to negotiate for the settlement of labor disputes, in the exercise of the com-merce power, was so arbitrary as to infringe upon the employer's due process of law guaranteed by the Fifth Amendment.[206] Thus for the first time a statute compelling an employer to bargain col-lectively with his employees through their chosen representatives was held not to be violative of the due process clause.

Twelve days later the Court upheld the National Labor Rela-tions Act,[207] which guaranteed the right of collective bargaining to all employees who could be reached by the congressional power to regulate interstate commerce.[208] The right to organize and to bargain collectively was held by the Court, with Chief Justice Hughes as spokesman, to be a "fundamental" right protected by the due process of law clause of the Fifth Amendment. The Court made it plain that the right of the employee to bargain was being incorporated in the due process of law clause. As a result, there had to be a balancing of two qualified rights—that of the employer to freedom of contract and property as against that of the em-

---

[203] 300 U.S. 515, 558 (1937).   [204] *Ibid.,* p. 558.
[205] Hardware Dealers Mutual Fire Insurance Co. *v.* Glidden Co., 284 U.S. 151 (1931).
[206] 300 U.S. 515, 559 (1937).
[207] 49 *Stat.* 449. See Charles M. Buford, *The Wagner Act* (New York, 1941), pp. 1–66.
[208] National Labor Relations Board *v.* Jones-Laughlin Steel Corp., 301 U.S. 1 (1937).

ployee to organize and bargain collectively. "Due process of law" was here interpreted as a positive guarantee of the employee's fundamental right.[209] Apparently the National Labor Relations Act was only an expressed recognition of an existing right of employees to organize and bargain collectively. Presumably the majority of the Court in March, 1937, was saying in effect that such right existed with or without national legislation on the subject.

In the light of the Parrish case the Court might have found that in protecting the rights of the employees the freedom of contract of the employer was necessarily infringed, but not so as to deny due process of law. This the Court did not choose to do. Rather, it was said that the employer's freedom of contract was not infringed.[210]

In National Labor Relations Board v. Mackay Radio Co.[211] the employees' right to strike was sustained, and the board's order for reinstatement with pay for the time lost during the strike was held not to deprive the company of property without due process of law. It was said that Congress, in the exercise of its commerce power, might, consistently with due process of law, impose upon contractual relationships reasonable limitations calculated to protect commerce against threatened industrial strife.[212] Nor was a denial of due process found in the investiture of the courts with jurisdiction to review the board's order on its merits only after the filing of a transcript of the record exhibiting the board's final action. A district court granted Republic Steel Corporation a writ of mandamus to force the board to vacate its order because it refused to send up the record so that the court could take action on the merits of the order. The Supreme Court held that the writ was invalid and that the company had not been denied due process by the board's refusal to file the record.[213]

A state statute forbidding a labor organization to deny membership to any person "by reason of his race, color, or creed" or on like ground to deny him equal treatment in designation for em-

[209] See Edward S. Corwin, *Liberty Against Government: The Rise, Flowering and Decline of a Famous Juridical Concept* (Baton Rouge, 1948), pp. 160–61; and Corwin, *Constitutional Revolution, Ltd.*, p. 89.

[210] 301 U.S. 1, 44–45 (1937).

[211] 304 U.S. 333 (1938).

[212] *Ibid.*, p. 347. See Advance-Rumley Thresher Co. v. Jackson, 287 U.S. 283 (1932).

[213] *In re* National Labor Relations Board, 304 U.S. 486 (1938).

ployment was upheld by the Court in Railway Mail Ass'n *v.* Corsi.[214] It was said that "A judicial decision that such legislation violates the Fourteenth Amendment would be a distortion of the policy manifested in that Amendment which was adopted to prevent state legislation designed to perpetuate discrimination on the basis of race or color. We see no constitutional basis for the contention that a State cannot protect workers from exclusion solely on the basis of race, color, or creed, by an organization, functioning under the protection of the State." [215]

Thus within one decade the Court completely reversed its attitude toward the relative rights of employees and employers. Until the Court's decision in the Parrish case [216] the employer had been able to invoke "freedom of contract" as guaranteed by the due process clause to have the Court void labor legislation. Under such a guarantee the Court invalidated regulations of hours and wages, except in particular industries held to be affected with a public interest. Beginning in 1937 the Court apparently recognized that the welfare of the employee was itself a matter of public concern. While the decision in the Parrish case was made possible by the fact that Justice Roberts decided that state regulation of wages for women was not a violation of due process, the approach to the problem in that case was carried into other fields of social legislation. New justices, favorable to labor and willing to give much weight to state legislative findings in support of specific social policies, replaced the more conservative justices who had consistently voted against legislation for the benefit of labor.[217]

CORPORATE HOLDINGS

In order to procure more land for agricultural purposes in the state, North Dakota in 1933 passed a law requiring domestic and foreign corporations to dispose of all lands used or usable for

[214] 326 U.S. 88 (1945).

[215] *Ibid.*, pp. 93–94. See pp. 54–56 for instances in which the Court has upheld anti-closed-shop legislation of several states against the challenge that such statutes infringe upon labor's freedom of speech and right to peaceful assembly.

[216] 300 U.S. 379 (1937). See pp. 38–54 for other types of labor legislation challenged as a violation of the rights named in the First Amendment and therefore in violation of the due process clause of the Fourteenth Amendment.

[217] See p. 419, *supra*, for the changes in the personnel of the Court.

farming except such lands as were necessary to the conduct of their business.[218] Any lands falling within the provisions of the statute, which had not been disposed of within the ten-year period allowed by the law became subject to escheat to the county in which they were located. The county was authorized to sell the property at public auction and pay to the owner the proceeds, less the costs of the sale. In Asbury Hospital *v.* Cass County, North Dakota,[219] the Court upheld the legislation as not inconsistent with due process of law. The principal ground for the ruling seems to be that the state might, without denying the due process guaranteed by the Fourteenth Amendment, exclude a foreign corporation from entry into the state. Apparently the Court, speaking through Chief Justice Stone, assumed that the right to exclude the corporation carried with it the power to expel a corporation already doing business in the state. It was said that if the corporation was excluded from the state, it would have to dispose of all of its property, and that under the law of North Dakota, corporations were required to do no more. Therefore, appellant was said to have no reason to seek the protection of the due process clause in this instance.[220]

Assuming that the Court had shown that the state had authority to compel the corporation to sell its property, Chief Justice Stone found no ground on which the owner could complain because he had not been able to sell at a profit. The Chief Justice explained that "The due process clause does not guarantee that a foreign corporation when lawfully excluded from ownership of land in the state shall recapture its costs. It is enough that the corporation, in complying with the lawful command of the state to part with ownership is afforded a fair opportunity to realize the value of the land, and that the sale, when required, is to be under conditions reasonably calculated to realize its value at the time of the sale." [221]

A somewhat similar restriction was embodied in the Public Utilities Holding Company Act of 1935,[222] in which Congress

---

[218] *North Dakota Laws,* 1933, c. 89.   [219] 326 U.S. 207 (1945).
[220] *Ibid.,* p. 211.
[221] *Ibid.,* pp. 212–13. Cf. our complaints that a "denial of justice" in international law had been perpetrated by the enforcement of Mexico's Alien Land Law of 1926, which was very much like this North Dakota law.
[222] 49 *Stat.* 803.

authorized the Securities Exchange Commission "to act to bring
about the geographic and economic integration of holding company systems." The commission took action to compel North
American Company to sever relationships with all of its properties
which, in the commission's judgment, did not comply with the
standards set forth in the law.[223] In North American Company v.
Securities Exchange Commission [224] the statute was challenged as
a violation of the commerce clause and the due process of law
clause of the Fifth Amendment.

As to the objection raised under the due process clause, Justice
Murphy, for the Court, said that Congress balanced the various
interests and considerations and concluded that the right of North
American's shareholders to pool their investments and obtain the
benefits of common management of diversified interests was
"clearly outweighed by the actual and potential damage to the
public, the investors, and the consumers resulting from the use
made of pooled investments." [225] Congress, it was said, had concluded that the "economic advantages of a holding company at
the top of an unintegrated, sprawling system are not commensurate with the resulting economic disadvantages." Justice
Murphy declared that the "reasonableness of that conclusion is
one for Congress to determine." [226] No question was raised concerning the procedure followed by the Commission.

This seems to be the most extreme expression of the Court's
"new" approach to social or economic legislation which is challenged as violative of due process of law. Since "due process" has
come to mean "reasonable" law, it would seem that the Court
has virtually relieved itself of the power or duty to review such
legislation by making "reasonableness" a matter for legislative
determination.

The constitutionality of this statute was again challenged in
1946 by American Power and Light Company and Electric Power
and Light Corporation. In American Power and Light Co. v.

---

[223] *Ibid.*, par. 11 b (1).   [224] 327 U.S. 686 (1946).
[225] *Ibid.*, p. 708.
[226] *Ibid.* Justice Murphy said that "Congress, in the exercise of its discretion,
has decided that it is necessary to reorganize the holding company structures.
And inasmuch as it has the constitutional power to do so, we cannot question the
appropriateness or propriety of its decision."

Securities Exchange Commission,[227] Justice Murphy again spoke for the Court. The due process issue was said to have been disposed of largely by the Court's decision in North American Company v. Securities Exchange Commission of 1945.[228] Justice Murphy conceded that the challenged section of the statute "materially affects many property interests . . . it may even destroy whatever right there is to continued corporate existence on the part of a holding company that is found to complicate a system unnecessarily and to serve no useful function." [229] But on the other hand the legislative body "carefully considered" these interests and concluded that they were "outweighed by the political and general economic desirability of breaking up concentrations of financial power in the utility field too big to be effectively regulated in the interest of either the consumer or the investor and too big to permit the functioning of democratic institutions." [230] Said Justice Murphy: "It is not our function to reweigh these diverse factors or to question the conclusion reached by Congress." [231]

Sales in Interstate and Intrastate Commerce. Congress found that the substitution of vegetable oils for food in milk products was harmful to the public in that it facilitated fraud and did not provide a nutritious food.[232] The congressional committee investigating this particular subject also found that the dairy industry was very important in the national economy and concluded that Congress should take steps to protect it from the competition offered by the sale of "filled" milk.[233] To remedy this evil situation which was said to exist, Congress passed the Filled Milk Act of 1923,[234] prohibiting the shipment of filled milk in interstate or

[227] 329 U.S. 90 (1946). Justices Reed, Douglas, and Jackson did not participate in the consideration or decision of this case. Justices Frankfurter and Rutledge concurred with the majority decision but dissented in part.
[228] 327 U.S. 686 (1946).   [229] 329 U.S. 90, 106 (1946).
[230] *Ibid.*, citing 74 Cong., 1 Sess., S.R. No. 621, p. 12.
[231] *Ibid.*, p. 107.
[232] 67 Cong., 1 Sess., H.R. No. 355 (Ser. 7921), p. 2.
[233] 67 Cong., 4 Sess., S.R. No. 987 (Ser. 8155), p. 3. The committee reported that the "civilization" of the nation was dependent upon the dairying industry. It suggested that the time "to prohibit the filled-milk traffic is now before it has done greater damage to our health or to one of our basic and indispensable industries." *Ibid.*, p. 7.   [234] 42 *Stat.* 1486.

foreign commerce. The Carolene Products Company, in United States *v.* Carolene Products Co.,[235] challenged the ban of its products from interstate commerce as a deprivation of property without due process. Justice Stone, for the majority, said that the Court might rest its decision entirely on the "presumption of constitutionality" of the statute, for "no persuasive reason" was given for departing from the general rule under which Congress had the right to secure a minimum of a particular nutritive element in widely used foods and to protect the public against fraudulent substitutions.[236]

In the light of the findings made by Congress fifteen years before, Justice Stone thought that the Court must sustain the validity of the law and its application here. And, he said, "Even in the absence of such findings, the existence of facts supporting the legislative judgment is to be presumed, for regulatory legislation affecting ordinary commercial transactions is not to be pronounced unconstitutional unless in the light of the facts made known or generally assumed, it is of such a character as to preclude the assumption that it rests upon some rational basis within the knowledge and experience of the legislators." [237] To the company's contention that other food substitutes are not so regulated and that therefore it has been denied the equal-protection clause,[238] Justice Stone replied that the Fifth Amendment contains no "equal protection" clause. In any case, the law would be sustained, he said, as a valid act to promote public health and to prevent the fraud which could so easily be perpetrated by the sale of such a product.[239]

Six years later Carolene Products Company again challenged the application of the law to its products.[240] The company contended that the validity of the law had been sustained on the ground that Congress might protect the public from an unwholesome food product and from fraud caused by the sale of filled milk under false labels. Carolene products, it was said, were wholesome and were sold under proper labels and trade names. To pro-

---

[235] 304 U.S. 144 (1938).   [236] *Ibid.*, p. 148.
[237] *Ibid.*, p. 152.   [238] *Ibid.*, p. 151.
[239] *Ibid.*, pp. 150–51.
[240] Carolene Products Co. *v.* United States, 323 U.S. 18 (1944). See the "Annotation: Constitutionality of Regulations as to Milk," 155 *A.L.R.*, 1383–1412.

hibit their shipment in interstate commerce, it was urged, deprives the company of its property without due process. Justice Reed spoke for the Court in upholding the application of the law to the milk products of the appellant, even though the food was found to be as "wholesome and nutritious as milk, with the same content of calories and vitamins." Justice Reed, conceding these things, was of the opinion that the Court must consider that the products banned by the law were "manufactured foods which are cheaper to produce than similar whole milk products." [241] He concluded from the findings of Congress that "evidently" that body had determined that the remedy for the possibility of fraud lay in the exclusion of the products from interstate commerce. As the law had not been repealed, it must, he thought, be assumed that Congress was still of the same opinion. It was said that "Congress might prohibit the sale of a wholesome article if that sale makes other evils harder to control." [242] Such a regulation, the Court held, did not deny the company the due process protected by the Fifth Amendment.

The Kansas Filled Milk Act,[243] prohibiting the sale or keeping for sale of any milk product to which oils other than milk fats have been added, was upheld in Sage Stores v. Kansas.[244] Here the Court said that "the power of the legislature to classify is as broad as its power to prohibit. A violation of the Fourteenth Amendment in either case would depend upon whether there is any rational basis for the action of the legislature." [245] With reference to this particular law, the Court found that such a rational basis did exist and that the regulation was a valid exercise of the police power.

WEIGHTS AND MEASURES

A Nebraska statute authorizing the governor of the state and the secretary of agriculture to prescribe weights and measures for a standard loaf of bread was upheld in Peterson Baking Co. v. Bryan.[246] The Court found that the regulation was intended to

[241] 323 U.S. 18, 23 (1944).   [242] Ibid., pp. 29–30.
[243] Kansas Laws, 1927, c. 242.   [244] 323 U.S. 33 (1944).
[245] Ibid., p. 35.
[246] 290 U.S. 570 (1934). A regulation for this purpose had been held uncon-

prevent fraud and that a regulation for such a purpose was a valid exercise of the police power, hence not a violation of due process. The delegation of authority to the secretary of agriculture was said not to involve a denial of due process, because there had to be some agency to make changes in the maximum weights and measures to suit prevailing conditions, and the minimum standards, which would not need to be varied, were fixed by the law.[247] Nor was there found to be any denial of due process involved in an Oregon statute fixing the standard measurements for berry baskets.[248] The state was said to have the power to prescribe standard containers in order to "facilitate trading, to preserve the condition of the merchandise, and to protect the buyer from deception, or to prevent unfair competition." [249] The appellant contended that there were in use in the United States thirty-four types of containers and that therefore the state should not be permitted to ban all except one. The company urged that it would be deprived of property without due process of law because it had in stock a large number of baskets which it would not be able to sell. The Court found none of the complaints, even if true, sufficient bases for invalidating the statute. The state, it was said, had perhaps decided that so many styles and shapes of baskets were confusing to the buyers at retail and that to prescribe a single standard container would tend to lessen the chances of fraud. Since such a regulation was found to be a legitimate exercise of the police power, necessarily it was not a violation of due process.[250]

A Chicago ordinance requiring that any merchandise sold in load lots by weight be weighed by a public weighmaster and a certificate of the weight delivered with the goods to the purchaser was upheld in Hauge v. Chicago.[251] South Carolina's law requir-

---

stitutional by the Court in Burns Baking Co. v. Bryan, 264 U.S. 504 (1924). However, the power of the state to regulate was not in question. Rather, the Court found that the maximum tolerances were unreasonable.

[247] 290 U.S. 570, 573–74 (1934).

[248] Pacific States Box and Basket Co. v. White, 296 U.S. 176 (1935).

[249] Ibid., p. 181.

[250] Ibid. "Different types of commodities require different types of containers. . . . Whether it was necessary for Oregon to provide a standard container for raspberries . . . involve[s] questions of fact and of policy, the determination of which rests with the legislative branch of the state government. . . . With the wisdom of such regulation we have, of course, no concern." Ibid., p. 182.

[251] 299 U.S. 387 (1937).

ing that manufacturers of fertilizers affix to each sack the chemical analysis, as well as a statement of the pounds of the materials used, was held not to be arbitrary or unreasonable or beyond the police power of the state,[252] hence not in violation of the due process clause.

LABELS FOR FOOD PRODUCTS

The legislature of Florida found upon investigation that persons engaged in importing into Florida citrus fruits and fruit juices produced and canned elsewhere were labeling these products as Florida-grown fruits. As a result Florida producers and canners were injured. To protect the Florida producers the legislature enacted a law requiring that every can of such fruit sold in the state bear a label showing where the fruit was grown and canned. All containers used for fruits produced in Florida were to have stamped into, or embossed onto, them the word "Florida." The constitutionality of the regulation was in issue in Polk Company v. Glover,[253] in which the company alleged that if the law were enforced, it would be deprived of valuable property without due process of law. In a *per curiam* opinion, from which Justice Black dissented, the Court held that the plaintiff should have been given an opportunity in the Federal District Court to prove its contentions. The Court did not pass on the due process aspects of the law and did not indicate that the company's allegations, if proved, would support the invalidation of the regulation.

Justice Black, in his dissent, pointed out that there were grave consequences in such a decision, for, he said:

> State laws are continually subjected to constitutional attacks by those who do not wish to obey them. Accordingly, it becomes increasingly important to protect the state government from needless expensive burdens and suspensions of their laws incident to federal injunctions issued on allegations that show no right to relief. The operation of this Florida law has been suspended. Complainants seeking to invalidate and suspend the operation of state laws by in-

[252] National Fertilizer Association v. Bradley, 301 U.S. 178, 181 (1937).
[253] 305 U.S. 5 (1938).

voking the "vague contours" of due process can irreparably injure state governments if we accept as a "salutary principle" the rule that all such complaints—though failing to state a cause of action—raise grave constitutional questions which require that the essential facts be determined.[254]

Justice Black urged that the question of the wisdom of the policy embodied in the statute here challenged should rest with the state legislature, "subject as it is to the veto of the governor of the State." If, he said, the petitioner in this case is to obtain relief on the theory that the regulation violates the due process clause, it must prove that the statute was "fixed or arrived at through an exercise of will, or caprice, without consideration or adjustment with reference to principles, circumstances, or significance" or that it is "despotic, autocratic, or high-handed" or that it is "irrational." [255]

CONSERVATION MEASURES

Under the Texas legislature's authorization the Railroad Commission issued an order limiting the daily allowable production of oil for oil-well owners who owned pipelines to a low amount, so as to furnish a market for oil producers who did not have pipeline connections. In Thompson v. Consolidated Gas Utilities Corporation,[256] Justice Brandeis, for a unanimous Court, held that the order deprived the appellants of property without due process of law. For the Court, Justice Brandeis expressed reluctance to pass on the validity of a state law which had not been construed by the state courts; but, he said, "being under duty to make an independent study, we have done so." [257] On the basis of this study, he found that "the sole purpose of the limitation which the order imposes upon the plaintiff's production is to compel those who may legally produce because they have market outlets for permitted uses, to purchase gas from potential producers whom the statute prohibits from producing because they lack such market

[254] Ibid., p. 11.
[255] Ibid., p. 17. This, Justice Black said, is according to the dictionary definition.
[256] 300 U.S. 55 (1937). This decision is one of the last based on the "old-line" due process interpretation. See p. 330, infra.
[257] 300 U.S. 55, 75 (1937).

for their possible product." [258] He emphasized *that had the measure been primarily for the prevention of waste*, the Court would not have invalidated it.[259] But it was held that "The use of the pipeline owner's wells and reserves is curtailed for the benefit of other private well owners." [260] This was held to be a most "glaring" instance of the taking of one man's property to give it to another, and hence a violation of the due process guaranteed by the Fourteenth Amendment.[261]

The Oklahoma Well-spacing Act [262] was upheld in the case of Patterson *v.* Stanolind Oil and Gas Co.[263] Under the law, the oil fields were divided into ten-acre plots, and owners were allowed to drill only one well in each plot. The oil produced from such well had to be shared proportionately with other owners of land within the plot. Stanolind Company complained that, under the law, it would have to share one eighth of the production from its new well in the middle of a ten-acre plot on its own six and one-fourth acres with the owners of the other three and three-fourth acres. The Court considered that the Corporation Commission of Oklahoma had made its findings and order after adequate hearings. Though the facts on which it based its conclusions did not appear on the record, the Court assumed that there was sufficient evidence. The state had found that "the source of supply of the well in question is common to the land adjoining it and that said pool underlies not only the six and one-fourth acres of land on which the well is located but that it also extends beneath the three and three-fourths acre tract." [264] In view of such a finding the Court held that the state had applied "well-settled" principles in denying the plaintiff's contentions that the order was in violation of due process of law.[265]

[258] *Ibid.,* p. 77.

[259] *Ibid.,* p. 78. In Henderson Oil Co. *v.* Thompson, 300 U.S. 258, 264 (1937), the Court answered a challenge of the Texas regulation forbidding the use of sweet gas for the manufacture of carbon black with: "The needs of conservation are to be determined by the legislature."

[260] 300 U.S. 55, 78 (1937).   [261] *Ibid.,* p. 79.

[262] *Oklahoma Statutes,* 1933, c. 59, Art. 4.

[263] 305 U.S. 376 (1939). For the background of this case see J. Howard Marshall and Norman L. Meyers, "Legal Planning of Petroleum Production," *Yale Law Journal,* XLI (1931), 33–67.

[264] 305 U.S. 376, 379 (1939). See p. 329, *infra.*

[265] 305 U.S. 376, 379 (1939).

An order of the Railroad Commission of Texas formulating a method of distributing among well owners the total amount of oil to be produced in the East Texas Fields was upheld in Railroad Commission of Texas v. Rowan & Nichols Oil Co.[266] After investigation the commission had found that, considering the bottomhole pressure and the quality of the sands surrounding the wells, a minimum of twenty barrels per day would be permissible. In its acceptance of the figure set by the commission the Court indicated the deference now to be paid to the findings of "expert" commissions. Justice Frankfurter, speaking for the Court, said that "Nothing in the Constitution warrants a rejection of these expert conclusions. Nor, on the basis of intrinsic skills and equipment, are the federal courts qualified to set their independent judgment on such matters against that of the chosen state authorities. For its own good reason, Texas vested authority over these difficult and delicate problems in its Railroad Commission. . . . It is clear that the Due Process Clause does not require the feel of the expert to be supplanted by the independent view of judges on the conflicting testimony and prophecies and impressions of expert witnesses." [267] Whatever inequalities might exist as a result of the order were to be remedied by a "continuing supervisory power of the expert commission," [268] for, said Justice Frankfurter, the Constitution does not provide the federal courts with the power to "strike a balance" between facts and inferences underlying such a complicated situation.[269]

In sustaining a California statute requiring a license for canning fish and prohibiting the reduction of fish into meal or fertilizer, Justice Sutherland, for a unanimous Court, said that the right to enter into a contract is "with some exceptions . . . a liberty

[266] 311 U.S. 570 (1941). A previous order which based the daily allowable production on the hourly potential and provided that a well which could not produce twenty barrels per day at 2.32 per cent of its hourly potential would be permitted a twenty-barrel minimum was upheld in Railroad Commission of Texas v. Rowan & Nichols Oil Co., 310 U.S. 573 (1940). Justice Frankfurter spoke for the Court; Chief Justice Hughes and Justices Roberts and McReynolds dissented.

[267] 310 U.S. 570, 575–76 (1941).

[268] Ibid., p. 577. Chief Justice Hughes and Justices Roberts and McReynolds dissented for reasons stated in Railroad Commission of Texas v. Rowan & Nichols Oil Co., 310 U.S. 573 (1940).

[269] 310 U.S. 570, 576–77 (1941).

which falls within the protection of the due process clause of the Fourteenth Amendment." [270] But he found that the law did not prevent appellant from making a contract for the purchase of fish; it only prevented his using the fish as he saw fit after they were purchased. Justice Sutherland did not see in this any denial of due process of law, for, he said, "A statute does not become unconstitutional merely because it has created a condition of affairs which renders the making of a related contract, lawful in itself, ineffective." [271]

Thus due process of law as guaranteed by the Fourteenth Amendment has not been successfully invoked to invalidate a state regulation enacted for the purpose of conservation of the state's resources. The mere fact that such regulations may or do interfere with freedom of contract or the use of property as the owner sees fit is of no judicial import. In this instance, as in many others, the Court holds that the due process which is protected by the Fourteenth Amendment does not comprehend a guaranty of the owner's right to use his property as he likes.

RESTRICTIONS ON CONTRACT TERMS

The power of the state to restrict the freedom of an individual to contract away certain rights was upheld in Advance-Rumley Thresher Co. v. Jackson.[272] The legislature of the state found that the farmers depended upon the operation of certain farm machinery for the harvesting of their crops and that in many instances it was impossible for a farmer to know that the machine which he bought would perform adequately unless he had an opportunity to try it on his own land. To protect the farmer from purchasing, at a heavy outlay of money, a piece of machinery which was not suited to his needs, the legislature provided by statute that, any contract provision to the contrary notwithstanding, the farmer must be allowed a period of time adequate for testing the machine before the sale became final. If the test showed any

[270] Bayside Fish Co. v. Gentry, 297 U.S. 422, 427 (1936).

[271] Ibid., p. 428. Justice Sutherland cites Chicago, B. & Quincy Railroad Co. v. McGuire, 219 U.S. 549, 569 (1916), to support the decision to leave matters of policy and appropriateness to the legislature.

[272] 287 U.S. 283 (1932).

defect in operation of the machine, the farmer would be permitted to return it to the company without cost to himself. The Court found no valid objection to such a restriction of the right to contract.

A state statute which provides, contrary to the express provisions of a surety contract, that the surety company's insurance must inure to the benefit of the subcontractor or the materialman as well as the owner or contractor was held not to deny the surety company the due process guaranteed to it by the Fourteenth Amendment. The Court said that neither the owner nor the contractor objected to such a provision in the contract and that the company could not hope to contract on better terms than they.[273]

RESTRICTIONS ON OCCUPATIONS

The state may, without violating due process of law, forbid dentists to advertise their profession. The statute prohibits the advertising of professional superiority, prices for services, free dental service, etc. The legislature, it was said, was striking at "bait advertising." Advertising of the kind prohibited by the statute was, as a rule, said the Court, "the practice of charlatans and quacks." The state was held to have authority to provide safeguards against deception and against "practices which would tend to demoralize the profession by forcing its members into an unseemly rivalry. . . ." Violation of the statute may validly entail the revocation of the offender's license to practice.[274] Likewise, the state may deny admittance to the state bar to any person who refuses to take the prescribed oath of allegiance to the state constitution.[275] In effect this would mean that all pacifists and conscientious objectors would be barred, for, held the state, a person who does not believe in the use of force even to prevent wrong or to enforce the law cannot sincerely take an oath to uphold and defend the constitution of the state. No denial of due process was

[273] Hartford Accident and Indemnity Co. v. Nelson Co., 291 U.S. 352, 360 (1934).

[274] Semler v. Oregon State Board of Dental Examiners, 294 U.S. 608, 612 (1935). Chief Justice Hughes wrote the opinion for a unanimous Court.

[275] In re Summers, 325 U.S. 561 (1945). Justice Reed spoke for the Court; Justice Black filed a dissenting opinion in which Justices Murphy, Douglas, and Rutledge concurred.

found to result from Michigan's law prohibiting beer dealers in the state from selling any beer manufactured in a state which, by its laws, discriminated against Michigan beer.[276] Nor was there any deprivation of property without due process of law involved in a state statute requiring that only licensed persons be allowed to transport or sell liquor within the state and providing that violation carried a penalty, in addition to confiscation of the liquor. The Court held that property rights in liquor depended upon state law and that such rights ceased to exist the moment the liquor became contraband.[277] But even the unlawful denial by the state of the opportunity to be a candidate for public office was held not to be a violation of due process. The liberty protected by due process, it was said, does not include the right to hold political office under the state.[278]

Under the South Carolina Mortuary Act of 1948 insurance companies and their agents may not operate an undertaking establishment and morticians may not serve as the collecting agents for any life-insurance company.[279] The Family Security Life Insurance Company, whose funeral-insurance policies were sold through undertaker-agents, challenged the statute as violative of the due process of law clause of the Fourteenth Amendment on grounds of its unreasonableness and inappropriateness. In Daniel v. Family Security Insurance Co.,[280] Justice Murphy spoke for the Court in upholding the statute against these com-

[276] Indianapolis Brewing Co. v. Liquor Control Commission, 305 U.S. 391 (1939). The opinion was written by Justice Brandeis.

[277] Ziffrin, Inc. v. Reeves, Commissioner of Revenue of Kentucky, 308 U.S. 132, 140 (1939). Justice McReynolds wrote the opinion for eight justices. Justice Butler took no part in the decision.

[278] Snowden v. Hughes, 321 U.S. 1, 7 (1944). According to the tabulation made by the Canvassing Board of Cook County and sent to the secretary of state for Illinois, Snowden's name should have been placed on the ballot for the election of state senators. Certification by the Canvassing Board was a prerequisite for candidacy. In this instance, the board failed to certify Snowden. He contended that the right to be certified, since he received the required vote, was a right conferred by the state and protected by the due process clause of the Fourteenth Amendment. Chief Justice Stone declared: ". . . the unlawful denial by state action of a right to political office is not a denial of a right of property or liberty secured by the due process clause. . . ." Ibid.

[279] 45 Stat. at Large, S.C., p. 1947. For similar laws, see New York, Consol. Laws, c. 28, par. 165 (c); Florida Code, par. 639.02; Georgia Code, 56-9920; Ohio General Code, par. 666; Maryland Code, 48A, par. 110; Maine Rev. Stat., c. 56, par. 138; Kentucky Rev. Stat., par. 303.120; Illinois Rev. Stat., c. 73, par. 956.

[280] 336 U.S. 220 (1949).

plaints. The Court did not conceive of its authority as extending to a consideration of the "desirability" of an action by the state. "The forum for the correction of ill-considered legislation is a responsive legislature." [281] In a footnote the Court suggests that the judicial deference to the legislature in this case is partially due to the particular business regulated. However, deference for the judgment of the legislative bodies in the states, which had been stated in the Texas cases of 1932, had been a well-established practice long before the case at bar originated.[282]

PROTECTION OF FREE LABOR

In the exercise of its police power the state may forbid the shipment into its territory of convict-made goods.[283] To facilitate the enforcement of such restriction, Congress may prohibit the shipment in interstate commerce of convict-made goods destined for sale or use within a state in violation of that state's laws.[284] The Court found that these regulations were not unreasonable nor arbitrary and therefore not violative of the due process of law guaranteed by the Fifth or the Fourteenth Amendment. The government was said to have a right to protect free labor from unfair competition offered by the sale of goods produced by convict labor.

SAFETY REGULATIONS

By statute New York declared that the owner of an automobile would be liable for any damage caused by his car, whether he or someone else was driving it at the time of an accident. The validity of the law was challenged when the state applied it to a resident of New Jersey whose car was involved in an accident in New York.[285] Appellant contended that the law violated due process

[281] *Ibid.*, p. 224.   [282] *Ibid.*, p. 224, n. 4.
[283] Whitfield *v.* Ohio, 297 U.S. 43, 439 (1936).
[284] Kentucky Whip and Collar Co. *v.* Illinois Central Railroad Co., 299 U.S. 334 (1937).
[285] Young *v.* Masci, 289 U.S. 253 (1933). See Morf *v.* Bingaman, 298 U.S. 407, 411 (1936), in which the Court sustained the validity of the statute of New Mexico requiring that all cars brought within the state for sale be driven by drivers licensed in the state and that the cars be inspected by state officers. In

in that it was an attempt to extend the legislative authority of the state into a neighboring state. To this, the Court replied: "A person who sets in motion in one state the means by which an injury is inflicted in another, may, consistently with due process of law, be made liable for that injury, whether the means employed be a responsible agent or an irresponsible instrument." [286]

In Queenside Hill Realty Co., Inc. v. Saxl [287] the Court upheld a New York regulation of lodginghouses, which required that all such houses constructed prior to the enactment of the law be equipped with automatic wet-pipe sprinkler systems. Justice Douglas, who voiced the opinion of the Court, thought there was little need to discuss the due process question. The Court, he said, was not concerned with the wisdom of the regulation or the need for it. The question of what regulations will best serve the purpose of reducing fire hazards is a matter for the legislature to determine. The fact that the value of the property may be diminished or the owner required to spend large sums in repairs was held to be immaterial in a consideration of the constitutionality of the law. Justice Douglas explained that the police power of the state was one of the "least limitable" of governmental powers, and "its operation often cuts down property rights." [288]

NOTICE OF PROCESS

A statute of Washington provided that if a foreign corporation withdrew from the state leaving no agent through whom notice of process might be served, the state would authorize a public official to accept such notice for the corporation. The law did not require that the designated official notify the corporation. The validity of the law was challenged when a company was forced to pay a judgment which had resulted from a court proceeding of which it had not been notified. The Court in Washington v. Superior Court [289] held that the provision of the statute was sufficient notice to the company. The burden was upon appellant to make such ar-

---

Clark v. Paul Gray, Inc., 306 U.S. 583 (1939), the Court upheld a California law imposing a tax of $75 for each automobile brought within the state for sale.
[286] 289 U.S. 253, 258 (1933).   [287] 328 U.S. 80 (1946).
[288] Ibid., p. 83.   [289] 289 U.S. 361 (1933).

rangement for notification as it deemed desirable. The omission of any requirement that the official of the state notify the company proceeded against was not a denial of due process.[290]

In Voeller v. Neilston Warehouse Co.[291] the Court upheld an Ohio statute which provided for the remuneration of stockholders in a building association who wish to withdraw from the association when the corporate assets are sold. Such persons might indicate what they considered a fair value of their stock. Within six months after such action the other shareholders might take action to determine the actual value of the stock of the withdrawing members. If, however, no such action is taken, the value fixed by the members who have given notice of their intention to withdraw must be accepted and that amount paid by the association. The company alleged that if the law were enforced it would result in a deprivation of the remaining shareholders' property in that they had not been notified that this amount would be paid. The Court held that notice to the company is equivalent to notice to the shareholders and that therefore no denial of due process was involved.[292]

ALIEN CREDITORS

In United States v. Pink,[293] Justice Douglas, speaking for the Court, declared that aliens as well as citizens were protected by the due process clause of the Fifth and Fourteenth amendments. However, that clause does not preclude a state from according priority to local creditors as against creditors who are nationals of a foreign state.[294] "By the same token," it was said that the federal government is not barred by the due process clause from "securing for itself and our nationals priority against such creditors." [295] If the President had power to make the agreement with Russia, due process of law will not stand in the way of its effectiveness.[296]

LEGISLATIVE RATE MAKING

The Court has shown a much greater leniency toward legislative rate making than toward rate making by administrative

---

[290] Ibid., p. 365.
[292] Ibid., p. 537.
[294] Ibid., pp. 227–28.
[291] 311 U.S. 531 (1940).
[293] 315 U.S. 203 (1942).
[295] Ibid.
[296] See "United States v. Pink—A Reappraisal," Columbia Law Review, XLVIII (1948), 890, 897–99.

agencies. Frequently legislators, in the exercise of this power, have been more concerned with the problem of preventing the imposition of exorbitant charges than with seeing that the utility received a "fair return." Such was the case in the tobacco-marketing industry in Georgia. The tobacco farmer was forced to employ the services of one of a very few warehousemen because there were one or two warehouses available to him at the time his tobacco became marketable. The legislature of the state enacted a statute fixing the maximum rates which the warehousemen might charge for handling and selling the tobacco,[297] and its power to enact such a law was upheld by the Court in Townsend v. Yoemans.[298] Chief Justice Hughes, for the Court, said that "So far as the present controversy turns upon the power of the State to give this sort of protection to this industry, *provided its regulation is not arbitrary or confiscatory*, and in the absence of conflict with federal power over commerce, our rulings are decisive in support of the state action." [299] This evidences an attitude quite different from that expressed by the Chief Justice in the St. Joseph Stock Yard case, though only a year had elapsed since that decision. Apparently the Court was saying that if the state possessed the power to fix a rate, the actual figure decided upon is of no concern to the Court.

In this instance the state legislature, as rate-making agent, had not made an investigation as to the value of the property involved, the conditions of the industry which might justify the regulation of its rates, or the adverse effects which the particular rates fixed might have upon the warehousemen. The tobaccomen based their complaint of arbitrary action on this lack of findings. But the absence of any specific findings of fact was thought by the Court not to detract from the validity of the legislation. The "presumption of reasonableness" attaching to state legislation of this character was not overthrown.[300] In this connection, it was explained:

> There is no principle of constitutional law which nullifies action taken by a legislature, otherwise competent, in the absence of special investigation. The result of particular

---

[297] *Georgia Laws*, 1935, No. 393. Similar laws had been enacted in other tobacco-producing states. See *Code of North Carolina*, 1931, c. 91.6; *Virginia Code*, 1936, pars. 1376–81; *Code of the Laws of South Carolina*, III, par. 7197.
[298] 301 U.S. 441 (1937).   [299] *Ibid.*, p. 450. (Italics added.)
[300] *Ibid.*

legislative inquiries through commissions may be most help-
ful in portraying the exigencies to which the legislative action has been addressed. But the *legislature, acting within its
sphere, is presumed to know the needs of the people of the
state.* Whether or not special inquiries should be made is a
matter for legislative discretion. . . . The necessity of protecting the growers from exorbitant charges must be presumed to have been fully known to the members of the
legislature.[301]

Here the legislature was actually prescribing a rate to be charged
for services rendered. Nevertheless, it did not attempt to ascertain
a rate base or the return which might be expected under the rates.
In spite of this, confiscation was not proved, for the "presumption
of reasonableness was not overthrown." Reasonableness of the
rate in this instance bears no relation to a fair return on a fair value.
Apparently the Court treated this legislation as though it were a
price regulation. It was at least five years before the Court evidenced the same degree of respect for administrative rate making
as it showed in this case.

In 1941 the Court was called upon to pass judgment upon the
state's power to fix maximum rates to be charged by employment
agencies. In Olsen *v.* Nebraska,[302] Justice Douglas, for the Court,
upheld the statutory provision fixing the charge to be made by a
private employment agency at not more than 10 per cent of the
applicant's first month's salary. He concluded that the decisions
of the Court upholding price fixing represented more than "scat-
tered examples of constitutionally permissible price-fixing." [303]
To him they indicated a "basic departure from the philosophy
and approach of the majority in the Ribnik case." The affected
with a public interest doctrine had been abandoned, and Justice
Douglas was able to cite a previous Court as saying that "such
criteria are not susceptible of definition and form an unsatisfactory
test of the constitutionality of legislation directed at business practices and prices." [304] Strangely enough, the Court dismissed

[301] *Ibid.,* pp. 451–52. (Italics added.)
[302] 313 U.S. 236 (1941).
[303] *Ibid.,* p. 245. Justice Douglas cited price-fixing as well as rate-making cases
in support of his statement.
[304] *Ibid.*

former decisions on the same question with: "Since they do not find expression in the Constitution, we cannot give them continuing vitality as standards by which the constitutionality of economic and social programs of the states is to be determined." Once again the Court has tested a rate case by the price rules and has not seen fit to apply the fair-value criterion.

Not only did the Court uphold the regulation of rates for this particular business but also it reaffirmed its ruling that such regulations are matters for legislative determination. Justice Douglas declared that the Court did not concern itself with the "wisdom, need, or appropriateness of the legislation." There would be differences of opinion on the issue, and the choice, said he, "should be left where . . . it was left by the Constitution—to the States and to Congress." [305] To the extent that the Court, by such decisions, has avoided the duty or the right to pass upon the necessity of the regulation or the appropriateness of the measure adopted, it has relieved itself of the duty or right to pass upon the reasonableness of such regulation. The import of this situation looms large when one considers that in such matters due process is "reasonable law." [306]

PRESUMPTION OF VALIDITY IN FAVOR OF LEGISLATION ACTION

Since 1932 the restrictive scope of the due process of law clause of the Fifth and Fourteenth amendments has been steadily contracted insofar as economic and social regulation by Congress

[305] *Ibid.*, p. 246. R. E. Cushman, in "Social and Economic Interpretation of the Fourteenth Amendment," *Michigan Law Review*, XX (1922), 737, 763–64, thought that he saw the beginning of such a trend in the decisions of the Court even then. Such an attitude on the part of the Court, he said, would "correct the only actual defects which have ever existed in our system of judicial review." See Charles G. Haines, *The Revival of Natural Law Concepts* (Cambridge, Mass., 1930), Chap. VII; and Rodney L. Mott, *Due Process of Law* (Indianapolis, 1926), pp. 593–94. In United States v. Trenton Potteries Co., 273 U.S. 392 (1927), Justice Stone had said: ". . . in the absence of express legislation requiring it, we should hesitate to adopt a construction making the difference between legal and illegal conduct stand upon so uncertain a test as whether prices are unreasonable —a determination which can be satisfactorily made only after a complete survey of our economic organization and a choice between rival philosophies."

[306] See Robert P. Reeder, "Constitutional and Extra-Constitutional Restraints," *University of Pennsylvania Law Review*, LXI (1913), 441, 446, 456; and Ray A. Brown, "Due Process of Law, Police Power, and the Supreme Court," *Harvard Law Review*, XL (1927), 943–68.

and the state legislatures is concerned. This is the logical result of the Court's approach to due process cases involving property rights during this period. In 1932, Justice Sutherland declared that "if the legislature concluded" that the particular regulation in question was an appropriate remedy for evils which it had found to exist in the state, "that conclusion must stand," for the Court would not pass judgment upon the findings of the legislative body. Two years later Justice Roberts found that due process of law, as applied to economic regulations, required only that there be a "rational basis" for the legislation embodying the challenged restriction. With few exceptions the trend in the Court's decisions has been toward an acceptance of state findings which would indicate the existence of such rational basis for the legislation in issue. This trend has culminated in the Court's assumption that adequate findings upon which to base the regulation were made by the legislative body though they do not appear on the record. Apparently a majority of the Court, at present, will assume that such findings might have been made, though the legislature has not attempted to support its restriction by any specific findings of fact.

Among the exceptions to this mode of approach to due process cases are numbered, in terms of social and economic significance, some of the Court's most momentous decisions of the past decade and a half. Those instances in which the Court, prior to 1937, deviated from its "presumption of validity" rule for economic regulations assumed an importance far beyond their number because of the subject matter involved. On May 6, 1935, nine justices found the first railway-pension plan unconstitutional as a deprivation of property without due process. Five of these men thought that Congress had no power to legislate on the subject of pensions for railway employees.[307] On May 27, 1935, Justice Brandeis, speaking for a unanimous Court, held that the operation of the federal farm-mortgage-moratory legislation resulted in the taking of property without due process and said that if Congress found it necessary to take the property of one for the benefit of the general public, it must do so through the process of eminent domain, so that the burden of just compensation would be borne

[307] Railroad Retirement Board v. Alton Railway Co., 295 U.S. 330 (1935).

by the public.[308] The New York minimum-wage law fell under the ban of due process on June 1, 1936, on the ground that in its operation the law deprived the employee and the employer of the freedom of contract guaranteed by the due process clause of the Fourteenth Amendment.[309] The decision handed down on March 29, 1937, voiding the Texas Railway Commission's order that the daily allowable production of oil for producers owning pipelines be cut to furnish a market for those producers having no pipeline facilities, is one of the last based on the old-line restrictive interpretation of due process as applied to property rights.[310]

And what has been the result of this attitude on the part of the Court toward its role in the application of due process of law to state and national economic regulation which in almost every instance involves a restriction upon the use and enjoyment of property? Simply that the Court has, for the time, relieved itself of what former majorities on the Bench thought to be its power and duty in reviewing such legislation. It has not divested itself of the power to review and strike down legislation as violative of due process. In only a few instances has there been any suggestion that under the presumption of validity rule the Court should refuse jurisdiction for the lack of a federal question.[311] Rather, the Court has assumed jurisdiction but in effect has found that a restriction embodied in a law which the legislative branch has deemed necessary and appropriate to the welfare of the state is, for that reason, due process of law. Following this approach, the Court has extended widely the area within which the legislature may regulate and restrict the use of property without violating due process as guaranteed by the Fifth or the Fourteenth Amendment.

Price fixing has come to be a legitimate mode of regulation avail-

[308] Louisville Joint Stock Land Bank v. Radford, 295 U.S. 555 (1935).
[309] Morehead v. New York ex rel. Tipaldo, 298 U.S. 587 (1936).
[310] Thompson v. Consolidated Gas Utilities Corporation, 300 U.S. 55 (1937). In Connecticut General Life Insurance Co. v. Johnson, 303 U.S. 77 (1938), the California privilege tax on reinsurance contracts effective in the state was invalidated on the ground that the tax applied to contracts not made in California and therefore not within the jurisdiction of that state and so deprived the company of property without due process.
[311] See Justice Frankfurter's dissent in Mayo v. Lakeland Highlands Canning Co., 309 U.S. 310 (1940), and the dissent by Justice Black in Polk Company v. Glover, 305 U.S. 5 (1938).

able to Congress and the state legislatures. The power to fix prices is not confined to businesses affected with a public interest but extends to private industry as well. The state or federal legislature may, consistently with due process, provide for the establishment of maximum and minimum prices for any industry within its respective jurisdiction. Only once since 1932 has the Court voided a commodity-price regulation as violative of due process of law.[312] Legislatures may, within the bounds of due process, authorize individual producers as well as administrative agencies to determine the prices to be charged for particular commodities. As the decisions now stand, the Court will not invalidate, on due process grounds, such price regulation either as an invalid mode of regulation or as an unconstitutional delegation of price-fixing authority.

Not only may the legislatures provide for commodity-price fixing as such. It is now permissible under the due process clause of the Fifth Amendment for Congress to regulate the prices of certain farm products by restricting the amount of the product to go into interstate commerce. As a corollary, Congress does not run afoul of the due process clause by restricting the amount of such products to be produced by an individual farmer though no part of his crop enters interstate commerce. It was held that control of the intrastate supply was essential to the effective working of the congressional program. The fact that an individual farmer may be injured by the regulation is immaterial insofar as due process is concerned. The due process which is guaranteed by the Fifth Amendment does not mean that an individual may carry on his business or sell his products as he sees fit. He may be required to curtail his production in order to furnish a market for goods flowing through the interstate market, thus boosting the general price. Such restrictions for the benefit of larger groups of individuals is now *ipso facto* due process of law.

Under the present interpretation of due process of the Fifth and Fourteenth amendments that clause does not protect an employer's freedom of contract or any right to conduct his business as he likes. In 1937 the Court held that the employer was not deprived of his property without due process of law by the operation of the

[312] Carter v. Carter Coal Co., 298 U.S. 238 (1936). In this instance, the case did not turn on the price provisions. The merits of such regulations were not discussed.

Washington minimum-wage law. Nor was he thought to have been denied due process by a law requiring him to contribute to an unemployment-insurance fund, the rate to be determined without reference to his unemployment record. Such restrictions on the use and enjoyment of property were for the benefit of an entire group of employees whose interests and welfare were of greater public concern than the employer's property. However, not until the Court's decision in the Jones-Laughlin case [313] was due process held to be a positive guarantee of any right of labor. In that case the Court declared that among the fundamental rights of labor was the right to organize, to bargain collectively, and to strike to enforce its rights. If one may assume that the Court's ruling to the effect that due process guarantees all rights which are fundamental applies in cases other than those involving civil liberties, this decision may mean that the Court was in effect ruling that the rights would exist even in the absence of national legislation on the subject. Two months later Justice Brandeis declared that under the due process guarantee of free speech, labor had a right to picket with or without state legislative authorization to do so.

Due process no longer protects an industry from extrastate regulation if, in the judgment of the Court, the regulating state has a substantial governmental interest in the activity it seeks to regulate. The state was held not to have deprived an insurance company of property without due process by a restriction upon the percentage of the agent's commission which might be shared with an out-of-state broker, even though the actual contracts for insurance were executed outside the state. Nor did the Court find that the due process clause prohibited a state from requiring that an insurance company set aside a reserve fund, the amount to be determined by reference to the premiums and membership fees collected in all states in which the company operated. Due process is not denied by the operation of a law regulating the activities of reciprocal insurance companies, even though the contracts were made wholly within the bounds of another state. In each instance the state was held to have, in the activity it sought to regulate, an interest which outweighed any complaint of the com-

[313] 301 U.S. 1 (1937).

pany under due process of law. Thus "jurisdiction" has ceased to be a territorial limitation coincident with the boundaries of the state. It has been extended beyond these bounds to include business activities in which the state, through its legislature, finds that it has a vital interest.

Due process does not protect a corporation in its ownership of land if the state finds that such ownership runs counter to, or makes less effective, a policy which the legislature has found essential to the public welfare. The corporation may by legislative enactment be required to sell its property within the state. The Court has held that in such a case the property owner was not denied due process because it was forced to dispose of the property or because it was unable to make a profitable return on the lands sold. Likewise, Congress does not deprive a holding company of property without due process by requiring that it sever relations with any of its properties which, in the judgment of the Securities Exchange Commission, fall within the prohibitions of the law. The determination of the reasonableness of the legislation rests with the legislature.

Congress may exclude or restrict the sale of certain products on the interstate market if it finds that such products are not wholesome, that they facilitate fraud, and, at least the Court has implied, if it finds that a product is one which, because of the low cost of production, competes favorably with other products that the Congress wishes to protect from undue competition. Similar restrictions may be imposed by the state. It may be assumed that the state legislature and Congress, to the extent that it may reach industry through its commerce power, may consistently with due process of law regulate public or private industry in any of its aspects.

During the period since 1932 the Court has held consistently that emergencies do not create power. An emergency, it is said, does nothing more than present the occasion for the exercise of an already existent power. Though this was the Court's ruling in the Minnesota mortgage-moratorium case, the legislation was upheld in spite of the fact that the operation of the law resulted in an impairment of the obligations of the contract, in violation of the specific provision of the Constitution prohibiting such impair-

ment. If the temporary nature of the provisions was a factor of
the Court's consideration in upholding the Minnesota law, the
ruling seems to have been made ineffective by the numerous extensions of the moratory legislation of various states far beyond
the dates fixed in the original laws. Not until 1945, however, did
the Court place the question of the existence of an emergency
in the category of matters for legislative determination. Under
present rulings, the mortgagee cannot successfully invoke the
protection of due process of law against emergency legislation
which impairs the mortgage contract nor may he challenge successfully the state's determination that the legislation is an emergency measure. In actual effect, whether or not one concedes that
an emergency does create power, such rulings as these have
greatly diminished the scope of the due process protection of
contract and other rights. In this, as in other instances, due process
has come to protect a type of legislation supposedly enacted for
the benefit of the public at large, even though the operation of
such legislation results in the violation of some specific constitutional provision.

Since 1937 the due process of law clause of the Fifth and Fourteenth amendments has not been employed to hamper Congress
or the state legislatures in the enactment of legislation for the
benefit of labor. In addition to the regulation of hours and wages
and a recognition of the right to organize, to bargain collectively,
and to strike, the Court has sustained social-security and unemployment-insurance laws which were alleged to be violative of
due process of law. That the individual employer's money was
taken to provide a fund for the benefit of other individuals was
not found to be inconsistent with the then prevailing concept of
due process of law. The reasoning underlying the decisions in the
unemployment-insurance, pension, and social-security cases seems
to have been that such a contribution on the part of the employer
was actually for a public purpose, that the state as well as the employer has a vital interest in the alleviation of the plight of unemployed persons, and that due process of law does not prohibit the
state from legislating on a subject in which it has such an interest.
Due process as reasonable law was held to comprehend a sub-
ordination of individual property rights to the larger needs of the

group, not because it is a group but because a solution of the problems prevalent among its members was viewed as a matter of vital concern to the public as a whole. This does not represent an abandonment of substantive due process so much as the introduction of a new type of substantive due process protection—that protection due the collectivity in its right to maintain an orderly society.

From this brief summary, which does not include all of the regulations and restrictions imposed upon the use and enjoyment of property by social and economic legislation since 1932, several significant conclusions may be drawn. Since the reasonableness of such restrictive legislation depends upon its appropriateness in attaining the ends for which it was passed as well as upon the appropriateness of the ends themselves, the determination of the reasonableness requires a balancing of interests. The Court has maintained its power to weigh the interests of the parties concerned and to determine on the basis of its findings whether the challenged regulation meets the requirements of due process of law. However, in very few instances during the years under consideration has the Court exercised this power to make an independent finding of facts and review legislation in the light of its findings. The principle of the presumption of the validity of economic and social legislation challenged as resulting in a deprivation of property without due process of law has become the settled doctrine of the Court for the present. The majority of the Court assumes that the legislature is the best judge of the regulations and policies most adequate to the needs of the people. As a general rule, the Court does not question the legislative finding that a particular measure is a necessary and appropriate remedy for ills which the legislature has found to exist in the state. The presumption of validity no longer needs to rest on an expressed finding of the legislature; rather it operates to support legislation unless there is presented specific evidence that the regulation is an arbitrary exercise of power. Thus the determination of the need for, and the appropriateness of, the legislation is left to the legislature. Necessarily this means that the legislature, in effect, determines the reasonableness of the regulation also. In several instances the Court has pointedly declared that the matter of reasonableness was for the legislature to decide. This leads to the conclusion that at present there is no judicially enforcible substantive due process protection available to those individuals who allege that their property rights have been infringed.[314] In making this shift from the more restrictive interpretation of due process of law in the matter of property rights, the Court has not actually ignored or abandoned the rights of the individual as such. Rather it has found that he, as well as the state, has an interest in the maintenance of an orderly society and that to maintain such a society under the present social and economic structure, restrictions upon the use and enjoyment of property are necessary and justified.

It appears that due process has ceased to be a restriction upon Congress in the exercise of its enumerated powers. If a statute embodies a regulation valid under the commerce power or the tax power, it will not be challenged successfully under the due process of law clause of the Fifth Amendment. Nor does the due process guaranteed in the Fifth Amendment include equal protection of the laws. The restriction may be discriminatory to such a degree as to be arbitrary and so violative of due process, but the mere fact that there is some discrimination is not enough to invalidate it.

[314] See Carl Brent Swisher, *The Growth of Constitutional Power* (Baltimore, 1946), pp. 107–27.

III

Criminal Proceedings in
State and Federal Courts

For more than half a century the Supreme Court interpreted the due process clause of the Fourteenth Amendment as protecting an accused person in his right to be heard by a regularly constituted tribunal of the state. But it was generally held that the state, through its legislature, should determine what would meet the requirements of a "hearing" and a "duly constituted tribunal." In 1884, Justice Matthews reasoned that "due process of law" in the Fourteenth Amendment "refers to the law of the land in each State, which derives its authority from the inherent and reserved power of the State, exerted within the limits of those fundamental principles of liberty and justice which lie at the base of our civil and political institutions, and the greatest security of which is the right of the people to make their own laws and to alter them at their pleasure." [1] And so it was said to follow that any legal procedure "enforced by public authority" whether it had the sanction of age and custom or was "newly devised in the discretion of the legislative power, in the furtherance of a general public good, which regards and preserves those principles of liberty and justice must be held to be due process." [2]

As late as 1915, Justice Pitney held that the state court's determination on the question of the mob domination of the trial was entitled to great, if not conclusive, weight. Only by a "show-

[1] Hurtado v. California, 110 U.S. 516, 535 (1884). See p. 192, n. 10, *infra*.
[2] *Ibid.*, p. 537. The same construction was used in Howard v. Fleming, 191 U.S. 126 (1903), concerning the sufficiency of an indictment, and in Twining v. New Jersey, 211 U.S. 78 (1908), on the matter of protection against self-incrimination.

ing of fact" rather than a "preponderance of evidence" could this determination be challenged successfully.[3] To Justice Pitney it was "well settled" that a criminal proceeding in the courts of a state "based upon a law not in itself repugnant to the Federal Constitution and conducted according to the settled course of proceedings as established by the law of the State" was due process in the constitutional sense "so long as it [included] notice and a hearing, or an opportunity to be heard before a court of competent jurisdiction, according to the prescribed modes of procedure. . . ."[4] The Court did not look behind the record of the case to see if the proceedings actually met these requirements. It did hold that a trial conducted in a mob-dominated courtroom would not accord due process to the accused. The burden of proof, however, was allowed to rest entirely upon the accused person who challenged the adequacy of the proceedings, and the presumption of validity which attached to the trial court's finding weighed heavily against him.

Justice Holmes showed a markedly different approach to the settlement of issues concerning the due process of criminal proceedings in state courts. He declared that when facts were alleged by the accused, which if true would make the trial void as lacking in due process, the appellate court was obligated to examine the situation surrounding the trial and make an independent determination of the truth or falsity of the allegation.[5] If it failed to do this, the Supreme Court, he said, would protect the constitutional rights of the accused by making such a determination. From this ruling it was but a step to the Court's method of deciding due process cases in the matter of criminal proceedings as exemplified in Powell v. Alabama.[6] The gap between the two cases was bridged by the speech cases, especially Whitney v. California[7] and Fiske v. Kansas.[8] Since 1932 "due process of law" has been applied to protect many individual accused persons against unfair

[3] Frank v. Mangum, 237 U.S. 309 (1915).

[4] Ibid., p. 326.

[5] Moore v. Dempsey, 261 U.S. 86, 91–92 (1923).

[6] 287 U.S. 45 (1932). For a detailed discussion of this gradual development, see Charles B. Nutting, "The Supreme Court, the Fourteenth Amendment and State Criminal Cases," University of Chicago Law Review, XIII (1933), 92–98.

[7] 274 U.S. 357 (1927). See p. 5, supra.

[8] 274 U.S. 380 (1927). See p. 4, supra.

action in state courts. However, very little progress has been made in the development of a concept of due process as a procedural guarantee; for in 1949 it would have been difficult, if not impossible, for an accused person to know that he was guaranteed a given procedural right.

THE RIGHT TO COUNSEL

Prior to the Court's epochal decision in Powell v. Alabama [9] in November, 1932, a person accused of crime in a state court had no right to counsel expressly guaranteed by the national Constitution. In this case petitioners, Negroes, were tried, convicted, and sentenced to death on a charge of rape. They alleged that they had been denied a fair trial, because, among other things, they had been deprived of the right to counsel with the accustomed incidents of consultation and opportunity to prepare a defense. The Supreme Court granted certiorari, and contrary to previous decisions in cases of this nature, declared that the "fact that a right is expressly stated in the Bill of Rights does not exclude such right from the meaning of due process." [10] Justice Sutherland, speaking for the majority, did not attempt to bring the specific provisions of the Sixth Amendment into the meaning

[9] 287 U.S. 45 (1932). For a compilation of cases on the right of an accused to the benefit of counsel, see "Annotation—Accused's Constitutional Right to Assistance of Counsel," Lawyers' Edition, LXXXIV (U.S. Reports, 308–10), 338–96. See also Felix Frankfurter's comment on this case in New York Times Magazine, November 13, 1932, p. 1.

[10] 287 U.S. 45, 66–67 (1932). In Hurtado v. California, 110 U.S. 516, 534 (1884), the Court had taken the position that since no part of the Constitution could be thought of as superfluous, the presence in the Bill of Rights of the provision that "no person shall be held to answer for a capital crime except on indictment of a grand jury" and the provision that no person should be deprived of "life, liberty, or property without due process of law" precluded the notion that "due process of law" in the Fourteenth Amendment, as applied to state courts, could include the right to indictment by a grand jury. Neither of the due process clauses could be interpreted to guarantee any of the rights specifically listed in the Bill of Rights. The right to freedom of speech and press had already been read into "due process of law." But this mode of interpretation was not completely abandoned until the decision in Near v. Minnesota, 283 U.S. 697 (1931). For a discussion of this approach in the Powell case, see Vernon Wilkerson, "The Federal Bill of Rights and the Fourteenth Amendment," Georgetown Law Journal, XXVI (1938), 439–57; and Ernst Friedler, "The Right to Counsel in State Courts," Wisconsin Law Review, VIII (1933), 370–71.

of the due process of law clause of the Fourteenth Amendment.[11] Instead he based the Court's ruling on a consideration of what he deemed to be a *fair hearing on a criminal charge* and declared that in the circumstances of this particular case the assistance of counsel was essential to a "hearing" as intended by the Fourteenth Amendment.[12] Here for the first time it was held that *in some circumstances* the right to counsel in a state court is "so vital and imperative that the failure of the trial court to make an *effective appointment* of counsel [is] . . . a denial of due process within the meaning of the Fourteenth Amendment." [13] The specific circumstances taken into account were "the ignorance and illiteracy of the defendants, their youth, the circumstance of public hostility, the imprisonment of the defendants by the military forces, the fact their friends were all in other states and communication with them necessarily difficult, and above all, that they stood in deadly peril of their lives." [14]

Not only did the Court hold that there existed a right to counsel under the due process clause; it declared that the right was to the "effective" appointing of counsel. The trial judge had appointed "all the members of the bar" for the "limited purpose of arraigning the defendants." There was no indication that such a designation meant that the entire bar would defend the accused at the trial if no counsel appeared in their behalf. Justice Sutherland was of the opinion that such a designation fell short of the requirements of due process, for counsel thus collectively named would not have that "clear appreciation of responsibility" nor be "im-

---

[11] The guarantee of the Sixth Amendment is that of an absolute right to counsel in every criminal trial in a federal court. However, the Supreme Court may at times determine that a given proceeding does not constitute a criminal case within the meaning of the amendment. See District of Columbia *v.* Clawans, 300 U.S. 617 (1937), in which the Court, after a consideration of the legislation of the Colonies before 1787 and of the states at the time of the adoption of the amendment, concluded that a proceeding against one charged with the violation of a law when conviction entailed only a 90-day prison sentence and a $300 fine did not constitute a criminal proceeding, and therefore, that the guarantee of a trial by jury did not apply.

[12] 287 U.S. 45, 71 (1932). Justices Butler and McReynolds dissented on the ground that by injecting the requirement of "effective appointment" of counsel into the meaning of due process, the Court had extended federal power "into a field hitherto occupied exclusively by the several states."

[13] *Ibid.* (Italics added.)   [14] *Ibid.*

pressed with that individual sense of duty" which would naturally accompany the proper appointment of counsel "specifically named and designated." [15]

"Effective assistance of counsel" was held to mean that competent counsel must be appointed at such time and in such manner as to make possible the preparation of a defense for the accused. The Court found that the defendants were not given an opportunity by the trial judge to obtain counsel of their own choosing had they been able otherwise to do so. Moreover, the indefinite appointment made by the judge was so close upon the opening of the trial that substantial aid was rendered impossible.[16]

The novelty of the case does not lie entirely in the fact that the right to counsel in a state court was successfully asserted under the national Constitution. The unwillingness of the Court to accept the state's record as disproof is also important. The Court did not hesitate to go behind the record of the proceedings to determine if, in fact, the accused had been given a fair hearing. It was found that the trial did not meet the requisites of due process because petitioners had not been effectively represented by counsel and therefore had not been afforded a fair hearing. A fair hearing or a fair trial in the future would be judged according to the Court's standards of fairness rather than the state's.[17]

The Court had an opportunity further to interpret the due process requirements of assistance of counsel in Avery v. Alabama.[18] In this case counsel was appointed by the trial court to defend Avery, but both attorneys designated were, at the time of

---

[15] *Ibid.*, p. 56.

[16] *Ibid.*, p. 58. See Joseph Sugarman, "The Right to Counsel," *Boston University Law Review*, XIII (1933), 98. The case was remanded to the state court, but Powell was never given an opportunity to have his case presented fairly. He was shot by a sheriff who was bringing him back to Birmingham from Decatur, where he had been taken to testify in the trial of Patterson. *International Juridical Association Bulletin*, IV (1936), No. 8, p. 6.

In Application of Yamashita, 327 U.S. 1 (1946), and Application of Homma, 327 U.S. 759 (1946), by a vote of six to two (Justices Murphy and Rutledge dissenting in each case), the Court determined that this right to counsel was not extended by the due process clause of the Fifth Amendment to war criminals on trial before American military commissions.

[17] See the note "The Emergence of a Nationalized Bill of Rights: Due Process and a 'Higher Law' of Liberty," *Brooklyn Law Review*, VII (1938), 490, 511; and Nutting, "The Supreme Court, the Fourteenth Amendment and State Criminal Cases," *loc cit.*, p. 260.

[18] 308 U.S. 444 (1940).

appointment, employed in another case. Within four days Avery had been arraigned, tried, convicted of murder, and sentenced to death. Counsel moved for a continuance on the ground that there had not been time to prepare an adequate defense. The trial judge denied the motion and Avery's counsel appealed to the Supreme Court on the ground that in denying the continuance, the judge in effect deprived petitioner of effective assistance of counsel. The Court, speaking through Justice Black, affirmed the ruling of the Powell case, declaring that had petitioner been denied "all" assistance of counsel he would have been deprived of his liberty without due process of law.[19] He did not rely upon the facts of the case to justify the holding that due process included the right to counsel. Thus it is possible that Justice Black intended to make some kind of assistance of counsel an absolute requirement of due process. Further, if petitioner had not been given an opportunity to confer and consult with the attorneys, the appointment would have been converted into a "sham and nothing more than a formal compliance with the Constitution's requirement that the accused be given the assistance of counsel." [20] But Justice Black considered that "The offense for which the petitioner was convicted occurred in a county largely rural. The County Seat, where court was held, has a population of less than a thousand. Indictments in Bibb County Circuit Court, as in most rural counties throughout the nation, are most frequently returned and the trials held during the fixed terms or sessions of court. And these rural 'Court Weeks' traditionally bring grand and petit jurors, witnesses, interested persons, and spectators from every part of the County for court. . . . Because this was so, petitioner's attorneys were able to make the inquiries during court week at the County Seat. . . ." [21] And so the majority concluded that the time allowed had been sufficient and that the mere fact that the continuance had been denied did not deprive the accused of due process of law. Justice Black was of the opinion that the Fourteenth Amendment did not limit the power of the state to deal with crimes committed within its borders. The authority to grant or deny a continuance was left to the discretion of the trial judge, and ordinarily, it was said, the

[19] *Ibid.*, p. 445.   [20] *Ibid.*, p. 446.
[21] *Ibid.*, pp. 451–52.

question of whether he had abused that discretionary power would not be reviewed by the Court.[22] The Court's ruling in this case seems to rest on the failure of petitioner's attorneys to indicate anything definite in the way of further evidence or other witnesses which they might have obtained for the defense had more time been allowed. The Court refused to overthrow the state's judgment unless it appeared that a different conclusion would have been reached had there been additional time for the preparation of the defense.[23]

Once again the Court read into "due process of law" a new meaning: How much time shall counsel be given to obtain testimony and prepare a defense? The counsel appointed by the trial court insisted that more time was needed. One of them testified that he had had two days and the other one day in which to make the investigations necessary for the defense. In spite of this brief time, Justice Black held that petitioner had been given adequate assistance of counsel and that counsel had performed their duties intelligently and competently. Counsel's appointment and representation rendered under it were not mere formalities, said Justice Black, for they "have contested every step of the way to the final disposition of the case." [24] And so the question of the adequacy of the time allowed becomes a determining factor in judging the competency of counsel appointed, and the final determination must depend upon the circumstances of the case.

By its decision in Smith v. O'Grady [25] the Court extended the rule of Johnston v. Zerbst [26] and Walker v. Johnston [27] to noncapital cases in a state court. In this case the accused alleged that he had not had the assistance of counsel at the time he pleaded

---

[22] *Ibid.*, p. 446.   [23] *Ibid.*, p. 452.
[24] *Ibid.*, p. 450.   [25] 312 U.S. 329 (1941).

[26] 304 U.S. 458, 464–65 (1938). Here the Court, with reference to a criminal case in a federal court, declared that "waiver" of the right to counsel means the "intentional relinquishment of a known right or privilege." If the individual wishes to waive this right, he must do so "competently" and "intelligently" with full understanding of the consequences of his act. See the note in *Columbia Law Review*, XLII (1942), 271–82.

[27] 311 U.S. 275, 286 (1941). In this case the rule of "competent" waiver of the right to counsel as stated in Johnston v. Zerbst (see n. 26, *supra*) was made applicable to a criminal trial in a federal court when the accused had pleaded guilty without the advice of counsel. The Court held that the accused should have had counsel in determining which plea to enter.

guilty and that he had been deceived by the state's attorney into entering a plea of guilty to an offense which actually was much more serious than that with which he had been led to believe he was charged. Justice Black declared that if these allegations were true, petitioner had been deprived of his liberty without due process of law; for he had entered a plea of guilty without legal advice, although he had not waived his right to counsel.

The question of a proper appointment of counsel by a federal court for a person accused of conspiracy to defraud the government was raised in Glasser *v.* United States.[28] Justice Murphy, speaking for the Court, declared that the right to counsel guaranteed to one accused of crime "is so fundamental that the denial by a state of a reasonable time to allow for the selection of counsel of one's own choosing" or the failure of that court to make an "effective appointment" of counsel "may so offend our concept of the basic requirements of a fair hearing as to amount to a denial of due process of law contrary to the Fourteenth Amendment." [29] Likewise, he was of the opinion that the assistance of counsel assured by the Sixth Amendment "contemplates that such assistance shall be untrammeled and unimpaired by a court order requiring that one lawyer shall simultaneously represent conflicting interests." [30] To interpret the right to the assistance of counsel to mean less than this, would be to impair substantially a valued constitutional right.

In this case one attorney had been appointed to defend two persons charged with the same crime and put on trial at the same time. Glasser alleged that the fact that the attorney had to defend the second person led him to admit and suppress evidence to his, Glasser's, detriment. He alleged that perhaps unintentionally, but inevitably, he was incriminated in the minds of the jurors far beyond what was reasonable in the light of the evidence presented against him. The district-court judge argued that Glasser, himself a competent attorney, had acquiesced in the appointment of counsel and therefore had waived his right to object that he had been denied the assistance of counsel. To this Justice Murphy replied that the Court must "indulge every reasonable presump-

[28] 315 U.S. 60 (1942).   [29] *Ibid.*, p. 70.
[30] *Ibid.*

tion" against waiver of the right to counsel.[31] The petitioner's standing as an attorney was immaterial so far as his constitutional right to the advice and assistance of legal counsel was concerned.[32] Justice Murphy thought that it would be almost impossible for the Court to determine the degree of prejudice against Glasser's interests which had resulted from the fact that the attorney had to defend two clients in the same proceeding. Furthermore, it was said that the assistance of counsel is "too fundamental" and "absolute" a right for the Court to "indulge in nice calculations as to the amount of prejudice arising from its denial." [33] For this reason, Justice Murphy thought that "Irrespective of any conflict of interest, the additional burden of representing another party *may conceivably impair counsel's effectiveness*." [34]

Thus the Court added another possible prerequisite for effective assistance of counsel: "Assistance of counsel" may mean the exclusive services of competent counsel during the entire course of the trial. While in this same case the fact that the interests of the two defendants were in conflict made the action of the trial court a clear denial of the petitioner's right, the Court went further to indicate that the mere fact that an attorney is called upon to assist a second party "may" impair his effectiveness so as to deprive the accused of his constitutional right to counsel as guaranteed by the Sixth Amendment and, impliedly at least, of the due process of law guaranteed by the Fourteenth Amendment should the action be taken by a state court.

It might reasonably have been assumed that the Court's ruling in the Glasser case meant that the right to counsel would be found equally as fundamental in a criminal trial in a state court. But the unpredictability of the Court was evidenced forcefully by its decision in Betts v. Brady [35] nearly six months later. Betts was indicted in a Maryland district court on a charge of robbery. For

---

[31] *Ibid.*   [32] *Ibid.*

[33] *Ibid.*, p. 76. Justice Frankfurter, joined by Chief Justice Stone, dissented. They did not disagree with the Court's rule of the "fundamental" nature of the right to counsel, but they could not agree with the conclusion that the trial court's action denied Glasser that assistance.

[34] *Ibid.*, p. 75. (Italics added.)

[35] 316 U.S. 455 (1942). For one of the few favorable comments on the ruling in this case, see George I. Haight, "Betts v. Brady," *American Bar Association Journal*, XXIX (1943), 61–63.

lack of funds, he was not able to employ counsel and requested that the trial judge appoint an attorney to assist him in his defense. The judge refused on the ground that it was not the practice of the court to appoint counsel for indigent persons charged with crimes other than murder or rape. Betts was found guilty and was sentenced to eight years' imprisonment.

When the fairness of the trial was challenged before the Supreme Court, Justice Roberts voiced the opinion of the majority. He did not think that the due process clause of the Fourteenth Amendment incorporated the specific rights guaranteed by the Sixth Amendment. Only in certain situations would denial of the rights embodied in that amendment deprive the accused of life or liberty without due process. He explained that the due process of law clause of the Fourteenth Amendment "formulates a concept less rigid and more fluid than envisaged in the other specific and particular provisions of the Bill of Rights. Its application is less a matter of rule. Asserted denial is to be tested by an appraisal of the totality of the facts in a given case. That which may in one setting constitute a denial of fundamental fairness, shocking to the universal sense of justice, may in other *circumstances and in the light of other considerations, fall short of such denial.*" [36] This case was distinguished from the Powell case [37] on the basis of the facts. In that case the rule had been applied in a "capital case where the defendant [was] unable to employ counsel and [was] incapable of making his defense because of ignorance, illiteracy, or the like. . . ." But the age of the defendant in the present case —forty-three years—his ordinary intelligence, and the fact that he had been in court on previous occasions were thought to qualify him adequately to defend himself.[38] Also the law of Alabama required the court to appoint counsel for indigents brought before it; Maryland had no such requirement. The rule of the O'Grady case was said not to apply, for that case involved factors

[36] 316 U.S. 455, 462 (1942). (Italics added.) Cf. the statement concerning the right to counsel made in Grosjean *v.* American Press Corp., 297 U.S. 233, 244 (1936).

[37] 287 U.S. 45 (1932).

[38] Cf. Glasser *v.* United States, 315 U.S. 60 (1942), in which the fact that the defendant was himself a competent lawyer—Assistant Attorney for the United States for four years—was not thought to qualify him to make his own defense.

other than denial of counsel which made the trial a mere pretense. There, too, the law of the state provided for the appointment of counsel.[39] On the basis of these distinctions, Justice Roberts explained that the issue in the case at bar was quite different from anything presented in previous cases. The Court, he said, was now called upon to decide if due process requires that in every criminal case, whatever the circumstances, a state must furnish counsel to an indigent. Actually the Court must decide, it was said, if the guarantee laid down in the Sixth Amendment "expresses a rule so fundamental and essential to a fair trial that it is made obligatory upon the States by the Fourteenth Amendment." [40] He concluded that the right itself was fundamental only in some instances.

In view of the attitude which the Court had assumed with regard to the right to the assistance of counsel, it is singular that Justice Roberts should have leaned so heavily upon the legislative policy of the states in determining the extent of the right in this case. Upon a consideration of state constitutional and statutory provisions and upon an investigation of colonial legislation on the matter of counsel, he found that in a majority of the states "it has been the considered judgment of the people, their representatives, and their courts that appointment of counsel is not a fundamental right, essential to a fair trial. . . ." [41] In the light of such evidence Justice Roberts felt precluded from deciding that the due process concept incorporated in the Fourteenth Amendment "obligated the States, whatever their view, to furnish counsel in every such case." [42]

Apparently the majority justified this decision by the fact that it had no doubt as to the guilt of the accused. Betts had been identified, to the satisfaction of the trial court, as the perpetrator of the robbery, and his defense consisted only of an alibi. Justice Roberts concluded that the case before the trial court was a simple one turning entirely upon the "veracity of the testimony for the state and the defendant." The majority overlooked the fact that if it were possible to divine the "veracity" of the testimony in any case the trial would be a simple one. Justice Roberts did not believe that the due process of law clause of the Fourteenth

---

[39] 316 U.S. 455, 464 (1942).   [40] *Ibid.*, p. 465.
[41] *Ibid.*, p. 471.   [42] *Ibid.*

Amendment should be interpreted to embody "an inexorable command that no trial for any offense, or in any court, can be fairly conducted and justice accorded a defendant who is not represented by counsel." [43]

Justice Black, speaking for Justices Murphy, Douglas, and himself, dissented. He urged that the due process clause of the Fourteenth Amendment made applicable to trials in state courts the same guarantee which the Sixth stated for trials in the federal courts. Denial of counsel in any case, he said, makes it impossible to conclude that the defendant's case was properly presented. Only when there can be such a conclusion can it be said that an accused has been accorded due process. [44] Though Justice Black would make the assistance of counsel per se an essential element of due process of law, [45] he did not think that the Court would be forced to apply an inexorable rule in this instance. The minority insisted that in the light of the facts of the case at bar petitioner had been denied the procedural protection guaranteed by the Fourteenth Amendment.

Does due process require that an accused be advised by legal counsel on the question of whether to plead guilty to the charge made by the state? Must he specifically request that the court appoint counsel? These questions were before the Court in two cases appealed from Missouri courts, Williams v. Kaiser [46] and Tomp-

---

[43] *Ibid.*, p. 473. See Snyder v. Massachusetts, 291 U.S. 97 (1934). For a discussion of the implications of the "fair trial" rule as laid down by the Court in this case, see Green, "Liberty Under the Fourteenth Amendment, 1942–1943," *Washington University Law Quarterly*, XXVIII (1943), 251–71; and Green, "Liberty Under the Fourteenth Amendment, 1943–1944," *loc. cit.*, pp. 437, 467. The author speaks of the rule as having been used to "sabotage" the right which the Court had declared to be fundamental and within the protection of the due process of law guaranteed by the Fourteenth Amendment. Lusky, "Minority Rights and Public Interest," *loc. cit.*, pp. 1, 28–29, explains the Court's action by the fact that the accused did not belong to any minority group.

[44] 316 U.S. 455, 476 (1942).

[45] *Ibid.*, p. 475. To Justice Black any other practice would defeat the "promise of our democratic society to equal justice under law." *Ibid.*, p. 477. Benjamin V. Cohen and Erwin N. Griswold writing in the New York *Times*, August 2, 1942, IV, 6:5, said: ". . . at a critical period in world history, Betts v. Brady dangerously tilts the scales against the safeguarding of one of the most precious rights of man. For in a free world no man should be condemned to penal servitude for years without having the right to counsel to defend him. The right to counsel for the poor, as well as for the rich, is an indispensable safeguard of freedom and justice under law."

[46] 323 U.S. 471 (1945).

kins *v.* Missouri.[47] The first of these involved a plea of guilty, entered without the advice of counsel, to a charge of "robbery by means of a deadly weapon." On the basis of the Powell case Justice Douglas ruled that "the right to counsel in cases of this type is a right protected by the Fourteenth Amendment of the federal constitution. The question of whether that federal right has been infringed is not foreclosed here, even though the action of the state court was on the ground that its statute requiring the appointment of counsel was not violated." [48] Petitioner alleged that he had entered the plea of guilty without legal advice, that he did not waive his constitutional right to such advice, and that because he lacked counsel, he was unable to make a defense and was forced to make that plea. Justice Douglas said that since the accused appeared before the court without counsel, it must be assumed that he was not able to employ an attorney and that he desired the court to appoint counsel for his defense.[49] The majority considered that "robbery by means of a deadly weapon" is a capital offense under the laws of Missouri and that in that state there are important distinctions between the various degrees of robbery. Because of this, the technical requirements of the indictment or information and the kinds of evidence necessary for a conviction as well as the defense available "are a closed book to the average layman." Necessarily then, the right to counsel was held to be guaranteed in connection with a plea of guilty as well as the manner in which the trial is conducted. In the light of the circumstances peculiar to this case and the complicated law involved, it was held that only a trained attorney could discern from the facts whether a plea of guilty to the charge or to a lesser offense would be appropriate. "A layman is usually no match for the skilled prosecution whom he confronts in the courtroom. He needs the aid of counsel lest he be the victim of over-zealous

[47] 323 U.S. 485 (1945).

[48] 323 U.S. 471, 473 (1945). Cf. the statement in Betts *v.* Brady, 316 U.S. 455, 473 (1942), that since the charge against the defendant Betts was robbery and since the Fourteenth Amendment protected property rights as well as life and liberty, "if we hold with the petitioner, logic would require the furnishing of counsel in civil cases involving property." Though this was suggested by counsel, Justice Roberts cited it without indication of disapproval.

[49] 323 U.S. 471, 474 (1945).

prosecutors, of the law's complexities, or of his own ignorance." [50] And so the right to the aid of counsel was held to be so fundamental that its denial was a deprivation of due process of law. The failure of the trial judge to inform the accused of his right to counsel was said to be equivalent to a denial of the right. The fact that the accused failed to appeal his case was thought to emphasize his need for legal advice. That failure could not be made a bar to the issuance of a writ of habeas corpus.[51]

Justice Frankfurter dissented for Justice Roberts and himself on the ground that the Supreme Court of Missouri had decided the case on the basis of state law and the United States Supreme Court should assume, when no evidence to the contrary appeared on the record, that the state court had decided the issue properly.[52]

In the second of these cases, Tompkins v. Missouri,[53] petitioner alleged that he did not waive his right to counsel, although he had not specifically requested the trial judge to assign counsel for his defense. Again Justice Douglas spoke for the Court and stated that an indigent accused *need not specifically ask* that counsel be assigned him. If such an accused appears before the court without an attorney, the trial judge is required to appoint counsel. Thus the Court virtually read into due process of law an absolute right to counsel in a state criminal proceeding. Justice Douglas may

[50] *Ibid.*, pp. 475–76. In Adams v. McCann, 317 U.S. 269, 279 (1942), Justice Frankfurter, for the Court, held that one accused of crime in a federal court might waive trial by jury without the advice of counsel as to the advantage of such action. "The right to the assistance of counsel," he explained, "and the correlative right to dispense with a lawyer's help are not legal formalisms. They rest on considerations that go to the substance of the accused's position before the law. The public conscience must be satisfied that fairness dominates the administration of justice. An accused must have the means of presenting his best defense. He must have time and facilities for investigation and the production of evidence. . . . Essential fairness is lacking if an accused cannot put his case effectively in court. But the Constitution does not force a lawyer upon a defendant. He may waive his constitutional right to the assistance of counsel if he knows what he is doing and his choice is made with open eyes." Justices Murphy, Black, and Douglas dissented in this case.

[51] 323 U.S. 471, 477 (1945). Cf. Mooney v. Holohan, 294 U.S. 103 (1935), in which the fact that appeal had not been taken to secure a writ of habeas corpus from the Supreme Court of California deprived petitioner of relief before the Supreme Court of the United States because he was held not to have exhausted the remedies afforded by the state.

[52] 323 U.S. 471, 480–81 (1945).

[53] 323 U.S. 485 (1945). Justices Frankfurter and Roberts dissented.

have been led to restate the ruling of the previous case because the petitioner alleged that he did not know that he was entitled to make such a request of the judge.[54] Here again the complexity of the law involved was considered. To the majority

> The nature of the charge emphasizes the need for counsel. Under the Missouri law one charged with murder in the first degree may be found guilty of second degree murder or of manslaughter. . . . The differences between them are governed by rules of construction meaningful to those trained in the law but unknown to the average layman. . . . And the ingredients of the crime of murder in the first degree as distinguished from lesser offenses are not simple but ones over which skilled judges and practitioners have disagreements. The guiding hand of counsel is needed lest the unwary concede that which only bewilderment or ignorance could justify or pay a penalty which is greater than the law of the state exacts for the offense which they in fact and in law have committed.[55]

If under the due process clause of the Fourteenth Amendment the trial court must appoint counsel for an accused appearing before it without a defense attorney, is the court required by that same clause to allow the accused to consult with the attorney whom he has employed? The Court answered this in the affirmative in its *per curiam* opinion in House *v.* Mayo.[56] Petitioner alleged that when he was brought before the court to be sentenced on two burglary charges to which he had pleaded guilty, he was handed an information charging him with a third burglary. His request that he be allowed to consult his lawyer who was at the time out of town was refused, and in the absence of legal advice, he pleaded guilty to the information. The Court held that the refusal on the part of the trial court was a "denial of petitioner's right to a fair trial, with the aid and assistance of counsel whose presence he had requested." [57]

---

[54] *Ibid.*, pp. 487–88. See De Meerleer *v.* Michigan, 329 U.S. 663, 665 (1947), where in a *per curiam* opinion the Court held that petitioner had been deprived of liberty without due process of law; for "At no time was assistance of counsel mentioned to him, nor was he appraised of the consequences of his plea."

[55] 323 U.S. 485, 488–89 (1945).   [56] 324 U.S. 42 (1945).

[57] *Ibid.*, p. 46. Justice Roberts dissented on the ground that no federal question was involved here.

Justice Black was of the opinion that when a petitioner alleged that the crime with which the state charged him was supposedly committed on an Indian reservation within federal jurisdiction there was raised an involved question "posing a problem that is obviously beyond the capacity of even an intelligent layman, and which clearly demands the counsel of experience and skill." [58] But the state had assumed jurisdiction because petitioner had entered a plea of guilty. Justice Black said that such action on the part of the state was equivalent to a ruling that an accused who pleads guilty, by that act, waives his right to counsel. That assumption was said to be "inconsistent with this Court's interpretation of the Fourteenth Amendment." [59]

The question of whether a refusal of a motion for continuance denied the accused his right to effective assistance of counsel was again before the Court in Hawk v. Olson.[60] Petitioner was tried in a Nebraska district court on a charge of first-degree murder. More than a month elapsed between the preliminary hearing and the verdict. Hawk was represented by counsel during this period but contended that counsel needed more time in which to prepare the defense. The request for continuance was denied on the ground that neither the accused nor his counsel presented any evidence in support of his innocence which had not been entered as evidence at the trial. Upon appeal to the United States Supreme Court it was found that there was no reason to believe that the accused was unfamiliar with the court procedure or the law governing his case. But there was an allegation that he had been without counsel between the time he entered the plea of not guilty and the calling of the jury. Because of this, Justice Reed said that "continuance may or may not have been useful to the accused but the importance of the assistance of counsel in a serious charge after arraignment is too large to permit speculation on its effect." [61] And so Justice Reed ruled that the denial of the right to

[58] Rice v. Olson, 324 U.S. 786, 789 (1945). "It is enough that a defendant charged with an offense of this character is incapable of making his defense, that he is unable to get counsel and that he does not intelligently and understandingly waive counsel." Ibid., pp. 788–89. Justice Frankfurter, joined by Justices Roberts and Jackson, dissented.

[59] Ibid., p. 788.

[60] 326 U.S. 271 (1945). See Avery v. Alabama, 308 U.S. 444 (1940), p. 195, supra.

[61] 326 U.S. 271, 278 (1945).

counsel "does violate due process," likewise the denial "of opportunity to consult with counsel on any material step after indictment on similar charge and arraignment violates due process." [62]

In December, 1946, for the first time in four years and the second time since 1932 the Court found that conviction of an accused not represented by counsel did not amount to a denial of due process of law. In 1928 the accused—a Negro, thirty years of age, of slight schooling and no previous experience in court proceedings—entered a plea of guilty to a murder charge and was sentenced to ninety-nine years in prison. In 1946 he sought release, contending that his conviction was void, for it was in violation of his right under the due process of law guaranteed by the Fourteenth Amendment inasmuch as he had not been assigned counsel until the sentencing stage of the proceeding.[63] Justice Frankfurter, speaking for five members of the Court, declared "There is . . . nothing in the statement of the Illinois Supreme Court alone from which we can infer that [the] normal requirements of Illinois law prejudiced this defendant or made their observance in this case incongruous with his constitutional rights." [64] This case was distinguished on the basis of the facts from previous cases in which the assistance of counsel had been deemed essential. Here was the "unchallenged finding by the trial court that the accused was duly appraised of his rights . . . and chose to plead guilty." [65] But here such factors as the age, experience, and intelligence which had been held determinative in previous cases were not considered. Justice Frankfurter explained that "From the common law record, we do not know what manner of man the defendant was. Facts bearing on his maturity, capacity of comprehension, or the circumstances under which a plea of guilty was tendered and accepted are wholly wanting." [66]

The majority conceded that inherent in the concept of a fair trial is the "opportunity to meet an accusation," and that "under pertinent circumstances" the opportunity is adequate only when

[62] *Ibid.*

[63] Carter *v.* Illinois, 329 U.S. 173 (1946). See Betts *v.* Brady, 316 U.S. 455 (1942).

[64] 329 U.S. 173, 179 (1946). See Hysler *v.* Florida, 315 U.S. 411, 422 (1942), where Justice Frankfurter followed this method of decision.

[65] 329 U.S. 173, 177 (1946). Cf. Rice *v.* Olson, 324 U.S. 786 (1945).

[66] 329 U.S. 173, 178 (1946).

the accused person is assisted by legal counsel.[67] Thus the Court still holds that there are situations when justice cannot be assured unless the person charged with crime is aided by competent legal advice. But from the meager record upon which Justice Frankfurter based his opinion nothing was found to indicate that the circumstances of this case "made it necessary for Carter to have professional guidance other than that given by the trial court." [68] In the face of these vague statements of the scope of the guarantee afforded by due process of law within the meaning of the Fourteenth Amendment, what does the Court conceive to be the extent of freedom left to the states? The answer given in the majority opinion is too general and vague to serve as a criterion. "Due process of law" has not been "perverted" so as to demand uniform procedures in each of the forty-eight states, but it does command that the states assure a "fair judgment" to an accused. The details of the procedures for securing this fairness, however, have been left to the states.[69] As long as "due process" means so indefinite a thing as a "fair judgment," it is inevitable that in individual cases counsel may or may not be deemed essential. In this case, the majority failed to follow what had become the established path of majorities since the Powell case in 1932. The Court did not look behind the common-law record which had been before the state supreme court. Apparently this shift in method takes the Court back to the pre-1932 mode of approach to due process cases involving the right to the assistance of counsel.[70] But four justices disagreed with the Court's opinion. To Justices Douglas, Black, and Rutledge it was immaterial that the accused had not requested counsel.[71] Since the Supreme Court of Illinois had based its decision on the fact that petitioner had not asked for legal assistance, these three would have the case remanded to the state court.[72]

Justice Murphy wrote a separate dissenting opinion in which he declared that upon a consideration of the facts before the

[67] *Ibid.*, p. 179.   [68] *Ibid.*

[69] *Ibid.*, p. 175. Said Justice Frankfurter: "So long as the rights under the United States Constitution may be pursued, it is for the State and not this court to define the mode by which they may be vindicated." *Ibid.*, p. 176.

[70] See pp. 191–92, *supra*.

[71] See Tompkins *v.* Missouri, 323 U.S. 485 (1945); and Williams *v.* Kaiser, 323 U.S. 471 (1945).   [72] 329 U.S. 173, 186 (1946).

Court, facts not in dispute in the trial court or the state supreme court, it became obvious that due process had been denied. To the majority's acceptance of the decision that the accused had waived his right to counsel, Justice Murphy answered that it is no excuse that the accused is willing to waive certain constitutional rights "unless we are certain that he has a full and intelligent comprehension of what he is doing. Otherwise we take from due process a substantial part of its content." [73]

Six months later, June 23, 1947, Justice Frankfurter again spoke for the majority of the Court on the issue of the right to counsel and again ruled that *under the circumstances of the case* the trial court was not required by due process of law to assign counsel. Foster *v.* Illinois [74] involved two petitioners who without counsel had been indicted, arraigned, their pleas of guilty accepted, and their sentences imposed in a single day. Justice Frankfurter explained that the "due process of law which the Fourteenth Amendment exacts from the States is a conception of fundamental justice." [75] But the states are not confined to the absolute rule of the Sixth Amendment.[76] The state must allow an accused "ample opportunity to meet an accusation." Therefore, "in the circumstances of a particular situation" the assignment of counsel may be prerequisite to a fair trial within the meaning of due process as guaranteed by the Fourteenth Amendment. The duty of the Court, however, in the judgment of Justice Frankfurter "does not go beyond safeguarding 'rights essential to a fair hearing' by the State." [77] On the common-law record before the Court, the majority found no reason to impeach the decision of the state court on due process grounds.

Justice Black spoke for the minority, which consisted of Justices Murphy, Rutledge, and himself. The dissenters appraised the Court's opinion in this case as "a watering down" of the Fourteenth Amendment "to make it compatible with the Court's standards of decency and fair trial." [78] Again Justice Black ex-

---

[73] *Ibid.*   [74] 332 U.S. 134 (1947).
[75] *Ibid.*, p. 136.
[76] In support of this ruling Justice Frankfurter cites Betts *v.* Brady, 316 U.S. 455 (1942). See Palko *v.* Connecticut, 302 U.S. 319, 327 (1937).
[77] 332 U.S. 134, 139 (1947). See Mooney *v.* Holohan, 294 U.S. 103, 112–13 (1935).   [78] 332 U.S. 134, 139 (1947).

pressed fear of the consequences of the Court's "natural law justice" criteria for applying the due process clause of the Fourteenth Amendment.[79]

Justice Rutledge wrote a separate dissenting opinion, in which Justices Black, Douglas, and Murphy joined. "I think," he said, "that the Sixth Amendment guaranty of the right to counsel in criminal causes is applicable to such proceedings as this in state courts." [80] These four justices spoke out against the majority's presumption of regularity in favor of the state court's decision even in spite of a record indicating irregularity. Said Justice Rutledge: "Adding to this blindness [to the pleadings placed by petitioners before the Court] a presumption of regularity to sustain what has thus been done makes a mockery of judicial proceedings in any sense of the administration of justice and a snare and a delusion of constitutional rights for all unable to pay the cost of securing their observance." [81]

In April, 1948, the Court again rejected a petitioner's plea that his trial had been unfair because he had not been assigned counsel. Justice Burton wrote the opinion for the majority in Bute *v.* Illinois,[82] which involved a fifty-eight-year-old man convicted of having taken indecent liberties with two small girls. Petitioner sought relief on the ground that he had not been represented by counsel and had not been advised of his right to request counsel. Said Justice Burton: "This *due* process is not an equivalent for the process of the federal courts or for the process of any particular state. It has reference rather to a standard of process that may cover many varieties of processes that are expressive of differing combinations of historical or modern, local or other juridical standards, provided they do not conflict with 'the fundamental principles of liberty and justice which lie at the base of our civil and political institutions.' " [83] This phrase taken from the opinion in the case of Hebert *v.* Louisiana in 1926 has been used so in-

[79] See Justice Black's dissent in Adamson *v.* California, 332 U.S. 46 (1947), for a more detailed exposition of this issue.

[80] 332 U.S. 134, 141 (1947).   [81] *Ibid.,* p. 145.

[82] 333 U.S. 640 (1948).

[83] *Ibid.,* p. 649. In this instance Justice Burton reaches back to the opinions of Hebert *v.* Louisiana, 272 U.S. 312 (1926); and Holden *v.* Hardy, 169 U.S. 366 (1899), for support of his position.

discriminately by the Court that it has been rendered almost meaningless. What are these immutable principles held so dear by the Court? None of the justices ever say exactly, but surely to many laymen the particular right here in question should be included among them. The Court, it was said here, has not in the past and does not now find it necessary to "define with precision" the term "due process of law." It is enough, thought Justice Burton, to say that "there are *certain immutable principles of justice,* which inhere in the very idea of free government, which no member of the Union may disregard, as that no man shall be condemned in his person or property without due notice and an opportunity of being heard in his defense." [84] But the states are free to choose what procedures shall be used, and "a substantial presumption arises in favor of, rather than against, the lawfulness of those procedures and in favor of their right to continued recognition by the Federal Government as due process of law." [85] Justice Burton found no reason for assuming that in 1868 the Fourteenth Amendment was directed particularly against the practice complained of in this case; therefore, he found no basis for an impeachment of the decision reached by the trial court. By way of summarizing what he considers to be the holding of the Court on the subject, he says:

> After exhaustive consideration of the subject, the Court has decided that the Fourteenth Amendment does not, through its due process clause or otherwise, have the effect of requiring the several states to conform the procedures of their criminal trials to the precise procedure of the federal courts, even to the extent that the procedure of the federal courts is prescribed by the Federal Constitution or the Bill of Rights. There is nothing in the Fourteenth Amendment specifically stating that the long recognized and then existing power of the states over the procedures of their own courts in criminal cases was to be prohibited or even limited. Unlike the Bill of Rights, the Fourteenth Amendment made

[84] 333 U.S. 640, 649 (1948). (Italics added.)
[85] *Ibid.*, pp. 653–54. It is of some significance that the Court cites Hurtado *v.* California, 110 U.S. 516 (1884), in support of its ruling. The approach followed in the Hurtado case had been virtually supplanted in 1932 by Justice Sutherland's opinion in Powell *v.* Alabama, which opinion had been viewed as a landmark of progress in the protection of the rights of accused persons.

no mention of any requirements of grand jury presentments or indictments as a preliminary step in certain criminal prosecutions; any universal prohibition against the accused's being compelled, in a criminal case, to be a witness against himself; any jurisdictional requirement of juries in all criminal trials; any guaranty to the accused that he have a right to the assistance of counsel for his defense in all criminal prosecutions; or any need to observe the rules of the common law in the re-examination of all facts tried by a jury.

. . . .

So here the procedure followed by Illinois should not be held to violate the standard of permissible process of law broadly recognized by the Fourteenth Amendment unless the Illinois procedure violates "the very essence of a scheme of ordered liberty" so that to continue it would "violate a principle of justice so rooted in the traditions and conscience of our people as to be ranked fundamental." [86]

And so it was concluded that the states are free to adopt whatever rule they choose concerning the right to the assistance of counsel so long as they do not "deprive an accused of life, liberty or property without due process of law." Thus we find ourselves precisely where we started—petitioner contending that the procedure adopted did deny him due process and the Court in a very unsatisfactory manner explaining that the particular right in question is not necessarily covered by the due process clause.

Had this been a capital charge, due process of the Fourteenth Amendment would have required that the accused be informed of his right to request counsel and that the court assign competent counsel if he desired it.[87] Also, it was said that where the charge is a noncapital one, there may be "special circumstances" leading to the conclusion that the accused would not enjoy "that fair notice and adequate hearing which constitute the foundation of due process of law in a trial on a criminal charge" unless he were represented and advised by a competent attorney.[88] In the case at bar, however, no such extenuating circumstances were found.

[86] 333 U.S. 640, 656–57 (1948), citing among other cases, Palko v. Connecticut, 302 U.S. 319, 325 (1939); Snyder v. Massachusetts, 291 U.S. 97 (1934); Twining v. New Jersey, 211 U.S. 78 (1908); and Hurtado v. California, 110 U.S. 516 (1884).
[87] 333 U.S. 640, 674 (1948).   [88] Ibid., p. 677.

Justice Douglas, speaking for Justices Murphy, Black, Rutledge, and himself, voiced dissent. In his opinion the Bill of Rights should apply to all courts under any circumstances.[89] "The basic requirements of a fair trial," said Justice Douglas, "are those which the Framers deemed so important to procedural due process that they wrote them into the Bill of Rights and thus made it impossible for either legislatures or courts to tinker with them." [90] The dissenters admitted no basis for the ruling that due process of law guaranteed counsel in capital cases only. "Certainly due process shows no less solicitude for liberty than for life." [91] Assuming that perhaps there are instances when legal advice is not essential, Justice Douglas' understanding of where the line of demarcation should be drawn is worthy of note. To quote him:

It might not be nonsense to draw the Betts v. Brady line somewhere between that case and the case of one charged with violation of a parking ordinance, and to say that the accused is entitled to counsel in the former and not in the latter. But to draw the line between this case [Bute v. Illinois] and cases where the maximum penalty is death is to make a distinction which makes no sense in terms of the absence or presence of *need* for counsel. Yet it is the *need* for counsel that establishes the real standard for determining whether the lack of counsel rendered the trial unfair. And the need for counsel, even by Betts v. Brady standards, is not determined by the complexities of the individual case or the ability of the particular person who stands as an accused before the court. That need is measured by the *nature* of the *charge* and the ability of the *average* man to face it alone, unaided by an expert in the law.[92]

On June 14, 1948, the Court handed down opinions in three cases involving the right to counsel under the due process of law

[89] *Ibid.*, pp. 678–79.   [90] *Ibid.*
[91] *Ibid.*, p. 681. See Justice Black's statement in Chambers v. Florida, 309 U.S. 227, 241 (1940). In Carter v. Illinois, 329 U.S. 173, 186 (1946), Justice Murphy explained that the insistence upon the advice of counsel at all stages of a capital case was "merely a recognition of our attempt to be civilized, a recognition that the process of condemning human life is to be judged by standards higher than those applied to a prosecution for violation of a minor ordinance or regulation."
[92] 333 U.S. 640, 682 (1948). (Italics added.)

clause of the Fourteenth Amendment. The first of these, Townsend *v.* Burke,[93] involved an accused who without legal advice pleaded guilty to two robbery charges and two burglary charges. His own complaints were that he had been held incommunicado for a period of forty hours and that he did not have counsel at the time he pleaded guilty. Justice Jackson repeated the recent ruling that the state court may accept an uncounseled defendant's plea of guilty to a noncapital charge.[94] But in this case "the court's facetiousness casts a somewhat somber reflection on the fairness of the proceeding" in view of the fact that the accused had been found not guilty of the charge, about which the trial judge joked. The judge had recited a number of charges which at some time in the past had been made against Townsend. The judge acted on the assumption that defendant had been found guilty on each charge. Thus by a reading of the record Townsend was made to appear to be a "habitual criminal." It was this misreading or misconstruing of the record by the judge in such a way as to prejudice the court to which Justice Jackson objected. In this instance he found extenuating circumstances which made counsel essential to a fair trial, for

> We believe that on the record before us, it is evident that this uncounseled defendant was either overreached by the prosecution's submission of misinformation to the court or was prejudiced by the court's own misreading of the record. Counsel, had any been present, would have been under a duty to prevent the court from proceeding on such false assumptions and perhaps under a duty to seek remedy elsewhere if they persisted. Consequently, on this record, we conclude that, while disadvantaged by lack of counsel, this petitioner was sentenced on the basis of assumptions concerning his criminal record which were materially untrue. Such a result, whether caused by carelessness or design, is inconsistent with due process of law. . . .[95]

[93] 334 U.S. 736 (1948).

[94] *Ibid.*, p. 739. But the majority reiterated the ruling that the disadvantages from the absence of counsel, when aggravated by circumstances showing that it resulted in the prisoner's actually being taken advantage of, or his cause prejudiced, does make out a case of violation of due process. *Ibid.*, p. 739.

[95] *Ibid.*, p. 740. The Chief Justice and Justices Reed and Burton dissented without writing an opinion.

The majority indicated that neither the severity of the sentence nor the possibility of error formed the basis of decision. Even "an erroneous judgment, based on a scrupulous and diligent search for truth, may be due process." The due process of law guarantee was violated by the lack of any search for truth or by the intentional use of false statements.[96]

The second of the trio, Gryger v. Burke,[97] involved an individual, eight times convicted of crimes of violence, who challenged the trial judge's interpretation of the Habitual Criminal Act of Pennsylvania and alleged that the judge would have given it a different interpretation had the defendant been represented by counsel. The judge, it was alleged, assumed that the act required him to impose a life sentence, while actually the statute made the sentence discretionary. Justice Jackson found nothing in the nature of the charge or the plea of the defendant to indicate that the absence of counsel invalidated the proceeding or that the defendant had requested counsel and had been refused. The fact that one of the convictions entering into the calculations by which defendant became a "fourth offender" occurred before the law was passed did not make the imposition of the penalty violative of due process.[98] A sentence as a fourth offender is said not to be a "new jeopardy" nor an additional penalty for earlier crimes but rather a more severe sentence for the latest offense because it is a repetitive one.

Justice Rutledge, joined by Justices Black, Murphy, and Douglas, dissented on the ground that "even upon the narrow view to which a majority of this Court adhere concerning the scope of the right to counsel," the decision in the instant case cannot be squared with the ruling in Townsend v. Burke.[99] The dissenters were of the opinion that the judge's misunderstanding of the discretionary aspect of the statute applied did place the accused at a disadvantage which could have been overcome only through the advice of a lawyer. Said Justice Rutledge: "The denial of the very essence of the judicial process, which is the exercise of discretion where discretion is required, is in itself a denial of due process, not merely

[96] Ibid., p. 741.
[98] Ibid., p. 732.

[97] 334 U.S. 728 (1948).
[99] Ibid., p. 733. See n. 94, supra.

an error of state law of no concern to this Court." [100] The dissenting members of the Court once again expressed their disapproval of the present majority's approach to the due process issue. Speaking for them, Justice Rutledge concluded: "Perhaps the difference [between the case at bar and the Townsend case] serves only to illustrate how capricious are the results when the right to counsel is made to depend not upon the mandate of the Constitution, but upon the vagaries of whether judges, the same or different, will regard this incident or that in the course of particular criminal proceedings as prejudicial." [101]

The Court's opinion in the third of the counsel cases decided June 14, Wade v. Mayo,[102] was written by Justice Murphy. Wade, charged with breaking and entering the property of another, requested the trial judge to appoint counsel for him. His request was refused and he was sentenced to five years in the penitentiary. But, said Justice Murphy, "There are some individuals who, by reason of age, ignorance or mental capacity are incapable of representing themselves adequately in a prosecution of a relatively simple nature. This incapacity is purely personal and can be determined only by an examination and observation of the individual. Where such incapacity is present, the refusal to appoint counsel is a denial of due process of law under the Fourteenth Amendment." [103] Justice Murphy does not further the development of a practicable rule by such a statement, for once again judges may honestly differ in their estimation of the capacity of an accused to make his way through the maze of a criminal proceeding. To have the guarantee of the right to counsel depend upon such an estimate does not spell progress in its protection. It can mean only that the judge, either the trial judge or a majority of the members of the Supreme Court, finds that the accused

---

[100] 334 U.S. 728, 734 (1948). [101] *Ibid.*, p. 736.

[102] Wade v. Mayo, 334 U.S. 672 (1948). Justice Reed, joined by Chief Justice Vinson and Justices Jackson and Burton, dissented on the issue of the jurisdiction of the Federal District Court. He expressed no opinion on the merits of the trial-court proceeding.

[103] *Ibid.*, p. 684. This ruling was restated in Uveges v. Commonwealth of Pennsylvania, 335 U.S. 437 (1948). In this case, the right to counsel was based on the age (seventeen years) of the accused and the seriousness of the crime. Justice Reed wrote the Court's opinion.

should have had counsel. Justice Murphy, it would seem, would advance his fight for the protection of the right of accused persons by attempting to lead a majority of his colleagues to an acceptance of such a right as belonging to accused persons regardless of the circumstances of the case.

If the right to counsel is to depend upon the circumstances of the particular case, surely such factors as age, experience, and the nature of the crime should not be given greater weight than the actual conduct of the trial. In the case of Gibbs v. Burke,[104] Justice Reed, expressing the views of the Court, recognized this to a larger extent than had been the case in previous instances when the question was before the Court. Here the accused person was thirty years of age and apparently had had some experience with law-enforcement officials. He was arrested and charged with the theft of some personal belongings from the home of one who at least was a prior acquaintance. He was indicted and pleaded not guilty. Without the aid of legal advice he was tried by a jury, found guilty, and sentenced to two and one-half years in prison. He appealed to the Supreme Court on the ground that because of the conduct of the trial he was not able to defend himself without counsel.

The Court's decision here was based primarily upon the actual manner in which the judge conducted the trial proceedings. Justice Reed found several occurrences in the course of the trial that made it unfair to the defendant. For instance: The judge admitted a considerable amount of hearsay evidence which any competent attorney would have taken exception to. He did not permit the accused to prove that the plaintiff had made similar accusations, proved to be false, at previous times and that he had taken the articles from plaintiff's house according to an agreement between himself and the owner. Justice Reed was of the opinion that these facts and the additional fact that the judge prejudiced the jury by allowing the accused to be deterred from taking the stand in his own behalf through the prosecution's threat to cross-examine him

---

[104] 337 U.S. 773 (1949). Justice Reed wrote the Court's opinion. Justices Black and Douglas concurred in the result on the basis of the Betts v. Brady rule but expressed the opinion that Betts v. Brady should be overruled and the right to counsel declared the absolute right of any accused person. Justices Rutledge and Murphy concurred in the results.

about other convictions indicated the lack of a fair trial. If the petitioner had been advised by counsel, it is possible that the judge would have been more careful of the manner in which the trial was conducted or possibly the accused would have been in a position to make objection and correct the situation. Therefore, said Justice Reed, due process of law required the assistance of counsel in this case.[105]

Thus by a series of decisions beginning in 1932, the Court has read into "due process of law" the right of an accused to the effective assistance of counsel if in the opinion of the Court the circumstances of the case make counsel essential to a fair hearing. The weight of the Court's opinions leads to the conclusion that there is no absolute right to counsel nor any definite criteria by which the Court determines whether denial of the right resulted in a deprivation of liberty without due process. Such factors as the age of the accused, his previous experience in court, the nature of the crime with which he is charged, and the atmosphere surrounding the trial have been considered. The trend at present seems to be toward the application of an even more subjective criterion—was the accused, in the estimation of the judge, capable of defending himself. Along with this vague standard, though expressed by different members of the Court, is the application of the rule of a presumption of regularity of state-court proceedings. This latter rule, applied far beyond anything warranted by the words or history of the Fourteenth Amendment, marks a trend dangerous to the protection of the individual rights of one accused before the courts of the state. Its application shifts the burden of proof from the accuser to the accused, who is rarely in a position to offer concrete proof of the alleged infringement of his right to a fair trial. If the Fourteenth Amendment was not intended to place some restrictions upon the procedures to be followed in state courts, its *raison d'être* is completely lacking.

Where the right to counsel exists, it includes the right to the effective assistance of a competent, specifically designated attorney who has had time to prepare for the defense. Depending

[105] The Court reiterated the ruling that the failure to request the assistance of counsel does not constitute a waiver of the constitutional right where the accused is not apprised of his right. 337 U.S. 773, 780. See also, Uveges v. Commonwealth of Pennsylvania, 335 U.S. 437 (1948).

upon the circumstances of the case, legal advice may be required for a decision to enter a plea of guilty. In no instance may such plea be considered equivalent to a waiver of the right. For a brief span of time the Court held that it was not necessary for the accused to request the appointment of counsel, that if on the basis of the facts the right exists, the trial judge must assume that an accused appearing before the court without a lawyer desires the court to assign an attorney for his defense. Between Powell *v.* Alabama in 1932 and Betts *v.* Brady in 1942 the Court consistently found that the facts of the case warranted the decision that counsel was essential to a fair hearing. In several recent instances, however, the Court has found that due process of law did not require the assignment of counsel. In these cases, beginning in 1946, appears the reinstatement of the pre-1932 mode of approach to due process cases. The present majority does not see that its duty extends to an investigation into the actual situation within which the accused alleges a violation of his rights, unless that situation is spread upon the record of the court from which the last appeal was taken. Thus the constitutional status of the right to legal counsel becomes increasingly precarious. It will be seen, moreover, that the same trend is apparent in due process cases involving other rights.

SELF-INCRIMINATION

Coerced Confessions. In February, 1936, Chief Justice Hughes handed down a decision, in Brown *v.* Mississippi, which for the first time virtually extended due process protection against a kind of self-incrimination in a state court.[106] The issue before the Court was whether, consistently with due process of law, the state could base a conviction on a confession obtained by the state law-enforcement officers through means of physical force and torture. Here the confessions were admittedly procured only after long hours of questioning under torture and the threat of mob violence. Chief Justice Hughes thought it would be "difficult to conceive

---

[106] 297 U.S. 278 (1936). See the note "Privilege Against Self-incrimination," *Indiana Law Journal,* XII (1936), 66; and Green, "Liberty under the Fourteenth Amendment, 1943–1944," *loc. cit.,* pp. 437, 467, 533, where this case is discussed as extending due process protection against self-incrimination.

of methods more revolting to the sense of justice than those taken to procure the confessions of these petitioners." He held that the "use of the confessions thus obtained as the basis for conviction was a clear denial of due process." [107]

The Court declared that this was not self-incrimination in the usual sense. The right of the state to withdraw the privilege of immunity from self-incrimination was said not to be involved. The freedom of the state in establishing its policies and enforcing its criminal law is limited by the requirements of due process of law, and though the state is free to dispense with a trial by jury, "it does not follow that it may substitute a trial by ordeal." [108] Due process requires that the state procedures be consistent with the "fundamental principles of liberty and justice which lie at the base of our civil and political institutions." [109] To meet this requirement the state must afford the accused an opportunity to be heard in his defense. No such hearing is possible when he has been forced to confess his guilt before the trial begins. On the other hand, the information so obtained is not reliable and therefore must not be the basis of a conviction.

The Court, said Chief Justice Hughes, will not attempt to correct "mere errors" on the part of the trial judge. But the failure of the judge to exclude the coerced confession from the evidence was thought to be more than a mere error. Rather it was said to be "a wrong so fundamental that it made the entire proceeding a mere pretense of a trial and rendered the conviction and sentence wholly void." [110]

[107] 297 U.S. 278, 286 (1936). The dissenting judge in the case, when it was before the Supreme Court of Mississippi, described the record as one which "reads more like the pages torn from some medieval account than a record made within the confines of a modern civilization which aspires to an enlightened constitutional government." 173 Miss. 542, 161 So. 465, 470 (1935).

[108] 297 U.S. 278, 285–86 (1936).

[109] Ibid., p. 286, citing Hebert v. Louisiana, 272 U.S. 312, 316 (1926).

[110] 297 U.S. 278, 286 (1936). See "Judicial Errors, Unfair Trials, and the Fourteenth Amendment," Harvard Law Review, XLIV (1931), 447–51. Cf. Buchalter v. New York, 319 U.S. 427, 430–31 (1943), where the Court held that "due process of law" did not enable it to review errors as to the state law "however material under that law. . . ." The case involved a charge that Buchalter, manager of a racketeering outfit in New York, had ordered the murder of one Rosen, who had been forced out of the New York and New Jersey Transportation Company because he refused to co-operate with Buchalter in a hauling stoppage. At the time of the murder the "Dewey Racketeering" investigation was at its height, and it was thought that Buchalter feared that Rosen would talk. The "errors"

The importance of the decision in this case does not lie in any protection extended by the Court to a racial minority, for there is no indication that the Court made race a factor for its consideration. The real significance rests on the fact that the Court went behind the findings of the state court and made an independent determination that on the basis of the methods of the law-enforcement officers—methods not in dispute in this instance—the confessions were coerced and therefore not admissible as evidence against the accused. The Court did not make any independent findings of fact, because the facts were admitted by the state and appeared on the record of the case. In effect the Court did attempt to correct an error of the trial judge and in so doing indicated that there are degrees of errors, some of which are of such import that they become not "mere errors" but "wrongs" which invalidate the entire proceeding. Once again the Court injected into its concept of due process of law a new element which has proved to be the basis of much litigation concerning criminal trials in state courts.

Not until four years later did a second confession case come before the Court. In 1940, Justice Black wrote the opinion for the Court in Chambers v. Florida,[111] which involved the admission in evidence of a confession obtained only after seven days of constant gruelling. The state contended that the issue of fact upon which the verdict and sentence were based had been finally determined by the jury, that the Supreme Court had no jurisdiction to look behind the judgments of the trial court. To this Justice Black replied that the Court "must determine independently whether petitioner's confessions were [obtained by duress] by review of the facts upon which the issue necessarily turned," for the accused had seasonably asserted a right under the Constitution to

---

complained of concerned chiefly the court's charge to the jury to the effect that the jurors might reconcile the conflicting testimony and find that the accused did or did not order the murder. The errors were said not to be so substantial as to deprive the accused of a fair trial. In Holiday v. Johnston, 313 U.S. 342 (1941), the Court held that the erroneous imposition of two sentences for a single offense of which the accused had been found guilty did not deprive him of liberty without due process of law. See the note in Harvard Law Review, LVII (1944), 919–20.

[111] 309 U.S. 227 (1940). Eight justices agreed that the accused had been denied due process. Justice Murphy took no part in the consideration of the case.

have their guilt or innocence determined without reliance upon such confessions.[112] The due process clause of the Fourteenth Amendment was held to have made operative against the states the requirement that court procedures conform to the fundamental standards of justice. Among such standards is that of a fair hearing for an accused. The use of coerced confessions is *ipso facto* a denial of a fair trial, hence of due process.[113]

Here mental as well as physical torture was placed under the due process ban. Said Justice Black: "From the popular hatred and abhorrence of illegal confinement, torture, and extortion of confessions in violation of the 'law of the land' evolved the fundamental idea that no man's life, liberty, or property be forfeited as criminal punishment for violation of that law until there had been a charge fairly made and fairly tried in a public tribunal free of prejudice, passion, excitement and tyrannical power." [114] These conditions were not met when the very circumstances surrounding confinement and questioning were intended to terrorize the prisoners into confessing their guilt. In this instance the accused, strangers in the community, were interrogated amid the haunting fear of mob violence and in an atmosphere "charged with excitement and public indignation." The Court was of the opinion that "To permit human lives to be forfeited upon confessions thus obtained would make of the constitutional requirement of due process a meaningless symbol." [115] As to the role of the Court in preventing such a devolution of constitutional rights, Justice Black explained:

> We are not impressed by the argument that law enforcement methods such as those under review are necessary to uphold our laws. The Constitution proscribes such lawless means irrespective of the ends. And this argument flouts the basic principle that all people must stand on an equality before the bar of justice in every American court. Today, as in ages past, we are not without tragic proof that the exalted power of some governments to punish manufactured crime dictatorially is the handmaid of tyranny. Under our constitutional system, Courts stand against any winds that blow

[112] *Ibid.*, pp. 228–29.
[114] *Ibid.*, pp. 236–37.
[113] *Ibid.*, p. 238.
[115] *Ibid.*, p. 240.

as havens of refuge for those who might otherwise suffer because they are helpless, outnumbered, or because they are non-conforming victims of prejudice and public excitement. Due process of law, preserved for all by our Constitution, commands that no such practice as that disclosed by this record shall send any accused to his death. No higher duty, no more solemn responsibility rests upon this Court, than that of translating into living law and maintaining this constitutional shield deliberately planned and inscribed for the benefit of every human being subject to our Constitution— of whatever race, creed, or persuasion.[116]

The convictions in Brown v. Mississippi [117] and Chambers v. Florida [118] rested entirely upon confessions which had been obtained through duress. But where it was shown that the confession was not the result of coercion or that the conviction had not been based solely on the confession even if it had been extorted by force and violence, the Court refused to reverse the judgment of the trial court.[119] The purpose of the due process requirement was said to be "not to exclude presumptively false evidence but to prevent fundamental unfairness in the use of evidence whether true or false." [120] Due process would be denied if violence should be used to force an accused to incriminate himself. Likewise, said Justice Roberts, it would be denied if incriminating evidence should be obtained as a result of a promise or other inducements of a favorable nature.[121] In Lisenba v. California, however, the accused did not complain that his confession had resulted from "favorable inducements." Rather his complaint was that his confession had resulted from the story told by his accomplice, which had implicated him in the crime, and that that story had been procured by promises of leniency.

[116] Ibid., pp. 240–41. See Bennett Brodsky and John H. Pickering, "Federal Restrictions on State Criminal Procedures," University of Chicago Law Review, XIII (1946), 266, 284, n. 62. See also V. M. Barnette, "Mr. Justice Black and the Supreme Court," ibid., VIII (1940), 20–41.
[117] 297 U.S. 278 (1936).   [118] 309 U.S. 227 (1940).
[119] Lisenba v. California, 314 U.S. 219 (1942). Justice Roberts spoke for the Court; Justices Black and Douglas dissented. This was on reargument. On the original hearing the judgment of the trial court was affirmed by an evenly divided court. 313 U.S. 537 (1941). The decision in the present case was the first in the series of confessions cases to be affirmed by the Court. See Brodsky and Pickering, "Federal Restrictions on State Criminal Procedures," loc. cit., pp. 286–88.
[120] 314 U.S. 219, 236–37 (1942).   [121] Ibid., p. 237.

The Court held that the confession had not resulted from any coercive action on the part of the law-enforcement officers. From the record of the trial court it was found that Lisenba had been questioned through the entire night of, and most of the day after, his arrest. During that time he had made no incriminating statements. It was not until ten days later, when confronted with Hope's story, that he confessed his part in the crime. The issue, therefore, was whether the confession should be considered unreliable because of the questioning of the officers. The Court declared that if it were to hold that the action of the officers of the state rendered the use of the confession a violation of due process, "it must be upon the grounds that such a practice, irrespective of the result upon the petitioner, so tainted his statements that, without considering other facts disclosed by the evidence and without giving weight to discredited findings below that his statements were free and voluntary, as a matter of law they were inadmissible in his trial." [122]

Justice Roberts calls attention to the fact that in each case where the Court has set aside a conviction based on a coerced confession, the confession was the sole basis for the conviction and there were other factors which prompted the Court to think that the coercion affected the reliability of the information so obtained. The confessions were secured only after "protracted and repeated questioning of ignorant and untutored persons, in whose minds the power of officers was greatly magnified; who sensed the adverse sentiment of the community and the danger of mob-violence; who had been held incommunicado, without advice of friends or counsel, some of whom had been taken by officers at night from the prison into dark and lonely places for questioning." [123] The state's action with regard to Lisenba was said not to fall within these conditions.

[122] *Ibid.*, p. 239. Justice Roberts relied upon the fact that the accused had said that the interrogation on the part of the police would never have drawn a confession from him had his confederate not made a statement incriminating him. "He exhibited a self-possession, a coolness, and an acumen throughout his questioning and at his trial, which negatives the view that he had so lost his freedom of action that statements made were not his but the result of the deprivation of his free choice to admit, deny, or to refuse to answer." But this picture of the petitioner was based upon the record of his accusers. *Ibid.*, p. 240.

[123] *Ibid.*, p. 238. The Court has held that a conviction based on a plea of guilty coerced by federal law-enforcement officers is "no more consistent with due process than a conviction supported by a coerced confession." Waley *v.* Johnston, 316 U.S. 101 (1942).

The state did not deny the accused due process of law by admitting testimony concerning the death of his first wife. The purpose of admitting such testimony was to "establish intent, design, and system." Nor did the trial judge's refusal of continuance deprive him of liberty without due process. Counsel for the defense was said to have had notice at the opening of the trial that the evidence would be introduced. He had waited until the state rested its case before asking for continuance, which the judge in his discretion had refused. Justice Roberts did not think that "The Fourteenth Amendment gives this Court any mandate to review his action or to inquire whether he abused his discretion in such a field." [124]

Justice Byrnes, speaking for the Court in Ward v. Texas, summarized the previous rulings of the Court as follows: "This Court has set aside convictions based on confessions extorted from ignorant persons who have been subjected to persistent and protracted questioning, or who have been threatened with mob-violence, or who have been held unlawfully incommunicado without the advice of friends or counsel, or who have been taken at night to lonely places for questioning—*any one of these grounds would be sufficient for a reversal.* The use of a confession obtained under such circumstances is a denial of due process." [125] In this case the petitioner had been taken from his home town and driven about for three days, being continuously questioned during the time. The Court considered the fact that the accused was a Negro and was at a disadvantage at best. Justice Byrnes did not consider the Court bound by the facts as presented on the record nor the verdict of the jury that the confession had been voluntary.[126]

In each of these cases, where a conviction had been set aside

---

[124] 314 U.S. 219, 228 (1942). See Avery v. Alabama, 308 U.S. 444 (1940). To Lisenba's contention that the trial court, by introducing into the courtroom snakes identified as those bought by the accused for the purpose of murdering his wife, denied him of due process, Justice Roberts answered: "The fact that the evidence admitted as relevant by the court is shocking to the sensibilities of those in the courtroom cannot, for that reason alone, render its reception a violation of due process." *Ibid.*, p. 229.

[125] Ward v. Texas, 316 U.S. 547, 555 (1942). (Italics added.) In the opinion of the author of a note on the use of coerced confessions as evidence, "Use by State of Perjured Evidence Denies Due Process," *Lawyers' Guild Review*, III (1943), 47, this states the most objective standard for determining the admissibility of confessions so far devised by the Court.

[126] 316 U.S. 547, 555 (1942). See Lusky, "Minority Rights and Public Interest,"

because it was found to have been based on a coerced confession, the "coercion" existed because of the manner in which the information had been obtained. The atmosphere of violence and fear surrounding the accused at the time of questioning was held to have made the testimony unreliable. In Ashcraft v. Tennessee [127] the Court went further to declare that the mere fact that the accused had confessed only after thirty-six hours of constant questioning invalidated the conviction based on the confession. The situation was said to be "inherently coercive," and therefore the confession was of necessity not voluntary and not admissible in evidence. In this case Ashcraft was charged with the murder of his wife. He was questioned over a period of thirty-six hours without food or rest and under other disconcerting circumstances. At the end of that time he signed a confession which was the sole basis for the conviction. Justice Black, for the majority, declared that in the case of one charged with crime the procedure of questioning away from the courtroom must not be such as would be condemned if used against a witness in open court. He expressed the majority opinion that

> a situation such as is here shown by uncontradicted evidence is so inherently coercive that its very existence is irreconcilable with the possession of mental freedom by a lone suspect against whom its full coercive force is brought to bear. It is inconceivable that any court in the land conducted as our courts are, open to the public, would permit prosecution serving in relays to keep a defendant witness under continuous cross-examination for thirty-six hours without sleep or rest in an effort to extort a "voluntary" confession. Nor can we, consistently with constitutional due process of law, hold voluntary a confession where prosecutors do the same thing away from the restraining influence of a public trial in an open court.[128]

---

loc. cit., p. 27. The author's thesis is that the Court has since 1938 become minority-conscious and has faced more realistically the situation of the Negro before a "white" court.

[127] 322 U.S. 143 (1944). Justice Black spoke for the Court. Justice Jackson, with whom Justices Roberts and Frankfurter joined, dissented, saying: "The use of the due process clause to disable the States in the protection of society from crime is quite as dangerous and delicate a use of federal judicial power as to use it to disable them from social and economic experimentation." Ibid., p. 174.

[128] Ibid., p. 154.

Here the Court set up an *irrefutable presumption of the involuntariness of any confession obtained as a result of long hours of incessant questioning.*[129] The due process protection was thereby extended far beyond its scope in the previous confession cases. The Court expressly refused to "resolve any of the disputed questions of fact." Such questions, except that of the length of time required to procure the confession, become relatively unimportant when there is a presumption of coerciveness, hence illegality, which the state cannot refute.[130]

A new difficulty was introduced into the confession cases in Lyons *v.* Oklahoma.[131] The petitioner made two confessions, the first of which was admittedly procured through duress. He contended that the coercive nature of the first confession invalidated the second because the fear engendered in obtaining the first resulted, twelve hours later, in the second. The jury had accepted the second confession as voluntary and had based a conviction upon it. The question before the Court was whether the facts surrounding the procurement of the first confession might be said to have controlled the character of the second so that the admis-

[129] See the note "Illegal Detention and the Admissibility of Confessions," *Yale Law Journal,* LIII (1944), 758, 772. The author of the note had thought that in the light of the decision in Buchalter *v.* People of New York, 319 U.S. 427 (1943), it was unlikely that the "presumption" established in McNabb *v.* United States, 318 U.S. 322 (1943)—that any evidence obtained from an accused between the time of his arrest and the time of arraignment before a judge was per se coercive and inadmissible and if used would invalidate the entire proceeding—would be applied to state action. The presumption set up in the present case allows for greater interpretation by the Court than that of the McNabb case because of the indefinite time element involved. The rule of the McNabb case was not applied in United States *v.* Mitchell, 322 U.S. 65 (1944), but was not overruled by that case. Cf. the presumption in the present case with that upheld in Atlantic Coast Line Ry. Co. *v.* Ford, 287 U.S. 502 (1933); and that invalidated as a denial of due process in Tot *v.* United States, 319 U.S. 463 (1943); or in Morrison *v.* California, 291 U.S. 82 (1934).

[130] 322 U.S. 143, 152 (1944). The case was remanded and Ashcraft was again convicted by the use of all the evidence produced at the first trial with the exception of the actual confession. In addition, the prosecuting attorney called attention to the fact that the accused, ten days after his arrest, had said that he knew the identity of the murderer. On certiorari, 327 U.S. 274 (1946), Justice Black, for the majority, again remanded the case to the state court on the ground that the evidence presented in the state court and the emphasis on the statement that the accused admitted having knowledge of the murderer's identity had denied Ashcraft a fair trial. Justice Frankfurter concurred.

[131] 322 U.S. 596 (1944). Justice Reed wrote the opinion for the Court. Justices Rutledge, Murphy, and Black dissented.

sion of the latter denied the accused due process of law. Justice Reed explained that an involuntary or coerced confession is offensive to the fundamental standards of justice, "not because the victim has a legal grievance against the police, but because the declarations procured by torture are not premises from which a civilized forum will infer guilt. *The Fourteenth Amendment does not provide review of mere error in jury verdicts, even though that error concerns the voluntary character of a confession.*" [132] Justice Reed held that when "conceded facts" exist which indicate the absence of mental freedom, the Court has toward the victim of the injustice a responsibility which it cannot avoid by leaving the burden of adjudication in the hands of the trial court and jury. But "where there is a dispute as to whether the acts which are charged to be coercive actually occurred, *or where different inferences may be fairly drawn from admitted facts*, the trial judge and jury are not only in a better position to appraise the truth or falsity of the defendant's assertions from the demeanor of the witnesses but the legal duty is upon them to make the decision." [133]

In this case the jury had been instructed as to the character of each of the confessions and their admissibility as evidence against the accused. It was not shown to the satisfaction of the jury that the coercion employed to obtain the first confession had any effect on petitioner's second confession. In ruling that the jury's determination as to the character of the confession is conclusive, the Court ignores the fact that the question of the nature of the confession and its effect upon the reliability of the evidence had in previous cases been considered a matter ultimately to be decided by the Court. Certainly Justice Reed should have indicated the factors present in this case which distinguished it from previous cases where the judgment of the state court was set aside because it was based on evidence accepted by the jury but found to be inadmissible by the Supreme Court.

[132] *Ibid.*, p. 605. (Italics added.)
[133] *Ibid.*, p. 602. (Italics added.) Cf. the attitude of the Court here with its position in Brown *v.* Mississippi, 297 U.S. 278, 286 (1936); Chambers *v.* Florida, 309 U.S. 227 (1940); or Ashcraft *v.* Tennessee, 322 U.S. 143 (1944). In each of these cases it was the interpretation of admitted facts upon which the Court's decision turned. In each case the state entered in evidence the confessions, knowing that an involuntary confession would void the entire proceeding.

New York police practices were reviewed by the Court in Malinski v. New York.[134] Malinski had been arrested as a suspect in the murder of a police officer. Instead of taking him to the police station for questioning, the officer in charge of his arrest took him to a hotel room, supposedly for a medical examination. Malinski was stripped and left naked for several hours during which time he made an oral confession. Later, and under different circumstances, he signed a confession. On the basis of the two he was convicted in the trial court. He appealed on the ground that his conviction was based solely on coerced confessions. To dispose of the case, the Court had to determine whether the first confession had resulted from coercion and, if so, whether the circumstances under which it had been made controlled the character of the second so as to taint it with coerciveness. Heretofore the Court had held that the conviction would be void if it rested wholly on the coerced confession, that is, if the conviction could not have been sustained without such confession.[135] In the present case Justice Douglas held that if the circumstances indicated that the confession had been procured through duress, it could not be used as evidence against the accused. "And if it is introduced at the trial, the judgment of conviction will be set aside *even though the evidence apart from the confession might have been sufficient to sustain the jury's verdict.*" [136] Thus the Court indicated that it assumed the task of determining the existence of "uncertainties" which would support the "conclusion of the judge or jury as to the nature of the voluntary character of the confession." [137] The accused man had been held incommunicado. He had been allowed to see only one person—an inmate of Sing-Sing—through whom the police hoped to get incriminating information. In the words of the prosecutor the accused was not "hard to break." On the basis of these considerations Justice Douglas concluded that "If we take the prosecutor at his word, the confession of October 23 was the product of fear—one on which we could not permit a person to stand convicted for a crime." [138]

---

[134] 324 U.S. 401 (1945).

[135] Brown v. Mississippi, 297 U.S. 278, 287 (1936); Chambers v. Florida, 309 U.S. 227, 238 (1940). But cf. Lisenba v. California, 314 U.S. 219, 239 (1942).

[136] 324 U.S. 401, 404 (1945). (Italics added.)

[137] *Ibid.*, pp. 408–409.   [138] *Ibid.*, p. 407.

Malinski had not been put on trial immediately after this confession was obtained; rather he had been held five days. On October 27 he signed a written confession and went on trial the next day. Upon investigation the Court found that the first confession had been mentioned, though it had not been entered as evidence. Justice Douglas was of the opinion that the mention of the confession was as effective in corrupting the trial as if it had been specifically entered and its details made known to the jury. The use of inadmissible evidence was said to be but a subtle intrusion upon the accused's constitutional rights and was held to be abusive as a disregard for constitutional guarantees.[139] Therefore, for the majority Justice Douglas held that "the case was one in which a coerced confession was used to obtain a conviction." Since the first confession was held to have been coerced, the majority did not consider it necessary to consider the nature of the subsequent one.[140] The conviction must be set aside.

Justice Frankfurter wrote a separate opinion explaining what he thought to be the Court's role in applying the due process of law clause in such cases:

> The Due Process of Law clause thus has a potency different from and independent of the specific provisions contained in the Bill of Rights. Apart from all other consideration, how could it be otherwise without charging Madison and his great contemporaries with writing into it a meaningless clause? The Fifth Amendment specifically prohibits prosecution of an infamous crime except by indictment; it forbids double jeopardy and self-incrimination, as well as deprivation of "life, liberty, or property without due process of law." Not to attribute to due process of law an independent function but to consider it a shorthand statement of other specific clauses in the same amendment is to charge those who secured the adoption of this amendment with meretricious redundancy by indifference to a phrase—"due process of law"—which was one of the great instruments in the very arsenal of constitutional freedom which the Bill of Rights was to protect and strengthen. Of course the due process clause of the Fourteenth Amendment has the same meaning.[141]

[139] *Ibid.*, p. 410.   [140] *Ibid.*   [141] *Ibid.*, pp. 414-15.

Justice Frankfurter thought that the issue before the Court was, not whether any of the specific provisions of the Bill of Rights had been violated, but whether the accused had been deprived of a fair hearing, by which he was entitled to have his guilt or innocence determined. He continued:

> Judicial review of the guarantee of the Fourteenth Amendment inescapably imposed upon this Court an exercise of judgment upon the whole course of the proceedings in order to ascertain whether they offend those canons of decency and fairness which expresses the notice of justice of English-speaking peoples toward those charged with the most heinous offenses. . . . But neither does the application of the Due Process clause imply that judges are wholly at large. The judicial judgment in applying the Due Process clause must move within the limits of accepted notions of justice and is not to be based on idiosyncracies of a merely personal judgment. . . . An important safeguard against such individual judgment is an alert deference to the judgment of the state court under review. But there cannot be blind acceptance even of such weighty judgment without disregarding this historic function of civilized procedures in the progress of liberty.[142]

Considering the entire proceeding against Malinski from the time of his arrest, the willful delay in arraignment, and the prosecutor's justification of the illegalities perpetrated by the law-enforcement officers, Justice Frankfurter held that "all these in combination are so far below the standards by which criminal law, especially in a capital case, should be enforced as to fall short of due process." [143]

Justice Murphy concurred with the majority opinion insofar as it concerned the conviction of Malinski. He concurred with Justice Rutledge's dissent with respect to the conviction of Malinski's accomplice Rudish. Justice Murphy expressed the opinion that "Once an atmosphere of coercion or fear is created, subsequent confessions should automatically be invalidated *unless there is proof beyond doubt that such atmosphere has been dispelled and that the accused has completely regained his free indi-*

[142] *Ibid.*, pp. 416–17.   [143] *Ibid.*, p. 418.

vidual will." [144] Aside from the use of the coerced confession to sustain the conviction, Justice Murphy thought that the prosecutors attempted to prejudice the jury against the accused because of race and creed. Malinski had been spoken of as the "jerk from the East Side" and as one who came from the East Side, "where one's life is not worth a pretzel." With reference to these remarks, which Justice Murphy took to be a reflection based on racial biases, he admonished:

> Those clothed with authority in the courtrooms of this nation have the duty to conduct and supervise proceedings so that an accused person may be adjudged solely according to the dictates of justice and reason. This duty is an especially high one in capital cases. Instead of an attitude of indifference and carelessness in such matters, judges and officers of the court should take the initiative to create an atmosphere free from undue passion and emotionalism. This necessarily requires the exclusion of attacks or appeals made by counsel tending to reflect upon the race, creed, or color of the defendant.[145]

Justice Rutledge concurred with the majority as to voiding Malinski's conviction. He felt that the use of such evidence in obtaining the conviction of the accused went beyond the prohibition against self-incrimination to "whatever extent this may have been applied to the states by the adoption of the Fourteenth Amendment." [146] Moreover, since the confession extorted from Malinski involved Rudish, his accomplice, Justice Rutledge would have had the Court set aside that conviction also.

Four members of the Court—Chief Justice Stone, Justices Reed, Roberts, and Jackson—voted to hold that both Malinski and Rudish should stand convicted. Their reasoning:

> It is not the function of the Court, in reviewing on constitutional grounds, criminal convictions by state courts, to weigh the evidence on which the jury procured its verdict,

---

[144] *Ibid.*, p. 433. (Italics added.) Cf. this with the reverse procedure followed in Lyons v. Oklahoma, 322 U.S. 596 (1944), where the Court found no evidence to show that petitioner had not regained his free and voluntary will, and therefore refused to hold the second confession coerced.

[145] 324 U.S. 401, 434 (1945).   [146] *Ibid.*, p. 431, n. 17.

also in the light of the arguments of counsel, to sit as a super-jury. We have, in appropriate cases, set aside state court convictions as violating due process of law where we were able to say that the case was improperly submitted to the jury or that the unchallenged evidence plainly showed a violation of the constitutional rights of the accused. . . . But we have not hitherto overturned the verdict of a state court jury by weighing the conflicting evidence on which it was based.[147]

Neither of the four was of the opinion that Malinski had been denied a fair trial. The mere fact that the police officers acted illegally did not, in their opinion, necessarily make the trial unfair. Said Chief Justice Stone: ". . . however reprehensible or even criminal the acts of state officers may be, insofar as the conduct of the trial is concerned they do not infringe due process of law unless they result in the use against the accused of evidence which is coerced or known to the state to be fraudulent or perjured, or unless they otherwise deny him the substance of a fair trial which is due process." [148]

There is no disagreement among the justices here as to the fact that due process of law requires a fair trial. The dissent rests upon a disagreement as to whether in this particular case there had been a fair trial. But to say that "due process" is a "fair trial" does not solve the problem. Since someone must determine if the accused has been given a trial which meets the requirements of due process, the issue becomes which court—state or national supreme court—shall decide finally and what standards that court shall apply. It would appear that the first of these issues has been resolved, even in the opinion of the dissenters, in favor of the national court. As to the latter, at least one significant thing was added by this decision, namely, the burden of proof was shifted. The state must refute beyond all doubt the presumption of coercion which attaches to confessions obtained under such circumstances as were indicated by the facts of this case.

Again, in Haley v. Ohio,[149] Justice Douglas announced the judgment of the Court in holding that a fifteen-year-old Negro

[147] Ibid., p. 438. Cf. Ward v. Texas, 316 U.S. 547, 550 (1942).
[148] 324 U.S. 401, 438–39 (1945).   [149] 332 U.S. 596 (1948).

boy had been coerced into confessing implication in a murder and had, by such coercion, been denied due process of law guaranteed by the Fourteenth Amendment. The accused had been taken into custody about midnight and questioned for five hours, after which he made an oral confession. In the opinion of Justice Douglas, "If the undisputed evidence suggests that force or coercion was used to extract the confession, we will not permit the judgment of conviction to stand *even though without the confession* there might have been sufficient evidence for submission to the jury." [150] Here the factors considered in judging the coerciveness of the police activity were petitioner's age, the time and duration of the questioning, the fact that neither friends nor counsel was present to advise, and the callous attitude of the police toward the rights of the accused. Justice Douglas felt that the whole situation precluded the assumption that the law-enforcement officers had not used compulsion to bring about the testimony. Since this was true, the conviction is invalid under the Fourteenth-Amendment guarantee of a fair trial.

Justice Frankfurter joined in this decision but felt compelled to amplify his reasons for so doing. In his judgment the state must be left as free as possible to choose its methods and procedures for law enforcement. "But these procedures cannot include methods that may fairly be deemed to be in conflict with deeply rooted feelings of the community." [151] He based his opinion on the ground that the determination of whether the confession of the boy was actually voluntary and so admissible in evidence against him or coerced, and thus a violation of due process involves a "psychological judgment that reflects deep, even if inarticulate, feelings of our society." [152] Whether the precise facts of the case at bar fall in the latter category "depends on an evaluation of psychological factors, or more accurately stated, upon the persuasive feeling of society regarding such psychological factors." [153] This is a very vague and indefinite standard to apply, but it is the standard which Justice Frankfurter feels compelled by the Constitution to attempt to apply when the issue of due

---

[150] *Ibid.*, p. 599. (Italics added.) Cf. Malinski *v.* New York, 324 U.S. 401, 404 (1945), cited in n. 134, *supra*.   [151] 322 U.S. 596, 604 (1948).
[152] *Ibid.*, p. 603.   [153] *Ibid.*, p. 605.

process in a criminal trial is before the Court. He concluded that
a finding that the confession could not be used as evidence against
the accused youth "reflects these fundamental notions of fairness
and justice in the determination of guilt or innocence which lie
embedded in the feelings of the American people and enshrined
in the Due Process clause of the Fourteenth Amendment." [154]

Dissent was voiced by Justice Burton, joined by Chief Justice
Vinson, Justices Reed and Jackson. The dissenters declared that
it is the business of the trial judge and jury, "under the safeguards
of constitutional due process of criminal law," to determine the
facts, one of which is the voluntary character of a confession.
In determining the due process of a criminal trial the Court must
"first make sure of its facts. Until a better way is found for testing
credibility than by the examination of witnesses in open court,
we must give the trial courts and juries that wide discretion in this
field to which a living record, as distinguished from a printed
record, logically entitles them. In this living record there are many
guideposts to the truth which are not in the printed record. Without seeing them ourselves, we will do well to give heed to those
who have seen them." [155]

Three recent confession cases show a sharp division of opinion
among the justices concerning the admissibility of confessions in
state criminal trials. In Watts v. Indiana,[156] Justice Frankfurter,
speaking for the Court, described ours as an "accusatorial" rather
than an "inquisitorial" system. This in his opinion entailed several
features having a direct bearing upon the use of evidence against
an accused. Under such a system, society carried the burden of
proving its charge against an alleged offender. It must establish
its case by evidence independently secured through skillful investigation, not through excessive interrogation of the accused,
even with judicial safeguards. The charges must be specifically
stated and proved beyond reasonable doubt. The accused must be
protected against extorted confessions, for they are not reliable
bases upon which to fix guilt. The accused must be given a prompt

---

[154] *Ibid.*, p. 607.   [155] *Ibid.*, pp. 624–25.
[156] 338 U.S. 49 (1949). Justice Frankfurter wrote the Court's opinion, in which
Justices Murphy and Rutledge joined. Justice Jackson concurred; Justice Douglas
concurred with a different rationale. The Chief Justice and Justices Reed and
Burton dissented.

hearing on the charges, with the assistance of an attorney when necessary. But Watts was held as a suspect in a criminal-assault case and later as a suspect of murder in connection with the assault. He was taken into custody on Wednesday afternoon and was not arraigned until the following Tuesday. Meanwhile he was illegally held without time or place for rest and was subjected to intermittent questioning for several hours each evening. During the day he was driven about town in an attempt to have him reconstruct the crime. At no time did he have legal advice or any protection against police grilling. After a week the accused confessed, led the officers to the scene of the crime, and described what happened, and took them across Indianapolis to the place where he had hidden the gun with which he had committed the murder.

The Court ruled that a confession, to be admissible in evidence, must be the expression of a free choice. It is not necessarily volunteered, but it must not result from sustained pressure on the part of police officers. Justice Frankfurter believed that the uncontroverted facts of the case would indicate that the confession was not the product of a free choice and therefore could not be made the basis of conviction without violating due process of law. Justice Frankfurter does not point out any one particular feature of the pretrial conduct of the investigation which tainted the confession and made it unreliable in the search for truth. It was the whole atmosphere of the proceedings which led him to classify the information obtained as "extorted" and inadmissible.

Again, in Harris v. South Carolina,[157] Justice Frankfurter spoke for the Court in reversing the conviction of a Negro whose guilt had been proved solely by the confession obtained after hours of incessant questioning by the police. No fingerprints had been available and the Federal Bureau of Investigation had not made a report on the question of whether the bullet which caused death had been fired from Harris' gun.[158] Said Justice Frankfurter, for

[157] 338 U.S. 68 (1949). Justice Frankfurter spoke for the Court in an opinion in which Justices Murphy and Rutledge joined. Justice Black concurred on the basis of Chambers v. Florida, 309 U.S. 227 (1940). Justice Douglas concurred. The Chief Justice and Justices Reed and Burton dissented. Justice Jackson wrote a dissenting opinion.

[158] People v. Harris, 46 S.E. (2d) 682, 691 (1948).

Justices Murphy, Rutledge, and himself: "The systematic persistence of interrogation, the length of periods of questioning, the failure to advise petitioner of his rights, the absence of friends or disinterested persons, and the character of the defendant constitute a complex of circumstances which invokes the same considerations which controlled our decision in Watts v. Indiana." [159] And on the same day, he spoke for the Court, remanding the case of Turner v. Pennsylvania; [160] for the facts alleged, if true, would vitiate the conviction. Here, too, the procedure complained of was the four to six hours of daily questioning over a period of days. Here again there was very little evidence to support the contention that the statements made in the confession were untrue. Turner corroborated the facts given by two companions. He described in detail the manner of the killing.

In each of these cases, Justice Douglas concurred with the majority decision but with the additional qualification that any confession obtained during an illegal detention should be outlawed.

Justice Jackson dissented in the Harris and Turner cases, apparently on the ground that in each instance the information so obtained could be verified and that therefore the argument that such a confession is unreliable breaks down. One might keep in mind that the state courts found no other evidence against Harris. Justice Jackson was willing to admit that the unhampered arrest on suspicion and interrogation without the assistance of counsel largely negates the benefits of the constitutional guarantee of counsel. On the other hand, the enforcement of that guarantee at this stage of the proceedings or the requirement that the suspect be taken immediately into the custody of the court for arraignment makes conviction impossible in many instances. He does not think that constitutional protection should be afforded in such a manner as to preclude the conviction of the guilty.

Here, as in almost every case where the due process issue is called to bear upon the procedure followed by a state in the administration of its criminal law, is the conflict of interests. On the one hand, sponsored by Justice Frankfurter for the majority, is the impelling desire to protect the innocent who may be trapped

[159] 338 U.S. 68, 71 (1949).
[160] 338 U.S. 62 (1949). See Commonwealth v. Turner, 58 A. (2d) 61, 63 (1948).

by such police methods as those apparent here. On the other hand, there is the state's interest in protecting society from criminals. It would seem from the opinions written in these cases, that the justices go on the assumption that the two are mutually exclusive. There is no reason to doubt that the dissenters here are persuaded that the law should shed its protection about the innocent. The assumption is that the innocent must at times be subjected to an all-too-rigorous investigation lest the guilty go free. This is the logical conclusion which follows from the premise that the only reason for not admitting a coerced confession is its unreliability. If, then, its truth is established at a later date, the unreliability argument must give way. But if the constitutional guarantee of protection against self-incrimination means less than the exclusion of any confession forced from a suspect by use of mental or physical torture or exacted by the police at a time when the victim was not even legally within their custody, it actually affords no protection of value to the accused. Surely we are not ready to admit that fascistic methods are essential to the enforcement of criminal law in our states. But the ultimate determination of whether or not such tactics will be countenanced lies with the justices on the Court. The application of the due process clause is their chief weapon in support of whatever system they choose.

Comment upon Failure to Testify. Only on rare occasions has the internal conflict among members of the Court concerning the scope of the due process clause of the Fourteenth Amendment been penned with such deliberate precision as in the case of Adamson *v.* California in 1947.[161] The specific issue before the Court was that of constitutional protection against self-incrimination in a state court. Justice Reed delivered the opinion of the Court, with Justice Frankfurter writing a concurring opinion, Justice Murphy, joined by Justice Rutledge, dissenting, and Justice Black, joined by Justice Douglas, offering a separate dissenting opinion which is a masterly defense of a return to what he is convinced was the original meaning and purpose of the due process

[161] 332 U.S. 46 (1947). See F. R. Coudert, "The Bill of Rights: The Decision in Adamson v. California," *American Bar Association Journal*, XXXIV (1948), 19–22.

of law clause of the Fourteenth Amendment. Under the California law the court or counsel may comment upon the failure of a defendant to explain or deny evidence offered against him by the prosecution. Petitioner had been arrested on suspicion of murder. The guilty person was not seen at the time and place of the crime, but there was evidence that entrance to the scene of the murder might have been obtained through a small door which was freshly broken. On the door were six fingerprints found to be those of the accused. It was known that several diamond rings were missing from possession of the deceased. There was also evidence that a few days after the crime petitioner had asked an unidentified person if he would be interested in purchasing some diamond rings. Petitioner refused to take the stand to refute this evidence when it was presented to the jury, on the ground that if he should, he would be cross-examined concerning former crimes he had admitted. In that case the truth of his testimony would be impeached and conviction would follow. The issue here is almost exactly the same as that decided in the Twining case forty years before. The question there was whether the privileges and immunities clause of the Fourteenth Amendment was violated by instructions to the jury permitting them to draw unfavorable inferences from Twining's refusal to testify in denial of evidence before the court. In that instance it was ruled that the clause did not protect an accused against self-incrimination. The action of the court did, however, impose self-incrimination upon the accused.

In considering the due process issue Justice Reed "assumed" but did not decide that "permission by law to the court, counsel, and jury to comment upon and consider the failure of defendant 'to explain or to deny by his testimony any evidence or facts in the case against him' would infringe defendant's privilege against self-incrimination under the Fifth Amendment if this were a trial in a Court of the United States under a similar law." [162] But the Fourteenth Amendment guarantees only a "fair trial." [163] "Specifically," it does not by its mere existence protect an accused from

[162] 332 U.S. 46, 50 (1947). See Boyd v. United States, 116 U.S. 616, 631 (1886); Wilson v. United States, 149 U.S. 60, 66 (1893); and Johnson v. United States, 318 U.S. 189, 199 (1943).
[163] 332 U.S. 46, 53 (1947).

giving testimony by compulsion in a state court.[164] "The due process clause forbids compulsion to testify by fear of hurt, torture, or exhaustion.[165] It forbids any other type of coercion that falls within the scope of due process." [166] In other words "due process" is anything which is not in violation of "due process." But such double talk is not conducive to much progress in formulating a concept of the term which can be used as a yardstick to measure the adequacy of the trial afforded by a state court in a specific case. Said Justice Reed, "It seems quite natural that when a defendant has an opportunity to deny or explain facts and determines not to do so, the prosecution should bring out the strength of the evidence by commenting upon defendant's failure to explain or deny it." [167] In making such a statement Justice Reed is only facing the situation realistically. Even if the judge or counsel does not comment upon the failure of the defendant to refute or explain, surely a reasonably intelligent jury will assume that the evidence could not be truthfully denied or explained. He implied, however, that had the instructions or comments imputed guilt to the accused because of his silence, the decision might have been different. In this respect the case is distinguishable from the Twining case. However, his opinion is far from a satisfactory statement of the concept of due process of law as a guarantee of protection.

Justice Frankfurter, concurring, was willing to assume that similar action in a federal court would violate the protection of the Bill of Rights against self-incrimination. He would not read the Fourteenth Amendment, however, as comprehending the specific provisions of the Bill of Rights or as being confined to those provisions. Due process has an "independent potency," and

[164] See Brown v. Mississippi, 297 U.S. 278, 285–86 (1936).

[165] 332 U.S. 46, 54 (1947), citing the cases involving coerced confessions.

[166] Ibid. This statement is supported by citing Malinski v. New York, 324 U.S. 401, 414, 428 (1945); Buchalter v. New York, 319 U.S. 427 (1943); and Palko v. Connecticut, 302 U.S. 319 (1937). It will be noted that due process in each of these cases was defined in very general terms as "fundamental principles of justice," "civilized standards of law," "rights the denial of which would be repugnant to the conscience of a free people," and "those canons of decency and fairness which express the notions of justice of English-speaking people even toward those charged with the most heinous offenses."

[167] 336 U.S. 46, 56, 59 (1947).

the phrase as used in the Fifth and Fourteenth amendments has an identical meaning. "To consider due process of law as a merely shorthand statement of other specific clauses in the same amendment is to attribute to the authors and proponents of this amendment ignorance of, or indifference to, a historic conception which was one of the great instruments in the arsenal of constitutional freedom which the Bill of Rights was to protect and strengthen." [168] But to attempt to find in the Fourteenth Amendment "due process" a guarantee against self-incrimination "in its protection of ultimate decency in a civilized society" would be to suggest that the due process clause "fastened fetters of unreason" upon the states.[169] "If," said Justice Frankfurter, "the basis of selection [from among the first eight amendments] is merely that those provisions of the first eight amendments are incorporated which commend themselves to individual justices as indispensable to the dignity and happiness of a free man, we are thrown back to a merely subjective test." [170] But with due respect for the opinion of Justice Frankfurter, a layman is certainly justified in asking what, if not this very subjective test, is being applied by the present majority on the Court, and inevitably so as long as its members attempt to apply a vague kind of natural-law justice in the selecting process. But Justice Frankfurter finds the "relevant" question to be whether the specific proceedings here challenged deprived the accused of the "due process of law to which the United States Constitution entitles him." One seeks in vain for anything definite by which to determine what the Constitution secures for him in the way of due process of law. The Court, says Justice Frankfurter, must exercise a judgment to ascertain whether the conduct of the trial offended "those canons of de-

[168] *Ibid.*, p. 66. See a somewhat similar statement in Malinski *v.* New York, 324 U.S. 401, 414–15 (1945).

[169] 322 U.S. 46, 61 (1947). He would affirm the conviction on the authority of Twining *v.* New Jersey, 211 U.S. 78 (1908), for that decision "shows the judicial process at its best."

[170] 322 U.S. 46, 65 (1947). Justice Frankfurter comments: "Between the incorporation of the Fourteenth Amendment into the Constitution and the beginning of the present membership of the Court . . . the scope of that Amendment was passed upon by 43 judges. Of all of these judges, only one, who may respectfully be called an eccentric exception, ever indicated the belief that the Fourteenth Amendment was a shorthand summary of the first eight amendments." *Ibid.*, p. 62.

cency and fairness which express the notions of justice of English-speaking peoples even toward those charged with the most heinous offenses." [171] But the determination of this question must not be based on "the idiosyncracies of merely personal judgment." To safeguard against such individual estimates the Court should show an "alert deference to the judgment of the state court under review." Here again, as in numerous instances in recent years, may be seen the tendency toward accepting to a greater and greater degree the judgment of the lower court concerning the regularity of the procedure. The trend toward Hurtado v. California is becoming more pronounced.[172]

Two dissenting opinions were written in Adamson v. California. Justice Murphy, joined by Justice Rutledge, affirmed his previous opinion that the due process clause of the Fourteenth Amendment incorporated all of the rights guaranteed by the Bill of Rights but was not limited to those rights. To them protection against compelled testimony is a constituent part of the Fourteenth Amendment. This protection was infringed by the application of the California law, for defendant's silence was used as a basis for drawing unfavorable inferences against him. "Thus he is compelled, through his silence, to testify against himself." If he chooses to take the stand "his testimony on cross-examination is the result of the coercive pressure of the provision rather than his own volition." Accordingly, Justices Murphy and Rutledge would reverse the judgment against the accused. Justice Black's dissent was based primarily upon a disagreement with the method or approach of the Court in reaching its decision. He is of the opinion that the natural-law theory of the Constitution which is relied upon by the majority "degrades" the constitutional safeguards and is of itself a violation of the Constitution.[173] Said Justice Black:

> I fear to see the consequences of the Court's practice of substituting its concept of decency and fundamental justice for the language of the Bill of Rights as its point of departure in interpreting and enforcing that Bill of Rights. If the

[171] Ibid., pp. 67–68.
[172] See Malinski v. New York, 324 U.S. 401, 414, 415 (1945), Justice Frankfurter speaking.
[173] 322 U.S. 46, 71–72, 75 (1947).

choice must be between the selective process of the *Palko* decision applying some of the Bill of Rights to the States, or the *Twining* rule applying none, I would choose the *Palko* selective process. But rather than accept either of these choices, I would follow what I believe was the original purpose of the Fourteenth Amendment—to extend to all people of the nation the complete protection of the Bill of Rights. To hold that this Court can determine what, if any, provisions of the Bill of Rights will be enforced, and if so, to what degree, is to frustrate the great design of a written constitution.[174]

He is persuaded that "one of the chief objects that the provisions of the Amendment's first section . . . were intended to accomplish was to make the Bill of Rights applicable to the states." [175] The framers of the amendment, he finds, purposed to overturn the effects of the Court's decision in Barron *v.* Baltimore. But the Court in the case at bar did not give due consideration to the purposes for which the amendment was passed. Said the dissenters, "The Court . . . again today declines to appraise the relevant historical evidence of the intended scope of the first section of the Amendment. Instead it relied upon previous cases, none of which had analyzed the evidence showing that one purpose of those who framed, advocated, and adopted the Amendment had been to make the Bill of Rights applicable to the states." In keeping with these views, Justice Black suggests that the natural-law formula which subtly conveyed to the courts "at the expense of the legislatures, ultimate power of public policies in fields where no specific provision of the Constitution limits legislative power" be abandoned as a violation of the Constitution.

In this instance the Court found itself in a dilemma which could have been resolved more readily had there been any precisely formulated notions of the meaning of self-incrimination in its historical setting and development. Surely the action of the trial court in this instance did not deprive the accused of a fair hearing. But just as surely the Court's explanation of that fact added nothing to the clarification of "due process of law" in such cases. Here there was presented to the Court an occasion for delineating

[174] *Ibid.,* p. 89.   [175] *Ibid.,* p. 71.

the scope of "self-incrimination." If the dissenters mean by their statements that the due process clause should prohibit the psychological effect of having an openly accused person refuse to answer "yes" or "no" to the charge or to decline any attempt to refute very pointed evidence, it would seem that they have extended the protection far beyond the possible. Surely it is enough to extend the guaranty to legal presumptions of guilt based upon that self-imposed silence.

THE RIGHT TO BE PRESENT AT A JURY VIEW

Does the due process clause of the Fourteenth Amendment guarantee an accused the right to be present while the jury views the site of the crime with which he has been charged? This question was before the Court in Snyder v. Massachusetts.[176] Justice Cardozo, speaking for the Court, reaffirmed the rule that the state "is free to regulate the procedure of its courts in accordance with its own conception of policy and fairness unless in so doing it offends some principle of justice so rooted in the tradition and conscience of our people as to be ranked as fundamental." [177] He assumed that the Fourteenth Amendment reinforced, in the state courts, the privilege of confronting one's accusers and the right to cross-examine those accusers face to face, "though this [had] never been specifically held by the Court." But Justice Cardozo also found that the Fourteenth Amendment did not say "in so many words" that an accused must be present at all times during the trial. "If words so flexible are to be taken as implied, it is because they are put there by a court, and not because they are there already, in advance of the decision. Due process requires that the proceedings be fair, but fairness is a relative, not an absolute, concept." [178]

Here it was decided that the accused could not have gained anything by being present at the view. Since this was true, he could not have been denied a fair hearing by the trial court's refusal to permit him to accompany the jury. "Justice," said Justice Cardozo, "though due to the accused, is due to the accuser also.

[176] 291 U.S. 97 (1934).   [177] Ibid., p. 105.
[178] Ibid., p. 116.

The concept of fairness must not be strained till it is narrowed to a filament. We must keep the balance true." [179]

The reasoning of the Court in this case represents a second step in the early thirties toward bringing state criminal proceedings under a closer federal supervision through the application of the due process clause. The implication is that the Court must decide in each instance whether presence at the jury would have been of benefit to the accused in making an adequate defense. Justice Cardozo would not commit the Court to any definite criteria for the application of the fair-hearing rule in this connection. That application must be made in the light of the circumstances of each individual case.

THE USE OF PERJURED TESTIMONY

In the case of Mooney v. Holohan [180] the Court held that the use of evidence known to the state to be perjured violated the due process clause of the Fourteenth Amendment in that it deprived the accused of a fair hearing to which he was constitutionally entitled. In a *per curiam* opinion it was said that due process "is a requirement that cannot be deemed to have been satisfied by mere notice and hearing if the state has contrived a conviction through the pretense of a trial which in truth is but a means of depriving a defendant of liberty through a deliberate deception of court and jury by the presentation of testimony known to be perjured." [181]

Thus the concept of due process was extended to protect an accused against false or perjured evidence, for the introduction of such evidence was said to violate the due process requirement of an "orderly procedure." A hearing within the meaning of the due process of law concept includes the opportunity for one charged with crime to make his defense. For a court to allow a conviction on the basis of false testimony is as much an infringement of that opportunity as to allow a conviction which has no pretense of a

---

[179] *Ibid.*, p. 122. Justices Roberts, Sutherland, Butler, and Brandeis dissented on the ground that the "view" was a "taking of evidence" and, as such, a part of the trial, and that the accused had a constitutional right under the due process clause to be present at all stages of the trial.

[180] 294 U.S. 103 (1935).   [181] *Ibid.*, p. 112.

basis. In either instance the accused is condemned without a hearing. In the present case, however, Mooney did not get the relief he sought, for the Court held that he had not exhausted the remedies afforded by the state.[182]

Again, in Hysler v. Florida,[183] the Court affirmed its rule that a conviction based on perjured evidence deprived an accused of a fair hearing. Justice Frankfurter, speaking for the Court, declared that if a state "whether by active conduct or the connivance of the prosecution" convicts an accused through the use of false or perjured testimony, "it violates civilized standards for the trial of guilt or innocence and thereby deprives an accused of liberty without due process of law." [184] The petitioner had been convicted on a murder charge. His conviction was based principally upon the testimony of two men who claimed to have been hired by him to commit the crime. After Hysler had been tried and sentenced, the two were convicted of murder and sentenced to death. Hysler claimed that evidence brought out in the trial of these two witnesses contradicted their stories as presented in his trial, and further that prior to their conviction they had rescinded their testimony as to Hysler's part in the crime and had indicated

---

[182] *Ibid.*, p. 113. So far as the state was concerned, Mooney had exhausted his legal remedies. The State Supreme Court had held that it was a settled law in the state that a judgment could not be set aside merely because it was based on perjured testimony. The majority opinion had stated that "If perjured testimony be produced or material evidence suppressed [by the District Attorney] insofar as the judgment is concerned, the injured party is without relief." 178 Cal. 525, 174 Pac. 325 (1935).

Mooney's case was remanded, without prejudice, to the state court. When it was again before the State Supreme Court, that court appointed a referee to make an investigation of the case. The referee decided against Mooney, and its decision was accepted by the state. 10 Cal. (2d) 1 (1937). The United States Supreme Court refused to grant certiorari to review the action of the state. Cf. Holiday v. Johnston, 313 U.S. 342, 351 (1941), in which the Court held that under the law of California prescribing habeas corpus procedures, petitioner should have been given a hearing before a judge. As a commissioner was held not comparable to a judge within the meaning of the law, the proceedings were held void. "One of the essential elements in the determination of the crucial facts is the weighing and appraising of the testimony. Plainly it was intended that the prisoner might invoke the exercise of this appraisal by the judge himself. We cannot say that an appraisal of the truth of the prisoner's oral testimony by a master or commissioner is, in the light of the purpose and object of the proceeding, the equivalent of the judge's own exercise of the function of the trier of the facts."

[183] 315 U.S. 411 (1942).   [184] *Ibid.*, p. 413.

that their testimony had resulted in part from the hope that by implicating him they would receive lighter sentences and in part
from coercion applied by state officers.

Justice Frankfurter asserted that "if Florida through her responsible officials knowingly used false testimony which was extorted from a witness by violence and torture, one convicted may
claim the protection of the Due Process clause against a conviction based on such testimony." [185] But Florida affords a remedy
for such an accused: He may make a substantial showing before
the supreme court of the state setting forth the bases for his claim
that his incarceration resulted from the lack of a fair trial and request a writ of *coram nobis* to have his petition passed upon by a
jury of the first instance. Justice Frankfurter found that this
remedy fulfilled the due process requirements of a corrective
process for one alleging a lack of fairness in his trial. The issue
before the Court, therefore, was whether the Supreme Court of
Florida, in denying a proper appeal to its corrective remedy, deprived the petitioner of his liberty without due process of law.[186]

Upon an independent consideration of the records of the case,
Justice Frankfurter concluded that if the records did not support
the state court's finding of a lack of substantial basis for the allegation, "It certainly precludes a holding that such a finding was not
justified." [187] The record, he said, did not permit the Court to
find that the petitioner had been denied due process.[188] In this case
the Court did not go behind the records of the case as presented to
the state supreme court by the trial court. Only an investigation
of the proceedings in the trial court itself could have produced
the evidence needed to support Hysler's contention that the testimony was known to be false at the time it was entered in evidence against him. The full burden of proof was shifted to the
convicted man, who ordinarily would have no opportunity to
obtain the evidence necessary to impeach the proceedings of
which he complained.

Almost the same set of facts was presented to the Court in Pyle

[185] *Ibid.*   [186] See Young *v.* Ragen, 337 U.S. 235 (1949).
[187] 315 U.S. 411, 422 (1942).
[188] *Ibid.* See Nutting, "The Supreme Court, The Fourteenth Amendment and
State Criminal Trials," *loc. cit.*, p. 256, for a discussion of the implications of the
Court's acceptance of the findings of the state courts.

v. Kansas.[189] Justice Murphy, applying the rule of the Mooney and Hysler cases, held that "The record of petitioner's conviction, while regular on its face, manifestly does not controvert the charge that perjured evidence was used, and that favorable evidence was suppressed with the knowledge of the Kansas authorities." [190] This record differed from that of the Hysler case in that there had not been a determination by the state as to the verity of these allegations. According to Kansas law, which allowed one imprisoned in violation of his constitutional rights to be heard through a writ of habeas corpus, the petitioner should have been granted the writ. Refusal on the part of the state to issue it was said to be a violation of due process.[191]

These cases serve to indicate the very great difficulty which an accused almost necessarily has in obtaining relief from a conviction based on false or perjured testimony. In the Mooney case petitioner's opportunity to present his claim to the Supreme Court was granted nearly twenty years after his conviction in the trial court.[192] By that time much of the evidence which might have served to exonerate him was unavailable. The Court would have had difficulty in doing more than considering the records of the state appellate court. But such an examination would not sustain the truth of his allegations. This difficulty may account, in part, for the disposition of this case, in spite of the fact that Mooney had been told by the state supreme court that his only remedy lay in executive clemency.[193] In the Hysler case the fact that the burden of proof was shifted, by state law, to the one who challenged the legality of the conviction made it impossible for the convicted man to present his case in such a way as to procure the relief sought even if it had been due him. The fact that the Kansas court had not made a determination as to the truth or falsity of the petitioner's allega-

---

[189] 317 U.S. 213 (1942).　　　　[190] *Ibid.*, p. 216.

[191] The case was remanded. Petitioner's amended petition was dismissed on the ground that it did not comply with the Kansas Supreme Court's order. 159 Kan. 458, 156 P. (2d) 509 (1945). The United States Supreme Court denied certiorari for the review of this action on the part of the state. Pyle *v.* Amrine, 326 U.S. 809 (1945).

[192] Mooney was denied certiorari by the Supreme Court in 1918 because the Court found, at that time, that no federal question was involved. 248 U.S. 579 (1918).　　　　[193] See n. 175, *supra.*

tions in the Pyle case was made the basis on which the Court remanded the case. What the outcome would have been had there been such a determination by the state is not indicated in the Court's opinion. Until the Court assumes an obligation to make an independent finding in cases of this type as it has in other criminal cases, the due process guarantee against conviction based on perjured testimony will not afford a very effective protection.

THE RIGHT NOT TO BE LYNCHED

Certainly the recent activities of lynch mobs have emphasized the need for federal action to protect individuals against lynching and mob violence as a part of the right to a judicial hearing guaranteed by the due process of law clause of the Fourteenth Amendment.[194] Only once has the Supreme Court rendered a decision in a lynch case, Screws v. United States, 1945.[195] In this case, Robert Hall, a Negro of Baker County, Georgia, complained to the grand jury that Screws, Sheriff of Baker County, had unlawfully taken and kept his revolver. Within twelve hours after this complaint was made, the sheriff arrested Hall on a warrant charging him with the theft of a tire. Hall was handcuffed and taken by the sheriff and two police officers to the courthouse yard and there beaten to death. When it became evident that the state authorities did not intend to take action against the law-enforcement officers, the Attorney General of the United States, with the aid of the Civil Rights Section of the Department of Justice, instituted proceedings against the three men in a federal district court.[196] Screws and his two confederates were indicted and convicted for having violated Section 20 of the United States Criminal Code, which provides: "Whoever, under color of any law, statute, ordinance,

---

[194] For a discussion of the background of this section, see Francis Biddle, "Civil Rights and Federal Law," in Biddle and others, *Safeguarding Our Civil Liberties Today*, pp. 109–44; Victor Rotnem, "Civil Rights During War: The Role of the Federal Government," *Iowa Law Review*, XXIX (1944), 409–14; Frank Coleman, "Freedom from Fear on the Homefront," *ibid.*, pp. 415–29; and Robert Carr, *Federal Protection of Civil Liberties* (New York, 1947).

[195] 325 U.S. 91 (1945).

[196] *Ibid.*, p. 114. (Justice Rutledge's opinion.)

regulation, or custom, willfully subjects, or causes to be subjected, an inhabitant of any State, territory, or District, to the
deprivation of any rights, privileges, or immunities secured or
protected by the Constitution, and laws of the United States,
or to different punishments, pains or penalties, on account of
such inhabitant's being an alien, or by reason of his color or
race, than are prescribed for citizens, shall be fined not more
than $1000, or imprisoned more than one year, or both." [197]
The Attorney General based the jurisdiction of the federal
courts on the principle that Screws and his two accomplices,
"acting under color of the law of Georgia, deprived Hall of his
right not to be deprived of life without due process of law; the
right to be tried on the charge on which he was arrested, by
due process of law, and if found guilty, to be punished in accordance with the laws of Georgia." [198]

Appeal from the conviction in the federal district court was
taken to the Supreme Court where four separate opinions were
filed and five justices agreed that Screws was entitled to a new
trial. Justice Douglas wrote the leading opinion, in which he
said that "it is plain that basic to the concept of due process of
law in a criminal case is a trial—a trial in a court of law—not
a trial by ordeal. It could hardly be doubted that they who,
under color of law, act with that motive violate Section 20.
Those who decide to take the law into their own hands and
act as prosecutor, jury, judge, and executioner, plainly act to
deprive a prisoner of the trial which due process of law guarantees him." [199] In spite of this and of the fact that there could be

[197] During the period 1932–45 there were 10 white and 108 Negro victims of
lynchings in the United States. (Figures are taken from the files of the Department of Records and Research, Tuskegee Institute, Tuskegee, Alabama.)
    Section 20 (section 52 of Title 18), United States Criminal Code, is one of the
few remaining fragments of the Enforcement Act, 1870, passed to make effective
the guarantees of the Thirteenth, Fourteenth, and Fifteenth amendments.
[198] Robert E. Cushman, "Constitutional Law, 1944–1945," *American Political
Science Review*, XL (1946), 241, 242. See Robert Carr, "Screws v. United States:
The Georgia Police Brutality Case," *Cornell Law Review*, XXXI (1945), 48,
49–50.
[199] 325 U.S. 91, 106 (1945). See James Barnett, "What Is State Action under the
Fourteenth, Fifteenth, and Nineteenth Amendments?" *Oregon Law Review*,
XXIV (1945), 227–43; Julius Cohen, "The Screws Case: Federal Protection of
Negro Rights," *Columbia Law Review*, XLVI (1946), 94–106; and Victor
Rotnem, "The Federal Right Not to be Lynched," *Washington University Law
Quarterly Review*, XXVIII (1943), 57–73.

little, if any, doubt of the willfulness of the act committed by
Screws and the other officers, Justice Douglas concluded that
there must be a retrial because the jury should have been told,
and was not, that "willful intent" to deprive Hall of his rights
was necessary to conviction.[200]

Justice Rutledge concurred with Justice Douglas because his
vote was necessary for the Court to dispose of the case.[201] He
was of the opinion that Section 20 was intended to aid in the
enforcement of the rights guaranteed by the Fourteenth Amendment. Justice Rutledge was convinced that Congress, in enacting Section 20, understood that there was danger of the
deprivation of rights by other persons than members of the
legislative and judicial branches of the government. Certainly
Congress intended to cover by this statute "abuse by whatever
agency the State might invest with its power capable of inflicting the deprivation." [202] To Justice Rutledge the due process
guaranteed by the Fourteenth Amendment included the right
not to be deprived arbitrarily of life itself, and by the lynching the accused had been deprived of that right. He concluded
that the right not to be lynched was as fully protected as any
of the other rights guaranteed by the phrase "due process of
law." As a matter of principle, Justice Rutledge said, he would
vote for the affirmation of the conviction; as a practical matter,
he voted for retrial.

Justice Murphy dissented, stating his views briefly thus:

> Robert Hall, a Negro citizen, has been deprived not only
> of the right to be tried by a court rather than by ordeal. He
> has been deprived of the right to life itself. That right be-
> longed to him, not because he was a Negro or a member
> of any particular race or creed. That right was his because
> he was an American citizen, because he was a human being.
> As such he was entitled to all the respect and fair treatment
> that befits the dignity of man, a dignity which is recognized
> and respected by the Constitution nor is foreign to the
> knowledge of the local police officers so as to cast any doubt
> on the convictions under Section 20 of the Criminal Code

[200] Retrial occurred and the defendants were acquitted. Cushman, "Constitutional Law, 1944–1945," *loc. cit.*, p. 242.
[201] 325 U.S. 91, 115 (1945).　　　　[202] *Ibid.*, p. 116.

of the perpetrators of this shocking and revolting episode in law enforcement.[203]

Justice Murphy voted for the affirmation of the conviction of the three officers.

A separate dissenting opinion was filed to state the position of Justices Roberts, Frankfurter, and Jackson. These three held that Section 20 did not apply in this case and that the convictions should be set aside.

The decision in this case has been described as "fully as significant as any single civil liberties case disposed of by the Court in the past fifteen years." [204] However, most lawyers and laymen alike would probably agree with Professor Cushman's characterization of it as a "masterpiece of confusion." [205] All nine justices considered the case and took part in the disposition of it. Five of the nine voted for retrial on the ground that the judge had failed to charge the jury properly rather than because of any doubt that the Supreme Court took jurisdiction rightly under Section 20 of the Criminal Code. But one of the five concurred, against his better judgment, only in order to permit the Court to dispose of the case. Actually, he agreed that Section 20 applied and that the conviction should not have been impeached because of such a minor technicality which, in his mind, was unimportant insofar as the trial court's decision was concerned. Three judges dissented as to the application of Section 20, holding that this provision was so indefinite and vague when made applicable to the rights protected by due process of law that it was unconstitutional. These justices said that if the statute were constitutional, it would not have been effective in this instance, for the police officers had acted beyond any authority granted them by state law. But, they said, if the first two barriers could be overcome, there was still another. The statute unconstitutionally interfered with the state's administration of its own criminal law. If Screws and his companions were guilty, they were punishable only by the state

---

[203] *Ibid.*, p. 134.

[204] Carr, "Screws *v.* United States: The Georgia Police Brutality Case," *loc. cit.*, p. 48. See Coleman, "Freedom from Fear on the Homefront," *loc. cit.*, pp. 415–29.

[205] Cushman, "Constitutional Law, 1944–1945," *loc. cit.*, p. 242.

in accordance with the law of the state. In their opinions the convictions were void. One member of the Court thought that Section 20 was applicable and that the convictions should stand.

In spite of the lack of agreement among the justices as to the proper disposition of the case it is significant that six of the nine agreed on one point, namely, that the right not to be deprived of life by the abuse of state power is within the protection of the due process of law guaranteed by the Fourteenth Amendment and is enforcible in the federal courts under Section 20 of the Criminal Code. What the effect of the decision will be must remain a matter of conjecture for the time. Certainly, little has been done with it in the five years since it was rendered. But even with its defects of uncertainty and confusion, the potentialities of federal protection will be strengthened by it. However, no rule guaranteeing one against deprivation of life by the abuse of "state power" is enough to lend protection in cases of this kind.

DOUBLE JEOPARDY

The question of the extent to which the due process clause of the Fourteenth Amendment protects an accused against double jeopardy in state criminal proceedings has not been settled by the Court.[206] Palko v. Connecticut [207] involved the validity of a Connecticut statute under which the state may appeal from a judgment in a criminal case if the court of errors finds that there was an error in the trial-court proceedings. Palko had been indicted for first-degree murder, which in Connecticut carries a death sentence, and was found guilty of murder in the

[206] In Dreyer v. Illinois, 187 U.S. 71, 86 (1902), it was said that "if" the Fourteenth Amendment embraced protection against double jeopardy, retrial after a hung jury did not constitute double jeopardy. Justice Brewer, in Keerl v. Montana, 213 U.S. 135, 137 (1909), found it unnecessary to decide whether the Fourteenth Amendment protected against double jeopardy or whether the fact that the judge dismissed a jury and had a second one impaneled did actually put the accused in jeopardy of his life twice for the same offense.

[207] 302 U.S. 319 (1937). L. B. Orfield, "Appeal by the State in Criminal Cases," Oregon Law Review, XV (1936), 306, 317, says that Connecticut is the only state allowing for an appeal by the state from an acquittal. The author is of the opinion that such an appeal "is certainly the antithesis of the prevalent American interpretation of double jeopardy, namely, that a defendant has been put in jeopardy as soon as the jury has been empanelled and sworn."

second degree, entailing a sentence of life imprisonment. The court of errors found that there had been substantial errors in the proceedings to the detriment of the state and granted a re-trial. In the second trial Palko was found guilty of first-degree murder and was given a death sentence. He appealed on the ground that he had been put twice in jeopardy of his life for a single offense and had thus been deprived of liberty without due process of law.

Speaking for the Court, Justice Cardozo declared that there was no rule which would make every action of a state a viola-tion of the Fourteenth Amendment simply because the same action by the federal government would be contrary to a pro-vision of the Bill of Rights.[208] He explained that though a hasty cataloguing of cases on one side or the other would lead one to think that the line of division between what is protected and what is not is "wavering and broken," reflection and analysis would show that there "emerges the preception of a rationaliz-ing principle which gives to discrete instances a proper order and coherence." [209] Some modes of procedure such as trial by jury or indictment by a grand jury might be abolished and justice still be done. According to the Court in this case, these are not of "the essence of a scheme of ordered justice." Nor are they "so rooted in the traditions and conscience of our people as to be ranked as fundamental." [210] The exclusion of some of the privileges and immunities from the protection of due process was said to have been "dictated by a study and appreciation of the meaning and essential implications of liberty itself." [211] Impliedly, at least, Justice Cardozo held that the guarantee against double jeopardy did not fall in the category of a "funda-mental" right and thus within the "implications of liberty it-self." Since this was so, the right to be protected against double

[208] 302 U.S. 319, 323 (1937).   [209] *Ibid.*, p. 325.
[210] *Ibid.*, the author of the note "The Emergence of a Nationalized Bill of Rights: Due Process and a 'Higher Law' of Liberty," *loc. cit.*, pp. 490, 492, says that these appeals to a "higher law" are the "essential means whereby the Court, in passing from case to case, pretends to travel the traditional road of the syl-logism, pursuant to the theory of written constitutionalism." For a discussion of the implications of this appeal to a "higher law," consult Edward S. Corwin, "The Supreme Court and the Fourteenth Amendment," *Michigan Law Review,* VII (1909), 643.
[211] 302 U.S. 319, 325 (1937).

jeopardy was not included in the rights so far guaranteed by the due process clause of the Fourteenth Amendment.

Justice Cardozo did not determine whether the procedure complained of constituted double jeopardy. Assuming that there was double jeopardy "of a sort," it was said not to be the kind against which the due process clause of the Fourteenth Amendment protected one accused of crime in a state court. Just as there were found to be "degrees" of errors in state court proceedings, there were found to be "kinds" of double jeopardy, some of which are permissible. Justice Cardozo said that the question to be answered by the Court was whether the kind of double jeopardy to which the statute subjected the accused worked a hardship so acute and shocking "that our polity will not endure it." [212] It was reasoned that had the proceedings been tainted with error to the detriment of the accused, he would have been entitled to a new trial. The state only provided itself with a reciprocal privilege; it merely sought a trial free from "substantial" error. The Court found no occasion to determine whether retrial of an accused who had been given a trial free from error would deny him liberty without due process of law.[213] There is no indication that the Court made an independent determination that in the first trial there had been substantial error, which alone would justify the appeal by the state. Rather, in this case it accepted the state court's finding of "fact," upon which the validity of the application of the law depended.

Here to a greater degree than in most of the Court's opinions in matters of criminal procedures is illustrated the sheer verbalism by which it has justified many of its extensions of the Fourteenth Amendment or its refusal to extend the protection of that amendment. In the first eight amendments are said to be embodied two levels of rights—those which are fundamental and those which are not. The due process which is guaranteed by the Fourteenth Amendment comprises only those classed as fundamental. But it is the prerogative of the Court to classify

[212] *Ibid.*, p. 328.
[213] *Ibid.* Edward D. Ransom, "Appeal by the State in Criminal Cases," *Michigan Law Review*, XXXVII (1938), 103–13, says that this relaxation of the rigid rule of appeals by the state in criminal trials is an indication of an awakened administration of criminal law, which will give the people protection equal to that accorded the accused.

rights as falling within one or the other of these groups. There is no particular standard by which the status of a right may be determined. In fact, the Court has said that the right may be so fundamental in some situations as to be guaranteed by the due process clause; in other situations not to be so fundamental, hence not guaranteed against infringement. Protection against the "kind" of double jeopardy perpetrated by Connecticut in Palko's case did not fall in the "fundamental" class. This decision, however, cannot be taken to mean that any procedure allowing for the retrial of an accused would be permissible under the Fourteenth Amendment. The Court went no farther in this case than to hold that upon a consideration of the record here there was not double jeopardy "of so shocking a nature" as to come within the prohibitions now embodied in the due process of law clause. "The tyranny of labels," said Justice Cardozo, "must not lead us to leap to the conclusion that a word which in one set of facts may stand for oppression or enormity is of like effect in every other." [214]

The due process protection against double jeopardy at the hands of the state was again before the Court in Louisiana ex rel. Francis v. Resweber.[215] The circumstances of the case were a bit unusual. Willie Francis, a Negro youth, was convicted on a murder charge and was sentenced to be electrocuted. He was placed in the electric chair and the switch was pulled, but death did not result. He was thereupon removed from the chair and returned to prison. The governor of the state issued a second date for the execution. Meanwhile, petitioner appealed to the Supreme Court on the ground that the carrying out of the execution would involve cruel and unusual punishment contrary to the protection guaranteed by the Eight Amendment and double jeopardy in violation of the Fifth Amendment. He contended that both of these amendments were made applicable to the states by the due process clause of the Fourteenth Amendment. Justice Reed announced the judgment of the Court; Chief Justice Vinson and Justices Black and Jackson joined in his opinion. Justice Frankfurter wrote a concurring opinion, and Justices Burton, Douglas, Murphy, and Rutledge dissented.

[214] 302 U.S. 319, 323 (1937).   [215] 329 U.S. 459 (1947).

Justice Reed, speaking for himself and three other justices, indulged the assumption, without so deciding, that violation of the Fifth and Eight amendments as to double jeopardy and cruel and unusual punishments would violate the due process guaranteed by the Fourteenth Amendment.[216] In resolving the issue of double jeopardy, Justice Reed explained that in principle the case was not different from that of Palko *v.* Connecticut.[217] There a new trial for error of law resulted in the execution of the death penalty; here an execution followed failure of equipment. "When an accident, with no suggestion of malevolence, prevents the consummation of a sentence, the state's subsequent course in the administration of its criminal law is not affected on that account by any requirements of due process under the Fourteenth Amendment." [218]

As to the charge that the execution would involve cruel and unusual punishment in violation of the Eighth Amendment, applicable to the state under the due process clause, Justice Reed replied that "The cruelty against which the Constitution protects a convicted man is cruelty inherent in the method of punishment, not the necessary suffering involved in any method employed to extinguish life humanely." [219]

Because four of his colleagues were of the opinion that due process of law had been denied, Justice Frankfurter felt compelled to be "explicit regarding the criteria by which the State's duty of obedience to the Constitution is to be judged." [220] The Fourteenth Amendment, he believes, "placed no restraints upon the States in the formulation or the administration of their criminal law." [221] In his judgment "The Fourteenth Amendment did not mean to imprison the States into the limited experience of the Eighteenth Century. It did mean to withdraw from the states the right to act in ways that are offensive to a decent respect for the dignity of man, and heedless of his freedom." [222] Again the standard of due process, according to Justice Frankfurter, is "the consensus of society's opinion." [223] Since the action challenged is not "repugnant to the conscience of man-

---

[216] *Ibid.*, p. 462.
[218] 329 U.S. 459, 463 (1947).
[220] *Ibid.*, p. 466.
[222] *Ibid.*, p. 468.

[217] 302 U.S. 319 (1939).
[219] *Ibid.*, p. 464.
[221] *Ibid.*
[223] *Ibid.*, p. 471.

kind," it is not, in the estimation of Justice Frankfurter, forbidden by the due process clause of the Fourteenth Amendment.[224] It is regrettable that the majority did not expressly declare that violation of the guarantee against double jeopardy would violate the due process of the Fourteenth Amendment, even though they did not find a case of double jeopardy here.

Justices Burton, Douglas, Murphy, and Rutledge dissented on the ground that the due process clause of the Fourteenth Amendment does protect an accused against cruel and unusual punishment as well as against double jeopardy and that both of these guarantees were violated by the procedure followed in Louisiana.[225]

Here the majority of the Court affirmed the Palko rule to the effect that the due process clause of the Fourteenth Amendment does not draw unto itself all the guarantees of the Bill of Rights but only those which are "fundamental" to an orderly scheme of justice. Among these latter may not be found protection against double jeopardy nor against cruel and unusual punishments. Justice Frankfurter lends to the confusion and vagueness of the due process concept by making it synonymous with "society's opinion," or rather what he thinks that opinion is. Obviously some persons did not find such a proceeding undesirable or unwarranted. But to say that the opinion of these represents the bounds of due process of law or that the phrase means nothing more than society's opinion at a given time is to strip it of much of its significance as a constitutional concept. There is no apparent justification for the Court's failure to bring protection against double jeopardy within the scope of due process. And whether or not they would have found that the procedure followed by the Louisiana court involved the infliction of cruel and unusual punishments, their decision that protection against such punishment is not guaranteed by the national Constitution to one accused in a state court bodes no good for the protection of accused persons, who must depend upon the national government for whatever protection they may require against arbitrary action on the part of the states. Regardless of the justification or lack of it for the action taken by

[224] *Ibid.*, pp. 471–72.   [225] *Ibid.*, pp. 481–83.

Louisiana in this instance, any interpretation of due process of law which makes it merely the consensus of society's opinion is dangerous. One must bear in mind that fascist societies have their opinions concerning criminal procedures. In some instances these procedures have been "according to the law of the land" such as it was. But surely Justice Frankfurter would not grace most of these by classing them due process of law.

THE RIGHT TO A PUBLIC TRIAL

In the case of *In re* Oliver,[226] which involved the issue of constitutional protection of the right to a public trial, Justice Black declared: "It is the 'law of the land' that no man's life, liberty, or property be forfeited as a punishment until there has been a charge fairly made and fairly tried in a public tribunal." [227] Oliver had been called upon to give testimony before a Michigan circuit court. The judge who was conducting a "one-man grand jury investigation" of alleged gambling and official corruption refused to believe petitioner's testimony, partly because of conflicting statements and partly because of testimony given by other witnesses without petitioner's knowledge. Based on his belief that Oliver had given false testimony, the judge–grand jury convicted him of contempt of court and sentenced him to sixty days in jail. At this point the proceeding ceased to be a grand-jury investigation and became a criminal-contempt proceeding in which there was no opportunity to make a defense and at which there were no persons present other than the judge and the accused. Under the law of Michigan, justices of the peace, police judges, and judges of courts of record are vested with inquisitorial powers traditionally conferred on grand juries and coroners. If a witness fails to appear when summoned by this one-man grand jury, or if the judge–grand juror believes that his testimony is false, he may be found guilty of contempt. This offense entails a fine of not more than $100 or imprisonment in the county jail not more than 60 days or both at the discretion of the judge–grand jury.[228]

[226] 333 U.S. 257 (1948).   [227] *Ibid.*, p. 278.
[228] *Michigan Laws*, 1917, Act 196.

Justice Black, for the Court, held that due process of law guarantees an accused the right to be given public trial with an opportunity to make a defense against the charge made by the judge in his capacity of judge-jury. The guaranty of a public trial has but one exception, namely, "Charges of misconduct, in open court, in the presence of the judge, which disturbs the Court's business, where all the essential elements of the misconduct are under the eye of the court and where immediate punishment is essential to prevent 'demoralization' of the court's authority before the public." [229] But since petitioner's statements were made in secret, the action of the judge does not fall within the narrowly limited category of contempt cases where sentence may be imposed without the incidents of a trial.[230] Due process also protects the accused in his right to hear the testimony used against him and his opportunity to cross-examine the witnesses and refute, if he can, their testimony. It is significant that in this connection Justice Black weighed the evidence available to the trial judge and found that "Nothing in the petitioner's testimony as reported could have remotely justified the judge-jury" in drawing certain of his conclusions. Therefore, the conclusions must have been based upon testimony given by other witnesses in petitioner's absence. Such procedure was said to violate due process.

Justice Rutledge, joining in the Court's opinion, thought that more needed to be said with regard to such procedure in the courts of Michigan. In his judgment the aggregated authority vested in the judge "denies to the accused not only the right to a public trial, but also those other basic protections secured by the Sixth Amendment. . . ." [231] By leaving to the committing officer's discretion the scope of the record on appeal, this authority deprives the accused of security against double jeopardy and denies the equal protection of the laws.[232] But the case had other significance in the estimation of Justice Rutledge. In his words: "The case demonstrates how far this Court departed from our constitutional plan when after the Fourteenth Amendment's adoption, it permitted selective departure by the states from the

[229] 333 U.S. 257, 275 (1948).
[231] Ibid., p. 278.

[230] Ibid.
[232] Ibid., p. 279.

scheme of ordered personal liberty established by the Bill of Rights. In the guise of permitting the states to experiment with improving the administration of justice, the Court left them free to substitute 'in spite of the absolutism of continental governments,' their 'ideas and processes of civil justice' in place of the time-tried 'principles of the common law' perpetuated for us in the Bill of Rights." [233] It is only by an exercise of such freedom, he thinks, that the procedure here challenged could have been adopted and applied. The remedy lay in "the agreement of a majority of this Court that the experiment violates fundamental notions of justice in civilized society."

With regard to the rather prevalent attitude today that the Bill of Rights is out of date and is a hamper upon the power of the courts of the land to track down and convict criminals and that even if the procedures guaranteed are adequate for trials in the federal courts, they are too restrictive to be imposed upon the courts of the states, Justice Rutledge explained:

> I do not conceive that the Bill of Rights, apart from the due process clause of the Fifth Amendment, incorporated all such ideas. [Notions of justice in civilized society.] But so far as its provisions go, I know of no better substitutes. A few may be inconvenient. But restrictions upon authority for securing personal liberty, as well as fairness in trial to deprive one of it, are always inconvenient—to the authority so restricted. But in times like these, I do not think that substitutions imported from other systems . . . offer promise on the whole of more improvement than harm, either for the cause of perfecting the adminstration of justice or for that of securing and perpetuating individual freedom which is the main end of our society as it is of our Constitution.[234]

In the opinion of Justice Rutledge this Bill of Rights is a charter which serves to mark only the minimum standard of justice to be guaranteed by the due process clause of the Fourteenth Amendment. To make it effective there must be an expressed attitude of the Court which will not tolerate any procedure violative of civilized standards of justice.

[233] *Ibid.*, p. 280.   [234] *Ibid.*

Justices Frankfurter and Jackson dissent from the Court's disposition of this case. Justice Frankfurter agrees that in a contempt proceeding "procedural safeguards of due process must be observed." These must include notice of the charge and a fair opportunity to meet it. "Opportunity to meet the charge" means the chance to refute it in open court rather than behind closed doors. Here Justice Frankfurter takes leave of his colleagues of the majority. He does not find that the state courts passed upon the issues decided by the majority here. The Court should not decide a constitutional issue before the state has been given an opportunity to pass upon it, he thinks. Once again the presumption of regularity appears to weigh heavily in favor of the action of the state. And once again concern over federal-state relations comes to the fore. The two dissenting justices would remand the case to the state court for determination of the constitutional issues raised.

In this connection the Court has been asked to rule that the right to a public trial includes the requirement that the judge consider only the evidence presented in open court before the jury. In the case of Williams v. New York [235] the petitioner was convicted of first-degree murder by a jury which recommended a life sentence. The judge, however, imposed a death sentence, explaining that he had made up his mind after due consideration not only of the information available to the jury but also of evidence obtained through the state's Probation Department and other sources. Williams contended that that violated due process of law, for he was not confronted with the additional evidence and thus had no opportunity to try to refute it. This, he insisted, was comparable to his not having been confronted by some of the witnesses against him. Justice Black, speaking for the Court, replied that due process of law requires that the accused be given reasonable notice of the charges against him and that he be given an opportunity to examine adverse witnesses. It does not, however, require that the judge not consider any circumstances not brought out in the trial which might have bearing upon the nature of penalty which should be imposed.

[235] 337 U.S. 241 (1949).

Justices Rutledge and Murphy dissented. Due process would, they thought, proscribe the use of any evidence which was not subject to examination by the defendant.

STATUTORY PRESUMPTIONS OF GUILT

By statute South Carolina provided that if a person was injured at a railroad crossing and it appeared that the train had not given the proper signals, the railway company would be held liable for all costs involved, unless it was proved that the accident resulted from gross and willful negligence or an unlawful act on the part of the injured person. In Atlantic Coast Line Ry. Co. *v.* Ford [236] the Court held that the statute did not deny the company due process. It was said that the conclusion to that effect reached by the lower court was sufficient for purposes of the Court's decision.[237] Proof that the train did not give the proper signals was said to raise a "presumption that such failure was the proximate cause of the injury." The Court held this to be a reasonable presumption and assumed that it was free from any infirmity under the due process clause. On the basis of that assumption the Court held that the company's citations of cases holding otherwise were without merit; for "If the assailed provisions as construed and applied in the present case afford due process, appellant cannot complain that in earlier cases they were so construed and applied to deny due process to other litigants." [238]

The Federal Firearms Act of 1938 [239] provided that it would be unlawful for any person "who has been convicted of a crime of violence or is a fugitive from justice" to receive firearms which have been shipped in interstate commerce. Such person's possession of firearms was to be "presumptive evidence" that the arms had been shipped through interstate commerce, in violation of the act. The validity of the law was challenged in Tot *v.* United States,[240] in which the Court held that a statutory presumption violated due process of law unless there is a "ra-

[236] 287 U.S. 502 (1933).
[238] *Ibid.*
[240] 319 U.S. 463 (1943).

[237] *Ibid.*, p. 505.
[239] 52 *Stat.* 1251.

tional connection between the fact proved and the ultimate fact presumed." [241] In this case Justice Roberts thought that the conclusion that mere ownership tended to indicate that acquisition had been in violation of the law did not rationally follow. The presumption created was said to be "violent" and "inconsistent with any argument drawn from experience," hence it was a violation of due process.[242]

As a means of enforcing the prohibition against aliens holding farm lands in the state, California provided by statute that the occupation of land by an alien ineligible for naturalization would create a presumption of conspiracy on the part of the landowner and the tenant alien. The constitutionality of such presumption was challenged in Morrison v. California.[243] The Court held that the provision violated due process because the burden of proof of ineligibility for citizenship should not fall on the individual. The state produced no evidence to indicate that Morrison knew or had any way of knowing that the tenant fell within the group forbidden to occupy farm lands in the state. As to him, the judgment of conspiracy denied due process.[244]

In these cases the Court seems to have followed a principle that due process will permit the state to create a presumption of the truth of one fact which logically follows proof of the truth of another; but due process is denied if the burden of disproof of a fact which is presumed to be true because of the truth of another fact falls upon an individual who would not ordinarily have the means of disproving the presumed fact. To meet due process requirements the fact presumed must bear a rational relation to the proved fact on which the presumption is based.

THE FOURTH AND FOURTEENTH AMENDMENTS

The Fourth Amendment guarantees that "The right of the people to be secure in their houses, papers, and effects, against unreasonable searches and seizures shall not be violated. . . ." This has been interpreted to mean that an officer is forbidden to

[241] *Ibid.*, p. 468.
[242] *Ibid.*
[243] 291 U.S. 82 (1934).
[244] *Ibid.*, p. 93.

search and seize papers or other kinds of evidence without a search warrant issued upon a showing of a probable cause and a stating of the things sought. The most difficult question which has arisen under this guarantee has been what to do with objects, valuable for evidentiary purposes, which have been obtained by a search without a warrant. In 1914 the Court ruled that in a federal prosecution the Fourth Amendment barred the use of evidence secured through an illegal search.[245] But when the issue concerning the use of such evidence in a state prosecution had been before the Court, the Court had found it unnecessary to consider the question of whether the Fourteenth Amendment made the proscription of the Fourth applicable to the states. In that instance the Court did affirm the judgment of the New York court that while the seizure was illegal, the documents, relevant to the truth or falsity of the charge, did not cease to be competent evidence in spite of the manner in which they had been obtained by police officers.[246]

The issue was again before the Court in June, 1949, in the case of Wolf v. Colorado.[247] Here the district attorney, who had definite information concerning Wolf's connection with conspiracy to perform abortions, went to Wolf's office, without warrant, arrested the doctor, and while in the place took further information from the office daybooks for 1943 and 1944. With the names of patients who had been attended by Wolf, the police were able to reconstruct the program of conspiracy.[248] Wolf, a licensed physician, and his accomplice Montgomery, a practicing chiropractor, were found guilty and given short prison sentences. Appeal was taken to the state supreme court and thence to the United States Supreme Court on the ground, among other complaints, that the "seizure" of the information from the office books constituted an "unreasonable" seizure con-

[245] Weeks v. United States, 232 U.S. 383 (1914).

[246] Adams v. New York, 192 U.S. 585 (1904). See N. B. Lasson, "The History and Development of the Fourth Amendment," *Johns-Hopkins Studies in History and Political Science,* IV (1937), 223–360.

[247] 338 U.S. 25 (1949). See S. Mezansky, "Battle of the Fourth Amendment," *Pennsylvania Bar Association Quarterly,* XX (1949), 231–40.

[248] People v. Wolf, 187 P. (2d) 926, 927 (1947). Approximately six weeks after the first conviction in the lower state court, Wolf was convicted a second time for similar conspiracy with different people. People v. Wolf, 187 P. (2d) 928 (1948).

trary to the provisions of the Fourth Amendment and that therefore the introduction of such evidence violated the due process of law clause of the Fourteenth Amendment. The only issue before the Court, so far as due process was concerned, was the extent to which the due process clause incorporated the protection of the Fourth Amendment, and the judicial interpretation that the guarantee against unreasonable searches and seizures, excluding the use of evidence illegally obtained, was actually a part of the amendment which would be comprehended by due process of law also.

Justice Frankfurter, speaking for the Court,[249] announced that security of privacy against the arbitrary intrusion of police is "implicit in the concept of ordered liberty" and hence enforcible against the states as a part of due process of law. In spite of this he declared that "in a prosecution in a state court for a state crime, the Fourteenth Amendment does not forbid the admission of evidence obtained by an unreasonable search and seizure." His rationale runs something like this: The due process of law clause of the Fourteenth Amendment does not subject criminal justice in the states to specific limitations. It conveys no formal or fixed requirements. Rather it is the "compendious expression for all those rights which the court must enforce because they are basic to our free society." When the Court is faced with the problem of determining what is and what is not due process, it must accept its responsibility to draw the line by the "gradual and empiric process of inclusion and exclusion."

Justice Frankfurter finds that the notion that illegally obtained evidence should not be admitted in the trial is not a part of the guarantee of the Fourth Amendment but rather nothing more than a judicial implication. While privacy should be protected, he would say that there are other methods which might be used. Anyway, he assumes, the people are in a position to remedy such undesirable features of law enforcement if they choose to do so, for the state officers are close to the people. The same argument, he finds, does not hold for federal law-enforcement offi-

---

[249] Justice Frankfurter wrote the Court's opinion; Justice Black concurred with the results, with opinion. Justice Rutledge, joined by Justice Murphy, dissented. Justice Murphy also wrote a dissent in which Justice Rutledge joined. Justice Douglas joined in both dissents but with slight modification.

cers, for they are remote from the people and can, if they choose, act in a much more arbitrary manner.[250]

Justice Black, concurring, re-emphasizes the rule that the Fourth Amendment is enforcible against the states. He also is of the opinion that the guarantee of that amendment does not include the exclusion of evidence obtained through illegal search and seizure.[251] He disagreed, however, with Justice Frankfurter's distinction between the need for such a rule with reference to state and to federal officers.

Justice Rutledge, dissenting, would like to have the Court declare that the due process of law clause of the Fourteenth Amendment includes the rights of the Bill of Rights. Therefore, he is in complete agreement that the Fourth Amendment is binding upon the states. He does not, however, agree that the majority has rightly interpreted the protection afforded by that amendment. Unless the guarantee excludes the use of illegally obtained evidence, its protection is of little value and "might as well be stricken from the Constitution." [252] And Justice Murphy, dissenting, adds one point of disagreement—the Court's approach to the case—the polling of the rules of various jurisdictions as a standard by which to judge the rightness of the rule. If the rule is wrong, the mere fact that all forty-eight states follow it does not make it less wrong.[253] Justice Douglas joins in this dissent, re-emphasizing the minority position that the admission of evidence obtained in violation of the Fourth Amendment is a violation of due process of law.

Here again the Court is caught between two equally valid interests, namely, the enforcement of a constitutional guarantee against unreasonable searches and seizures and the apprehension of a criminal. In the case at bar two individuals who do not contend that they are innocent of the charge lodged against them base their right to freedom upon the ground that their guilt would possibly not have been established had it not been for the information obtained from the physician's daybook containing his appointments. There is no contention that the in-

[250] 338 U.S. 25, 32–33 (1949).   [251] *Ibid.*, pp. 39–40.
[252] *Ibid.*, p. 47, citing Weeks v. United States, 232 U.S. 383 (1914).
[253] *Ibid.*, p. 46.

formation so acquired was misconstrued but only that it was the lead by means of which the truth was found. The notion that there must be a warrant giving specific information as to the place to be searched and the things to be looked for had its roots in the revulsion of the people against blank warrants or writs of assistance which left individuals without security in their homes. Under such warrants enforcement officers frequently sought information as probable evidence of crime but not directed to the detection of any particular offense. Those charged of crime as a result of such searches were without means of defense, for they did not always know what evidence would be used against them. In the present case the district attorney had definite evidence implicating the accused, and by use of the names of persons gotten from the daybooks, the truth of the charge was confirmed. He even had the testimony of one of the most recent patients. One could hardly call that an unreasonable seizure. Yet the solution to the problem seems to lie neither in ruling that the leading information was not obtained illegally nor in the exclusion of the evidence which followed from it, but rather in the personal liability of the officer thus violating the law and jeopardizing the position of the state. From the record there appears no reason why the district attorney should have entered the office to arrest the doctor without first securing a warrant.

"Due Process" Equals a "Fair Trial"

Perhaps the most significant conclusion which may be drawn from a consideration of these cases concerns the method of the Court in reaching its decisions and the consequent change in the position of the states in the administration of their own criminal law. In the Powell case [254] the Court showed its determination to test individually criminal cases in the state courts by the due process requirements. This could be done only by arriving at an independent finding of fact as well as of law by means of an investigation which reached beyond the record of the proceedings in the trial court. Thus the way was opened for almost

[254] Powell v. Alabama, 287 U.S. 45 (1932).

unlimited supervision by the Supreme Court over the manner in which the states enforce their criminal law. From 1932 to 1946, almost in every case where the procedures in a state court were challenged as violative of due process, the Court felt compelled to look behind the record of the trial court and reach its decision on the basis of what it found to be the actual situation surrounding the challenged proceedings. Since 1946 in several instances the Court has indicated its willingness to accept the record of the trial as set forth in the trial court's account. There have been enough such instances to cause some question as to whether the Court is reverting to its pre-1932 mode of approach, under which it was frequently impossible to afford the accused the protection necessary to assure due process of law in the determination of his guilt or innocence.[255] This role of guardian of the rights of accused persons by the Court has gone far in upsetting the balance of power between the states and the national government. In this particular sphere, until so recently considered, with few exceptions, as in the exclusive domain of the states, the state may no longer claim supremacy. The final adjudication of practically every step in a criminal proceeding conducted by the states might be shifted to the United States Supreme Court under the Court's recent interpretations of due process. The extent to which the new-found supervisory power will be used may depend in large part upon the adequacy of the procedures and protections afforded by the states to accused persons. It will certainly depend in greater part upon the personnel of the Supreme Court and the particular attitude of individual justices to the role of the Court in this matter. The shift from state to national court has been the inevitable result of the states' indifference toward the proper administration of the law or their inability to control their law-enforcement officers. In many instances the unfair conduct of criminal trials can be attributed to a deliberate policy on the part of the state officials to deal more harshly and severely with members of certain minority groups than with other persons. To understand the need of federal intervention for the protection of the basic rights

[255] See Carter v. Illinois, 329 U.S. 173, 177 (1946); Foster v. Illinois, 332 U.S. 134, 139 (1947); and Gayes v. New York, 332 U.S. 145, 147 (1947).

to which every individual is entitled, one has only to consider the number of lynchings which have occurred in the last two decades and the inhuman treatment accorded by law-enforcement officers throughout the nation. If the states hope to recover a semblance of control over the final disposition of criminal cases within their borders, they must see that their courts accord in fact a fair trial to accused persons brought before them. The existence of adequate criminal law on the statute books is not sufficient.

In dealing with criminal procedures in state courts, the Supreme Court has extended greatly the meaning of "due process of law" of the Fourteenth Amendment. In this the Court had performed a legislative as well as a judicial function. It has read into "due process" vague standards of procedural requirements which are at present as binding upon the states as if they had been embodied in legislative enactments. But the fact that today there are so many judicially made due process requirements is not the result of a recent development. The phrase could never have been made effective in any field without judicial interpretation, and with each new interpretation the equivalent of a new law has resulted. The significant feature of this judge-made law of the period 1932–46 is the marked tendency to enlarge due process in criminal procedures to protect minority groups, especially the Negro.

This tendency has at times appeared to be a deliberate discrimination in favor of the Negro. Particularly was this true in the manner in which the Court has distinguished such cases as Avery v. Alabama [256] and Betts v. Brady [257] from the Powell case,[258] or Lisenba v. California [259] from Brown v. Mississippi [260] and Chambers v. Florida.[261] Perhaps it was not intentional solicitude for the Negro so much as a recognition of the fact that in many state courts the color of the defendant may make the all important difference which results in a just or unjust application of the criminal law. This difficulty of applying a qualified right might have been partially remedied in the matter of the

[256] 308 U.S. 444 (1940).
[258] 287 U.S. 45 (1932).
[260] 297 U.S. 278 (1936).

[257] 316 U.S. 455 (1942).
[259] 314 U.S. 219 (1942).
[261] 309 U.S. 227 (1940).

right to counsel by making the right an absolute one as in the federal courts. Such a solution would be impossible in the case of coerced confessions or false or perjured evidence, since in each instance there must be a determination of the character of the evidence before the issue of its admissibility can be answered. In Malinski v. New York [262] the Court came near making absolute the prohibition against the admission in evidence of coerced testimony. So long, however, as the guarantees are held to apply only under certain circumstances, they will need to be interpreted by the Court in the light of the facts. Race is one of the facts which must be considered. In several recent cases the race factor was not considered because it had not been made an issue in the state courts. It is much too soon to conjecture upon the possibility of a return to the pre-1932 approach— the consideration of the record of the case as it came from the trial court without independent investigation into other factors which may have been significant.

In applying the due process clause to state criminal proceedings the Court nonetheless has not attempted to embody in the Fourteenth Amendment the specific guarantees of the Fifth and Sixth amendments. Rather it has read the Fourteenth Amendment due process clause to guarantee the "right to be heard," which in turn has been used to mean the "right to a fair trial." Those guarantees which the Court has found to be essential to a fair trial it has included in its meaning of due process in criminal cases. Among the specific rights so far brought within the meaning of the new due process is the right to effective assistance of counsel, if such assistance is essential to a fair hearing, and the right not to be convicted on the basis of evidence obtained through torture or promises of leniency, because such testimony is unreliable. It does not include protection against double jeopardy, the right to be present at all stages of the proceedings, unless such presence may be of help in making a defense, the right to a trial by jury, or the right to an indictment by a grand jury. Protection against self-incrimination has been included only as that may be thought a part of the protection against coerced confessions. In applying the specific prohibi-

[262] 324 U.S. 401 (1945).

tions embodied in these guarantees, the Court has considered the particular facts of the case as well as the general situation surrounding the trial. Such factors as the race, age, and experience of the defendant, the nature of the crime and the general attitude of the community toward one accused of the particular crime, the complexity of the state law under which the individual was tried, the question of jurisdiction which might have made the defense more difficult, and the obligation of the state, under its own laws, to furnish the protection said to have been infringed have been significant determinants. With respect to the guarantees against coerced confessions the Court has concerned itself only with that part of the proceedings which took place before the trial court. Due process has not been held to protect the individual against illegal acts on the part of police officers in obtaining the confession except insofar as such acts may affect the fairness of the hearing.

The "right to be heard" has been interpreted to include a "right not to be lynched." Only once has the Court had an opportunity to pass on the question of a federal court's jurisdiction, under Section 20 of the United States Criminal Code, in the case of a lynching by a state officer. The hesitancy on the part of the Court to assume the new responsibility of enforcing the guarantee against such acts was indicated by the fact that the case was remanded on a trivial technicality which would not have affected the trial in any way. However, the Court expressly recognized that the right to life, except when taken by due process of law, was an essential part of the constitutional guarantee of life and liberty and that the authority of the Court extended to the enforcement of this right. It also has been held to mean the right to be heard in a public trial with knowledge of the charge and an opportunity to meet the accusation.

The Court has couched its interpretation of "due process of law" guaranteed in criminal proceedings in terms of generalities which have little or no meaning apart from the particular set of facts which elicited them. While only fundamental rights are said to be embodied in the due process protection of the Fourteenth Amendment, it is the special prerogative of the Supreme Court to determine whether a right in question is fundamental in relation to the specific set of facts involved. This is necessary, since the Court itself has held that a right may be so fundamental as to come within the protection in some cases and not in other cases. One of the more undesirable aspects of such an interpretation is the natural-law-justice theory presently applied by some of the justices. Under such a theory "due process" has come to mean "principles of decency and fair play," "fundamental" rights which are "implicit in the concept of ordered liberty," or the "consensus of society's opinion" on the matter. The consequences of this natural-law-justice or decency-and-fairness standard are already apparent. In individual cases the scope of protection has been severely contracted during the past two years. The burden of proof is once again being placed upon the accused who challenges the court's procedures. There is more and more evident the excessive weight of a presumption of regularity in favor of the adequacy of the states proceedings. The implications of this go much deeper than the extensive supervisory powers of the Court over criminal trials in state courts. It has made the final disposition of every case potentially a matter of the subjective opinion of the majority of the Court. Though the result announced represents an agreement among the majority, the individual justice who writes the opinion may, by means of dicta, consciously or unconsciously open the way for new interpretations of due process in the future. Hence the personality and philosophy of the members of the Court assume a greater significance.

But whatever may be the weaknesses of the new interpretations of due process requirements in state criminal trials, extension in this sphere is one of the most worthy developments in the constitutional law of the past two decades. It has not eliminated the defects in state administration of criminal law, but at least it may have discouraged some of the most flagrant disregards of individual rights of accused persons. On several occasions individual justices have urged that all the guarantees of the Bill of Rights were incorporated into the due process clause of the Fourteenth Amendment.

IV

Administrative Actions

Though the development of administrative law and the extensive use of administrative agencies in government had their beginnings long before the 1930's, it was early in that decade that the fear engendered by them culminated in a drive to reform this field of government. In 1928, Professor John Dickinson, speaking before the Maryland Bar Association, had called attention to the alarmingly rapid growth of administrative agencies and the "prolific" making of administrative law, which he dubbed an "immigrant alien" on the American scene.[1] In 1931 none other than Charles Evans Hughes, Chief Justice of the Supreme Court, gave vent to the judiciary's fear of bureaucracy. He insisted that administrative agencies possessed an authority of "enormous consequence" in their fact-finding powers. He alluded to the possibility of their overriding the general principles of justice by a manipulation of findings of facts. He evidenced an anxiety lest these agencies "overwhelm" the traditional institutions of government.[2] This attitude may account for the Court's unwillingness

---

[1] John Dickinson, "Administrative Law and the Fear of Bureaucracy," *American Bar Association Journal*, XIV (1928), 513–16, 597–602. See Arthur T. Vanderbilt, *The Federal Administrative Procedures Act and the Administrative Agencies* (New York, 1947), Foreword.

[2] See New York *Times*, May 13, 1931, p. 18. See also Chief Justice Hughes's comment in St. Joseph Stock Yards Co. *v.* United States, 298 U.S. 38, 52 (1936), to the effect that to make the findings of these agencies conclusive regardless of the nature of the evidence "is to place those rights at the mercy of administrative officials and to impair the security inherent in our judicial safeguards." This, in view of the rapid multiplication of such agencies, was a matter not to be taken lightly, said he. Again, in Jones *v.* Securities Exchange Commission, 302 U.S. 1, 24–25 (1936), Justice Sutherland unmercifully castigated administrative agencies. There he declared: ". . . if the various administrative bureaus and commissions, necessarily called into existence by the increasing complexities of our modern social and political affairs, are permitted gradually to extend their powers by encroachments—even petty encroachments—upon the fundamental rights, privi-

to credit findings made in the name of such agencies, regardless of the expertness of the finders.

In spite of the distrust expressed in relation to administrative boards and commissions, little was done to allay the fear in the face of the mushrooming of administrative activities in the early thirties to take care of the difficult and complex situation engendered by the depression. On the national level the number of administrative agencies had grown to thirty-five by 1929 and had increased to fifty-one by 1940. During the economic crisis of the thirties and during the war more than two hundred emergency agencies were created on the national scene.[3] Concurrently, in the state and local units, innumerable activities were being turned over to administrative agents. The services of the expert have been sought in almost every field of government activity. But the uneasiness felt over the use of such officers did not stem altogether from the number of the agencies created. Until 1935 [4] the publication of the rules and orders of federal agencies had not been provided for, nor were their rules of procedures uniform or obtainable by the persons who might be affected by them. There is little doubt that ignorance breeds fear and distrust. Yet in few, if any, instances could the ordinary citizen find definitely prescribed rules to be followed by local administrative officers. In view of this situation, there was a warranted anxiety engendered by the ever increasing discretionary authority vested in the hands of commissions and boards so remote from the people.

---

leges, and immunities of the people, we shall in the end, while avoiding the fatal consequences of a supreme autocracy, become submerged by a multitude of minor invasions of personal rights, less destructive but no less violative of constitutional guarantees."

[3] "Administrative Procedure in Government Agencies," *Monograph of the Attorney General's Committee on Administrative Procedures*, 77 Cong., 1 Sess., *Senate Document* 8 (Ser. 10562), pp. 2–10. Walter Gellhorn, director of the research, found that these agencies increased as follows: 1789–1865, eleven; 1865–1900, six; 1900–18, nine; 1918–29, nine; 1930–40, seventeen. These figures took into account only those federal agencies "having the power to determine, either by rule or decision, private rights and obligations." See C. G. Haines, "Effects of the Growth of Administrative Law upon Traditional Anglo-American Legal Theories and Practices," *American Political Science Review*, XXII (1932), 875–94; and James M. Landis, *The Administrative Process* (New Haven, 1938), pp. 134–35.

[4] The Federal Register Act, 1935, 45 *Stat.* 500, provided for the publication of such orders.

But what could the Court do to remedy this unwholesome attitude toward an obviously permanent arm of government? In view of the fact that the services of specialized and expert persons have become almost indispensable to the execution of many legislative acts, the Court should content itself with checking, not supplanting, the administrative agents in their work. The due process of law clause of the Fifth and Fourteenth amendments has been read to require that the rates fixed by the government be high enough to allow a utility a fair return on a fair valuation of its property. Thus judicial review conferred upon the judiciary, so long as this interpretation was the law, the power to determine the fairness of the rate, which entailed a determination of the fairness of the valuation, which in turn required the Court to determine the fairness of the procedure by which the valuation was established.[5]

The Court has more grudgingly and infrequently acquiesced in the competence of these agencies than in other fields of government. Even its willingness to place property rights in a secondary position in the face of regulatory legislation has been reflected only lately in its decisions concerning the work of administrative officials. However, the period since 1932 has been marked by some very significant changes in the judicial attitude toward the work of these agencies.

The year 1932 is a milestone in the attempt to reduce the scope of power exercised by administrative agencies, for in that year Chief Justice Hughes recouped for the Court a large area of authority which for some years had been exercised by the agencies. The occasion arose over a piece of legislation of 1927 by which Congress had attempted to establish a workmen's-compensation system for workers in the maritime service of the United States. The application of the law depended upon a finding that the claim was based upon actual employment in the maritime service and that the injury occurred upon the navigable waters of the United States. In Crowell v. Benson the Court declared that these were "jurisdictional facts" which should be redetermined by the courts. It implied that a *de novo* trial could be had on a challenge of such facts. Resting its judicial authority on Article III of the

[5] See "Administrative Procedure in Government Agencies," *loc. cit.*, pp. 76–79, 115–21.

Constitution rather than on the due process clause, Chief Justice Hughes held that there must be a judicial determination with reference to jurisdictional facts, for the constitutional power of Congress could extend only to certain fact situations. The question of fact (that of the proper employer-employee relation and the actual place of the injury) is much broader, held the Court, than due process in its relation to notice and hearing. "It is rather a question of the appropriate maintenance of the Federal judicial power in requiring the observance of constitutional restrictions." It is a question of whether "Congress can substitute for constitutional courts, in which the judicial power of the United States is vested, an administrative agency . . . for the final determination of the existence of facts upon which the enforcement of the constitutional rights of citizens depend." [6]

Thus by a confused path of reasoning the Chief Justice recaptured for the Court the power to redetermine "jurisdictional facts" and left one to conjecture what facts could not be brought within that category and so would be left for final determination by the administrative agency.

For purposes of examining the application of "due process" as a restriction upon administrative actions, we may look at three kinds of cases: those involving rate making, those involving alleged deprivation of property by action other than rate making, and those concerned with rights named in the First Amendment.

RATE REGULATION

Within a decade after the passage of the Fourteenth Amendment the Court was faced with the state's power to regulate rates charged for use of a grain elevator which was in effect a public utility. The Court attempted to answer two questions, namely, "May the state regulate public utilities?" and "Is the grain elevator a public utility?" [7] The state might, it was said, within the re-

[6] Crowell v. Benson, 285 U.S. 22, 55, 56 (1932). See Reuben Oppenheimer, "The Supreme Court and Administrative Law," Columbia Law Review, XXXVII (1937), 1; and John Dickinson, "Crowell v. Benson: Judicial Review of Administrative Determinations of Questions of 'Constitutional Fact,'" University of Pennsylvania Law Review, LXXX (1932), 1055.

[7] Munn v. Illinois, 94 U.S. 113 (1877). See Bartemeyer v. Iowa, 18 Wall. 129 (1874), which seems to be the first indication that due process of law would restrict the state legislatures in enacting economic legislation of this nature.

quirements of due process of law fix maximum rates for businesses affected with a public interest. The Court would undertake to determine if a given enterprise was actually "clothed with a public interest" so as to come within the regulatory power of the state. But the amount of the rate was held to be a matter for legislative determination, and for protection against an abuse of this legislative power, the people must resort to the polls, not to the courts.[8] With slight additions this view was held until 1890, when the Court undertook to judge the validity of the amount of the charge as well as the existence of the power to regulate. In Chicago, Milwaukee, and St. Paul v. Minnesota,[9] the Court appropriated to itself the power to apply the due process test in such cases when the reasonableness of the rate was challenged. Said Justice Blachford:

> The question of the reasonableness of the rate of charge for transportation by a railroad company, involving as it does the element of reasonableness both as regards the company and the public, is eminently a question for judicial investigation, requiring due process of law for its determination. If the company is deprived of the power of charging reasonable rates for the use of its property, and such deprivation takes place in the absence of an investigation by judicial machinery, it is deprived of the lawful use of its property, and thus in substance and effect, of the property itself, without due process of law. . . .[10]

[8] 94 U.S. 113, 134 (1877). Ten years later, in Dow v. Beidelman, 125 U.S. 680, 690 (1888), the Court implied that due process of law protected a return from the original investment and that the bonded indebtedness and outstanding stock would be accepted as evidence of that original investment. In this instance no such evidence had been presented.

[9] 134 U.S. 418 (1890). Justices Bradley, Gray, and Lamar were of the opinion that "due process of law does not always require a court," that it only requires "such tribunals and proceedings as are proper to the subject in hand. . . ." See Justice Black's comment on this decision in his dissent in Federal Power Commission v. Natural Gas Pipeline Co., 315 U.S. 575, 600, n. 4 (1942), in which he distinguishes between types of cases now falling within the purview of due process of law.

[10] 134 U.S. 418, 420 (1890). In Stone v. Farmers' Loan and Trust Co., 116 U.S. 307, 331 (1886), Chief Justice Waite said that the railroad could not be required to carry persons or property without reward. Nor would the state be permitted, under the guise of regulating fares or freight, in effect "to take private property for public use without just compensation." Thus the notion of a "return" was related to compensation in eminent-domain cases.

Thus began one of the most disreputable and illogical lines of reasoning followed by the Court. By it, however, the field of rate regulation became subject to the test of substantive due process.

With this decision it became inevitable that the Court would be called upon to define more precisely and strictly the meaning of reasonableness in rate cases. This it attempted to do in 1898 in the case of Smyth *v.* Ames.[11] Here the Court held that due process of law demanded a rate great enough to assure the owner a "fair return on a fair value of the property used for the public convenience." The formula which it announced for determining fair value comprised a strange congeries of factors which, if taken too seriously, would have made effective rate regulation impossible. ". . . the original cost of construction, the amount expended for permanent improvements, the amount and market value of its stocks and bonds, and the present as compared with the original cost of construction, the probable earning capacity of the property under particular rates prescribed by statute and the sum required to meet operating expenses are all matters for consideration, and are to be given such weight as may be just and right in each case. . . ."[12] But the public was said to have a right to demand that "no more be exacted from it" than the services rendered by the highway were reasonably worth.[13]

Thus unceremoniously began the building of one legal fiction upon another, and in the process the Court opened the way through which it has been plagued for more than fifty years for answers to intricate questions concerning the effective determination of permissible rates for public utilities. It arrogated to itself not only the power to review the actual rate of return to be considered fair but also the obligation to determine the reasonableness of the charge relative to a fair valuation. To solve these problems it was forced into a position of having to decide the fairness of the valuation upon which a fair return was to be made. But fairness, in the minds of the justices, entailed more than mere accuracy. Between the Smyth case and 1933 the Court expended immeasurable effort upon the reproduction-cost theory as a reasonable rate base. At one time or another it was held that in accord-

[11] 169 U.S. 466 (1898).   [12] *Ibid.*, pp. 544-47.
[13] *Ibid.*

ance with due process of law, reproduction cost required that depreciation be deducted,[14] that good will be excluded but franchises included at original capitalized value if the law of the state permitted,[15] that land be included at present value,[16] that water rights be considered,[17] and going-concern value be included.[18] This strange array of factors in no wise comprehends all of those read into and out of the due process–reproduction cost standard. But with each addition the Court drifted farther and farther from the path of reality in a rate-making situation. The issue of procedures followed by the rate-making agency, which should have been the only issue before the Court in rate cases, came into greater prominence than it had been accorded previously; but the substance of the rate order, however arrived at, also became a matter of judicial concern.

Until recently the major dilemma in such cases revolved around the question of what elements should be included in the property and what standard of price should be applied to each in fixing its value. Actually a mergence of the concept of procedure and that of substance was taking place, so that no clear line could be drawn between them. The Court tried to make the Smyth rule fit the various occasions, but in each new case modifications of the rule had to be made. The intangible nature of the thing to be investigated and the bearing of social and economic conditions upon any determinations reached, as well as the economic predilections of the judges, made this field of judicial review even more subjective than most of those falling under the possible challenge of due process.

Minimum Rates for Contract Carriers. In 1932 the Texas legislature found that the increasing business of the private-contract motor carriers of the state offered serious competition to the railroads. To remedy this the legislature enacted a law requiring private carriers to obtain a permit, the issuance of which would depend upon the public's need of an additional carrier in the

---

[14] City of Knoxville v. Knoxville Water Co., 212 U.S. 1 (1909).
[15] Wilcox v. Consolidated Gas Co., 212 U.S. 19 (1909).
[16] Minnesota Rate Cases, 230 U.S. 352 (1913).
[17] San Joaquin Co. v. Stanislaus County, 233 U.S. 454 (1914).
[18] Des Moines Gas Co. v. Des Moines, 238 U.S. 153 (1915).

community. The contract carrier would be compelled to charge rates not lower than those charged by the railroads of the state for like services.[19] At this time the advisability of restricting undue competition of contract motor carrier with the railway service was receiving much publicity. The Interstate Commerce Commission reported that in 1932, 30 per cent of the truck traffic was being carried by private-contract carriers.[20] Economists and groups interested in the railway-transportation system urged the necessity of federal regulation in this field unless the states enacted measures to curb the "unfair" inroads made by the private carriers into the transportation field.[21] It was suggested that the loss occasioned to the railroads had become a matter of public concern, because the contract carriers, not being under state regulation, were less dependable than the railroads.[22] Railroad companies complained that they were being forced to compete disadvantageously with the motor carriers, especially the private-contract carriers.[23] Moreover, in Stephenson v. Sproles [24] the Court had recognized that Texas had a vital interest in the appropriate utilization of its railroads.

In such a setting, the Texas statute was challenged before the Court as a violation of due process of law. To what extent, if at

[19] *1934 Supplement to the 1928 Texas Complete Statutes, Art. 911b.*
[20] "Coordination of Motor Transportation," *Interstate Commerce Commission Reports,* CLXXXII (1932), 363, 380.
[21] By the end of 1932, each of the states with the exception of Delaware had in effect statutes imposing some regulations upon the motor carriers operating within the state. Some of these regulatory laws permitted the regulation of private-contract carriers as well as of common carriers. Bureau of Railway Economics, *Special Series,* Bulletin No. 60 (Washington, D.C., 1933), p. 133.
[22] *Ibid.,* 381. See *National Association of Railroad and Utilities Commissioners' Proceedings* (Washington, D.C., 1933), pp. 41–120; "An Economic Survey of Motor Transportation in the United States," Bureau of Railway Economics, *Report* (Washington, D.C., 1933), p. x. Here it was stated that on the basis of statistics gathered from government agencies and state authorities, the motor truck was the most important commercial competitor of the railroads.
[23] See L. J. Hackney, "The Railroads' Future and Motor Transport," *Review of Reviews,* LXXXVI (1932), 37, 38; Edward S. Jouett, *Digest of decisions relating to the validity of state statutes regulating the operation of motor vehicles,* prepared for the Research Committee of the Mississippi Valley railroads (Louisville, 1933).
[24] 286 U.S. 374, 394 (1932). In this case the Court said that "Debatable questions of reasonableness" were not for the courts but for the legislature to decide. The legislature, it was said, was entitled to form its own judgment, and the legislative action "within the range of its discretion" would not be set aside by the Court merely because compliance would be burdensome. *Ibid.,* pp. 388–89.

all, the majority of the Court was influenced by the fact that the statute was actually for the benefit of the railroads is not known. In Stephenson v. Binford,[25] Justice Sutherland for the first time considered the power of the state to prescribe minimum rates [26] and upheld the statute providing for such regulation.

The question of the state's power to regulate a private business was specifically before the Court. The legislature, however, had not indicated that it considered the contract motor carrier to be a business affected with a public interest, and the Court found it unnecessary to make any determination on that matter.[27] Apparently the status of the contract carrier as public or private was thought to be immaterial. Thus the Court surmounted one of the most difficult obstacles set up by its earlier decisions.

The carrier contended that the permit provision and the rate-fixing provision violated due process of law in that they infringed its freedom of contract. Justice Sutherland countered with the explanation that the power of Congress encompassed the right to regulate private contracts whenever reasonably necessary to effect any of its purposes. In his judgment the principle would apply equally to the states under like circumstances. To Justice Sutherland, who in many instances expressed great respect for the right of freedom of contract, freedom of contract is not an absolute right; and when the free exercise of the right conflicts with the "power and the duty of the state to safeguard its property . . . and preserve it for those uses for which it was primarily designed," it may be regulated and limited "to the extent which reasonably may be necessary to carry that power into effect." [28] He rationalized that the contract carrier was not required to obtain a cer-

[25] 287 U.S. 251 (1932). See "Regulation of Motor Carriers," *University of Pennsylvania Law Review*, LXXX (1932), 1008–17; Harry Spurr, "The New Curb on the Contract Carrier," *Public Utility Fortnightly*, X (1932), 369–73; and "The Regulation of the Business of the Contract Motor Carrier," *Michigan Law Review*, XXXI (1932), 395–408.

[26] Apparently the question of the state's power to pass a minimum-price regulation was considered for the first time by any court in the case of Economic Gas Co. v. City of Los Angeles, 169 Cal. 448, 143 Pac. 717 (1914), 1916A *Ann. Cas.* 931.

[27] 287 U.S. 251, 265 (1932). The author of a note, "The Regulation of Private Business," *Indiana Law Journal*, VIII (1933), 552, 554, calls this one of the most "revolutionary" decisions the Court has rendered in many years.

[28] 287 U.S. 251, 274–75 (1932), citing Highland v. Russel Car Co., 279 U.S. 253, 261 (1929). Corwin, *The Twilight of the Supreme Court: A History of Our*

tificate of public convenience and necessity. It was required only
to obtain a permit, the issuance of which would depend upon a
finding that the common-carrier service of a given community
would not be impaired by additional service.[29] The due process
of law clause was said to place only one restriction upon the legislature's power over such subjects, namely, that whatever condition it imposed bear a reasonable relation to the end sought, which
in this case was the conservation of the highways. That requirement would be deemed satisfied if it could be seen that "in any
degree, or under any . . . reasonably conceivable circumstances" there existed an actual relation between the means and
the end.[30] Justice Sutherland was of the opinion that such a relation did exist and that ". . . in any event, *if the legislature so
concluded, as it evidently did, that conclusion must stand*, since
the Court is not able to say that in reaching it that body was manifestly wrong." [31] Further, the majority of the Court reasoned
that if the state could regulate the use of the highways, it could
regulate the making of contracts which would contemplate the
use of them.[32] With regard to such a matter the state was said
to be "master in its own house." [33] The legislature had found

---

Constitutional Theory, p. 94, comments upon this "absentminded" procedure of
assuming, without argument, that a rule held for the due process clause of the
Fifth or the Fourteenth Amendment would be valid in the case of the other.
With specific reference to Heiner *v.* Donnan, 285 U.S. 312 (1932), Professor
Corwin states somewhat in detail five serious objections to the Court's supporting national power, by citing cases concerning the power of the state to take the
challenged action.

[29] 287 U.S. 251, 272 (1932). Cf. Michigan Public Service Commission *v.* Duke,
Doing Business as Duke Cartage Co., 266 U.S. 570, 577–78 (1925), where the
Court held that the requirement that a contract motor carrier obtain a certificate
of public convenience and necessity converted the private carrier into a common
carrier and thus deprived it of property without due process of law. In Smith *v.*
Cahoon, 283 U.S. 553, 563 (1931), Chief Justice Hughes, for the Court, said
that the Florida statute requiring contract carriers to obtain certificates of public
necessity denied due process by placing the private carriers on the same footing
as the common carrier.

[30] 287 U.S. 251, 272 (1932).

[31] *Ibid*. (Italics added.) See Gant *v.* Oklahoma City, 289 U.S. 98, 101–102
(1933), for an expression of this attitude toward legislative judgment. Cf. Pan-
handle Eastern Oil Pipeline Co. *v.* Highway Commission of Virginia, 294 U.S.
613 (1935), in which the Court held that the Highway Commission of Virginia
could not consistently with the requirements of due process of law order the
company to move its pipelines to conform with the commission's plans for a new
highway.

[32] 287 U.S. 251, 274 (1932).   [33] *Ibid.*, p. 276.

that for several years there had been a steadily increasing number of motor carriers in the state and that these were carrying much of the freight formerly carried by railroads. Beyond doubt this was one of the evils sought to be remedied by the legislation here in question. The Court chose to pass quietly over this factor and place the regulation solidly on the state's right to determine how best to conserve its highways. Justice Sutherland thought it unnecessary to inquire whether there were other aspects of the regulation which, if considered, would invalidate the law. "If plainly one of its aims is to conserve the highways," the legislation is valid. The mere fact that the legislature had other and unlawful purposes would not make the statute void as violative of due process of law.[34]

Without passing on the question of the delegation of the rate-fixing power to the Railroad Commission, a majority of the Court agreed that the fixing of a relative minimum rate had a "definite tendency to relieve the highways by diverting traffic from them to the railroads." [35] That this did interfere with the private carrier's freedom to contract was thought immaterial. The question of a fair value of the property used or of a fair return was not before the Court. Circumstances would have made a consideration of either of these standards impossible, for here the regulation was not to be applied to a single utility or even to an integrated transportation system which could be supervised by the state but rather to numerous small carriers over which supervision had not been exercised. Apparently, however, the Court did consider the fact that the challenged rate would be a minimum, not a maximum, rate. Furthermore, these carriers were not public utilities in the sense that they had been granted franchises under which they must supply any demand for services according to the rates fixed and under which they would not be permitted to discontinue services without permission from the state. Therefore, the usual rate-making rules did not apply. Freedom of contract was said to be a "general rule" rather than an absolute right. Though it had long been recognized that the state might, consistently with due

[34] *Ibid.*
[35] *Ibid.*, pp. 273–74. See Central Lumber Co. *v.* South Dakota, 226 U.S. 157 (1913), upholding legislative enactment forbidding charging lower prices in one locality than in another.

process of law, prescribe maximum rates for public utilities which serve the public at large, this appears to be the first time that the state was held to have the power, within the bounds of due process, to fix minimum rates for private businesses. The importance of the decision, however, does not lie in any benefits which may have accrued to the railroads of Texas but rather in the Court's approach to the problem presented.[36] Undoubtedly Justice Sutherland did consider the factual situation, not in Texas alone but throughout the country, which had called forth such legislation in almost every state. On the other hand, he expressed a willingness to accept the legislature's finding that the regulations were necessary. Due process of law was not to interfere with the fixing of minimum rates when the state determined that such a policy was in the public interest.[37]

Minimum Rates for Public Utilities. The issue of the state's power to prevent the evils of "free competition" by prescribing minimum rates for public utilities was before the Court in Public Service Commission of Montana v. Utilities Co.[38] Justice Butler, for a unanimous Court, reiterated the ruling that due process of law protected a utility company against *maximum rates* which were too low to permit compensation. But, said he, that clause does not "assure the public utilities the right under all circumstances to have a return upon the value of the property so used." [39] This appears to be the first time the Court made such a ruling. The appellee in this case was engaged in the business of selling natural gas in a small community which could support only one gas company. A rival company entered the field and with the consent of the Utilities Commission established rates lower than those charged by Utilities Company. In an attempt to retain its

---

[36] The Court's acceptance of the legislature's finding that the regulation was necessary, hence not violative of due process, had by 1946 culminated in the holding that the "reasonableness" of social and economic regulations is a matter for the legislatures to determine. Potentially this means that there is no longer any way of enforcing "substantive" due process protection against government regulation of property rights.

[37] See Public Service Commission of Montana v. Utilities Co., 289 U.S. 130 (1933).

[38] *Ibid.*

[39] *Ibid.*, p. 135. Apparently what Justice Butler meant was that due process did not guarantee an opportunity to make a profit.

customers, appellee company lowered its rates several times. Upon a finding by the Public Utilities Commission that the Utilities Company's rates were so low as to impair the services rendered, the commission fixed minimum rates at the level charged by the new company. Appellee charged that it had been deprived of its property without due process of law because it could not compete with the new company at the rates fixed.[40] Justice Butler replied that "The loss of, or failure to obtain, patronage due to competition does not justify the imposition of charges that are exorbitant and unjust to the public." [41] Thus the fixing of minimum rates for public utilities in order to prevent competition which appears to be dangerous to the public was held to be a valid exercise of the state's police power and therefore not violative of due process of law.

Maximum Rates for Public Utilities. In spite of the deviations from the usual rules for minimum rate fixing, the Court had its own notions of the nature of rate cases, and for those dealing with maximum rates for the traditional public utilities it continued to apply the rule of a fair return upon a fair value. Its decision in Los Angeles Gas and Electric Corporation v. Railroad Commission of California [42] indicated a probable turning point in the application of due process of law in rate-making cases. Here "reproduction cost," which as late as 1926 was demanded by the Court's interpretation of due process, was replaced by "prudent investment" as a measure of value in fixing a rate base.[43] The com-

---

[40] In Alton Railway Co. v. Commission, 305 U.S. 548 (1939), the Court held that the railway was not deprived of property without due process by the commission's order that it continue its services even though it operated at a loss.

[41] 289 U.S. 130, 135 (1933).   [42] 289 U.S. 287 (1933).

[43] The Commission had attempted to avoid one factor—that of reproduction cost—which had come to be almost a "must" in the determination of a rate base. In Bluefield Water Works and Improvement Co. v. Public Utilities Commission, 262 U.S. 679 (1923), Justice Butler declared that the reproduction theory "must" be considered in ascertaining fair value. Justice Sutherland, in Ohio Utilities Co. v. Commission, 267 U.S. 359 (1925), added the rule that "organizing expenses" should be included in reproduction cost. It appears that by 1926 the Court was supplanting the rule of Smyth v. Ames, insofar as that rule stated the factors to be considered in determining fair value, by the single factor—reproduction cost. See McCardle v. Indianapolis Water Co., 272 U.S. 400, 411 (1926). See F. G. Dorety, "The Function of Reproduction Cost in Public Utility Valuation and Rate Making," *Harvard Law Review*, XXXVII (1924), 173; and J. C. Bonbright,

mission had made two kinds of valuations of the corporation's property, one based on "historical cost" and the other on "prudent investment." By a consideration of both of these the Commission arrived at a rate base. The valuation had been made upon a consideration of the property as a going business valued at current levels of prices plus the intangible elements of value not taken care of in the usual current-expense allowance, the value of additions and betterments, working capital, and materials and supplies. The value assigned to the property as an original investment was that made by the commission in 1917, when the first rate base was fixed.[44]

When the rate, or more accurately the value, assigned to the company's property upon which it should be allowed a profit was challenged before the Court, Chief Justice Hughes held that reproduction cost could not be made an exclusive test of value [45] and that "actual cost" was not an adequate standard, for "the property is not always worth what it cost." [46] The Court insisted that it did not sit as a board of revision but only to see that constitutional requirements were met. The Constitution was found not to bind the rate-making agency to any artificial rule or formula.[47] However, the Court did restate the rule that only the property used or usable in the public service could be included in the rate base and that the company was guaranteed a fair return on this base. The Court seems to have returned to the latter part of the Smyth v. Ames rule that the weight to be given to specific factors in fixing a valuation must depend upon the facts of the particular case. Said Chief Justice Hughes: "The judicial ascertainment of a value for purposes of deciding whether rates are confiscatory is not a matter of formulas, but there must be a reasonable judgment, having its basis in a proper consideration of all relevant facts." [48]

"Economic Merits of Cost and Reproduction Cost," *Harvard Law Review,* XLI (1928), 593.

[44] The commission had decided that reproduction cost would have to be determined on an assumed reconstruction program and was entirely too uncertain for use as a rate base. 289 U.S. 287, 296 (1933).

[45] *Ibid.,* p. 307.   [46] *Ibid.,* p. 306.

[47] *Ibid.,* p. 304. Here the Court stated: "The legislative discretion implied in the rate-making power necessarily extends to the entire legislative process, embracing the method used in reaching the legislative determination as well as that determination itself."

[48] *Ibid.,* p. 306.

For three decades such rule had been quoted and ignored by a Court which demanded that one formula or another be used by the rate-making body. However, in spite of the Court's reluctance to impose a formula, in this case prudent investment or historical cost plus an amount for "going concern" seems to have been given priority. The Court accepted the historical cost excluding all "unnecessary facilities" in a reproduction-cost estimate. For example, the cost of a gas-manufacturing plant which had been used on only one occasion could not be included in the base.[49]

The fair return which was guaranteed by due process was thought to be one "equal to that generally made at the same time in the same general part of the country on investments which are attended by corresponding risks and uncertainties."[50] But, said the majority: "When rates are in dispute, earnings produced by rates do not afford a standard for decision."[51] The charges allowed should be sufficiently great to permit a rate of return which will "assure confidence in the financial soundness of the utility and should be adequate under efficient and economical management to maintain and support its credit and enable it to raise the money necessary for the proper discharge of its public duties."[52]

Justice Butler, joined by Justice Sutherland, voiced dissent. In his judgment the Constitution required that the commission take into account "actual original and estimated present cost of the property,"[53] based on cost of reproduction new. Again the minority, this time consisting of only two of the nine, favored the reproduction theory of valuation for rate-making purposes. Going-concern value, which the dissenters conceived of as a sum separate from, and in addition to, the full value of the physical plant, should be included in the valuation.[54] In their opinion the amount attributable to this item should be specifically ascertained

[49] *Ibid.*, pp. 306–307. See Franklin H. Cook, "History of Rate-Determination under the Due Process Clauses," *University of Chicago Law Review*, XI (1944), 297, 322–23. In the case of Lindheimer *v.* Illinois Bell Telephone Co., 292 U.S. 151 (1934), reproduction cost was not required because the actual experience of the company under the challenged rates was inconsistent with the charge that the rates were confiscatory.

[50] 289 U.S. 287, 319 (1933). [51] *Ibid.*, p. 305.
[52] *Ibid.*, p. 319. [53] *Ibid.*, p. 326.
[54] *Ibid.*, p. 334.

and stated upon some rational foundation. Justice Butler does not explain how this could possibly be done.

The prudent-investment formula for fixing a rate base was re-emphasized by Justice Cardozo for a unanimous Court in 1935.[55] Here the Court added a new factor to be considered as prudent investment, namely, the wise investment of money to procure new business. Said Justice Cardozo: "We take judicial notice of the fact that gas is in competition with other forms of fuel . . . within the limits of reason, advertising or development expenses to foster normal growth are legitimate charges upon the income for rate purposes as for others." [56] Also in current expenses must be included a sum to cover the costs of litigating cases on grounds of alleged unfairness. Since the company successfully challenged the validity of the commission's order, "The charges of engineers and counsel, incurred in defense of its security . . . were as appropriate and even as necessary as expenses could be." [57] Taking into consideration all these items, Justice Cardozo concluded that the company's annual income would be reduced to $23,185.25 and thus its rate of return lowered to 4.53 per cent. This he thought would be "too low to satisfy the requirements of the Constitution when applied to a corporation engaged in the sale of gas during the years 1928 through 1931, two at least of the four years being before the depression." [58]

Justice Stone concurred with this decision because he believed that the commission had arbitrarily omitted the expense incurred by unavoidable waste.[59] He would not, however, agree that the company should be permitted to make the cost of obtaining new business a charge against the income. "New business" is not a part of the property "used and usable in the public service." He found "no constitutional principle upon which this expenditure must be taken from the pockets of the patrons of the present business, any more than the cost of future service lines required to carry on the new business." [60] He did not think that a rate of 4.91 per cent based on reproduction cost as of 1928 could be called confiscatory when the rate fixed obtained for a period of five

[55] West Ohio Gas Co. v. Public Utilities Commission of Ohio, 294 U.S. 63 (1935). Justice Stone concurred. [56] Ibid., p. 72.
[57] Ibid., p. 73. [58] Ibid., p. 75.
[59] Ibid., p. 77. [60] Ibid., p. 78.

years, three of which were marked by declining prices and diminishing capital returns for all businesses.[61]

On this same day Justice Cardozo wrote the Court's opinion in a second case involving the West Ohio Gas Company. In 1933 the commission had accepted income of 1929 as the standard and did not consider the actual income of 1930–31. "We think the adoption of a single year as an exclusive test or standard imposed upon the company an arbitrary restriction in contravention of the Fourteenth Amendment and the rudiments of fair play made necessary thereby," [62] held the Court. The chief objection to the procedure followed by the commission was that it had chosen to depend upon forecast of the probable income even after the actual income was known and entered in evidence by the company. In the previous case Justice Cardozo had said that the Court's "inquiry in rate cases coming here from the state courts is whether the action of the state officials in the totality of its consequences is consistent with the enjoyment of the regulated utility of a *revenue something higher than the line of confiscation.* If this level is attained . . . there is not denial of due process though the proceeding is shot through with irregularity or error." [63] But the Commission in this instance was determining what the rate should have been for the previous three and a half years, and it had before it concrete evidence as to the actual income under the original rates so that there was no need to estimate the return.

In June of 1935, Chesapeake and Potomac Telephone Company of Maryland challenged the rates fixed by the state Public Service Commission as confiscatory because the value of the plant for rate-making purposes had not been properly ascertained. The commission had used a new method of arriving at "present value." It had made a translator of dollar-unit values for the years 1923 to 1933 based upon price indexes prepared to show price trends. Using the translator, the commission had taken the value of the physical plant of 1923 and by adjusting it to changes in price levels over a period of years arrived at the 1932 value in terms of price levels and purchasing power of that year.

[61] *Ibid.*

[62] West Ohio Gas Co. *v.* Public Utilities Commission, 294 U.S. 79 (1935). Again the Court was unanimous in its decision.

[63] 294 U.S. 63, 70 (1935). (Italics added.) Cf. the Morgan cases, pp. 315–22.

Likewise, it took depreciation reserve of 1923 and the yearly net additions to the reserve and trended them to the 1932 value. The rate base was said to be the 1932 value so determined less the depreciation reserve. Justice Roberts, for six members of the Court, held the rate order invalid.[64] In his judgment this method was "inappropriate for obtaining the value of a going telephone plant." [65] To quote Justice Roberts:

> The established principle is that the due process clauses [amendments Five and Fourteen] safeguard private property against a taking for public use without just compensation. Neither Nation nor State may require the use of privately owned property without just compensation. . . . To an extent value must be a matter of sound judgment, involving fact data. To substitute for such factors as historical cost and cost of reproduction, a "translator" of dollar value obtained by the use of price trend indices, serves only to confuse the problem and to increase its difficulty, and may well lead to results that are anything but accurate and fair.[66]

Once again rate making is related to the taking of property under the power of eminent domain. Present value becomes the measure of valuation for rate purposes, for market value at the time of the taking had been made the measure in eminent-domain cases.[67] So far as compensation is concerned, by assuming that regulating the use of property through the rate-making power is comparable to taking the property itself, Justice Roberts perpetuated one of the chief fallacies of the entire rate-fixing theory of fair value and fair return. Here the Court has failed to recognize that there is a fundamental difference in the purpose of compensation in the two cases. "Compensation" in an eminent-domain case is supposed to replace any economic advantage which the owner may be forced to lose. "Return" in a rate case is supposed to curb and delimit

---

[64] West v. Chesapeake and Potomac Telephone Co., 295 U.S. 662 (1935).

[65] Ibid., p. 670.

[66] Ibid., pp. 671–72. Chief Justice Hughes concurred with this opinion. Cf. his decision in the Lindheimer case, 292 U.S. 151 (1934). See p. 287, supra.

[67] See Bailey v. Anderson, 326 U.S. 203 (1945), where it was held that even in an eminent-domain case the value need not be fixed prior to changes by the agency taking the property. In this instance the changes permitted were such as would make "market value at the time of the taking" impossible to determine.

certain advantages which might, without regulation, accrue to the owner. The return is not the full value of the property nor necessarily a percentage of the full market value.

Justice Roberts held that to reach an adequate valuation of the property "actual cost, reproduction cost, and all other elements affecting value" must be given their proper weight in the final conclusion.[68] He would not give price levels much consideration in the valuation of a telephone company, which obviously was not to be put on the market as other commodities. But the Court was not willing to accept the valuation made by the District Court either. A valuation based on cost less depreciation reserve was said to be a "rough and ready approximation" which was as arbitrary as the method employed by the commission.

In spite of these holdings Justice Roberts insisted that ". . . it is not the function of a tribunal inquiring into the question of confiscation to set aside the legislative findings for mere errors of procedures." [69] In this case he did not base the finding of an inaccurate valuation upon any concrete evidence but upon his own judgment that any such method of determining value was faulty and must produce a faulty result. Perhaps the justices felt that the time had come when they should take stock of the accretions to the Smyth v. Ames rule and return to the pattern of the Court prior to the Smyth case, when the judges relied upon their own best judgment as to the adequacy of the valuations. This stock-taking was implemented by use of the due process of law clause.

Justice Stone, joined by Justices Cardozo and Brandeis, dissented from the Court's opinion on the ground that the majority did not find the rates to be confiscatory but only that the methods used in arriving at the valuation were "inapt." [70] The dissenting justices believed that a return of 4.5 per cent was not so out of line with current yields on invested capital that it should be condemned as confiscatory.[71] As for present value, said Justice Stone: "Present value at best is but an estimate. Historical cost appropriately adjusted by reasonable recognition of price trends appears to be quite as common sense a method of arrival at a pres-

---

[68] 295 U.S. 662, 672 (1935).
[69] This method had been approved in Clark's Ferry Bridge Co. v. Public Service Commission, 291 U.S. 227, 236–37 (1934).
[70] 295 U.S. 662, 681 (1935).   [71] Ibid., p. 683.

ent theoretical value as any other." [72] Regardless of the methods used by the Commission, confiscation was not found to result. Therefore, said the minority, the work of the Court was at an end. The findings and the order of the commission should have stood. To quote Chief Justice Stone:

> The legislative discretion implied in the rate-making power necessarily extends to the entire legislative process, embracing the method used in reaching the legislative determination itself. We are not concerned with either, so long as constitutional limitations are not transgressed. When the legislative method is disclosed, it may have a definite bearing upon the validity of the result reached, but the judicial function does not go beyond the decision on the constitutional question. . . . And upon that question the *complainant has the burden of proof*, and the *Court may not interfere with the exercise of the state's authority unless confiscation is established.*[73]

Here the justices have set forth the two opposing views of what reviewing authority the Court has under the due process clause. Six join in the opinion that if the valuation was not determined by what they consider a proper method, they may set aside the rate order as a violation of due process regardless of the substance of the order. Three believe that the Court should concern itself only with the substance of the final order. If the rate is not found to be confiscatory, the Court should not interfere. This latter view brings up the question of review when the issue is not that 6 per cent or 8 per cent is too low but that 6 per cent would not accrue to the company because the valuation upon which it was based is inaccurate.

In St. Joseph Stock Yards Co. *v.* United States,[74] Chief Justice Hughes spoke for the Court in reiterating the principle which previous Courts had stated but seldom followed in practice, namely: "The Court does not sit as a board of revision to substitute its judgment for that of the legislature or its agents as to matters within the province of either." [75] He went further,

---

[72] *Ibid.,* p. 692.

[73] *Ibid.,* p. 693, quoting from San Diego Land and Town Co. *v.* Jasper, 189 U.S. 439, 446 (1903). (Italics added.)

[74] 298 U.S. 38 (1936).   [75] *Ibid.,* pp. 50–51.

saying that within its field of discretion the findings of the legislative body are conclusive and that likewise the findings of an administrative agency created by the legislature are conclusive, "provided the requirements of due process which are specifically applicable to such agency are met, as in according a fair hearing and acting upon the evidence and not arbitrarily." [76] The question of the weight of the evidence lies with the legislative agency acting within its statutory authority,[77] it was said. The only function of the Court, said the Chief Justice, is to ascertain whether there is evidence to support the findings.[78] Theoretically this means that the Court must find evidence on one side only, not necessarily more evidence for than against.[79] When one considers these statements in the light of the rulings of the Court, it becomes obvious that if the result of the agency's work is not satisfactory, the Court is likely to find that the due process requirements of a fair hearing and supporting evidence were not met.

But one must not jump to the conclusion that Chief Justice Hughes intended for the Court to step aside and give the legislature or the administrative agency free rein in the rate-making business. The above-cited words are vague and general. The Court retains the authority, even within this opinion, to "ascertain whether there is evidence to support the findings." Previous court majorities had assumed that they were doing just that. The Court explains that in view of the increasing number of administrative agencies, it could not regard lightly the prospects for constitutional rights if it was precluded from an examination of the facts and the law where such rights may be involved.[80]

[76] *Ibid.*, p. 51.

[77] *Ibid.*, pp. 50–51. In Ohio Valley Water Co. *v.* Ben Avon Borough, 253 U.S. 287 (1920), Justice McReynolds, speaking for the majority, held that when the issue of confiscation is raised, "the reviewing Court must exercise its independent judgment upon the facts as well as the law."

[78] This decision diminishes almost to the vanishing point the force of the rule of the Ben Avon case. 253 U.S. 287 (1920).

[79] In this connection, see "Administrative Procedure in Government Agencies," *Monograph of the Attorney General's Committee on Administrative Procedures,* 77 Cong. 1 Sess., *Senate Document* 8 (Ser. 10562), pp. 210–11. The minority report inserted the formula: "substantial evidence on the whole record." See George Warren, *The Federal administrative procedures act and the administrative agencies,* proceedings of an institute conducted by the New York University School of Law, February, 1947 (New York, 1948), 558–60, 591.

[80] 298 U.S. 38, 52 (1936). Cf. Morgan *v.* United States, 298 U.S. 468 (1936).

The duty and right to make such an investigation applies equally where the rights are those of property and where they are rights of persons.[81] Chief Justice Hughes acquiesced in the ruling that a presumption of validity attaches to an administrative finding which has been made after a proper hearing and upon adequate evidence. But "as the question is whether the legislative action has passed beyond the lowest limit of the permitted zone of reasonableness into the forbidden reaches of confiscation, judicial scrutiny must of necessity take into account the entire legislative process, including the reasoning and findings upon which the legislative action rests." [82] Such a statement nullifies the protestations that the administrative agency has any authority to make findings and orders which are conclusive.

In determining the rates for the stockyard company, the company was said to be entitled to rates allowed on the fair market value of its land, including any element of value obtaining by reason of special adaptation to particular uses but not including any increment of value by virtue of its public use.[83] The buildings were valued at reproduction cost less depreciation. In this amount were included construction overheads, general salaries and expenses, legal expenses, compensation of architects and engineers, fire and tornado insurance, workmen's-compensation and public-liability insurance, and taxes during construction. As for going-concern value, no separate amount was allowed, for "that element was inextricably interwoven with other value." [84] There was no suggestion that the Court should refuse to examine both sides of the case and make a final decision concerning the validity of the rates. Indeed, the Court considered each item allowed by the secretary of agriculture and each item contended for by the company and concluded that the secretary's determinations should not be disturbed.

In a separate concurring opinion Justice Brandeis suggested that the concept of the due process guarantee did not necessarily mean that a court must decide whether the findings as to value

[81] 298 U.S. 38, 52 (1936). Cf. Justice Stone's statement in United States v. Carolene Products Co., 304 U.S. 144, 152, n. 4 (1938), in which he indicated that there was a significant difference between "due process" applied to protect rights of property and the same phrase applied to protect rights of persons. See p. 92, supra.   [82] 298 U.S. 38, 53 (1936).
[83] Ibid., p. 59.   [84] Ibid., p. 64.

or income are correct but "that the trier of the facts shall be an impartial tribunal. . . ." [85] In his opinion the difficulties involved in determining the rates to be charged are attributable to the application of the Smyth v. Ames rule. To circumvent the paralyzing effects of that rule, he urged the Court to apply a "rule of reason" under which it has sometimes sanctioned the legislative provision giving finality to quasi-judicial findings of value and income by administrative tribunals.[86] Justices Stone and Cardozo agreed that Justice Brandeis had stated the law "as it ought to be." Their chief objection to the majority opinion lay in the fact that it "reexamines the foundations of the rule that it declares and finds it to be firm and true." If the fair return on a fair value rule is to be reconsidered, they would like to go on record as opposing it.[87] Thus by April of 1936, three justices had gone on record as specifically opposing an interpretation of the due process of law clause as demanding a fair return on a fair value.

The Court remanded the case of McCart v. Indianapolis Water Co.[88] to the District Court, with the admonition that the "general and persistent rise in prices should have been given effect in fixing a fair valuation." [89] The regulation in question here was actually a price to be charged for water, but the Supreme Court applied rate-making rules in concluding that it violated the due process of law clause. In 1935 the District Court in fixing a rate base had excluded a group of farms owned by the company but not used in the public service. The cost of reproduction new had been included. In 1937 the Circuit Court of Appeals had remanded the case, ordering that the company's farms be included in the total valuation, the sum of $361,308 be added to the cost of reproduction new, and going-concern value be increased by $250,079. The principal basis for these changes had been the general rise in price levels between the time of the valuation and the time of the District Court's order in November, 1935. In making the changes, the Circuit Court had used price-index figures of much the same nature

[85] *Ibid.*, p. 73.   [86] *Ibid.*
[87] *Ibid.*, p. 93.
[88] 302 U.S. 419 (1938). Justice Cardozo took no part. Justice Black dissented.
[89] *Ibid.*, p. 424.

as those condemned by the Supreme Court in the telephone company's case the previous year.[90] According to its use of these figures price levels had ascended 25 per cent during the thirty-two months. The Circuit Court thought that if this rise were included in the valuation of the property, the charges permitted by the commission would have yielded a noncompensatory return. The Supreme Court remanded the case to the District Court, for now that court would have in evidence the actual results of the company's business during the intervening years and thus could make its decree upon known conditions. Thus the record would speak for itself and would prove "in the light of the economic changes which have occurred whether the rates prescribed are or are not of a confiscatory character. . . ."[91] But it is absurd to assume that any such ruling could be applied effectively. If the District Court had authority in 1935 to pass judgment upon the adequacy of the rates permitted, necessarily its decision must be appraised in the light of the evidence available at that time. In effect the Court might as well go on a "census" schedule and at the end of each decade, in the light of "actual results of the company's business" during that period, determine whether it had charged rates too high or too low. The Court did not discuss the adequacy of the rates or attempt to determine a fair value. These things were to be left to the lower court, apparently with a final appeal lying to the Supreme Court at a later day.

Justice Black, dissenting, finds the reproduction-cost theory of valuation completely unreliable for purposes of rate making.[92] In spite of any such theory, "the State of Indiana has the right to regulate the price of water in Indianapolis free from any interference by the federal courts."[93] This, he believed, was a

---

[90] See West v. Chesapeake and Potomac Telephone Co., 295 U.S. 662 (1935).

[91] 302 U.S. 419, 422–23 (1938).

[92] In this particular case he finds that the reproduction-cost theory would force the price of water to fluctuate with the cost of cast-iron pipe, which will not have to be replaced for about 125 years. He could not "believe that the constitutionality of action by a sovereign state of this union is dependent upon the market fluctuations of cast iron pipe." *Ibid.*, p. 437.

[93] *Ibid.*, p. 441. This was Justice Black's first significant expression of opinion on the content of the due process guarantee. See his dissent in Connecticut General Life Insurance Co. v. Johnson, 303 U.S. 77, 85 (1938), concerning the due process restriction upon the state's power to tax and the consequent due process protection of corporations.

general principle which had been followed for more than a hundred years by the Court. But assuming the validity of the recent restrictive doctrines under which the Court has undertaken to supervise the rate-making process in the states, they would not justify an extension of its jurisdiction to this case, he thought. This belief he based "on the record which does not show that the stockholders of Indianapolis Water Company have ever made any substantial investment which could be confiscated." [94] Since, in his judgment, "as applied to corporations, it is the interest of the stockholders and bondholders which the due process clause protects," [95] he would have the Court dismiss the case for lack of jurisdiction. Justice Black interpreted previous Court decisions to mean that "the states have full and complete right to regulate rates of local intrastate utilities and that the federal courts cannot and will not interfere with this regulation unless the rates are confiscatory." [96] The judicial function, he said, does not extend beyond the question of constitutionality and the presumption of validity demands that the company prove confiscation.[97] This the company had failed to do.

Again, in Railroad Commission of California v. Pacific Gas and Electric Co.,[98] Chief Justice Hughes spoke for the Court and stated that a commission was not bound by the due process clause to any particular formula for the determination of value. Here the company had complained that the commission's order violated due process because the valuation had included historical cost only. Apparently the Court assumed that reproduction cost had been considered in ascertaining the rate base, though historical cost, actual present cost, and reproduction cost were accepted as evidence of the fair value of the property. No one of the standards was accepted as an exclusive test of value.[99] The majority position was briefly that no principle of constitutional law requires the rate-making agency to base its decision as to value, or anything else, upon conjectural and unsatisfactory estimates. It is significant that the Court, in

[94] 302 U.S. 419, 441 (1938).   [95] Ibid., p. 434.
[96] Ibid., p. 424, citing Los Angeles Gas and Electric Corp. v. Railroad Commission, 289 U.S. 287, 305 (1933).
[97] 302 U.S. 419, 424, 428 (1938).   [98] 302 U.S. 388 (1938).
[99] Ibid., pp. 394–95. See Los Angeles Gas and Electric Corp. v. Railroad Commission, 289 U.S. 287, 304 (1933).

1938, should imply that a determination of reproduction cost would be conjectural when such a determination had for so many years been required of the rate-making agency. While it has been held that "in order to determine present value, the cost of reproducing the property is a relevant fact which should have appropriate consideration," Chief Justice Hughes pointed out that "the Court has not decided that the cost of reproduction furnishes an exclusive test." [100] The tenor of the Court's opinion appears to veer away from the restrictive interpretation of due process as applied to rate fixing.

Justice Butler, however, was not convinced that valuations should be based on so indefinite a standard. He insisted that the "value to be ascertained is the money equivalent of the property, the amount to which the company would be entitled upon expropriation." [101] He condemned the valuation fixed by the commission because it was based on "historical cost, actual or estimated," and in his opinion, cost is not the measure of value.[102] Value, he thought, must be determined upon a consideration of cost of reproduction new plus a sum for going-concern value.[103] Here again is an attempt by one of the "experts" on the Court to tie the fair-value idea to the just-compensation requirement in an eminent-domain proceeding. The property being valued consisted of a rambling gas and electric company which would not be put on the market. Even if market value could be ascertained, it would not necessarily represent the value of the utility.

When Chief Justice Hughes spoke for the Court in United Gas Public Service Co. v. Texas,[104] he was still of the opinion that the Court concerned itself only with the question of "whether the action of state officials in the totality of its consequences is consistent with the enjoyment by the regulated utility of something above the line of confiscation." [105] In this instance the commission had relied upon operating expenses and income over a period of the four preceding years rather

[100] 302 U.S. 388, 397–98 (1938).　　　[101] Ibid., p. 403.
[102] Ibid., p. 405.　　　　　　　　　　[103] Ibid., pp. 405, 409.
[104] 303 U.S. 123 (1938).
[105] Ibid., p. 143. See West Ohio Gas Co. v. Public Utilities Commission, 294 U.S. 63, 70 (1935).

than of the single preceding year. It did state that it had determined the fair value of the property used; thus it did not disparage the Smyth *v.* Ames rule, which was still applied by the Court in some cases. In spite of this the majority seems to have deviated considerably from the usual rate-making rules and procedures. The Court sustained the rate, for it was satisfied that *if* it should check upon the results of the company's operations for the period 1932–33, it would find that the rates permitted did not impose confiscation upon the company.[106] It did not actually make such a check but rather assumed that the valuation had been properly made. This was the greatest latitude announced and applied to a rate-making agency up to that time. Here the Court was determining the validity, under the Fourteenth Amendment, of a price of gas. In so doing, however, it condoned the application of the traditional rate-making rules and assumed that due process required that a fair value be ascertained and a price permitted which would assure the utility a fair return upon that value. Here, then, the content of due process was not specifically altered, though in effect it was modified by the Court's willingness to be less scrutinizing.

Justice Black concurred with the Court's holding but with a rather significant reservation. He could not agree that the Delaware corporation doing business in Texas derived any rights from the Fourteenth Amendment "or that the Fourteenth Amendment deprives Texas of its constitutional power to determine the reasonableness of intra-state rates in that state." [107] In his judgment the only issue to be determined by the Court should be the question of confiscation. The presumption of validity attaching to rates fixed by the state or commission could be overcome only if the company could prove that its operating expenses had not been properly ascertained. This it could do by a show of proof that each expenditure alleged to have been made or incurred by an associate of affiliate was in fact so made and was fair and reasonable.[108] The decision, he thought, should have been based on the company's failure to

106 303 U.S. 123, 146 (1938).
107 *Ibid.*, p. 147. Cf. Justice Black's dissent in Connecticut General Life Insurance Co. *v.* Johnson, 303 U.S. 77 (1938).
108 303 U.S. 123, 148 (1938).

prove confiscation. The dissent in the present case came just two weeks after his comparable dissenting opinion in Connecticut Mutual Life Insurance Co. *v.* Johnson. His position here is far from clear. If, as he says, due process of law of the Fourteenth Amendment does not restrict the right of the state to determine the reasonableness of the rates, it would seem that the Court would have had no reviewing authority over the question and therefore should have refused jurisdiction because no federal question was involved. Justice Black did express an opinion, not too long ago followed by the Court, that due process of law does not extend the authority of the federal courts to cases tried and settled in accordance with a valid law of a state.[109]

Justice McReynolds was joined in dissent by Justice Butler. These two were adamant in their belief that when a company challenges the due process of rates fixed by an administrative agency, "the Federal Constitution requires that fair opportunity be afforded for submitting the controversy to a judicial tribunal for determination upon its own independent judgment both as to the law and facts." [110] Because they did not believe that such opportunity had been given, they insisted that the proceedings violated due process and that the case should be remanded for retrial. The dissenters opposed the refusal of the state court to find in favor of the company when there was conflicting evidence as to the valuation. They held that in according a presumption of validity to the work of the commission, the state court dispensed with a judicial determination to which the company was entitled as a matter of due process.

Justice Butler spoke for the Court in Denver Union Stock Yards Co. *v.* United States.[111] In determining the value of the company's property for rate-making purposes, the Secretary of Agriculture had considered the present value of the land used in the performance of stockyard services, plus cost of reproduction less depreciation of structures and an allowance on the cost of a bridge then under construction, plus working capital. When the company challenged his action as a violation of due

109 *Ibid.,* p. 153.   110 *Ibid.,* p. 154.
111 304 U.S. 470 (1938). Justice Cardozo did not participate in the proceedings and Justice Black concurred with the majority.

process, Justice Butler spoke for the Court. Still clinging to the principle that the company was entitled to a fair return on a fair value of the property, he held that due process guarantees the right to charge rates "not *per se* excessive and extortionate." [112] He laid no particular stress upon this point, however, though it is quite the opposite of most of the Court's rulings. The company contended that it should have included in the valuation a sum for the land used for stock shows. Justice Butler ruled that a reasonable sum for this item should be added as advertising and charges for procuring new business.[113] The company, he said, is entitled under the due process clause to a fair return on the property as a going concern. Going-concern value, he observed, may be less than, equal to, or more than present cost plus necessary supplies and working capital.[114] It is measured by "profitableness." But for rate-making purposes value was said to depend upon "use and is measured, or at least significantly indicated, by the *profitableness of present or prospective service rendered at rates that are just and reasonable as between owner and those served by the property.*" [115] The value of the property, then, was not thought to have been reduced by a reduction of rates, for the value or profitableness guaranteed by the due process of law clause was only that attributable to reasonable rates. Any part of the profitableness which accrued as a result of excessive rates was not protected as a part of the going concern. In effect Justice Butler's reasoning was moving in a circle, for the reasonableness of the rates under Smyth v. Ames is dependent upon the value or profitableness of the business. Thus actually the value or the profitableness cannot be measured until reasonable rates have been fixed, but such rates are reasonable only in relation to the value or profitableness of the property.[116] For this particular case, then, Justice Butler

[112] *Ibid.*, p. 475. Cf. West Ohio Gas Co. *v.* Public Utilities Commission, 294 U.S. 63, 70 (1935), where revenue "something higher than the line of confiscation" was said to be the return granted by due process. Justice Butler had not opposed a minimum rate. See Public Service Commission of Montana *v.* Utilities, 289 U.S. 130 (1933).

[113] 304 U.S. 470, 476 (1938).   [114] *Ibid.*, p. 479.

[115] *Ibid.* (Italics added.) Frederick Blachly, "The Role of Smyth *v.* Ames in Federal Rate Regulation," *Virginia Law Review*, XXXIII (1937), 141, 160–61, calls this the "vicious circle doctrine."

[116] See Robert L. Hale, "Utility Regulation in the Light of the Hope Natural Gas Company," *Columbia Law Review*, XLIV (1944), 488, 492–93.

effectively indicated the absurdities inherent in the fair-value theory without overruling Smyth v. Ames. But the cat is out. A fair return on value is impossible to determine. The Secretary's finding that the company would have a return of 6.5 per cent and that such a return met due process requirements was left undisturbed.

One of the most recent important state rate cases to come before the Court was that of Driscoll v. Edison Light and Power Co.,[117] in April of 1939. In spite of the absurdities of the fair return–fair value rule the Court shrinks from abandoning it. Justice Reed spoke for seven members of the Court, upholding the rates fixed by the Pennsylvania Public Service Commission against the charge of confiscation made by the company and affirmed by the District Court. The fact that the commission had made no specific allowance of going-concern value was not thought to invalidate the rate order. But in so holding Justice Reed took cognizance of the fact that the commission had given "practical effect" to the consideration of the going-concern value when it fixed fair value of the property at several hundred thousand dollars in excess of the original and reproduction cost, both depreciated.[118] He found that actually the commission had considered all the elements required by the Smyth v. Ames rule, though it had not so stated in its report. At least the company had failed to prove otherwise.[119] The commission's work was sustained without damage to due process of law as embodied in Smyth v. Ames.

Justice Frankfurter concurred with the decision of the majority, though he disapproved of the opinion because it appeared to lend validity to the Smyth v. Ames doctrine.[120] To quote him:

> The force of reason, confirmed by events, has gradually been rendering that formula moribund by revealing it to be useless as a guide for adjudication. Experience has made it

[117] 307 U.S. 104 (1939). C. Herman Pritchett, *The Roosevelt Court: A Study in Judicial Politics and Values, 1937–1947* (New York, 1948), pp. 79–80, believes that this case has actually marked the reversal of Smyth v. Ames so far as state rate regulation is concerned.
[118] 307 US. 104, 117 (1939).   [119] *Ibid.*
[120] *Ibid.*, p. 122. Justice Black joined in this opinion.

overwhelmingly clear that Smyth *v.* Ames and the uses to which it has been put represented an attempt to erect temporary facts into legal absolutes. *The determination of utility rates*—what may fairly be exacted from the public and what is adequate to enlist enterprise—*does not present questions of an essentially legal nature in the sense that legal education and a lawyer's learning afford peculiar competence for their adjustment.* These are matters for the application of whatever knowledge economics and finance may bring to the practicalities of business enterprise. *The only relevant function of law in dealing with this intersection of government and enterprise is to secure observance of those procedural safeguards in the exercise of legislative powers which are the historic foundations of due process.*[121]

At this time the rule set forth in Smyth *v.* Ames was still the law of the land, but reproduction cost as a rate base had been supplanted by other methods. The requirement is, apparently, only that the method used does not actually confiscate the property. There is not the careful scrutinizing of each element considered by the commission as though the Court is certain before it starts that it will find something wrong with the procedure followed and the method used.

In 1942, Chief Justice Stone, speaking for the Court, sustained the Federal Power Commission's reduction of rates for Natural Gas Pipeline Company and indicated a significant shift in attitude toward administrative rate making.[122] The validity of the price-fixing provisions of the Natural Gas Act of 1938 was upheld on the ground that "The price of gas distributed through pipelines for public consumption has been too long and consistently recognized as a proper subject of regulation under the Fourteenth Amendment to admit of doubts concerning the propriety of like regulation under the Fifth Amendment." [123] In this statute Congress authorized the commission to reduce rates for any interstate industry whenever it found that the

[121] *Ibid.* (Italics added.) But see his opinion in Federal Power Commission *v.* Natural Gas Pipeline Co., 315 U.S. 575 (1942); and in Federal Power Commission *v.* Hope Natural Gas Co., 320 U.S. 591, 625 (1944).

[122] Federal Power Commission *v.* Natural Gas Pipeline Co., 315 U.S. 575 (1942).

[123] *Ibid.,* p. 582.

charges imposed were unreasonable. The commission, in its own discretion, could reduce rates to the "lowest reasonable" rate. Since the statute required that the rates fixed be "fair and reasonable" and supported by adequate evidence, the law was not unconstitutional on its face.

The commission issued an interim order for the reduction of rates charged by Natural Gas Pipeline Company that would result in an annual reduction of $3,750,000 in operating revenues. In determining the rate base in accordance with which it reached this figure, the commission had accepted the company's estimate of the reproduction cost of the physical properties and their estimated present value of the gas reserves. No separate amount was included as going-concern value, and the amortization period was taken for the entire life of the company, twenty-three years, rather than the sixteen-year period from the date of the commission's order to 1954, when the business would be exhausted.

Upon the company's complaint that the order deprived it of property without due process of law, the Court declared that its work would come to an end "if viewed in its entirety" the order "produces no arbitrary result." [124] Once again the Constitution was said not to bind the rate-making agency to any particular formula or combination of formulas.[125] In addition the commission was said to be free to make "pragmatic adjustments" called for by the circumstances of the case. Thus it appeared that Chief Justice Stone would lead the Court back to the rulings of the Los Angeles case [126] of 1933. Nonetheless, he proceeded to judge the work of the commission by the conventional standards. Each factor in the making of the rate base was considered. It was concluded that the commission had ascertained the fair value of the property and that the return of 6.5 per cent met the constitutional requirements of due process. Though no separate item for going-concern value had been listed, the Court thought that the "liberal" estimate of reproduction cost covered that element of value adequately. The

[124] *Ibid.*, p. 586.
[125] *Ibid.*
[126] Los Angeles Gas and Electric Corporation *v.* Railroad Commission, 289 U.S. 287, 304 (1933). See n. 31, *supra.*

company's contention that the amortization period should have dated from the time of the commission's order was answered in the negative. The Court found that though the company had been unregulated for the first seven years, the earnings of that period were available and adequate for amortization. Therefore, the requirement that they credit earnings of the years 1932–38 in the amortization account did not, in the judgment of the Court, deprive them of property without due process.[127] The order was upheld because the Court was of the opinion that under the rates prescribed the company would be able to earn a fair return on a *reasonable* value of the property they used in the public service. Justice Frankfurter supported this opinion, for he believed that the legislature had committed to the Court the duty to review rate cases arising under the Natural Gas Act. In addition to the law itself Justice Frankfurter cited numerous decisions in support of review in such cases. He did not explain the nature of the reviewing process under the law.[128] The justices with whom he agreed had, however, made a careful examination of the work of the Commission before rendering their decision.

In spite of the fallacies which at one time or another most of the justices had discovered in the traditional fair-value rule, they appear very reluctant to desert that rule. In the present case the order of the commission was upheld without any great detriment to the Smyth *v.* Ames rule. The majority opinion went no farther than to state that the commission's order produced no arbitrary results in the particular case. There is no indication that the Court was about to go out of the rate-reviewing business.[129]

But this opinion did not go far enough to please all of the justices. Justice Black, for Justices Murphy and Douglas, concurred, offering an opinion which evidenced the willingness of three members of the Court to be relieved of this exercise of

[127] 315 U.S. 575, 595 (1942).
[128] *Ibid.*, p. 610. See his opinion in Driscoll *v.* Edison Light and Power Co., 307 U.S. 104, 122 (1939), where he seems to have expressed quite a different attitude.
[129] See Clifford Hynning, "Price Control and the Profit System," *University of Chicago Law Review*, IX (1942), 561–83; Robert L. Hale, "Does the Ghost of Smyth *v.* Ames Still Walk?" *Harvard Law Review*, LV (1942), 1116–40.

power. Justice Black could find nothing in the Constitution which would authorize the Court to invalidate a rate order whenever it found such order "unreasonable." In his opinion "due process" does not extend such discretionary power to the Court.[130] "Rate-making is a species of price-fixing." [131] He called attention to the rulings of the Court which had declared that legislative price fixing did not violate the due process clause of the Fifth or the Fourteenth Amendment. The substance of the rate order, he insisted, was a matter for determination by the legislature or its agent. Insofar as the Court sanctioned any scheme for ascertaining the value of the property in order to determine the validity of the rate, it went beyond what he held to be its constitutional power. Courts should not concern themselves with the economic merits of the rate base.[132] In his judgment the question of "just and reasonable" is at an end "if the rate permits the company to operate successfully and to attract capital." [133] Since various routes to that end might be taken by those charged with the duty of fixing rates, the courts should not attempt to prescribe the use of any formula. "The decision [as to fair value] in each case must turn on considerations of justness and fairness which cannot be cast into a legalistic formula." The determination of a return to be allowed in each instance calls for highly expert judgment—judgment which, held Justice Black, was entrusted to the commission and "There it should remain." [134]

Not until two years later was the demise of the Smyth v. Ames rule consummated, and then not explicitly but rather in effect by an opinion which was in principle similar to that of the Lindheimer case of 1934. In 1944, Hope Natural Gas Company challenged rates fixed for its products.[135] Because the commission had used actual legitimate cost and prudent investment and had not considered reproduction cost, the Circuit Court had set aside the order. By the time this case came to the Su-

[130] 315 U.S. 575, 599 (1942).   [131] *Ibid.*
[132] *Ibid.*, p. 606.   [133] *Ibid.*, p. 607.
[134] *Ibid.* See Hale, "Does the Ghost of Smyth v. Ames Still Walk?" *loc. cit.*, p. 1116.
[135] Federal Power Commission v. Hope Natural Gas Co., 320 U.S. 591 (1944). See Hale, "Utility Regulation in the Light of the Hope Natural Gas Case," *loc. cit.*, pp. 488–530.

preme Court, Justice Rutledge had joined the group and voted with Justices Douglas, Murphy, and Black. Justice Douglas, speaking for the Court majority of five, repudiated the fair-value theory and urged that rate making be placed on a par with other kinds of price fixing. "The fixing of prices, like other applications of the police power, may reduce the value of the property which is being regulated. But the fact that the value is reduced does not mean that the regulation is invalid. [Citing Block v. Hirsh and Nebbia v. New York.] *It does, however, indicate that fair value is the end product of the process of rate-making and not the starting point.* . . . The heart of the matter is that rates cannot be made to depend upon fair value when the value of the going enterprise depends upon earnings under whatever rates may be anticipated." [136] Thus, at least for the time, rate making was made a subject of the police power rather than an exercise of the power of eminent domain. A valid rate would be any rate which "enables the company to operate successfully, to maintain its financial integrity, to attract capital, and to compensate its investors for the risks assumed, . . . even though they might produce only a meager return on the so-called 'fair value' rate base." [137] Instead of a fair value to be determined with reference to the cost of the physical property, value was said to depend upon earnings from whatever rates were permitted, not just from "reasonable rates." [138] The Court did not say that the rate must meet these requirements—only that a rate which did would not be held invalid. Nor did the majority find it necessary to determine whether the valuation ascertained by the commission was actually in accordance with the prudent-investment theory of rate-base making. [139] The rates, to be reasonable, must represent a balance between investor and consumer interests. [140] This notion had been expressed by Justice Black in his concurring opinion in the previous natural-gas case.

[136] 320 U.S. 591, 601 (1944). (Italics added.)   [137] *Ibid.*, p. 605.
[138] *Ibid.*, p. 601. See Justice Butler's opinion in Denver Union Stock Yards Co. v. United States, 304 U.S. 470, 479 (1938).
[139] 320 U.S. 591, 601 (1944).
[140] *Ibid.*, p. 603. See Market Street Railway Co. v. Railroad Commission of California, 324 U.S. 548 (1945), where the Court sustained a rate based upon an amount less than investment but equal to the price at which the company had offered to sell its street-railway system to San Francisco.

There he added that the interests of consumers and investors might collide so that the rate-making agency would be warranted in concluding that a return on historical cost or prudent investment would be fair to the investor but grossly unfair to the consumer. He stops just short of indicating which interest will prevail. The situation is, however, that the facts formerly assumed by the Court to be "constitutional" facts have ceased to be such. But Justice Douglas did not insist that the Court renounce its power to overrule the rate-making authority. The mere fact that the Court assumed jurisdiction means that the due process of law clause still extends to substance as well as procedure in rate cases. There is this modification—if the statutory authorization to the rate-making agency prescribes a rate base arrived at by a rule other than that laid down in Smyth v. Ames, the Court will not, as a matter of due process, require the latter standard. Regardless of the method used by the rate-making body, unless the result could be termed unreasonable and confiscatory, the order must not be called unconstitutional.

Justice Reed dissented on the ground that the rights here in dispute were derived, not from the Constitution, but from the provisions of a congressional statute. Since the Natural Gas Act had, in his opinion, provided for "just and reasonable" rates in the light of the traditional relation of "fair and reasonable" to fair value, the Court must insist upon that standard until the legislature changes the prescriptions.[141] He agreed that the Court should not impose the prudent-investment rule alone in the determination of the value of the property. But "this leaves the Commission free, as I understand it, to use any available evidence for its findings of fair value, including both prudent investment and cost of installing at the present time an efficient system for furnishing the needed utility service." [142] He would have the case remanded with the direction that the commission accept the disallowed capital investment (that for exploratory operations and other capital costs prior to the time the company was first regulated) in determining the fair value of the property for rate-making purposes.

Justice Frankfurter, following the line of reasoning expressed

141 320 U.S. 591, 621 (1944).   142 *Ibid.*

in the previous natural-gas case, reminds his colleagues that "it was decided more than fifty years ago that the final say under the Constitution lies with the judiciary and not the legislature." He thought that "Congressional acquiescence" in that doctrine "may be fairly claimed." [143] "Just" and "reasonable" are relative terms and must be tied to some standard. In his estimation the Court is making little progress by attempting to substitute for the "hodge-podge" of the Smyth v. Ames rule "an encouragement of conscious confusion in reaching a result, on the assumption that so long as the result appears harmless its basis is irrelevant." [144] To say that this expression of opinion is not understandable in the light of previous pronouncements by Justice Frankfurter is to err by understatement. While in the first natural-gas case he seems to have based his support of judicial scrutiny in the field on the specific provisions of the Natural Gas Act, it may be worth noting that in the present case he does not refer to judicial-review provisions of the statute as representing the will of Congress but rather to the "acquiescence" in a judicial policy which had remained intact for nearly fifty years. On the other hand, the Court had long ago made it plain that such a statute must permit review by the judiciary or it would be found in violation of due process of law.

Justice Jackson was of the opinion that neither the Constitution nor the Natural Gas Act of 1938 required the Commission to conform to the standards fixed in Smyth v. Ames.[145] The theory which ties the rate-making process to the fair value–reproduction cost formula should be overruled, he insisted, as inconsistent with the decision of the Court in the Natural Gas Pipeline case.[146] But Justice Jackson viewed the natural-gas company as a unique public utility especially serviceable for domestic use. Regulation of this utility should be directed toward conserving this particular fuel for home use and discouraging its

[143] *Ibid.*, p. 625.

[144] *Ibid.* In the Driscoll case he had stated that the determining of rates presented no questions of a legal nature. 307 U.S. 104, 122 (1939). See Louis L. Jaffe, "The Judicial Universe of Mr. Justice Frankfurter," *Harvard Law Review*, LXII (1949), 357, 368–69.

[145] 320 U.S. 591, 603 (1944).

[146] *Ibid.*, p. 628. See Federal Power Commission v. Natural Gas Pipeline Co., 315 U.S. 575 (1942).

use for industrial purposes.[147] He would divorce price fixing in this utility from the rate-base theory. A determination of the value of the property is of little help in judging the reasonableness of the price of the gas sold.[148] As for prudent investment, the "service one renders to society in the gas business is measured by what he gets out of the ground, not by what he puts into it, and there is little more relation between the investment and the results than in a game of poker." [149]

He was prepared to rule that the requirements read into the Fourteenth Amendment as applicable in rate-making cases do not apply in a natural-gas rate fixed under authority of the Natural Gas Act. In his opinion if the majority had adopted his view, the commission would have been free to fix maximum and minimum prices for natural gas just as for coal, oil, or any other commodity. Such a price would not be designed to produce a "fair return on the synthetic value of a rate base of any individual producer, and would not undertake to assure a fair return to any producer." [150] Thus "price" would assume a social function. It would be fixed at a point to "induce private enterprise completely and efficiently to utilize gas resources, to acquire for public service any available gas or gas rights and to deliver gas at a rate and for uses which will be in the future as well as in the present public interest." [151]

Thus by 1944 at least eight members of the Court had at some time expressed a willingness to disavow the doctrine that the Constitution prohibited the state and national governments from reducing rates below a level to produce a fair return upon the present value of the property used. They would disassociate rate making from expropriation and eminent domain and make rate making a kind of price fixing. Their position is not to be construed to mean that judicial review in this field has ceased to exist. The exercise of the power to overthrow rate regulations no longer appears to be the order of the day, but nonetheless the Court retains unbattered the potential exercise of this power.

---

[147] 320 U.S. 591, 653–54 (1944).   [148] *Ibid.*, p. 648.
[149] *Ibid.*, p. 649.   [150] *Ibid.*, p. 652.
[151] *Ibid.*, p. 653. See Colorado Interstate Gas Co. *v.* Federal Power Commission, 324 U.S. 581, 612 (1945), for Justice Jackson's statement concerning the social function of "price."

The result of the natural-gas cases seems to be a resolution on the part of the Court not to require as a matter of constitutional law that a commission use some artificial scheme for determining a valuation of the utility. Apparently rate making is to be considered as just one kind of price fixing and therefore not to be held to the close scrutiny formerly given the rate cases.

Rate of Return. The Court has, at various times, held rates from 4 per cent to 8 per cent adequate to meet the prerequisites of due process of law. The basis for the determination that a rate of return of 5 per cent rather than 6 or 7 or 3 is required by the due process of law clause of the Fifth or the Fourteenth Amendment in the particular case is of some significance in understanding the peculiar difficulties involved in this exercise of power. In Wabash Valley Electric Co. *v.* Young,[152] Justice Sutherland explained that a rate of 7 per cent was sufficient; first, because the company had a monopoly on the services it sold, and, secondly, because it had affiliations which provided it with financial security. In 1935 due process of law was said to be denied to West Ohio Gas Company if it was allowed only 4.91 per cent on its fair value during 1928–31. Justice Cardozo considered the fact that two of these years were not depression years and therefore the company should have earned more.[153] Justice Stone, concurring, believed that this rate of return upon reproduction cost as of March, 1928, was above the confiscation mark. In so deciding he took into consideration the fact that between March, 1928, and April, 1933, price levels and earnings generally had declined greatly.[154] In 1939 the Court, speaking through Justice Reed, in Driscoll *v.* Edison Light and Power Co.[155] delved much more deeply into the problem of an adequate rate of return under the due process of law clause. The Public Utilities Commission of Pennsylvania fixed charges to be imposed by the company high enough to yield a return of 6 per cent upon the fair value of its property as determined by the commission. The company contended that a rate of return

[152] 287 U.S. 488, 500 (1933).
[153] West Ohio Gas Co. *v.* Public Utilities Commission, 294 U.S. 63, 75 (1935).
[154] *Ibid.*, p. 78.   [155] 307 U.S. 104 (1939).

so low would be noncompensatory and therefore would deprive
it of property without due process of law. In holding that under the circumstances 6 per cent "cannot be confiscatory,"
Justice Reed explained that the answer to the utility-rate problem does not lie alone in "average yields of seemingly comparable securities or even in deductions drawn from recent sales of
issues authorized by the same commission." [156] The utility challenging the rate was said to operate in "a stable community, accustomed to the use of electricity and close to the capital markets, with funds readily available to secure investments." [157]
Also, the company had operated there over a long period of
time and had adequate records upon which to forecast net
operating revenues. Under such favorable circumstances a return of 6 per cent was sufficient, said the Court, to meet the
due process requirements. Justice Stone, writing the Court's
opinion in Federal Power Commission v. Hope Natural Gas
Pipeline Co.,[158] held that a return of 6.5 per cent upon the rate
base was a reasonable and fair return on the property used.[159]
Apparently this conclusion seemed proper upon a consideration of the profits made by other utility companies and the
favorable circumstances under which Hope operated. Justice
Stone pointed out the steady decline in profits in private industry
as well as in public utilities during the years 1929–38. Further,
he found that the "regulated business here seems exceptionally
free from hazards which might otherwise call for special consideration in fixing a fair rate of return." [160] For instance, substantially all of the company's product is distributed in the metropolitan area of Chicago, which provided a stable and growing
market. In addition the company had entered long-term favorable contracts for the distribution of the greater portion of the
gas; thus it stood in no immediate danger of additional expenditures for distribution costs and expenses to invite new business.[161]
But in the development of a due process rule requiring a fair
return upon a fair value of the property used and usable in the
public service, thus necessitating a judgment by the Court, the

[156] Ibid., p. 120.   [157] Ibid.
[158] 315 U.S. 575 (1942).   [159] Ibid., p. 596.
[160] Ibid., p. 597.   [161] Ibid.

concurring opinion of Justice Black, joined by Justices Murphy and Douglas, is of much significance. These three dissenting justices refused to join the majority insofar as it "assumes that, regardless of the terms of the statute, the due process clause of the Fifth Amendment grants it power to invalidate an order as unconstitutional because it finds the charges to be unreasonable. . . ." [162] In the opinion of these rate making is just another kind of price fixing which should be governed by the same rules and measured by the same standards. Because the Court had for so long allied rate making with "taking" under the power of eminent domain and held that the property must not be diminished in value by its regulation, no adequate standards on the issue of confiscation could be applied. The Court, however, had upheld the price-fixing power as an exercise of the state police power unhampered by many of the strings attached to the determination of rates.[163] It was noted that the doctrine of due process which grants to the courts an unlimited power to reject or approve legislative attempts to fix prices charged by public utilities "in accordance with the judges' notion of reasonableness" has had a paralyzing effect.[164] These justices would, once and for all, renounce the rule laid down in Smyth v. Ames and put rate making and judicial review of the rate-making process on a sounder basis. Nonetheless, these men did not suggest that the Court divest itself of the power to review, and that issue, though much in controversy for a number of years, remained yet unsettled.[165] Nor was it settled in the next important rate case, which involved Hope Natural Gas Company [166] and in which Justice Douglas voiced the opinion of the Court, Justices Reed, Frankfurter, and Jackson dissenting. Rate making, it was held, is but one species of price fixing.[167] Like other applications of the police power, rate making may decrease the value of the thing so regulated, but that does not invalidate the regulation.[168]

---

[162] *Ibid.*, p. 599.
[163] *Ibid.*, p. 599. "Like other forms of social legislation, rate-making or price-fixing may diminish the value of the property used. That, however, does not make such legislation invalid under the due process clause."
[164] *Ibid.*, p. 601.   [165] *Ibid.*, p. 602.
[166] Federal Power Commission v. Hope Natural Gas Co., 320 U.S. 591 (1944).
[167] *Ibid.*, p. 601.   [168] *Ibid.*

However, the Court retained the power to determine the reasonableness of the rate fixed. The change lies in what the Court will be willing to call reasonable in such a case. Justice Douglas veers away from any particular figure but declares that the due process of law concept demands that the rate of return "to the equity owner should be commensurate with returns on investments in other enterprises having corresponding risks." Moreover, the return "should be sufficient to assure confidence in the financial integrity of the enterprise so as to maintain its credit and to attract capital." [169] Since, in the opinion of the majority, the rate fixed by the commission permits such a return, it is held to meet the requirements of the due process of law of the Fifth Amendment as well as the statutory requirements of a just and reasonable rate. The power to review is not impaired nor is it confined to any less subjective standards.

Fair Hearing. Due process has always encompassed the notion that one must have the opportunity to be heard in his defense whenever his rights are endangered by action of the government. With respect to property rights this requirement has frequently been made, though the danger lay in prospective government action.[170] This, as a matter of principle, was no less true when the action was contemplated by an administrative agency than when it was to be taken by any other agent of government. In spite of the Court's idea that an administrative proceeding had to be judicial in character, the nature and purpose of the administrative process early gave rise to a slightly different kind of procedure. By assuming that hearing, whenever provided, entailed a process of argument and evidence before a court or body acting like a court, the justices have been inclined to add judicially pronounced requirements which for a time bade fair to counteract the advantages to be gained by the use of boards and commissions.

[169] *Ibid.*, p. 603. The commission had fixed prudent investment at $33,712,526, and the company insisted that it should have been $17,000,000 more.

[170] See Railroad Commission *v.* Pacific Gas and Electric Co., 302 U.S. 388, 393 (1938), where a "fair hearing" was held to be "one of the rudiments of fair play" and a "minimal requirement" of the Constitution. See also Ohio Bell Telephone Co. *v.* Public Utilities Commission, 301 U.S. 292 (1937).

Perhaps the decisions in the first two of the Morgan cases can be taken as the culmination of the Court's basic dissatisfactions with the manner in which administrative agencies were functioning. For many years the Court had concerned itself almost entirely with the results of the rate-making process and had looked chiefly at the actual rate of return and the factors which had gone into the rate base. The first Morgan case,[171] however, called for an investigation of the proceeding to determine if there had been afforded an adequate hearing. Perhaps it is for this reason that the Court's action appeared a bit severe and radically different. In April of 1930 the United States Secretary of Agriculture began proceedings contemplated to fix reasonable rates for some fifty stockyard companies. In 1936 these determinations were challenged as violative of due process of law on the ground that a "hearing" within the meaning of that term had not been granted. The plaintiff company complained because (1) the different companies had not been heard separately, (2) the trial examiner had not made a tentative report subject to oral argument and exceptions, and (3) the Secretary of Agriculture had made the final decisions without having heard the arguments. It should be noted that although this was a rate case, the elements considered as a part of the value of the property were not in issue nor was the actual rate decided upon questioned.

The opinion of the Court was voiced by Chief Justice Hughes, who declared that no denial of due process had resulted from failure to hear the fifty cases separately. Nor was it necessary for the examiner to prepare a tentative report, though, said he, it would have been "good practice."

The significant question was whether the final determination of the rate must be based upon the Secretary's personal participation in the argument. Said the Chief Justice, the "fundamental procedural requirements" must be met in such a case. Among these was a "full hearing," that is, a hearing which produced "evidence adequate to support pertinent and necessary findings of fact." [172] In such a proceeding "Nothing can be treated as evidence which is not introduced as such. Facts and

[171] Morgan v. United States, 298 U.S. 468 (1936).
[172] Ibid., p. 480.

circumstances which ought to be considered must not be excluded. Facts and circumstances must not be considered which should not legally influence the conclusion. Findings based on the evidence must embrace the basic facts which are needed to sustain the order." It was said that the mere fact that the evidence supports the findings is no answer to the challenge, for regardless of evidence to support the findings, their conclusiveness rests on the "assumption that the officer who makes the findings has addressed himself to the evidence. . . ." [173] Congress, in requiring a "hearing" had reference to "the traditional judicial proceeding," said the Court. In such a proceeding evidence is taken and weighed by the trier of the facts. This is intended to provide the essential safeguard that "the one who decides shall be bound . . . to consider the evidence and be guided by it alone." [174]

The need for such a requirement is obvious when one considers that at the time the Secretary of Agriculture administered forty-two regulatory statutes.[175] While it would impose an onerous burden upon the administrative officer, it is necessary as a guard against arbitrary action based on ignorance of the real situation. It would mean, however, a tremendous increase in the number of agents authorized to make important decisions and rules.[176]

Into this opinion crept one disturbing element so far as judicial review is concerned. With all the complaining, the plaintiff companies made no attempt to prove that the actual rates fixed were confiscatory. In other instances this had become a prerequisite to a consideration of the issues by the Court. There is no explanation given of why that question was not found necessary in this instance. Apparently the Court decided that if the procedure was defective, the action and its results should be invalidated without

---

[173] *Ibid.* See P. M. Berkson, "Due Process Requirements of a Fair Hearing in Rate Proceedings," *Columbia Law Review*, XXXVIII (1938), pp. 978–1007.

[174] 298 U.S. 468, 480–81 (1936).

[175] See O. R. McGuire, "Federal Administrative Action and Judicial Review," *American Bar Association Journal*, XXII (1936), pp. 492–96. As a result of this decision the Schwellenback Act, 54 *Stat.* 81, authorized the Secretary of Agriculture to delegate regulatory functions to officers in the department when he deemed such delegation necessary.

[176] See A. H. Feller, "Prospectus for Further Study of Federal Administrative Law," *Yale Law Journal*, XLVII (1938), 647, 662–64; and Walter Gellhorn, *Administrative Law: Cases and Comments* (Chicago, 1940), pp. 746–47.

consideration of the merits of the results.[177] The Court was not bothered by the fact that persons dealing with these companies had rights which needed protection also. As a practical matter, the decision remanded the case to the District Court where the Secretary would be called upon to answer the company's inquiries.

The case was before the Court a second time in 1938.[178] In this instance, the Secretary testified that he had considered the findings made by the men in the Bureau of Animal Industry. The Court assumed "that the Secretary sufficiently understood" the import of those findings.[179] Thus was answered the specific ground for complaint in the 1936 case. But here another prerequisite for a fair hearing was imposed. "The right to a hearing embraces not only the right to present evidence but also a reasonable opportunity to know the claims of the opposing party and to meet them." [180] The Court believed that Congress surely had reference to a hearing according to judicial standards with respect to the "fundamental requirements of fairness which are the essence of due process in a proceeding of a judicial nature." [181] The examiner, it was held, should have made a tentative report, indicating the government's claims and proposed findings. This ruling was in direct conflict with that of the earlier case, but the Chief Justice explained that the preliminary report was necessary since the

[177] See Justice Butler's dissent (joined by Justice Sutherland) in the Los Angeles Gas Corporation case, 289 U.S. 287, 327 (1933), where he declared that an arbitrary method should invalidate the action regardless of the correctness of the results. Cf. the decision in West Ohio Gas Co. v. Public Utilities Commission, 294 U.S. 63, 70 (1935); and West v. Chesapeake and Potomac Telephone Co., 295 U.S. 662, 692 (1935), as well as the dissent in the same case at p. 693, where it was said that confiscation must be shown. See Justice Black's dissent in McCart v. Indianapolis Water Co., 302 U.S. 419, 424-28 (1938).

[178] Morgan v. United States, 304 U.S. 1 (1938). Justice Black dissented. Justices Reed and Cardozo took no part. In United Gas Public Service Co. v. Texas, 303 U.S. 123, 138 (1938), the Court, speaking through Justice Hughes, did not dwell upon the question of the adequacy of the hearing. However, he did note that the Commission's findings were available and open to argument by the company.

[179] 304 U.S. 1, 18 (1938).

[180] Ibid., pp. 18-19.

[181] In his concurring opinion in St. Joseph Stock Yards Co. v. United States, 298 U.S. 38, 73 (1936), Justice Brandeis declared that due process did not necessarily assure a judicial review of the determinations. He added, however, that the proceeding must be conducted "in such a way that there will be opportunity for a court to determine whether the applicable rules of law and procedure were observed."

Secretary had not participated in the oral arguments. Apparently the Court assumed that had the Secretary, who decided upon the rates, taken part in the oral arguments concerning these, the companies would have become acquainted with the thinking of the government's agents and would have been in a better position to defend themselves. This, however, was as true in 1936 as in 1938. Chief Justice Hughes in 1936 had said that a tentative report would have been in keeping with good practice but was not essential to the fairness of the proceeding. In the present case he considered the absence of it "more than an irregularity in practice." [182] To see the full import of this pronouncement one must remember that this is not a new set of hearings the Court is passing upon but rather a continuation of proceedings which had been in progress for seven years. One glance at the actions taken during these years would assure us that the companies had been given every opportunity to know the government's attitude and proposed action. Suppose, in spite of this, the Court had made a mistake in 1936. More respect for its work would have been engendered had the Chief Justice admitted the error rather than so casually assuming that the Secretary of Agriculture had misunderstood his previous holding.

Obviously the Court in 1938 was not interested in administrative agencies which acted like administrative agencies. Said Chief Justice Hughes: ". . . as we have said at the outset, if these multiplying agencies deemed to be necessary in our complex society are to serve the purposes for which they are created and endowed with vast powers, they must accredit themselves by acting in accordance with the cherished judicial tradition embodying the basic concepts of fair play." [183] If this was intended to be a lesson to the Department of Agriculture, it came a little too late, for the "preliminary report" method had been in use there for nearly two years.[184] One must remember that if there was an injustice, it occurred before such procedural reform.

[182] Note that in National Labor Relations Board v. Mackay Radio and Tel. Co., 304 U.S. 333, 350–51 (1938), Justice Roberts wrote that a tentative report was not necessary if the issues were otherwise clearly defined.

[183] 304 U.S. 1, 22 (1938). It is possible that a majority of the justices were influenced by the current investigations of administrative procedures.

[184] See Secretary Wallace's letter to the New York Times, May 8, 1938, IV, 8:5. See also J. A. Doyle, "Federal Administrative Hearings: Significance of the Morgan Cases," Nebraska Law Journal, XIX (1940), pp. 125–45; and John Dickinson,

Since the issue of the report had been deleted from the case by the Court itself in 1936, the Solicitor General of the United States petitioned for a rehearing. If the plaintiff marketing agents were entitled to know what the government proposed to do, surely the defendant agency of the government was entitled to know on what issues the Court planned to have its decision turn. In a *per curiam* opinion [185] the petition was refused. It was said that the Solicitor's complaint of a reversal of decision was unwarranted. True, the 1936 opinion had left the door open for this decision. But that in itself represents one of the grave defects of a system in which a Court, certainly with less information about, or consideration of, the matter at hand, can override the determination of the administrative agency and prescribe rules for its proceedings.

This was not to be the end of this spree of litigation. Impounded in the District Court was a large sum representing rates charged in excess of those fixed by the Secretary. The disposition of the fund was left to the District Court and the Secretary. The District Court granted commissionmen's petition to have the money distributed among them, and upon that decision the case came again to the Supreme Court.[186] Justice Stone declared that the District Court should not distribute the money but should await a final order from the Secretary. Thus after nine years the rate issue remained unsettled. To clarify the Court's position to those who might be in doubt, Justice Stone explained: ". . . in construing a statute setting up an administrative agency and providing for judicial review of its actions, court and agency are not to be regarded as wholly independent and unrelated instrumentalities of justice, each acting in the performance of its prescribed statutory duty without regard to the appropriate function of the other in securing the plainly indicated objects of the statute."

On the fourth hearing before the Court, Justice Frankfurter

"Judicial Review of Administrative Decisions: A Summary and An Evaluation," *Minnesota Law Review*, XXV (1941), pp. 588–621. The new procedure was required as of September 14, 1936. For the new rule as meeting the standards of this decision, see Kathryn Pearlman, "The Effect of the Morgan Decisions on the Position of the Trial Examiner," *George Washington Law Review*, X (1942), 43, 47–50.

[185] Morgan *v.* United States, 304 U.S. 23 (1938). Again Justice Black dissented and Justices Reed and Cardozo took no part.

[186] United States *v.* Morgan, 307 U.S. 183 (1939).

expressed the Court's opinion that the Secretary of Agriculture never should have been subjected to examination before the courts. In his opinion, the Secretary, as guardian of the public interest, was not supposed to reflect the items on a profit-and-loss sheet and nothing more. In such a duty the agency making the rates must exercise some judgment, for the elements involved doubts and difficulties which are not susceptible of exact resolution. There was no reason for believing that the Court's judgment was any more sound than the Secretary's. Justice Frankfurter described the Court's action as taking the judiciary into the "legislative realm of fixing rates." Such a task, he finds, requires ". . . striking a balance and reaching a judgment on factors beset with doubts and difficulties, uncertainty and speculation. On ultimate analysis, the real question is whether the Secretary or the courts should make an appraisal of elements having delusive certainty. Congress has put the responsibility on the Secretary and the Constitution does not deny the assignment." [187] He was of the opinion that the Court's function had been performed when it found that the Secretary was responsibly conscious of conditions affecting the market during the years following 1933. Said he: "Just as a judge cannot be subjected to such a scrutiny, so the integrity of the administrative process must be equally respected." [188]

Justice Roberts dissented because he felt that the majority had been too lax in its scrutiny of the Secretary's work. While Justice Frankfurter was sure that the Secretary had considered the changes in the market during the period 1933–37, Justice Roberts was just as certain that he had not.

Justice Cardozo, for a unanimous Court, had in 1935 found the rates fixed for the West Ohio Gas Company invalid because of the defective method used in arriving at the company's income. The commission had ignored actual evidence available, choosing to forecast a probable income instead.[189] Approximately six

[187] United States v. Morgan, 313 U.S. 409, 417 (1941). Note that this attitude had been embodied in the opinion in Railroad Commission of Texas v. Rowan & Nichols Oil Co., 310 U.S. 573 (1940).

[188] 313 U.S. 409, 422 (1941). See James M. Landis, "Administrative Policies and the Courts," Yale Law Journal, XLVII (1940), 519–31.

[189] West Ohio Gas Co. v. Public Utilities Commission, 294 U.S. 79 (1935).

months later Justice Roberts wrote the opinion in the case of West *v*. Chesapeake and Potomac Telephone Co.,[190] holding that the rate was invalid because the method of arriving at fair value was "inappropriate." He assumed that the faulty method of determining value inevitably resulted in an invalid rate base. But "procedure" in each instance is distinguishable from the "procedure" as challenged in the Morgan cases. In the earlier cases "procedure" or "method" referred to a manner of computation, while in the Morgan cases "procedure" referred to both the manner of getting the figures and the way of using them after they had been obtained. These cases represent a shift from the overemphasis of the Court on the substance of the order made by the agency to the actual procedure which went into the making of such order.

Here we have four hearings before the Supreme Court, all arising from a single rate-fixing action by the Secretary of Agriculture. So far as the scope of due process of law is concerned, these cases are significant for several reasons. First, the Court has concentrated upon procedural aspects to a greater extent than in previous rate cases. In the important rate cases between 1933 and 1936 the Court majorities had referred in passing to a fair hearing as one of the requirements of due process of law but had considered almost exclusively the factors which comprised the basis of the fair value of the utilities' property and the actual rate of return permitted. "Formulas" for ascertaining the fair value had been discussed at length, and various formulas had been in vogue at different times. In the first two of the Morgan cases no mention was made of the particular recipe for fair value nor did the companies prove that any confiscation would be entailed in the enforcement of the prescribed rates. The complaint was not even that the procedure by which the evidence had been gleaned was inadequate but that the use made of the evidence was invalid. In other words, assuming that the evidence was accurate and sufficient to support the findings made, the person who made the findings had not personally gathered the evidence and had not participated in the oral arguments concerning evidence or findings. But the case was remanded to the District

[190] West *v*. Chesapeake and Potomac Telephone Co., 295 U.S. 662 (1935).

Court by the 1936 decision, and the "ignorance" of the Secretary was eliminated as an issue. Before the case came to the Supreme Court in 1938, the "one who decides" had acquainted himself with the evidence to the satisfaction of the Court. Thus there remained only one defect, namely, that of the inability of the plaintiff companies to have information about the proposed actions to be taken by the government. If actually these companies had not been informed of the Secretary's proposals, they would have been placed at a great disadvantage in refuting the findings, at least so the Court decided. This, it seems, involves two alternative aspects of procedural due process. Granted the companies should have been well informed of the proposed findings and actions, should not they have gotten this information from the administrative agency involved rather than from unofficial observation? This would place the burden of making available the information upon the agency itself. Certainly such a requirement could not possibly work to the detriment of any party concerned, for presumably every action by the Secretary of Agriculture is in the interest of the general public, including the companies as well as those who use their facilities. On the other hand, nothing would have prevented the companies from challenging the validity of any specific finding. This would only shift the burden of proof to the plaintiff, and such has been the rule in previous rate cases. The opinions submitted in these two cases indicate the Court's reading of "due process," as pertains to a fair hearing, to place the burden upon the rate-making agency.

A second significant aspect of the Morgan decisions is the facility with which the Court is able to use "due process of law." There is no indication in the second opinion that there had been made available to the Court additional information which caused it to add the requirement of a tentative report in order to have a fair hearing. There is no explanation given of why "due process" applied to exactly the same agent and the same action at two different times implied such divergent standards. The Chief Justice wrote the opinion in the first and second cases and in each instance was able to find justification for his decision in the due process of law clause. On the third round Justice Stone wrote the Court's opinion, and on the fourth Justice Frankfurter spoke for the

Court. These two had one thing in common, namely, they each believed that administrative agencies should be placed on a level at least close to par with the courts. Thus by "judicial review" under due process of law, in 1941 the Court relinquished for the time the extension of its power which it had gotten in 1936 and 1938 by the same means.

In Market Street Railway Co. *v.* Railroad Commission of California [191] the company complained that it had been deprived of property without due process, for the commission had based its decision partially on company reports which had not been entered in evidence at the hearing. Justice Jackson explained that "due process . . . requires that commissions proceed upon matters in evidence and that parties have an opportunity to subject evidence to the test of cross-examination and rebuttal." But due process deals with the substance of the hearing and is not to be "trivialized by formal objections" which have no significant bearing upon the alternate rights of the parties. Reference to the company's revenue for the months January to August of 1943, though it did not appear formally as evidence, did not violate the tenets of due process.[192]

In spite of its careful scrutiny of administrative activities, the Court has not held that the hearing must be granted at the initial stage of the proceedings.[193] It is enough to satisfy due process standards that the hearing is afforded before the order becomes effective.[194] In some instances the stage at which the hearing may be had becomes very important. In Bailey *v.* Anderson,[195] for instance, the plaintiff, whose property was being torn up to build a highway, was not given a hearing before the construction began. Hence it was almost impossible for the Highway Commission to determine a fair price of the property taken.

Not much had been said about what would constitute a fair hearing before an administrative body since the last of the Morgan cases, which left much doubt on the subject. Though the Court

[191] 324 U.S. 548 (1945).   [192] *Ibid.,* p. 562.
[193] See American Surety Co. *v.* Baldwin, 287 U.S. 156, 168 (1932).
[194] See United States *v.* Illinois Central Railroad Co., 291 U.S. 457, 463 (1934), Justice Sutherland for the Court; and Opp Cotton Mills *v.* Administrator of Wage and Hour Division of the Department of Labor, 312 U.S. 126, 152–53 (1941), Chief Justice Stone rendering the Court's opinion.
[195] 326 U.S. 203 (1945).

has consistently held that due process required an administrative agency to allow a full hearing, or "judicial hearing," before rendering a final hearing, it has not always interpreted such a hearing to include oral argument. The absence of an oral argument was not a question in issue in the first of the Morgan cases. However, in describing the kind of hearing demanded by the due process of law clause, Chief Justice Hughes said that oral argument was not an essential part of a hearing. Apparently at that time the Court was willing to allow an alternative, namely, the use of written evidence, provided that the trier of the facts acquaints himself with such evidence. But when the case was before the Court a second time, Chief Justice Hughes declared that the plaintiff companies were entitled, as a matter of due process of law, to know the findings which the government proposed to make. This standard of "fair play" could be met by oral argument in which both company and administrative agent participated or by a trial examiner's tentative report upon which oral argument could be had and exceptions made.

The question was specifically before the Court in the case of Federal Communications Commission v. WJR, the Goodwill Station.[196] The Federal Communications Commission was considering the desirability of new rules governing clear-channel stations to permit certain stations to increase their broadcast strengths. Meanwhile, the Coastal Plains Broadcasting Company filed application for a permit to construct a "Class II Station" to broadcast from Tarboro, North Carolina. This Class II station would operate on a clear channel and would be designed to render service over a primary service area which is limited by, and subject to, such interference as may be received from Class I stations. WJR, a clear-channel, Class I station, filed a petition asking that the question of this permit be postponed until the matter of new regulations for clear-channel stations had been decided upon. It alleged that the operation of the Tarboro station would cause objectional interference with its broadcast signal, especially in areas where its field intensity averaged less than 32 microvolts.

Without a hearing on this request the Federal Communications Commission granted the permit for the construction of the Class

[196] 337 U.S. 265 (1949).

II station at Tarboro, and WJR filed a petition for reconsideration and hearing. Several months later the commission denied the petition without prior oral argument. It explained that the new station would not cause interference within the normally protected service area of WJR, for areas of signal intensity lower than 100 microvolts per meter were outside the normally protected contours. The Court of Appeals held that WJR's claim of objectional interference presented a question of law and that the due process of law clause of the Fifth Amendment assured WJR an oral argument as to the merits of its allegations.

The commission appealed to the Supreme Court, and Justice Rutledge wrote the opinion for eight members of the court.[197] Procedural due process guaranteed by the Fifth Amendment has "no fixed and invariable content," it was said.[198] The right of oral argument varies from case to case according to the circumstances of the cases. To make any broad general rule that there must be opportunity for oral argument on all questions of law would "do violence" to the constitutional power of Congress to devise differing administrative and legal procedures appropriate for the disposition of issues of widely different kinds. Here, as in previous cases, the Court defers to congressional determinations of proper procedures, judicial and administrative. In the Communications Act of 1934, Congress provided for oral argument in "proceedings initially heard before an examiner," and none other. The holder of an outstanding license was guaranteed "reasonable opportunity to show cause" why a modification should not be made, but this, thought the Court, did not necessarily include opportunity for oral argument. Since WJR did not contend that it was denied the chance to present any matters of fact or law or that the commission failed to give due consideration to those matters presented, there was found no basis for the complaint that due process was denied.

Perhaps so far as the conduct of administrative actions is concerned, the chief significance of the decision lies in the apparent willingness of the Court to credit the judgment of the commission in its selection of a given procedure. The due process clause,

[197] Justice Murphy did not participate in this case.
[198] 337 U.S. 265, 268 (1949).

it was said, requires that the parties affected be given an opportunity to present the facts of the case and to have these facts considered. If that much is afforded, mere technicalities of procedure will not vitiate the decision reached.

THE STATUS OF FINDINGS OF ADMINISTRATIVE AGENCIES

Findings Involving Property Rights. The Court has not always recognized the competency of administrative boards even in fields in which the individual members are supposed to be experts. Legislative findings have, generally speaking, been accorded much greater credit. A statement by Justice McReynolds in Southern Railway Co. *v.* Virginia [199] gives some insight into the attitude of the justices. There he remarked: "There is an obvious difference between a legislative determination and the finding of an administrative official not supported by evidence. In theory, at least, the Legislature acts upon adequate knowledge after full consideration and through members who represent the entire public." [200] In this instance a Virginia statute authorized the State Highway commission to determine when the public safety required the elimination of a grade crossing. Upon such determination the commission would authorize expenditures for a new structure, one half of the cost to be met by the railroad. The railroad was not granted a hearing nor could it appeal on the question of whether the public safety required the elimination of the crossing. It could demand a hearing and judicial review only of the questions concerning the type of structure which would replace the crossing. The Highway Commission made its determination on the basis of the large amount of traffic over the particular crossing and the number of accidents which had occurred there.[201] Certainly such was the only reasonable basis for

[199] 290 U.S. 190 (1933). Chief Justice Hughes, joined by Justices Stone and Cardozo, dissented.

[200] *Ibid.,* p. 197.

[201] Letter from C. C. Bowles, Assistant Attorney General of Virginia, to the author, April 22, 1949. Apparently, however, the Highway Commission did not keep a record of specific findings made. Since the ruling in this case, the Virginia statute was amended (1934) to accord the railway companies a hearing before the state Corporation Commission. See *Virginia Code,* 3974a.

the determination. The Virginia court held that this particular question was not judicial but was one which could best be decided by the commission. The Southern Railway Company challenged the statute as falling short of due process by failing to provide for judicial review and determination of the initial issue of the public need.

In 1933, when the case reached the Supreme Court, Justice McReynolds was not favorably inclined toward such a procedure as that provided for by the Virginia law. He assumed that the commission might disregard "all the rules of evidence" and could "capriciously" make findings by "administrative fiat." [202] Such a *possibility* was thought to be incompatible with "rational justice" and to fall under the constitutional ban of "all arbitrary exercise of power." [203] But the state courts had interpreted the statute as permitting judicial review of the original question if "arbitrary" action could be shown.[204] This was not enough to meet the due process requirements as read by the members of the Supreme Court. Presumably, Justice McReynolds thought that the railroad company should be allowed to have a court make the original determination, even though such a tribunal could not have based a reasonable decision upon a kind of evidence different from that before the Highway Commission.[205] Nonetheless, with all the talk about procedures, obviously Justice McReynolds was more concerned with the substance of the order than with the procedure followed.

Though Justice McReynolds would admit that the state could protect the public against "imminent danger," he did not believe

[202] 290 U.S. 190, 195 (1933). See Chief Justice Hughes's comments to the American Law Institute, *Proceedings* (1938), 23.

[203] 290 U.S. 190, 195 (1933). By 1948 *possibility* of injury was no longer basis for complaint under the due process clauses except in cases involving civil liberties, especially those named in the First Amendment.

[204] In Southern Railway Co. *v.* Commonwealth of Virginia, 159 Va. 779, 167 S.E. 578 (1933); and *ibid.*, 124 Va. 36, 97 S.E. 343 (1918), the Virginia Supreme Court had held "If such action is arbitrary, control is vested on the courts." See E. E. Olson, "Due Process—Notice, Hearing, and Review," *Southern California Law Review*, VIII (1935), 330.

[205] 290 U.S. 190, 197-98 (1933). By 1938, the Court had come to hold that evidence which "a reasonable mind might accept as adequate" would meet due process standards. Consolidated Edison Co. of New York *v.* National Labor Relations Board, 305 U.S. 197, 229.

that such danger existed. His reason—the statute itself contemplated a sixty-day delay, during which time the railroad might seek to have the proposed plans modified.[206]

Chief Justice Hughes and Justices Cardozo and Stone dissented on the ground that this was a lawful delegation of power to the commission and that the power to determine the requirements of safety might be exercised without notice and hearing.[207]

In the Lindheimer case [208] quite a different attitude is evidenced. In that case it was "enough that the rates have been established by competent authority and their invalidity has not been satisfactorily proved." [209] And in Illinois Commerce Commission v. United States [210] the Court held that the question of whether the cost study was adequate and dependable evidence of the reasonableness of the rates was one for the commission to decide.[211] The Court examined the "abundance" of the evidence and found adequate support for the commission's conclusions. Determination must be grounded in facts which appear as evidence, however. In the "Hot Oil" case the president's orders were said to be invalid because they were not accompanied by supporting findings of fact.[212] In some instances the commission may be required to incorporate into its report the sources of its information.[213]

But in Nashville, C. & St. L. Ry. Co. v. Walters,[214] Justice Brandeis found the commission's order arbitrary and violative of due process, not because the state lacked power to afford the protection it sought to offer the public, but because the railroad, which would be required to pay for the underpass, would not benefit from it. The highways that would be constructed would

---

[206] 290 U.S. 190, 197 (1933).   [207] Ibid., p. 199.

[208] Lindheimer v. Illinois Bell Telephone Co., 292 U.S. 151 (1934).

[209] Ibid., p. 175. "It is not the function of the Court to attempt to construct out of this voluminous record independent calculations to invalidate the challenged rates."

[210] 292 U.S. 474 (1934).

[211] Ibid., p. 481. "There is no basis," held Justice Stone, "upon which the courts, not authorized to weigh the evidence could reexamine or disregard its conclusions."

[212] Panama Refining Co. v. Ryan, 293 U.S. 388 (1935). When the determinations are reached by the legislature, findings are not essential. See Pacific States Box and Basket Co. v. White, 296 U.S. 176 (1935).

[213] West Ohio Gas Co. v. Public Utilities Commission, 294 U.S. 63, 69 (1935).

[214] 294 U.S. 405 (1935).

not feed the railways but would offer competition for them.[215] Justice Brandeis called attention to the effect of federal aid for highway building, upon the revenues of the railroads. Not only would the improvement sought here reduce the amount of rail freight and passenger traffic but it would also compel the railroads to reduce their rates in order to compete favorably with new kinds of transportation.[216] In addition the Court considered the fact that the railroads were already paying a disproportionately large share of the taxes of Tennessee.[217] Said Justice Brandeis: "When the police power of the state is exercised for a valid purpose but in such a way as to single out one group to pay the cost, the imposition must bear a reasonable relation to the evil to be eradicated or the advantages to be secured." [218] He did not find such relation in this instance. Here there was no complaint concerning the procedure followed by the Highway Commission. Nor were the findings upon which the order was based attacked. Rather the substance of the order was found to be arbitrary under the peculiar circumstances of the case. Apparently this was not the kind of question to be affected by the competence or expertness of the person who answered it.

Three divergent views of the status to be accorded administrative findings were put in focus in United Gas Public Service Co. v. Texas.[219] Here Chief Justice Hughes could see no reason for nullifying rates fixed by the commission, for evidence had been received and weighed, the amounts of revenue and expenses considered appeared on the record, and judicial review was granted.[220] Justice Black, concurring, was of the opinion that the state proceedings were valid, for they had been conducted in accordance with regular court procedures fixed by state law applicable to such cases.[221] Under these circumstances he did not

---

[215] Ibid., pp. 424–26. The police power of the state, it was held, may not be exercised unreasonably. Ibid., p. 415.

[216] Ibid., p. 426.   [217] Ibid., p. 428.

[218] Ibid., p. 429. Justices Stone and Cardozo dissented. They did not think a consideration of the special facts led to the conclusion that the action had been arbitrary. In St. Joseph Stock Yards Co. v. United States, 298 U.S. 38, 83 (1936), Justice Brandeis apparently thought that the test of validity was the existence of evidence upon which a reasonable man might base a similar conclusion.

[219] 303 U.S. 123 (1938).   [220] Ibid., p. 138.

[221] Ibid., p. 153. The facts had been submitted to a jury as the constitution and laws of Texas required.

think that any "proper interpretation of due process" would justify an invalidation of the order. On the other hand, Justice Butler dissented; for he was of the opinion that when rates are fixed by an administrative agency, the Constitution guarantees "that a fair opportunity will be afforded for submitting the controversy to a judicial tribunal for determination upon its own independent judgment both as to the law and the facts." [222] Under such a ruling it would seem useless for the state to go to the expense of supporting a commission to determine rates. Surely even Justice Butler would not have wished to saddle the Supreme Court with this duty.

When the Texas proration order limiting the allowable production of sweet gas by pipeline owners came before the Court, it was condemned by Justice Brandeis as an arbitrary taking of one person's property for the benefit of another in violation of due process.[223] He considered it the Court's duty to make an independent study of the Texas situation and the application of the order to producers of sweet gas. He found that the effect of the order was to limit the allowable production for pipeline owners to furnish a market for producers who did not own pipeline facilities. On the basis of this finding, he held the order unconstitutional as a deprivation of property without due process. In 1937, then, it was obvious that the Court had not forgotten its "duty" to protect the owner from arbitrary deprivation of his property.

Three years later the second of the Texas oil series was before the Court.[224] Justice Frankfurter embodied in the Court's opinion a statement of an almost complete change of attitude toward the "expert" administrative agencies. True, new members had been added to the Court [225] since the previous Texas oil case, and the plight of the oil producers had not been alleviated to any

[222] *Ibid.*, p. 154.
[223] Thompson v. Consolidated Gas Utilities Corporation, 300 U.S. 55 (1937). This decision is one of the last based on the "old line" due process interpretation.
[224] Railroad Commission of Texas v. Rowan & Nichols Oil Co., 310 U.S. 573 (1940). Meanwhile, the Court indicated a more trusting attitude toward the work of such administrative agencies in Patterson v. Stanolind Oil and Gas Co., 305 U.S. 376 (1939), in which it upheld the Oklahoma Well-spacing Act of 1933.
[225] Between June of 1937 and June of 1940 Justices Van Devanter, Sutherland, Cardozo, Brandeis, and Butler left the Court; and Hugo Black, Stanley Reed, Felix Frankfurter, William O. Douglas, and Frank Murphy were appointed to the Court.

great extent. One may reasonably assume that the Court recognized that oil production also was a matter for the application of "whatever knowledge economics and finance may bring to the practicalities" of the oil business.[226] The issue involved was the validity of the oil-proration order promulgated by the Texas Railroad Commission.

Justice Frankfurter considered the difficulty of finding a solution to the problem involved. The state commission had experimented for some years, trying to find a formula which would prescribe a fair allotment of the allowable production. The fact that many such experiments had been successfully challenged before the courts only indicated to him an "evolution of adjustment" of private and public interests. The commission, he thought, should guide this evolutionary process without interference from the federal courts. ". . . courts must not substitute their notions of expediency and fairness for those which have guided the agencies to whom the formulation and execution of policy have been entrusted." In his judgment the District Court and the Circuit Court of Appeals had done just that. He was willing to admit that the lower court might have presented a fairer and wiser program. In spite of this, however, "whether a system of proration based on an hourly potential is as fair as one based on estimated recoverable reserves or some other factor . . . is in itself a question for administrative and not judicial judgment."[227] Regulation in this field required judgment inevitably "beset by the necessity of inferences bordering on conjecture. . . ." Therefore, it would be "presumptuous" for the courts "on the basis of conflicting expert testimony to deem the view of the administrative tribunal, acting under legislative authority, offensive to the Fourteenth Amendment."[228] The state chose to use the commission because it believed that body of ex-

[226] See Driscoll v. Edison Light and Power Co., 307 U.S. 104, 122 (1939).

[227] 310 U.S. 573, 581 (1940). But this is not to be taken as an expression of faith in all administrative agencies or their actions. In 1947, Justice Frankfurter admitted that administrative experts "no doubt have antennae not possessed by courts. . . ." But also, "Courts charged as they are with the review of the action of the Commission, ought not to be asked to sustain such a mathematical coincidence as a matter of unillumined faith in the conclusion of experts." New York v. United States, 331 U.S. 284, 357 (1947).

[228] 310 U.S. 573, 582–83 (1940). Cf. S.C. State Highway Dept. v. Barnwell, 302 U.S. 177, 191–92 (1938), where Justice Stone held the determination as to weight and width of trucks for safety was matter for legislative determination.

perts to be competent. "It is not for federal courts to supplant the Commission's judgment even in the face of convincing proof that a different result would have been better." [229]

A year later Justice Frankfurter rendered the opinion of the Court in a second case involving the same company and a second order of the commission.[230] It was recognized that:

> The accommodation of conflicting private interests in the East Texas oil fields, with due regard to the public welfare, is beset with perplexities, both geological and economic.
>
> .   .   .   .
>
> Nothing in the constitution warrants a rejection of these expert conclusions. Nor, on the basis of intrinsic skills and equipment, are federal courts qualified to set their independent judgment on such matters against that of the chosen state authorities. . . . Presumably that body [the state legislature], as the permanent representative of the state's regulatory relation to the oil industry equipped to deal with its ever-changing aspects, possesses an insight and aptitude which can hardly be matched by judges who are called upon to intervene at fitful intervals.[231]

At last the administrative experts were to come into their own—their competency in given fields to be recognized. Once again the Court is willing to accept a division of competencies—courts and judges in their proper places and economic experts in other equally proper places. Continued Justice Frankfurter: "The Due Process Clause does not require the feel of the expert to be supplanted by an independent view of judges on the conflicting testimony and prophecies and impressions of expert witnesses." [232] Responsibility for the proper functioning of the commission was placed on the shoulders of the people through their

[229] 310 U.S. 573, 584 (1940). Justice Roberts dissented on the ground that the Court announced principles directly opposed to those previously established with regard to judicial review of administrative action. He thought Justice Brandeis had stated the correct principles in the Thompson case.

[230] Railroad Commission of Texas v. Rowan & Nichols Oil Co., 311 U.S. 570 (1941).

[231] Ibid., p. 575.

[232] Ibid., p. 576. See Justice Rutledge's statement concerning the "informed judgment" of the Interstate Commerce Commission over subjects "within its special competence." United States v. Jones, 336 U.S. 641, 665 (1949).

representative government. Here again is seen the relatively greater deference to be shown to elected legislative bodies in their choice of policy-making agents. Could it be that Justice Frankfurter believes that by such a shifting of responsibility he can force the states and the people into a greater consciousness of political processes?

In 1945 the Court went on record as being even more favorable to administrative commissions and boards. Justice Jackson, speaking for a unanimous Court,[233] declared that a commission "so experienced" with the affairs of the particular company involved as the Railway Commission "is entitled to draw inferences as to the probable effect on traffic of a given rate decrease" and to evaluate previous experience "without the aid of an expert." [234] Said Justice Jackson: "The process of keeping informed as to regulated utilities is a continuous matter with these commissions." [235] The Court was willing to accept the judgment of the commission as meeting all the requirements of due process.

On this assumption, boards and commissions find themselves vested with a great amount of discretionary authority which, by practice, is not reviewable by the Court. Justice Frankfurter has declared that "courts are not charged with general guardianship against all potential mischief" in the task of government.[236] In 1948, Justice Black accepted without question the findings of the Interstate Commerce Commisison to support an order commanding the railroad to carry products to Swift Company's meat-packing house, even over a track owned by the stockyard, regardless of the expense to the carrier.[237]

Findings Involving Civil Liberties. Just as the majority of the Court has been adamant in its position that the fundamental rights

---

[233] Market St. Railway Co. *v.* Railroad Commission of California, 324 U.S. 548 (1945).

[234] *Ibid.,* pp. 560–61.

[235] *Ibid.,* p. 562. In 1944, Justice Jackson had said that if the Court intended to take the commission's word of the reasonableness of the order, there was no need for judicial review at all. Federal Power Commission *v.* Hope Natural Gas Co., 320 U.S. 591 (1944).

[236] Federal Communications Commission *v.* Pottsville Broadcasting Co., 309 U.S. 134, 146 (1940).

[237] United States *v.* B. & O. Ry. Co., 333 U.S. 169 (1948). Justice Burton dissented in this case.

protected by the First and Fourteenth amendments were withdrawn from the decision of the ballot, so it has held fast to the
rule that these rights cannot be placed at the mercy of administrative officers. Only judges, apparently, possess that close affinity
with the "higher law of justice" which would fit a government
agent to determine when and under what circumstances such
rights may be restricted. This issue was before the Court in
Lovell v. Griffin,[238] which involved a city ordinance requiring
a permit to distribute handbills, circulars, and the like. The permit
could be obtained from the city manager, and the ordinance did
not indicate that he would have any discretionary authority over
the issuance of it. Plaintiff, in this instance, was arrested for
violating the ordinance. She challenged the constitutionality of
the requirement, though she had not sought a permit and could
not point to any specific injury arising from the ordinance. Chief
Justice Hughes, speaking for eight members of the Court,[239]
declared that legislation of this kind would "restore the system
of license and censorship in its baldest form." [240] An administrative officer could not be allowed to grant or withhold a permit
to distribute literature, for that right was guaranteed by the
national Constitution. The Chief Justice recalled that freedom
of the press became "a right to publish *without* a license what
formerly could be published only *with* one." [241]

The Court did not look into the record to see if the city
manager had refused to grant a permit to any applicant. The
assumption seems to have been that he would.[242] Again in
Schneider v. State, 1939,[243] Justice Roberts passed judgment on
the Irvington ordinance which required a license for door-to-
door canvassing. The administrative officer, in this instance, was
authorized to hear evidence of the good character of the applicant and to determine whether or not the literature might be

---

[238] 303 U.S. 444 (1938).   [239] Justice Cardozo took no part.
[240] 303 U.S. 444, 452 (1938).   [241] *Ibid.*, p. 451.
[242] 55 Ga. App. 609, 191 S.E. 152 (1937). The state court's opinion here is too
brief to indicate the issues or any facts as to actual operation of the ordinance.
In Coleman v. Griffin, 55 Ga. App. 123, 189 S.E. 427 (1936), the Court of Appeals for Georgia held that the complaint of unconstitutionality under due
process was too vague to stand.
[243] 308 U.S. 147 (1939).

distributed. Justice Roberts felt that such a provision struck at the very heart of the constitutional guarantee.[244] The city could not constitutionally enforce such a rule. "Conceding that fraudulent solicitations may be made in the name of charity and religion, we hold that a municipality cannot, for this reason, require all who wish to disseminate their ideas to present them first to police authorities for their consideration and approval, with a discretion in the police to say that some ideas may, while others may not, be carried to the homes of citizens." [245]

A more far-reaching discretionary authority was held in violation of due process in the case of Cantwell v. Connecticut,[246] in which the plaintiff challenged the validity of an ordinance authorizing the Secretary of the Public Welfare Council to grant licenses for solicitations. Before a permit could be issued, the secretary would determine the nature of the cause for which the solicitations were to be made and would grant the license only if he found it to be a bona fide religious cause or object of charity. He could revoke the license at any time. Justice Roberts declared that such "censorship of religion as the means of determining its right to survive" denies the freedom "guaranteed by the First and Fourteenth Amendments." [247] The ordinance was defended on the ground that if the administrative officer should abuse his discretionary authority, his action could be reviewed by the courts. But, held Justice Roberts, ". . . the availability of a judicial remedy for abuses in the system of licensing still leaves that system one of previous restraint upon the exercise of guaranteed freedom. A statute authorizing previous restraint upon the exercise of guaranteed freedom by judicial decision after trial is as obnoxious to the Constitution as one providing for like restraint by administrative action." [248] On the other hand, the state may by statute require one to obtain from the selectmen of the town or a licensing committee a permit to have a parade or procession in the public streets. A municipality must have the authority to "give consideration without unfair discrimination as to time,

[244] Ibid., p. 164.
[245] Ibid.
[246] 310 U.S. 296 (1940).
[247] Ibid., p. 304.
[248] Ibid., pp. 305–306. Cf. the explanation in Bourjois, Inc. v. Chapman, 301 U.S. 183, 189 (1937).

place or manner in relation to other proper uses of the street." [249]
Also, the state may impose a fee ranging from $200 to a nominal
amount. The fee, it was said, was not a revenue tax but one to
meet the expense of administering the statute.[250] The statute
could validly be applied to one using streets for religious processions. This decision was based on a recognition of the necessity
of regulating mass use of public thoroughfares and of knowing
when and in what manner the streets would be put into use for
parades and processions. It cannot be construed to mean that the
Court was becoming less ardent in its protection of the freedoms
guaranteed by the First and Fourteenth amendments. In Largent
v. Texas [251] the Court was again called upon to review an ordinance which required persons wishing to solicit orders for books,
wares, or merchandise to obtain a permit from the mayor. The
mayor was authorized to issue a permit when "after investigation
he deems it proper or advisable." Justice Reed, speaking for the
Court, did not find it necessary to determine whether distribution
of the publications by Jehovah's Witnesses constituted sales or
contributions. Under the ordinance in question "Dissemination
of ideas depends upon the approval of the distributor by the official." "This," said Justice Reed, "is administrative censorship in
an extreme form." [252]

In cases involving property rights the defects of the findings
of the commission or board may be corrected by provision for
judicial review. This is not true in cases where administrative
officers exercise authority in the field of civil liberties. "Judicial
review" will not save a statute which permits such official to
make findings on the basis of which fundamental civil liberties
may be exercised or restricted.

ADMINISTRATIVE AGENTS—INSTRUMENTS OF GOVERNMENT

The years between 1932 and 1948 have witnessed rapid and
significant changes in the development of constitutional law pertaining to the use of administrative agencies. In the field of rate

---

[249] Cox v. New Hampshire, 312 U.S. 569, 576 (1941). Chief Justice Hughes
spoke for the Court.

[250] Ibid., pp. 576–77.   [251] 318 U.S. 418 (1943).

[252] Ibid., p. 422.

regulation previous interpretations of due process of law which required a fair return on a fair value have been abandoned. Prior to 1933 due process had been used to prohibit a rate-making agency from determining a rate except by reference to the cost less depreciation or reproduction cost or some other standard compatible with the Court's attitudes toward the regulation. In that year the Court upheld a rate base arrived at by consideration of prudent investment.[253] This decision was affirmed in the Lindheimer case of 1934.[254] By 1935 a rate base equal to prudent investment seems to have been the order of the day. Prudent investment, in addition to expenditures for the improvement of current facilities, was said to include money spent in the procurement of new business as well.[255] The real test of a change had to come, however, when the Court was faced with a rate base which had not been determined on the basis of the old reproduction-cost standard nor on the newly accepted prudent-investment rule. Within a few terms of Court it became evident that change was in process. Consideration of shifts in price levels, which was prohibited by due process of law in 1935,[256] was required by the same clause in 1938.[257] In the latter year five members of the Court announced that confiscation must be proved before the rate order would be set aside. Apparently they meant that the factors considered in arriving at the rate base were no longer of prime importance. The Constitution no longer imposed any particular valuation formula upon the rate-making authority.[258] Meantime the Court had affirmed its authority to review both facts and law in determining whether the findings of the legislatures or legislative agents support the results.[259] The Chief Justice did not say that due process of law required the Court to make such an independent judgment on either facts or law. It

---

[253] Los Angeles Gas and Electric Corp. v. Railroad Commission, 289 U.S. 287 (1933).

[254] Lindheimer v. Illinois Bell Telephone Co., 292 U.S. 151 (1934).

[255] West Ohio Gas Co. v. Public Utilities Commission, 294 U.S. 79 (1935).

[256] West v. Chesapeake and Potomac Telephone Co., 295 U.S. 662 (1935).

[257] McCart v. Indianapolis Water Co., 302 U.S. 419 (1938). In dissent Justice Black insisted that if the rates were not so low as to confiscate the property, the work of the Court was at an end.

[258] United Gas Public Service Co. v. Texas, 303 U.S. 123 (1938). This had been the opinion of Justices Stone, Cardozo, and Brandeis in previous cases.

[259] St. Joseph Stock Yards Co. v. United States, 298 U.S. 38 (1936).

only permitted it to do so. By 1942 when the Natural Gas Pipe-line Company challenged a reduction of its rates, several changes had occurred in the personnel of the Court. Justices Black, Reed, Frankfurter, Douglas, Murphy, and Jackson had taken their places on the Court. Justice Stone, who had by now become Chief Justice Stone, wrote that the due process of law clause required only that the rate order be not arbitrary in its result.[260] He reluctantly failed to apply Smyth v. Ames standards but did cite decisions stemming from that case as authority for his conclusions in the present instance. Three justices—Black, Douglas, and Murphy—found this the time to declare open opposition to the Smyth rule. Justice Frankfurter, on the other hand, based the Court's power on the statute which be believed imposed the duty of review upon the Court. He also seems to have revitalized the ghost of Smyth v. Ames, just laid by his colleagues.

Two years later, with the decision in Federal Power Commission v. Hope Natural Gas Co.,[261] Justice Douglas disregarded the rule of Smyth v. Ames. It is safe to say that the present Court does not hold that the due process of law clause requires such a standard of state or of federal rate-making authorities. "Rates," it was said, "cannot be based on fair value when value depends upon rates." Rate making is just another species of price fixing and is to be guided by the same rules. But this opinion was not subscribed to by all of the justices. Justice Reed felt that so long as Congress did not change the statute which said that rates should be reasonable and that review should be available, the Court was obligated to review the order in the light of the traditional standards of "reasonable." In his opinion this meant a fair return on a fair value as determined by consideration of the usual factors. Justice Frankfurter seems stubbornly to hold to Smyth v. Ames in spite of his opposition to that rule in previous cases. Justice Jackson, agreeing that this is price fixing and should be treated as such, said further that the price should perform a social function. He seems to say that the Court should decide what is needed in the way of a natural-gas industry and make the price of gas accordingly.

What, then, does the due process of law clause require of a

---

[260] Federal Power Commission v. Natural Gas Pipeline Co., 315 U.S. 575 (1942).
[261] 320 U.S. 591 (1944).

rate-making agency? The agency must afford a fair hearing, but this does not imply any particular procedure. An oral argument, report, complete record, among other things, may be good practice, but none of them are demanded as a matter of due process of law. No longer does due process prohibit the reduction of rates below the point where they will yield a fair return on a fair value of the property. Eminent domain and rate regulation are no longer comparable. The owner of an industry whose rates are regulated need not be placed in a position as good pecuniarily as before the regulation. Rate fixing, like price fixing, falls within the police power of the state and therefore can be used in the public interest.

Administrative agents have been accorded a status of respect and competence so far as their activities touch property rights only. In 1940, Justice Frankfurter, for the Court, declared that "courts must not substitute their notions of expedience and fairness" for those of the experts entrusted with the power to formulate and execute policy. Here the Court was speaking of an agency authorized to regulate production in the East Texas oil fields. But an administrative agent, whether he be an appointed city manager, an elected mayor, a law-enforcement officer, or an employee or the secretary of the town's public welfare council, is forbidden by the due process of law clause to wield discretionary power over the exercise of those freedoms named in the First Amendment and incorporated into the Fourteenth. Not even the possibility of judicial review will remedy the evil seen to lurk in such a situation.

It is quite obvious that talk of the Court's abdication in the field of administrative activities, whether those activities deal with property or personal rights, is not supported by the facts. The Court has announced a policy of co-operation with these agencies except where civil liberties are concerned. Whereas in 1941, Chief Justice Stone explained that "court and agency are not to be regarded as wholly independent and unrelated instrumentalities of justice," in 1942, Justice Frankfurter warned the Federal Communications Commission that "Courts no less than administrative bodies are agencies of government." [262]

[262] Scripps-Howard Radio v. Federal Communications Commission, 316 U.S. 4, 15 (1942).

V

The Tax Power

As the services of government have been extended, the states have been faced with the problem of tapping new sources of revenue with which to defray the additional expenses. It has been the general rule that the state may tax all nonfederal property within its bounds. That is, the state is said to have "jurisdiction" to tax property situated within the borders of the state. If it levies a tax on property not within its jurisdiction, it is said to deprive the owner of property without due process of law in violation of the Fourteenth Amendment.

But a determination of the absence or presence of jurisdiction is not a simple one. As business enterprises came more and more to be matters of financial arrangements spreading over several states and as much of the economy of the nation involved intangibles which could not be tied to a specific place or business, the necessity for a more adequate definition of "jurisdiction" took on greater proportions. What if the economic interests of an individual involved several states? Does the state's power to tax attach to the owner of the interests, to the person who may receive some benefit from them, to the economic interest itself, or to each of these? In other words, could more than one state have jurisdiction to tax economic interests stemming from a single business undertaking or arrangement?

There have been members of the Supreme Court who thought that "double taxation," that is, the imposition of a tax on the same economic interest by two or more states, in itself deprived the owner of his property without due process of law. Therefore, we find, at times, the rule that only one state may have jurisdiction—the constitutional right—to tax a single economic interest. In this respect, jurisdiction is thought of as a juridical concept rather than a territorial limitation.

To help solve the problem arising from the situation in which an economic interest involves several states and the seeming necessity for determining the power to tax by the location of the thing taxed, a notion of "situs" was given prominence. By "situs" is meant the location of a subject for purposes of conferring jurisdiction to tax.

Prior to 1929, it appeared to be a settled doctrine of the Supreme Court that "due process of law" of the Fourteenth Amendment did not prohibit double taxation of intangibles.[1] But in the case of Safe Deposit and Trust Co. v. Virginia,[2] in 1929, the Court departed from its former rulings that double taxation did not per se violate due process. Virginia was denied the right to levy a property tax on the value of income from a trust consisting of stocks and bonds deposited in Maryland but providing for the accumulation of the income to be paid to the settler's two sons, residents of Virginia, when they reached the age of twenty-five. Double taxation was declared officially to be undesirable and contrary to the concept of due process of law embodied in the Fourteenth Amendment.[3] A few months later, in Farmers' Loan and Trust Co. v. Minnesota, Justice McReynolds, for the Court, declared that Blackstone v. Miller could no longer be considered a "correct exposition of existing law."[4] Intangibles were said

---

[1] Blackstone v. Miller, 188 U.S. 189, 202 (1903); Kidd v. Alabama, 188 U.S. 730, 732 (1903); Ft. Smith Lumber Co. v. Arkansas, 251 U.S. 532, 533 (1919); Cream of Wheat v. Grand Forks, 253 U.S. 325, 330 (1920); Baker v. Druesdow, 263 U.S. 137, 140–41 (1923). Of the doctrine embodied in these cases, it has been said: "The doctrine that the Fourteenth Amendment did not forbid multiple taxation of intangibles was no febrile growth rooted in the careless dicta of a few judges; it was the considered judgment of a number of painstaking decisions—a cardinal principle of the jurisdiction to tax." Charles L. B. Lowndes, "The Passing of Situs—Jurisdiction to Tax Shares of Corporate Stock," *Harvard Law Review*, LXV (1932), 777, 780.

[2] 280 U.S. 83 (1929).

[3] *Ibid.*, p. 93. Here Justice McReynolds said: "It would be unfortunate, perhaps amazing, if a legal fiction originally invented to prevent personalty from escaping just taxation, should compel us to accept the irrational view that the same securities were within two states at the same instant, and because of this to uphold a double and oppressive assessment."

[4] 280 U.S. 204, 209 (1930). For a comprehensive study of the theories of taxation during this period, see Arthur L. Harding, *Double Taxation of Property and Incomes* (Cambridge, Mass., 1933).

to be taxable at the domicile of the owner, and Justice McReynolds could find no good reason for saying that "they are not entitled to enjoy an immunity against taxation at more than one place similar to that accorded to tangibles." [5] Justice Holmes dissented, for he thought that Minnesota should have been allowed to levy its tax, since the party needed the help of that state to acquire a right. This was a benefit conferred by Minnesota in return for which that state had a right to exact a tax. Said Justice Holmes: ". . . a good deal has to be read into the Fourteenth Amendment to give it any bearing in this case. The Amendment does not condemn everything that we may think undesirable on economic or social grounds." [6]

But the Court was confronted with the question of which state would have jurisdiction to tax if the property had acquired a business situs elsewhere than the domicile of the owner. By 1932 it had solved that question "in respect to intangibles" by applying the maxim *mobilia sequuntur personam*.[7] Jurisdiction was not to be interpreted as coextensive with the territorial bounds of the state nor was it thought to be concomitant with benefits conferred. Regardless of whether jurisdiction in the usual sense existed, the power to tax was to be restricted by what the majority of the Court thought to be a desirable policy. "Practical considerations of wisdom, convenience, and justice" pointed to the necessity of a uniform rule confining the im-

[5] 280 U.S. 204, 212 (1930). However, the Court alluded to an exception to the rule. It was said that choses in action might acquire a situs for taxation other than that of the domicile of the owner if they became an integral part of some local business elsewhere. Business situs as conferring exclusive jurisdiction to tax intangibles was not before the Court.

[6] *Ibid.*, p. 218.

[7] First National Bank of Boston *v.* Maine, 284 U.S. 312, 328 (1932). The Court concluded that "shares of stock like other intangibles constitutionally can be subjected to a death transfer tax by one state only."

For a comprehensive study of the principles applied by the Court prior to the 1932-33 term, see Harding, *Double Taxation of Property and Incomes, passim*; Henry Rottschaefer, "Power of the State to Tax Intangibles," *Minnesota Law Review*, XV (1931), 741-66; Charles G. Haglund, "Double Taxation," *Southern California Law Review*, VIII (1935), 79-113; W. Wickersham, "Double Taxation," *Virginia Law Review*, XII (1926), 185-202; Forney Nowlin, "Jurisdictional Features of State Taxation—Property and Inheritance Taxes," *Texas Law Review*, IX (1931), 352-64; Charles L. B. Lowndes, "Bases of Jurisdiction for the Purpose of Imposing Inheritance Taxes," *Michigan Law Review*, XXIX (1931), 850-93; and David R. Mason, "Jurisdiction for the Purpose of Imposing Inheritance Taxes," *ibid.*, pp. 324-38.

position of death-transfer taxes on intangibles to the state of domicile.[8] Among the dissenters from such rulings were Justices Stone and Holmes. Justice Stone held that "control and benefit" together comprise the "ultimate and indubitable justification for all taxation."[9] Justice Holmes declared: "I have not yet adequately expressed the more than anxiety that I feel at the ever increasing scope given to the Fourteenth Amendment in cutting down what I believe to be the constitutional rights of the States. As the decisions now stand, I can hardly see any limit but the sky to the invalidating of these rights if they happen to strike a majority of this Court as for any reason undesirable. I cannot believe that the Amendment was intended to give us *carte blanche* to embody our economic or moral beliefs in its prohibitions."[10]

To indicate what principles the Court has followed in applying "due process" to the question of state jurisdiction to tax, its opinions will be considered according to the type of tax involved.

Income Taxes. The first departure from the recently adopted doctrine that the due process clause of the Fourteenth Amendment prohibited the imposition of more than one tax on a single

[8] First National Bank of Boston v. Maine, 284 U.S. 312, 327 (1932). Justice Sutherland said: "A transfer from the dead to the living of any specific property is an event single in character, and is effected under the laws, and occurs within the limits, of a particular state; and it is unreasonable and incompatible with sound construction of the due process of law clause of the Fourteenth Amendment, to hold that jurisdiction to tax that event may be distributed among a number of states."

[9] *Ibid.*, p. 334. Justice Stone went further, saying: "but as the stockholder could secure complete protection and effect a complete transfer of his interest only by invoking the laws of both states, I know of no principle of constitutional interpretation which would enable us to say that taxation by both states, reaching the same economic interest with respect to which he has sought and secured benefits of the laws of both, is so arbitrary or oppressive as to merit condemnation as a denial of due process of law." *Ibid.*, p. 333.

[10] Baldwin v. Missouri, 281 U.S. 586, 595 (1930). In commenting upon this decision to a friend, Justice Holmes said that it was too late to prevent the extension of due process to an artificial meaning, "but the Court has gone farther than I can possibly believe to be warranted on the question of the right of the State to tax." Howe (ed.), *Holmes-Pollock Letters*, II, 267. Justice Stone concurred with the majority in this case but stated: ". . . that one must pay a tax in two places, reaching the same economic interests, with respect to which he has sought and secured the benefits of the laws of both, does not seem to me so oppressive or arbitrary as to infringe constitutional limitations." 281 U.S. 586, 597 (1930).

subject is seen in the Court's decision in Lawrence *v.* Mississippi,[11] handed down just before the close of the 1931–32 term. A resident of Mississippi brought suit to have set aside the assessment of a tax on that part of his income derived from work in Tennessee. The tax was challenged on the ground that by imposing it on income earned outside the state, Mississippi had deprived him of property without due process of law. Justice Stone wrote the Court's opinion, in which he held that "Enjoyment of the privileges of residence within the state and the attendant right to invoke the protection of its laws" were inseparable from the responsibility of sharing the costs of government. On the other hand, he said that the obligation to pay taxes to one's domiciliary state arose "from the unilateral action of the state government in the exercise of the most plenary of sovereign powers, that to raise revenue to defray the expenses of the government and to distribute its burden equally among those who enjoy its benefits." [12] He found it sufficient to satisfy due process requirements that the state levied the tax upon one of its own citizens with reference to the receipt and enjoyment of income, regardless of the place where the income was earned.[13]

Two years later the Court confirmed the doctrine that the state had jurisdiction to tax nonresidents on the basis of income earned within the state, thus in effect permitting double taxation of incomes.[14] The Court held valid a Virginia tax imposed on the net income of the Imperial Coal Company, though the business was evidenced in Virginia only by intangibles. Chief Justice Hughes found that the property had acquired a business situs in the state and was taxable there. The opinion in this case, as well as that in Lawrence *v.* Mississippi, must be read in the light of the fact that in neither instance was there actually double taxation,[15] for in neither case did the second state have a tax law to

---

[11] 286 U.S. 276 (1932). Francis C. Nash, "Maguire v. Trefry Reclaimed: A New Approach to an Old Problem," *Georgetown Law Journal,* XXVII (1938), 281, 296, sees this decision as the beginning of the change from the prohibition against double taxation of all kinds. Cf. Chief Justice Hughes's statement in Burnet *v.* Brooks, 288 U.S. 378, 401 (1933).

[12] 286 U.S. 276, 279 (1932).   [13] *Ibid.,* pp. 280–81.

[14] Virginia *v.* Imperial Coal Co., 293 U.S. 15 (1934).

[15] Arthur L. Harding, "State Jurisdiction to Tax Income from Foreign Land," *California Law Review,* XXV (1937), 444–50.

reach the income here taxed. When, however, Ohio purported to levy a tax equal to 5 per cent of the income received from beneficial interests in parcels of land, some located in Ohio and some in other states, the Court held that the certificates evidencing a beneficial interest in the land held in trust in another state were in reality not choses in action but interests in the land itself, and as such they were not taxable except where the land was located.[16]

Said Justice Stone, dissenting: "When new and different legal interests, however named, are created with respect to land or a chattel, of such character that they do enjoy benefits of the laws of another state and are brought within the reach of its taxing power, I know of no articulate principle of law or of the Fourteenth Amendment which would deny the state the right to tax them." [17]

Here the Court either attempted to ban double taxation in the field of income taxes [18] or it merely confused the nature of the thing upon which the state sought to levy the tax.[19] Perhaps the more plausible conclusion is that the Court, speaking through Justice McReynolds, did both of these. Justice McReynolds did not recognize this as a tax on income. The case at bar was distinguished from Maguire v. Trefry [20] on the ground that in the latter case the Massachusetts statute undertook to tax incomes.[21] On the other hand, Justice McReynolds pointed out that the opinion relied upon by the state was based on Blackstone v. Mil-

---

[16] Senior v. Braden, 295 U.S. 422, 432 (1935).

[17] Ibid., p. 435. Justice Stone was of the opinion that the doubt which existed as to the obligation to pay the tax rested on no more substantial foundation than a lack of jurisdiction to tax and the "assertion that the Fourteenth Amendment is endowed with a newly discovered efficacy to forbid double taxation when the sovereignty imposing the tax is that of two or more states." See Walter Tuller, A Treatise on the Taxing Power with Particular Application to the State Income Tax (Chicago, 1937), pp. 297–300.

[18] Turner H. McBaine, in a comment on this case in California Law Review, XXIV (1936), 200, interprets the opinion as representing the greatest extension of the "no double taxation" doctrine. See Walter Land, Trusts in the Conflicts of Laws (New York, 1940), Chap. XII; and Walter Nossaman, "State Taxation of Incomes," California Law Review, XXIV (1942), 525–44.

[19] See Robert C. Brown, "The Present Status of Multiple Taxation of Intangible Property," Michigan Law Review, XL (1942), 806, 811.

[20] 253 U.S. 12 (1920). In this case the Court held that income from a trust outside the state was taxable by the domiciliary state.

[21] Senior v. Braden, 295 U.S. 422, 431 (1935).

ler,[22] which was not in harmony with the views "now accepted here in respect to double taxation." [23]

Two years later virtually the same issue arose in Cohn v. Graves,[24] which involved the validity of a New York income-tax law according to which rents and interests derived from lands situated in New Jersey were included in the computation of taxable income. Justice Stone, for the majority, held that "income derived from real estate may be taxed to the recipient at the place of his domicile, irrespective of the location of the land." [25] There was an attempt to distinguish this case from Senior v. Braden [26] on the ground that the transferable certificates entitling Senior to income made the legal interest of a nature different from that involved in the present case. But along with this distinction is the statement: "Neither the privilege nor the burden is affected by the character of the source from which the income is derived. For that reason, income is not necessarily clothed with the tax immunity enjoyed by its source. A state may tax its residents upon net income from a business whose physical assets, located wholly without the state, are beyond its taxing powers." [27] He continued that the protection from taxation offered to the property in one state does not extend to the receipt and enjoyment of the income from it in another.[28] Thus the holding of Maguire v. Trefry reappeared [29] and Senior v. Braden was in effect overruled. On the other hand, the Court held that this was not actually double taxation, since the two taxes were assessed on *different legal interests*. The fact that the recipient of the income is "subject to its control and enjoys the benefits of

[22] 188 U.S. 189 (1903).   [23] 295 U.S. 422, 432 (1935).
[24] 300 U.S. 308 (1937).   [25] *Ibid.*, p. 315.
[26] 295 U.S. 422 (1935).

[27] 300 U.S. 308, 313 (1937). In his dissent Justice Butler cites Senior v. Braden, 295 U.S. 422 (1935), as authority for the fact that a tax on the income from the land is a tax on the land itself.

[28] 300 U.S. 308, 314 (1937). See Harding, "State Jurisdiction to Tax Income from Foreign Land," *loc. cit.*, pp. 444, 447. The author thinks that the test which has been applied in these cases is not whether the property was taxable but whether it had been taxed elsewhere. In Senior v. Braden, 295 U.S. 422 (1935), the land had been taxed to its full value; in Cohn v. Graves, 300 U.S. 308 (1937), New Jersey had not imposed a tax.

[29] This case, which had held that the income from a trust outside the state was taxable by the domiciliary state, had been practically read out of the law in Senior v. Braden, 295 U.S. 422 (1935).

its laws" was thought by Justice Stone to be sufficient basis for the state's tax.

When a resident of Massachusetts sold his right to one fourth a new membership in the New York Stock Exchange and New York imposed an income tax on the profits from the sale, the Court upheld the tax, explaining: "When we speak of a business situs of intangible property in the taxing state, we are indulging in a metaphor. We express the idea of localization by virtue of the attributes of the intangible right in relation to the conduct of affairs at a particular place." The right may grow out of the actual transaction of a localized business or it may be identified with a particular place because its exercise is fixed exclusively or dominantly at that place. In the latter case the "localization for the purpose of transacting business may constitute a business situs itself." [30] The Court did not discuss the right of Massachusetts to impose a tax on the same income.[31]

The first actual instance of double taxation of income was challenged before the Court in Guaranty Trust Co. v. Virginia.[32] Virginia taxed a resident on the income derived from a trust fund in New York set up by the will of a resident of that state. New York had collected a tax on the full amount of the income. Justice McReynolds, expressing the views of the majority, explained that the cases cited by the company as opposing double taxation turned on the theory that the state's taxing power was restricted to her confines and could not be exerted in respected to subjects beyond them. In this instance, he said, Virginia had not sought to tax something beyond her jurisdiction. The taxable event was the receipt of income by a resident of the state. And, it was said, "The mere fact that another state lawfully taxed funds from which payments were made did not necessarily destroy Virginia's right to tax something done within her borders." [33]

---

[30] Whitney v. Graves, 299 U.S. 366, 372 (1937). Charles L. B. Lowndes, *National Tax Association: Proceedings* (Lancaster, Pa., 1937), p. 334, thinks that this decision read with that in the Cohn case indicates that there are no substantial jurisdictional limitations on the states' power to impose an income tax.

[31] J. Mark Jacobson, "State Jurisdiction to Tax Incomes," *University of Pennsylvania Law Review*, LXXXV (1937), 795, 800, is of the opinion that the implication of the Whitney case is that only New York would be allowed to tax.

[32] 305 U.S. 19 (1938).

[33] *Ibid.*, p. 23.

In Welch *v.* Henry [34] the Court held that the Wisconsin special income-tax law of 1935, applying retroactively to income received in 1933, did not violate due process of law. Prior to 1935, Wisconsin had exempted dividends, in whole or in part, from the income tax. In 1935 it placed a tax on the dividends received in 1933 and 1934 which had not been subject to an income tax in those years.[35] It was said that the tax did not deny due process merely because it operated retrospectively. The state legislature met biennially, and this was the first opportunity there had been since the 1933 session to make a change to meet the increased expenses of government. The Court was willing to consider the financial plight of the state and not use the due process clause as an obstacle to government. Said Justice Stone:

> The equitable distribution of the costs of government through the medium of an income tax is a . . . difficult task. In its performance, experience has shown the importance of reasonable opportunity for the legislative body, in the revision of tax laws, to distribute increased costs of government among its taxpayers in the light of the present need for revenue and with knowledge of the sources and amounts of the various classes of the taxable period preceding the revision. Without that opportunity, accommodation of the legislative purpose to the need may be seriously obstructed, if not defeated. We cannot say that the due process which the Constitution exacts denies that opportunity to the legislature.[36]

[34] 305 U.S. 134 (1938). For a discussion of retroactive legislation and due process of law, see Edward S. Stimson, "Retroactive Application of Law—A Problem of Constitutional Law," *Michigan Law Review,* XXXVIII (1939), 30–56; Ralph Neuhoff, "Retrospective Tax Laws," *St. Louis Law Review,* XXI (1935), 1–11; Frederick A. Ballard, "Retroactive Federal Taxation," *Harvard Law Review,* XLVIII (1935), 592–619.

[35] R. J. Traynor, "Tax Decisions of the Supreme Court," *National Tax Association: Proceedings* (Lancaster, Pa., 1939), pp. 27, 36.

[36] 305 U.S. 134, 149 (1938). In Demorest *v.* City Bank, 321 U.S. 36 (1944), the appellant challenged the validity of the New York personal-property tax law which took away the remainderman's right to a judicial examination of the trustee's computation of the income as applied to an estate whose administration began before the act was passed. The Court replied that "Nothing in the Federal Constitution would warrant us in holding that judicial rules tentatively put forward and leaving much to discretion will deprive the legislature of power to make further reasonable rules which in its opinion will expedite and make more equitable the distribution of millions of dollars of property locked in testamen-

This concern for the financial status of the state and the assumption that the taxpayer's position had not been changed in reliance upon the tax as it stood in 1933 seem to explain the Court's decision in this case. Apparently the taxpayer might reasonably anticipate that someday the public coffers would require additional revenue. Although he had disposed of the income for 1933 and 1934 and possibly would not have done so had the tax been assessed at that time, he was thought not to have altered his financial position because of the absence of the tax.[37]

The Wisconsin statute which imposed upon domestic and foreign corporations a tax on that part of a corporation's income derived from its business in the state was challenged by J. C. Penney Company [38] as a violation of due process. This tax was in addition to the general income tax and was, according to the state, payment for the privilege of declaring and receiving dividends. The company challenged the law as violative of due process in that it reached money beyond the state's jurisdiction; for the dividends were declared in Connecticut, the state of incorporation, and paid to shareholders, many of whom were not residents of Wisconsin.

The Court found that the tax, rather than being a privilege tax, was actually a supplementary income tax and as such was a valid exercise of the state's tax power. Justice Frankfurter declared that "For constitutional purposes the decisive issue turns on the operating incidence of the challenged tax. A state is free to pursue its own fiscal policies, unembarrassed by the Constitution, if by the practical operation of a tax the state has exerted its power in relation to opportunities it has given, to protection which it has afforded, to *benefits which it has conferred by the fact of being an orderly, civilized society.*" [39] The question of

---

tary trusts, even if they do affect the values of various interests and expectancies under the trust. The Fourteenth Amendment does not invalidate the Act in question." See United States *v.* Hudson, 299 U.S. 498, 500 (1937), where a 50 per cent tax on the profits from the sale of silver bullion was imposed retroactively 35 days and was held not to violate due process.

[37] 305 U.S. 134, 147–48 (1938).

[38] Wisconsin *v.* J. C. Penney Co., 311 U.S. 435 (1940).

[39] *Ibid.,* pp. 444–45. (Italics added.) The Court went on to say: "The substantial privilege of carrying on business in Wisconsin, which has here been given, clearly supports the tax, and the state has not given the less merely because

whether the state had given something for which it might ask a return was found to be the ultimate test of the validity of a tax when challenged as a violation of due process of law.[40] Such a rule would leave few limitations on the state's power to tax capital exports. As applied in this case that rule permitted the tax to be based on dividends declared outside the state and the amount of the tax to be taken from the funds set aside for the payment of dividends.

Here again is evidence of the fact that due process of law as formerly interpreted to restrict the taxing power of the state is more and more giving way to the practical need of revenue by the states. Justice Frankfurter recognized that the responsibility for devising a just and productive tax policy for the state was a challenge to legislators acquainted with the revenue sources and the financial needs of the state. In his opinion the least the Court could do was to be very cautious not to restrict the tax power unnecessarily by a misapplication of the due process clause.[41] Professor Corwin thinks that the Court was forced to make a choice between having the federal government subsidize the state and allowing the local units greater freedom in the selection of tax subjects and the methods of enforcement.[42]

The validity of the Wisconsin tax was in question again in the case of International Harvester Co. *v.* Department of Taxation of Wisconsin.[43] Here the company alleged that the tax upheld in the J. C. Penney case, if applied in the present case, would violate the due process guaranteed by the Fourteenth Amendment in

---

it has conditioned the demand of the exaction upon happenings outside its own borders. The fact that a tax is contingent upon events brought to pass without a state does not destroy the nexus between such a tax and transactions within a state for which the tax is an exaction." A California tax imposed on the net income of domestic corporations, including interstate and foreign income attributable to California, was sustained in Matson Navigation Co. *v.* State Board of Equalization, 297 U.S. 441, 445 (1936).

[40] 311 U.S. 435, 444 (1940).

[41] *Ibid.,* pp. 435, 445. Justice Roberts dissented on the ground that the tax was invalid if considered as an income tax in that the burden of the tax, in reality, fell on persons outside the state. It was equally invalid if considered as a privilege tax in that it placed an additional condition on doing business in the state, thus violating the company's charter. The Chief Justice and Justices McReynolds and Reed joined in the dissent.

[42] Corwin, *Constitutional Revolution, Ltd.,* p. 112.

[43] 322 U.S. 435 (1944).

that the tax was measured by reference to Wisconsin income earned and carried over the company accounts before the tax law became effective. But the "taxable event" on which Justice Frankfurter, speaking for the Court, based the validity of the application of the law was "the distribution of the dividends paid from earnings," and the fact that "the deduction of them occurred subsequent to the enactment of the taxing statute. . . ." [44] He could see no constitutional barrier to the state's prorating the burden of the tax among the shareholders "as the ultimate beneficiaries of the corporation's activities within the state." [45]

The company challenged the tax on the ground that actually it would fall on persons domiciled in another state. In the words of Justice Frankfurter:

> The power to tax the corporation's earnings includes the power to postpone the tax until the distribution of those earnings, and to measure it by the amounts distributed. In taxing such distributions, Wisconsin may impose the burden of the tax either upon the corporation or upon the shareholders who derive the ultimate benefit from the corporation's Wisconsin activities. Personal presence within the state of the stockholder-taxpayers is not essential to the constitutional levy of a tax out of so much of the corporation's Wisconsin earnings as is distributed to them. A state may tax such part of the income of a non-resident as is fairly attributable to property located in the state or to events or transactions which, occurring there, are subject to state regulation and which are within the protection of the state and entitled to numerous other benefits which it confers. [46]

The fact that the dividends were declared outside Wisconsin was said not to deprive that state of its power to tax. The tax power was based on the fact that the withdrawal from the state of the income earned there was subject to some regulation by the state. Justice Frankfurter does not indicate what regulations had been placed upon the withdrawal of the earnings, but the fact that restrictions could be imposed by the state was said to satisfy due process requirement that there be a relation between

[44] *Ibid.*, p. 445.   [45] *Ibid.*, p. 442.
[46] *Ibid.*, pp. 441–42.

the subject taxed and the taxing power.[47] Moreover, the Fourteenth Amendment was said not to prohibit "unwise taxes merely because they are unwise, or unfair or burdensome taxes, merely because they are unfair or burdensome." [48] It would seem that this decision has effectively laid to rest all bases for challenging a state income tax under the due process of law on jurisdictional grounds. Apparently the only question left unsettled is that of how far the event upon which benefits are conferred may be from actual earnings to bring the income within the taxing power of the protecting state.

From the decisions in the foregoing cases, it is seen that the Court has not made an effort to prohibit double taxation of incomes. The due process clause of the Fourteenth Amendment has been interpreted as placing no limitations on the state's power to tax incomes of residents derived from activities outside the state, or to tax the income of nonresidents derived from activities within the state. Likewise, the Court has found that income from land outside the taxing state may be taxed to residents and that intangibles may acquire a business situs in a state other than the domiciliary state and be taxed at that situs as well as at the domicile of the owner. Actual instances of double taxation of income were specifically held to be not inconsistent with the due process of law concept. Few jurisdictional limitations under the due process clause remain after the decision that the state may tax the privilege of declaring and receiving dividends, the amount of the tax to be deducted from the amount of the dividend owing to the shareholder.

Ad Valorem Property Taxes. In 1925 the Court was of the opinion that stocks could be taxed at the domicile of the owner *and* by the state of incorporation.[49] By 1932 it had become the doctrine of the Court that the transfer, at the death of the owner, of shares of stock and other kinds of intangibles could be taxed by only one state. The domiciliary state had jurisdiction to tax if the property had not acquired a business situs elsewhere. If the intangibles had acquired situs in another state, they became taxable

[47] *Ibid.*, pp. 443–44. Justice Jackson dissented.
[48] *Ibid.*, p. 444.
[49] Frick *v.* Pennsylvania, 268 U.S. 473 (1925).

there, and domicile of the owner did not confer jurisdiction to tax. It was reasonable to assume that this doctrine of no double taxation would be extended to the field of the general property tax on intangibles. However, the beginning of a different principle in the realm of property taxation was foreshadowed by the implication in earlier decisions that intangibles might acquire a business situs outside the owner's domicile and be subject to taxation at the situs.[50] It was not held that situs conferred exclusive jurisdiction.

"Business situs" as the basis for a general property tax was invoked by West Virginia in Wheeling Steel Corp. *v*. Fox.[51] The question was that of the validity of an ad valorem property tax laid by the state on bank deposits and accounts receivable of the Wheeling Steel Corporation, incorporated under the laws of Delaware but having its principal place of business in Wheeling, West Virginia. Chief Justice Hughes, speaking for the majority, restated the principle that in general intangible property might be taxed only at the domicile of the owner.[52] But in this case the Court found that the intangibles had a business situs in West Virginia, because the company conducted its business through the Wheeling office, and therefore were taxable in that state. The implication was that West Virginia's jurisdiction was exclusive, though the Court did not commit itself on this point.[53] It reserved that question, for "upon the record, the question before the Court was with regard to the constitutional validity of the tax as assessed in West Virginia and not as to the amount of the tax assessed elsewhere." [54]

The next case in line with this holding was that of First Bank Stock Corp. *v*. Minnesota.[55] Here the issue was whether a Dela-

[50] For instance, Farmers' Loan and Trust Co. *v*. Minnesota, 280 U.S. 204 (1930), which was decided after the Court had changed its mind as to the permissibility of double taxation under the due process clause.

[51] 298 U.S. 193 (1936).   [52] *Ibid.*, p. 209.

[53] *Ibid.*, p. 212. R. L. Howard, "State Jurisdiction to Tax Intangibles: A Twelve-year Cycle," *Missouri Law Review*, VIII (1943), 155, 161, finds that the Court's language on this matter is "less than clear."

[54] 298 U.S. 193, 215 (1936). Chief Justice Hughes, who wrote the opinion in this case, concurred with Justice Butler's dissent in Curry *v*. McCanless, 307 U.S. 357, 383 (1939), to the effect that business situs should have priority over domicile for a tax and that only one state should tax.

[55] 301 U.S. 234 (1937). Edward S. Stimson, "Jurisdiction to Tax Intangibles," *Cornell Law Quarterly*, XXIII (1937), 806, 827.

ware corporation doing business in Minnesota could be required, consistently with due process of law, to pay a property tax laid by Minnesota upon shares of stock in Montana and North Dakota bank corporations. These two states had levied a tax on the stocks in the banks of the respective states.[56]

In upholding Minnesota's power to tax, Justice Stone restated the recent ruling that the enjoyment by the resident of a state of the protection of the state's laws "is inseparable from responsibility for sharing the costs of its government." To measure the tax by the value of the rights which the state protects was said to be an "equitable method of distributing the burdens of government among those who are privileged to enjoy its benefits." [57] The Court implied, at least, that the states of incorporation had power to tax, though that issue was not before it in this case. Justice Stone said that he could find no lack of due process in the taxation of the corporate shares in Minnesota irrespective of the control over them which the due process clause saved to North Dakota and Montana as the states of incorporation.[58] Minnesota was said to have jurisdiction to impose the tax because, as the commercial domicile, it conferred certain benefits upon the property. As to what these were, the Court explained:

> The economic advantages realized through the protection, at the place of domicil, of the ownership rights in intangibles the value of which is made the measure of the tax, bear a direct relationship to the distribution of burdens which the tax affects. These considerations support the taxation of intangibles at the place of domicil, at least where they are not shown to have acquired a business situs elsewhere, as a proper exercise of the power of government. Like considera-

[56] See Brown, "The Present Status of Multiple Taxation of Intangible Property," *loc. cit.*, pp. 806, 827.

[57] 301 U.S. 234, 241 (1937). For a discussion of the application of this theory prior to 1931, see Harding, *Double Taxation of Property and Income*, pp. 95–96; and Lowndes, "The Passing of Situs . . . ," *loc. cit.*, p. 779. See also Maurice Merrill, "Jurisdiction to Tax—Another Word," *Yale Law Journal*, XLIV (1935), 582–84. But the power to tax does not depend upon the taxpayer's receiving any special benefit. See Inter-Island Steam Navigation Co. *v.* Hawaii, 305 U.S. 306 (1938); Georgia Railway and Electric Co. *v.* Decatur, 297 U.S. 620 (1936); Roberts *v.* Irrigation District, 289 U.S. 75 (1933); and Nashville, C. & St. L. Ry. Co. *v.* Wallace, 288 U.S. 249 (1933).

[58] 301 U.S. 234, 241 (1937).

tions support their taxation at their business situs, for it is there that the owner in every practical sense invokes and enjoys the protection of the laws, and in consequence realizes the economic advantages of his ownership.[59]

Thus double taxation of the intangibles was upheld by the Court. The tax power of Delaware, as the state of incorporation of the First Bank Stock Corporation, was not in question in this case.

Though the reasoning was different, the rule of the First Bank Stock Corporation case was followed in Schuylkill v. Pennsylvania,[60] in which the jurisdiction of the state of the corporation's legal domicile was challenged. Justice Roberts, speaking for the Court, upheld the state's power to tax—"notwithstanding the ownership of the stock may be a taxable subject in another state." [61] The power to tax was based on the fact that the state had retained the power to alter or amend the corporate charter and the fact that "every stockholder acquired his shares with the full knowledge that his interest in the corporation was subject to regulation and taxation." [62] The Court found that the state had construed the statute as reaching nonresidents as well as residents, and the Court considered itself bound by that construction. The fact that a nonresident shareholder was taxed on his shares was not a violation of due process of law. While not expressly overruling Farmers' Loan and Trust Co. v. Minnesota [63] and First National Bank of Boston v. Maine,[64] the decision in this case makes them inapplicable to property taxes on intangibles, limiting their scope strictly to death-transfer taxes.

Much the same issue was before the Court in Newark Fire Insurance Co. v. State Board of Tax Appeals,[65] in which a New

---

[59] Ibid.

[60] 302 U.S. 506 (1938). See Edward S. Stimson, "Jurisdiction to Tax Intangibles, Again," Georgetown Law Journal, XXVI (1938), 666.

[61] 302 U.S. 506, 516 (1938).

[62] Ibid., p. 516. C. L. B. Lowndes, "Taxation and the Supreme Court, 1937 Term," University of Pennsylvania Law Review, LXXXVII (1938), 1, 27, thinks that if this was the basis of the power to tax in this instance, the Court could have made it a special case. That it did not choose to do so is evident from subsequent decisions.

[63] 280 U.S. 204 (1930).   [64] 284 U.S. 312 (1932).

[65] 307 U.S. 313 (1939).

Jersey corporation contended that its intangible property had acquired situs in New York and was not taxable in New Jersey. New York's tax law did not provide for the taxation of the property in issue here. The Court was not called upon to decide whether both states could tax.[66] Justice Reed wrote an opinion, in which Chief Justice Hughes and Justices Butler and Roberts concurred, saying: "When a state exercises its sovereign power to create a private corporation, that corporation becomes a citizen, and domiciled in the jurisdiction of its creator. . . . In accordance with the ordinary rule of *mobilia sequuntur personam* to determine the taxable situs of intangible personalty, the presumption is that such property is taxable by the state of the corporation's origin." [67] The corporation failed to show to the satisfaction of the majority that its intangible property had actually acquired situs in New York. Justice Reed was of the opinion that the mere fact that the corporation's general offices were located in New York did not destroy the taxability of a part of its intangibles by the state of the corporation's legal domicile.[68] He did not say what effect a New York situs would have had on New Jersey's power to tax.

Justice Frankfurter wrote a separate opinion upholding the tax power of New Jersey.[69] He was of the opinion that the Court had no authority to review the desirability or wisdom of the tax measure. His conclusion was based on the fact that he did not find any specific constitutional prohibition against this tax law. He held that the Court's work was ended when "a tax appropriately challenged before us is not found to be in plain violation of the Constitution." [70] The flaw in this line of reasoning lies in the fact that whatever is a constitutional prohibition under the due process of law clause is such only because the Court has said so. Thus it would be difficult to find a "plain violation of the Constitution" if a majority of the Court interpreted the clause in such a way as to permit the tax.

[66] *Ibid.*, p. 319. New York had not assessed a personal-property tax against the corporation. New Jersey courts had treated this as a personal-property tax on property having a situs in New York.

[67] *Ibid.*, p. 318. See Philip Kraus, "Jurisdiction to Tax Intangibles," *Southern California Law Review*, XIII (1940), 453–61.

[68] 307 U.S. 313, 322 (1939).

[69] Justices Stone, Black, and Douglas concurred in this opinion.

[70] 307 U.S. 313, 323–24 (1939).

Until very recently the due process of law guaranteed by the Fourteenth Amendment prohibited double taxation of tangible movable property. In the case of Johnson Oil Refining Co. *v.* Oklahoma [71] the Court ruled: "When a fleet of cars is habitually employed in several States—the individual cars constantly running in and out of each State—it cannot be said that any one of the States is entitled to tax the entire number of cars regardless of their use in other States." [72] Oklahoma was said to have jurisdiction to tax the average number of cars physically within the state during the tax year.[73]

The decision of the Court in Northwest Airlines *v.* Minnesota [74] indicated a marked departure from this "well-settled" doctrine of property taxation. Northwest Airlines, a Minnesota corporation, had its principal place of business in St. Paul. All of the corporation's planes were in Minnesota during the 1939 tax year. That state assessed its property tax on the entire fleet of planes. The company alleged that since some of its planes had been taxed in other states, the application of Minnesota's law deprived it of property without due process. Justice Frankfurter rendered the decision of the Court: "On the basis of rights which Minnesota alone originated and Minnesota continues to safeguard, she alone can tax the personalty which is permanently attributable to Minnesota and no other State." And "The fact that Northwest paid personal property taxes for 1939 on 'some proportion of its full value' of its airplane fleet in some other States does not abridge the power of taxation of Minnesota as the home State of the fleet in circumstances of the present case." [75] The home state was said to have jurisdiction to tax all of the corporation's property which had been within its bounds during

[71] 290 U.S. 158 (1933). See Ott *v.* Mississippi Valley Barge Line Co., 336 U.S. 169 (1949).

[72] 290 U.S. 158, 162 (1933). The Court said that the state of incorporation had no jurisdiction to tax personal property where its actual situs was in another state.

[73] *Ibid.*, p. 163.

[74] 322 U.S. 292 (1944). See William H. Page, "Jurisdiction to Tax Tangible Movables," *Wisconsin Law Review* (1945), 125–68; Thomas Reed Powell, "Northwest Airlines *v.* Minnesota: State Taxation of Airplanes—Herein Also of Ships and Sealing Wax and Railroad Cars," *Harvard Law Review*, LVII (1944), 1097–1112.

[75] 322 U.S. 292, 295 (1944). Justice Frankfurter thought that the particular benefits accruing to Northwest as a result of its relation with Minnesota were sufficient to justify a tax on the entire value of the property.

the tax year "even if every item of that property should be taken successively into another State for a day, a week, or even six months and then brought back." [76] Justice Frankfurter did not think that any of the planes had acquired in another state situs which would bar the home state from levying its tax. He explained that the statement ". . . the State of origin remains the permanent situs of the property, notwithstanding its occasional excursions to foreign parts" [77] was simply a recognition of the "legally significant fact that neither any specific cars nor any average of cars was so continuously in any other state as to have been withdrawn from the home state and to have established for tax purposes an adopted home State." [78] Thus the decision, relying on Justice Holmes's reasoning, might mean that Minnesota's power to tax is exclusive or that double taxation of movable tangible property will be permissible. The question of double taxation was not before the Court in this case.

Justice Jackson refused to accept the majority opinion because it failed to commit the Court to the doctrine that the jurisdiction of Minnesota as the home state was exclusive.[79] He concurred with that reservation. Justice Stone filed a dissenting opinion in which Justices Roberts, Reed, and Rutledge joined. With such a difference of opinion as to the validity of the tax and the basis of that validity it is impossible to determine just what a majority of the Court thought other than that there had been no deprivation of property without due process of law. Professor Powell thinks that Justice Frankfurter did not condone double taxation in this case.[80] However, since the Court recognized the fact that there had been taxation by other states but did not let that interfere with the tax jurisdiction of the home state, an answer to the double taxation question must wait until a corporation simi-

[76] *Ibid.*, p. 299, quoting Justice Holmes's dissent in New York Central & H.R.R. Co. *v.* Miller, 202 U.S. 584, 597 (1906). See Justice Frankfurter's opinion in Central Greyhound Lines *v.* Moaloy, 334 U.S. 653, 662 (1948), where he declares invalid New York's tax on gross receipts of public utilities when applied to a public-transportation company which has 42.53 per cent of its mileage in New Jersey and Pennsylvania. This tax was not challenged under the due process clause.

[77] Quoting New York Central & H.R.R. Co. *v.* Miller, 202 U.S. 584, 597 (1906).

[78] 322 U.S. 292, 299, n. 4 (1944).

[79] *Ibid.*, p. 307.

[80] Powell, "Northwest Airlines *v.* Minnesota . . . ," *loc. cit.*, p. 1105.

larly situated challenges the tax assessed by states other than the home state. Only the question of Minnesota's power to tax was in issue here.

With the Court's decision in Greenough *v*. City of Newport, Rhode Island,[81] the last remnants of due process limitations upon the state's taxing power seem to have disappeared. In this instance Rhode Island imposed an ad valorem property tax against a resident trustee upon one half the value of the corpus of a trust located in New York. The trustee contended that such a tax violated the due process clause of the Fourteenth Amendment because the state rendered no services nor offered any protection to the trust fund in return for the exaction. Justice Reed, speaking for the Court, took cognizance of the fact that "Although nothing appeared as to any specific benefit or protection which the trustee had actually received," the state "was willing, ready, and capable of furnishing either if requested." [82] The trustee might have occasion to call upon the courts of the state in connection with the administration of the trust and "third parties dealing with the trustee on trust matters or beneficiaries may have need to proceed directly against the trustee as an individual for matters arising out of his relation to the trust." Where federal jurisdiction depends upon diversity of citizenship, federal courts would not be open to the trustee, resident of Rhode Island, to enforce trust claims against a Rhode Island resident. Therefore, the trustee may be forced to call upon the courts of that state. A combination of these factors and others led Justice Reed to conclude that the state did actually offer the possibility of protection in the event that a need should arise and thus that the state might lawfully impose the tax here questioned.[83] Certainly the fiction of state protection and substantial benefits was extended beyond the bounds of reason, but by such extension the tax law was brought within the permissible limits of due process of law.

Justice Frankfurter concurred with the majority, for "Rhode Island's system of taxing its residents—subjecting them to the same measure for ascertaining their ability to pay whether they

[81] 331 U.S. 486 (1947).   [82] *Ibid.*, p. 495.
[83] *Ibid.*, pp. 495–96.

held property for themselves or for others—long antedated the Fourteenth Amendment. Rhode Island has imposed this tax 'it may be presumed, for the general advantages of living within the jurisdiction.' . . . It can hardly be deemed irrational to say, as Rhode Island apparently has said for a hundred years, that these advantages may be roughly measured, for fiscal purposes, by the wealth which a person controls, whatever his ultimate beneficial interest in the property." [84] Here as in other recent cases Justice Frankfurter implies that the Fourteenth Amendment worked no changes in the power of the state or in the position of the individual relative to the state. While in many instances the application of such a principle would entail no injustice, even its statement appears rather dangerous in view of the few recourses open to an individual who feels that he has been the victim of an injustice.

Four members of the Court dissented. The basis of disagreement by Justices Jackson and Murphy was that the tax had been levied on the trustee as such, therefore actually upon the trust funds. Such a tax, they would hold, is beyond the tax jurisdiction of the state, therefore in violation of due process of law. Justice Rutledge and Chief Justice Vinson dissented because to them the relationship existing between trustee and state of residence in this case is not sufficiently substantial to warrant the tax. In the words of Justice Rutledge: "Whether or not due process under the Fourteenth Amendment forbids state taxation of acts, transactions, events or property is essentially one of degree depending upon the existence of sufficiently substantial factual connections, having economic and legal effects, between the taxing state and the subject of the tax." [85] The mere fact that one trustee lived in the state was not thought to be sufficient connection to justify the tax.

Death-Transfer Taxes. From 1929 through 1938 the rule of the Court with regard to death-transfer taxation was that a trans-

---

[84] *Ibid.*, p. 499, citing Jackman *v.* Rosenbaum Co., 260 U.S. 22, 31 (1923), to the effect that "The Fourteenth Amendment, itself a historical product, did not destroy history for the states and substitute mechanical compartments of law all exactly alike."

[85] 331 U.S. 486, 501–502 (1947).

fer tax or an inheritance tax could be levied on a given subject by one state only.[86] If the property acquired situs at a place other than the domicile of the owner, it became taxable at the situs; otherwise, it was taxable by the domiciliary state. In theory, the Court applied the maxim *mobilia sequuntur personam*. But when "justice demanded," this maxim gave way to the doctrine of a business situs.[87] During this time the Court did not pass on the question of whether business situs in a state other than the domiciliary state conferred exclusive jurisdiction to tax. There were no significant decisions with regard to double taxation and due process of law in the field of death-transfer taxes between 1932 and 1939.[88] The Court, however, had indicated its willingness to cast aside what had come to be considered well-settled doctrines of taxation in other fields, and it was only to be expected that some shift would be forthcoming insofar as transfer taxes were concerned.

In 1939 the Court reversed completely its earlier attitude toward multiple taxation in the field of transfer taxes. In Curry v. McCanless [89] the doctrines of the Holmes-Brandeis-Stone dissents became the majority opinion of the Court. Here the holding that the due process clause of the Fourteenth Amendment prohibits multiple taxation of intangibles was rejected. The issue before the Court was whether both Alabama and Tennessee could impose a tax upon the transfer of intangibles held in trust by an Alabama trustee but passing under the will of a beneficiary decedent domiciled in Tennessee. The trust had devolved to the decedent by will, had remained at all times in Alabama, and had been, for many years, irrevocable. The only relation between the

[86] For a study of death-transfer taxation during this period, see Harding, *Double Taxation of Property and Income;* and Rottschaefer, "Power of States to Tax Intangibles," *loc. cit.,* pp. 741–66.

[87] Safe Deposit and Trust Co. *v.* Virginia, 280 U.S. 83, 93 (1929).

[88] In Worchester Bank *v.* Riley, 302 U.S. 292, 298 (1937), the Court held that a tax statute construed to impose a transfer tax upon intangibles of a decedent domiciled elsewhere violated due process. But, in this case, the courts of two states determined that the decedent was a resident of the state. The Court held that due process of law does not protect against erroneous judgments of courts. It refused to make a determination in favor of either state.

[89] 307 U.S. 357 (1939). Henry Brandis, Jr., "State Gift Taxes—Their Relation to Death Taxes," *Iowa Law Review,* XXVI (1941), 470–511; George Stimson, "The Due Process of State Taxation," *Georgetown Law Journal,* XXIX (1940), 271, 287.

decedent and the fund was the power of appointment which she exercised at her death by will. The Court found that the rule of First National Bank of Boston *v.* Maine [90] had not been given a completely logical application. And even if one could consider the various subjects taxed here as a "composite unitary interest and ascribe to it a single location in space," it would, Justice Stone thought, be difficult to find any "articulate principle" of the Fourteenth Amendment that would withdraw from either state the taxing jurisdiction which it possessed before the adoption of that amendment "by conferring on one state, at the expense of the other, exclusive jurisdiction to tax." [91]

In effect the Court said that the due process of law clause of the Fourteenth Amendment serves to restrict the tax power of the states in the same manner and to the same degree as the Fifth Amendment restricts the taxing power of the national government. Said Justice Stone: "If the 'due process' of the Fifth Amendment does not require us to fix a single exclusive place of taxation of intangibles for the benefit of their foreign owner, who is entitled to its protection, the Fourteenth Amendment can hardly be thought to make us do so here, for the due process clause of each amendment is directed at the protection of the individual and he is entitled to its immunity as much against the state as against the national government." [92] In the reasoning of the Court the doctrine of business situs was not made a factor. The jurisdiction of Alabama was said to rest on the domicile of the trustee. Justice Stone explained:

> If taxation is but a means of distributing the costs of government among those who are subject to its control and who enjoy the protection of its laws, legal ownership of the intangibles in Alabama by the Alabama trustee would seem to afford adequate basis for imposing on it a tax measured by their value. . . . This Court has never denied the constitutional power of the trustee's domicile to subject them to property taxation. And since Alabama may lawfully tax the property in the trustee's hands, we perceive no ground for saying that the Fourteenth Amendment forbids the state

[90] 284 U.S. 312 (1932).   [91] 307 U.S. 357, 369 (1939).
[92] *Ibid.*, pp. 369–70.

to tax the transfer of it to another merely because the transfer was effected by decedent's testamentary act is another state.[93]

Tennessee was said to have jurisdiction to tax the entire value of the property because of the domicile of the owner in that state. It was said:

> From the beginning of our constitutional system, control over the person at the place of his domicile and his duty there, . . . to contribute to the support of the government have been deemed to afford an adequate constitutional basis for imposing on him a tax on the use or enjoyment of rights in intangibles measured by their value. Until this moment that jurisdiction has not been thought to depend on any factor other than the domicile of the owner within the taxing state, or to compel the attribution to intangibles of a physical presence within its territory, as though they were chattels, in order to support the tax.[94]

The Court expressly denied that due process of law prohibited the imposition of a transfer tax on the same intangible property in more than one state. Justice Stone, for the Court, did not think that it was possible to apply the Fourteenth Amendment with "such mechanical nicety" without infringing upon powers which had not been withdrawn from the states. It was said to be "undeniable" that there were many circumstances in which more than one state might have jurisdiction to impose a tax measured by some or all of the taxpayer's intangibles.[95] Each state had conferred benefits for which it could, consistently with due process of law, exact payment. Since the Court did not find that either state had a prior right, both were said to have jurisdiction to tax the transfer, the amount of the tax to be measured by the full value of the trust property.

The Court seems to have gone out of its way in adding that the mere fact that a state in which a corporation carries on its business imposes a tax measured by the value of all its intangibles used in the business does not preclude the state of incorporation

[93] *Ibid.*, p. 370.   [94] *Ibid.*, pp. 366–67.
[95] *Ibid.*, p. 368.

from imposing a tax measured by the value of all the corporation's intangibles, wherever located.[96]

Justice Butler dissented on the ground that since the property had acquired situs in a state other than that of the owner's domicile, the state of situs should have exclusive power to tax.[97]

In Graves v. Elliott [98] the Court followed the rule of the Curry case. Here the issue was whether New York might constitutionally tax a domiciled resident's relinquishment, at death, of a power to revoke a trust of intangibles held by a Colorado trustee. Justice Stone, speaking for the majority, found that the legal interests in Colorado were so closely associated with the person of the decedent as to come within the jurisdiction of the state of domicile. He said, "Her right to revoke the trust and to demand the transmission to her of the intangibles by the trustee and the delivery of the physical evidences was a potential source of wealth, having the attributes of property. As in the case of any other intangibles which she possessed, control over her person and estate at the place of her domicile and her duty to contribute to the support of the government there afford adequate constitutional basis for the imposition of a tax measured by the value of the intangibles transmitted or relinquished at her death." [99] The decision in this case did not go quite so far as the rule of Curry v. McCanless,[100] for the relation of the decedent to the Colorado trust which was cited as sufficient to give the domiciliary state jurisdiction to tax did not exist in the Curry case.

The right of Oregon, as domiciliary state, to tax the transfer of a trust fund situated in Illinois and consisting in part of Federal Reserve Notes was challenged in Pearson v. McGraw.[101] Decedent had created a trust in Ilinois consisting of currency and

[96] Ibid., p. 374. Justice Reed concurred with the majority but with reservation as to this statement.

[97] Ibid., pp. 382–83. Chief Justice Hughes and Justices Roberts and Mc-Reynolds joined in this dissent.

[98] 307 U.S. 383 (1939). See Floyd Dix, "Must We Carry Our Stocks and Bonds in Our Pockets," Indiana Law Journal, XV (1940), 373–95; Stimson, "The Due Process of State Taxation," loc. cit., pp. 286–89.

[99] 307 U.S. 383, 387 (1939). Both states were held to have jurisdiction to tax the transfer; New York because of the domicile of the owner, and Colorado because of the location of the property in that state.

[100] 307 U.S. 357 (1939).

[101] 308 U.S. 313 (1939). See R. T. Rawlins, "State Jurisdiction to Tax Intangibles," Texas Law Review, XVIII (1940), 296, 312.

stocks. Six months before his death, he directed the trustee to sell the stocks and buy Federal Reserve Notes with the fund. Such notes were usually considered tangible property taxable at the place where they were located. Upon the death of the owner Oregon assessed a transfer tax against the full value of the trust. It had been taxed on its full value by Illinois. The Oregon Supreme Court had declared this invalid as a violation of due process in that it imposed a tax on a subject beyond the jurisdiction of the state.

Apparently the Court wished to avoid the difficulties inevitable in any ruling that tangibles might be taxed by a state in which they had never been, and at the same time not to deny the power of Oregon to tax. Therefore, Justice Douglas, for the majority, declared: ". . . we believe that the various steps in the series must be considered as constituting but one integrated and indivisible transaction—a transfer by decedent of intangibles in contemplation of death." [102] He found that it would not make any difference whether the notes were considered as tangible or intangible, for their taxability as such was not in question.[103] In his opinion "to hold that there is a constitutional barrier to the tax sought to be imposed would be to make a fetish of form." [104]

Stewart v. Pennsylvania [105] was decided, without opinion, on the basis of the rule of the Curry and McGraw cases. However, in this case the factors which had been thought adequate to confer jurisdiction in the former cases were not present. In the Stewart case the trustees were residents of New York, where the stocks and bonds were kept. The beneficiary, a resident of Pennsylvania, had no control over the trust property, no power to supervise the investments, no remainder interests in the trusts, and no rights under the deed except to receive income during the

[102] 308 U.S. 313, 317 (1939).
[103] *Ibid.*, p. 318. See Mortimer M. Kassell, "Death Taxation and the Fourteenth Amendment," *National Tax Association: Proceedings*, pp. 120, 123 (Lancaster, Pa., 1942). See also A. S. Guterman, "The Revitalization of Multiple State Death Taxation," *Columbia Law Review*, XLII (1942), 1249, 1254, who interprets the decision to mean that the state will be allowed to determine the character of the tax subject as tangible or intangible. Cf. Texas v. Florida, 306 U.S. 378 (1939).
[104] 308 U.S. 313, 318 (1939).
[105] 312 U.S. 649 (1941). Chief Justice Hughes and Justices Roberts and McReynolds dissented.

remainder of her life. Pennsylvania was held to have tax jurisdiction over the relinquishment and transfer of this right to receive income. Thus the domiciliary state of the beneficiary,
though it has no control over the owner of the property or the
trust itself, is held to have power to tax the transfer upon the
death of the beneficiary.[106]

The Court in Whitney v. Tax Commissioner [107] held valid, as
not violative of the due process clause, the New York estate-tax
law requiring that in the computation of the transfer tax the
gross estate consisting in part of trust funds be included. The
decedent had no "beneficial interest" in the corpus of the trust so
that she could use it or appoint it to her estate; but by her husband's will she had been given the power to appoint to her
children, as she saw fit, the property comprising the trust. The
Court held that the power to dispose of the property was a privilege afforded by the law of New York, and for that privilege
the state properly demanded a return. The disposition of the
property which she was free to make enhanced her freedom with
respect to her own estate. To the extent that the circle of beneficiaries was enlarged by the additional property which was hers
to appoint, there was compensation to those who succeeded to
any part of the estate.[108] To give the state jurisdiction to tax—
"It is enough that one person acquires economic interests in
property through the death of another person, even though such
acquisition is in part automatic consequence of death or related
to the decedent merely because of her power to designate to
whom and in what proportions among a restricted class the benefits shall fall." [109]

The issue before the Court in Graves v. Schmidlapp [110] was

---

[106] 338 Pa. 9, 12 A (2d) 444. See Walter F. Dodd, "The Relation of the Due
Process and the Commerce Clause to the Taxing Power," National Tax Association: Proceedings (Lancaster, Pa., 1941), pp. 113–16. The author assumed that
the decision indicated that the limitations of Curry v. McCanless and Pearson v.
McGraw were no longer effective.

[107] 309 U.S. 530 (1940).   [108] Ibid., p. 540.

[109] Ibid., p. 538. See West v. Oklahoma Tax Commission, 334 U.S. 717, 727
(1948), where Justice Murphy, speaking for six members of the Court, held that
an inheritance tax is imposed upon the shifting of economic benefits and the
privilege of transmitting or receiving such benefits rather than upon the property
of which the estate is composed.

[110] 315 U.S. 657 (1942).

whether the Fourteenth Amendment precluded New York from taxing the exercise of a general testamentary power of appointment of which the decedent, resident of New York, was donee under the will of a resident of Massachusetts, the property appointed being intangibles held by trustees under donor's will. Chief Justice Stone wrote the opinion for the majority. He could see no distinction, insofar as the jurisdiction to tax was concerned, between the right of disposition and the right of ownership. The power of New York to tax was based on the benefits and protection which the state had afforded the decedent in the enjoyment and appointment of the property. In Chief Justice Stone's opinion "Intangibles, which are legal relationships between persons and which in fact have no geographical location, are so associated with the owner that they and their transfer at death are taxable at the place of his domicile, where his person and the exercise of his property rights are subject to control of the sovereign power. . . ." [111] The rule of Wachovia Bank and Trust Co. v. Doughton [112] was expressly overruled, and the Court rejected the suggestion that the "benefit" criterion as applied in the present case should not hold if it would allow for multiple taxation.[113]

In Tax Commission of Utah v. Aldrich [114] the Court expressly overruled Farmers' Loan and Trust Co. v. Minnesota [115] and First National Bank of Boston v. Maine.[116] Once again it became the "settled" doctrine of the Court that double taxation in the field of death-transfer taxes was not per se inconsistent with the due process of the Fourteenth Amendment.[117] Here the issue involved the imposition of a tax upon the transfer at death of shares

[111] *Ibid.*, p. 660.

[112] 272 U.S. 567 (1926). In this case the situation was almost identical with that of the present case. Justice McReynolds held there that "The exercise of the power of appointment was subject to the laws of Massachusetts and nothing relative thereto was done by permission of the State where Mrs. Taylor happened to have her domicile." The domiciliary state was held not to have jurisdiction to tax.

[113] 315 U.S. 657, 660 (1942).

[114] 316 U.S. 174 (1942). See Guterman, "Revitalization of Multiple State Death Taxation," *loc. cit.*, pp. 1249–81; Howard, "State Jurisdiction to Tax Intangibles . . . ," *loc. cit.*, pp. 155–76.

[115] 280 U.S. 204 (1930). See p. 341, *supra.*

[116] 284 U.S. 312 (1932). See p. 343, *supra.*   [117] 316 U.S. 174, 176 (1942).

of stock in a Utah corporation forming a part of the estate of a decedent who, at the time of his death, was domiciled in New York and held there the certificates representing these shares. The decedent, at the time of his death, owned 10,000 shares of common stock and 400 shares of preferred stock in the Union Pacific Railway Corporation, a Utah corporation which maintained its executive offices and stock books in New York. Upon the death of the owner the stock certificates in New York were transferred to executors, residents of New York. It was the transfer of these stocks upon which Utah sought to impose a tax. The application of the law would not involve double taxation, for New York allowed, as a credit against the New York estate tax, the amount of constitutionally imposed tax elsewhere. Justice Douglas said that the "doctrine" which had "read into" the due process of law clause of the Fourteenth Amendment "a rule of immunity from taxation by more than one state" should not stand.[118] The right of Utah to impose the tax was upheld on the ground that if "freedom of transfer exists, it stems from Utah law. It finds its ultimate source in the authority which Utah has granted. It is indeed a benefit which Utah has bestowed. For it alone Utah may ask a return."[119]

The Court's opinion in this case embodies the ideas expressed by the minority of the First National Bank case and Baldwin v. Missouri.[120] The majority once again committed the Court to the rule that there could be found no constitutional immunity from double taxation of intangibles. Any state which could demonstrate the fact that it had conferred benefits or afforded protection to the subject might lawfully impose a tax on its transfer.[121] Justice Douglas declared that even if the Court felt that a system to protect against multiple taxation were desirable it was not within the province of the Court to provide it. For the Court to attempt such a thing would, he thought, be to indulge the "dangerous assump-

[118] Ibid.   [119] Ibid., p. 180.
[120] 284 U.S. 312 (1932), and 281 U.S. 586 (1930). Of these cases Justice Frankfurter, concurring, said: "That decision, as was made clear in its dissent, was an unwarranted deviation from the unbroken legal history and fiscal policy . . . due regard for the Constitution demands that the deviation be not perpetuated and that the power erroneously withdrawn from the States be again recognized." 316 U.S. 174, 183 (1942).
[121] 316 U.S. 174, 181 (1942).

tion" that the Fourteenth Amendment had provided the justices a free hand to embody their moral and economic beliefs in the law.[122]

In his concurring opinion Justice Frankfurter was willing to admit that the due process of law clause of the Fourteenth Amendment had some application to the taxing power of the states. To have jurisdiction to tax, he said, the state must have rendered some service in return for which it could levy a tax. If it has not conferred any benefit or has not afforded any protection to the subject taxed or the person upon whom the incidence of the tax falls, it has no jurisdiction to tax. The fallacy of the reasoning here, as in other cases where the Court has relied upon the benefit rendered, lies in the fact that in some cases it has held that benefit was not essential to jurisdiction to tax [123] and that the term "benefit" itself calls for interpretation by the Court.[124]

Justice Frankfurter was of the opinion that in order to make due process a restriction upon the state's power in this case, the Court would have to read into the Fourteenth Amendment the private economic and social theories of the justices. He was unwilling, apparently, to admit that every time the Court renders a decision on a piece of social or economic legislation challenged under the due process of law clause, it reads into the Constitution the private notions of policy of its members.[125]

Justice Jackson dissented because he thought that even though the benefit theory might be the proper criterion in determining the state's jurisdiction to tax, the benefits afforded by Utah in this instance were too slight to support such an extension of the state's tax power as was conferred by virtue of them. "Because Utah

[122] *Ibid.*

[123] In Georgia Railway and Electric Co. *v.* Decatur, 297 U.S. 620, 625 (1936), the Court said that the street-railway company could be assessed for the pavement of the street though it would receive no benefit. The California legislature was said to have the power to declare that making a given improvement in a special district would benefit the owners of land located in the district, and on the basis of such declaration levy a tax. Chesebro *v.* Los Angeles County Flood District, 306 U.S. 459, 465 (1939). In Rapid Transit Corp. *v.* New York, 303 U.S. 573, 585 (1938), the Court expressly held that a tax is not necessarily a payment for benefits received or to be received.

[124] See Greenough *v.* City of Newport, 331 U.S. 486, 495 (1947), for the most extreme interpretation of "benefit."

[125] For a statement of the power of the Court in this respect, see Justice Brandeis' dissent in the New State Ice Co. case, 285 U.S. 262, 311 (1932).

issued a charter to a corporation, which issued stock to a non-resident, which changed hands at his death, which required a transfer in the corporation's books, which transfer was permitted by Utah law, Utah got jurisdiction to tax succession to the stock." [126] He raised the question of whether the Court's opinion would necessitate an overhauling of its attitude toward multiple taxation of tangible property—"Since the Due Process Clause speaks with no more clarity as to tangible than as to intangible property." [127]

Once more due process protection against double taxation was contrasted in Central Hanover Bank and Trust Co. v. Kelly.[128] This case involved a decedent, resident of New Jersey, who executed an irrevocable trust in New York. The trustee was to pay to the grantor the net income for his lifetime. The principal was to be divided between his two sons upon his death, if his wife did not survive him. At the time of his death neither of the sons were residents of New Jersey. New Jersey collected a tax measured by the full value of the trust at the time of decedent's death, contending that the tax was upon the transfer at the time the trust was created in 1929, because the transfer had been made in contemplation of death. The Court upheld New Jersey's power to tax, saying: "The command of the State over the owner, the obligations which domicile creates, the practical necessity of associating intangibles with the person of the owner at his domicile since they represent the only rights which he may enforce against others—these are foundations for the jurisdiction of the domiciliary state to tax." [129]

The appellants alleged a deprivation of property without due process of law on the ground that the tax had been levied, not according to the value of the property at the time the trust was executed, but rather on its value at the time of the grantor's death. In effect the state had used its death-transfer tax law to reach a gift, for at the time the trust had been executed the state did not have a gift-tax law. The Court could find "no constitutional reason why a state may not make the transfer inter vivos the taxable event

[126] 316 U.S. 174, 187–88 (1942). [127] Ibid., p. 201.
[128] 319 U.S. 94 (1943).
[129] Ibid., pp. 96–97. Domicile of the grantor at the time of his death was said to be the controlling factor here.

and then measure the tax by the value of the property at the time of death. The significant facts are that the remaindermen derived solely from the trust agreement and that the grantor died domiciled in New Jersey." [130]

The Court held itself bound by the decision of the state court as to "the kind of interest transferred," [131] and it interpreted the due process clause as placing "no restriction on a state as to the time at which an inheritance tax shall be levied or the property valued for the purpose of such a tax." [132] It would seem that, following the rule of this decision, a state might lawfully reach the transfer of property by applying its gift-tax law but measuring the tax by the value of the trust property after years of accumulation even if it did not have a death-transfer tax. Though the power of other states to tax the transfer was not in question here, the rule applied by the Court in this case, along with those of Curry and Graves v. Elliott, brings such a transfer within the purview of the tax power of the grantor's domiciliary state as well as the state in which the trust property is located. The real significance of the decision lies in the extent to which the Court allowed the state to make the determinations upon which the validity of the tax turned.

Thus the due process of law clause in the realm of transfer taxation has been interpreted to permit double taxation of intangible property if there can be shown any beneficial relation between the subject and the taxing state. In many instances the benefits accorded are rather difficult to discover. Frequently the basis has not been actual benefit but the possibility of benefit, as where the protection of the laws of the state might have been invoked but the occasion for such protection never arose.[133] The protection granted may be to the person of the owner or to the tax subject. Such is the logical conclusion of the application of a "benefit" or "protection" criterion of jurisdiction to tax. In the face of such criterion territorial limitations on the jurisdiction to tax disappear.

[130] *Ibid.*, p. 97.   [131] *Ibid.*

[132] *Ibid.* Cf. Heiner v. Donnan, 285 U.S. 312, 332 (1932), where the Court held that the statute providing that the value of the gift be determined as of the date of decedent's death was so arbitrary as to violate due process of law of the Fifth Amendment.

[133] See Greenough v. City of Newport, 331 U.S. 486, 495 (1947), where this rule was applied to a property tax.

"Jurisdiction to tax" becomes almost anything the Court wants to make of it.[134]

Franchise Taxes. In only a few instances the franchise tax has been challenged on the basis of jurisdictional limits placed upon the states by the due process of law of the Fourteenth Amendment. The holdings in the few cases in which the validity of such tax has been questioned do, however, indicate the principles on which the Court has based its decision.

The validity of a Virginia law taxing the privilege of doing business in the state, the amount of the tax to be measured by the authorized capital stock of the company applying, was challenged in Atlantic Refining Co. *v.* Virginia.[135] The sole objection raised by the company was that the method of ascertaining the amounts to be paid placed the tax on property beyond the jurisdiction of the state and therefore violated the due process of law guaranteed by the Fourteenth Amendment. The Court decided in favor of the state,[136] saying that since the tax was in effect an entrance fee rather than a tax on a corporation already doing business in the state, Virginia could fix the rates as high as she liked. The basis for determining the amount of the tax was said to be a fair one, since "the greater the financial resources of the company, the greater the privilege." [137]

The California privilege tax, as applied to a company doing business in the state, was challenged in Connecticut General Life Insurance Co. *v.* Johnson.[138] The statute imposed a tax on all insurance companies operating in the state. The amount of the tax was to be measured by the gross premiums received by the companies on contracts entered into outside the state with other

[134] For a discussion of the benefit theory, see Merrill, "Jurisdiction to Tax—Another Word," *loc. cit.,* pp. 582–604. See also Harding, *Double Taxation of Property and Income,* pp. 35–45.

[135] 302 U.S. 22 (1937).

[136] The statute had been upheld previously in General Ry. Signal Co. *v.* Virginia, 246 U.S. 500 (1918); and Western Gas Construction Co. *v.* Virginia, 276 U.S. 597 (1928). But the taxation, in the form of a filing tax and license fee reckoned on the authorized stock, of a foreign corporation admitted to do business in the state was an attempt to reach property outside the jurisdiction of the state and therefore a violation of due process of law. Cudahy Packing Co. *v.* Hinkle, 278 U.S. 460 (1929).

[137] 302 U.S. 22, 30 (1937).   [138] 303 U.S. 77 (1938).

insurance companies authorized to do business in California, insuring the latter companies against loss on policies of life insurance executed by them in California. The Court, speaking through Justice Stone, found that the reinsurance transactions took place outside the state. Since "the due process clause denies to the state the right to tax or regulate the corporation's property and activities elsewhere," [139] the tax was held to be invalid. It was said that the limits prescribed by the due process clause were to be determined by reference to the "incidence of the tax" rather than the "ultimate thrust of the economic benefits and burdens of transactions within the state." [140] The Court held that by the reinsurance contracts the company agreed to indemnify the insured companies against loss upon policies contracted in California. But the reinsurance transactions called for no act in California and therefore did not fall within the jurisdiction of that state.[141]

In several cases the Court has held that the right to employ labor is a legitimate subject for a franchise tax. In Carmichael v. Southern Coal and Coke Co.[142] the validity of the tax provisions of Alabama's unemployment-insurance law was at stake; in Steward Machine Co. v. Davis,[143] that of the federal law on the same

[139] *Ibid.*, pp. 80–81. Whatever significance the decision of the majority might have had, it was, for the time at least, overshadowed by the vigorous dissent of Justice Black, who declared that the due process of law clause should not be invoked to protect corporations. "Persons" in the Fourteenth Amendment, he said, was not intended to include corporations. *Ibid.*, p. 85. Looking at the opinions in such cases as Hague v. C.I.O., 307 U.S. 496 (1939); Grosjean v. American Press Corp., 297 U.S. 233 (1936); Bridges v. California, 314 U.S. 252 (1941); and the present case, it seems that the Court itself has not made up its mind as to whether the "property" or "liberty" or both of corporations are protected by due process of law. See Orville C. Snyder, "Freedom of Press: Personal Liberty or Property Right," *Brooklyn Law Review*, VIII (1938), 4–27. See Justice Douglas' dissent, joined in by Justice Black, in Wheeling Steel Corporation v. Clander, 337 U.S. 562 (1949). The case was decided on the basis of the equal-protection clause, but the dissenters declared that "persons" in the Fourteenth Amendment referred only to "natural" persons.

[140] 303 U.S. 77, 80–81 (1938).

[141] *Ibid.*, p. 81. Cf. Osborn v. Ozlin, 310 U.S. 53 (1940); and State Farm Mutual Automobile Insurance Co. v. Duel, 324 U.S. 154 (1945). See Memphis Natural Gas Company v. Stone, 335 U.S. 80 (1948), in which the Court upheld Mississippi's franchise tax of $1.50 per $1,000.00 capital invested in the state. The tax was challenged as a violation of the commerce clause, but Justice Rutledge, concurring, specifically said that the state had "jurisdiction" to tax and had not violated due process by applying the tax to the gas company, which was engaged wholly in interstate commerce. 335 U.S. 80, 96 (1948).

[142] 301 U.S. 495 (1937).   [143] 301 U.S. 548 (1937).

subject. In each case the Court held that the state or federal government might tax employers for the privilege of employing labor. It was said that the right to select the subjects of taxation was an essential part of the state's inherent power to tax.[144]

The state tax law was challenged on the ground that a single group was chosen to bear the full burden of the tax, which was to be used for the benefit of another group, and that a company's share of the tax was in no way proportionate to its unemployment record. Considerations of practical convenience and policy were said to preclude the Court's condemnation of the measurement of the tax and the classifications on the ground that they were arbitrary.[145] Congress had found that the unemployment situation was a matter of public interest. The state, in compliance with the congressional policy set forth in the federal law, had found the unemployment situation in the state a matter of grave concern and had sought to translate its remedial policy into legislation. The fact that, in legislating on the subject, the state required an employer to pay a tax measured by his payroll, even though it could not be shown that he had contributed to the conditions sought to be remedied, was not thought to be a valid objection to the law.

The case of International Shoe Co. v. State of Washington Office of Unemployment Compensation and Placement [146] involved a privilege tax in the form of contributions to the unemployment-compensation fund imposed on all companies doing business in the state. Appellant company, a Delaware corporation having its principal place of business in St. Louis, Missouri, distributed shoes through branch offices located throughout the country. It had no office in Washington but conducted its business there through a group of salesmen hired in St. Louis and super-

---

[144] 301 U.S. 495, 509 (1937).

[145] Ibid., pp. 521–22. Justice Stone said that it was a familiar principle in taxation that the state could tax a class or individual who would enjoy no direct benefits from its expenditures and who were not responsible for the conditions to be remedied by the imposition of the tax or the expenditure of the funds. "A tax is not an assessment of benefits. . . . It is a means of distributing the burden of the costs of government. *The only benefit to which the taxpayer is entitled is that derived from his enjoyment of the privilege of living in organized society, established and safeguarded by the devotion of taxes to public expenses.*" Ibid., p. 522. (Italics added.)

[146] 326 U.S. 310 (1945).

vised from that office. The state brought suit to recover the unpaid unemployment-insurance tax assessed against the company. The company contended that for purposes of taxation it was not present in the state of Washington and was not, therefore, amenable to the proceedings in the courts of that state to recover unpaid contributions. Chief Justice Stone spoke for the Court and, in upholding the tax and the state proceedings for recovery, explained: "Since the corporate personality is a fiction, although a fiction to be acted upon as though it were a fact," it is clear that unlike an individual its "presence" without, as well as within, the state of its origin can be manifested only by activities carried on in its behalf by those who are authorized to act for it. To say that the "corporation is so far 'present' there to satisfy due process requirements, for purposes of taxation is to beg the question to be decided. . . . Those demands may be met by such contacts of the corporation with the state of the forum as to make it reasonable, in the context of our federal system of government, to require the corporation to defend the particular suit which is brought there." [147]

The Court considered the fact that the company employed labor in the state and explained that "The right to employ labor has always been deemed an appropriate subject of taxation." [148] Citing the decision in Carmichael v. Southern Coal and Coke Co.,[149] the Court said that a tax imposed upon the employer for employment benefits was within the tax jurisdiction of the state.[150] The benefits in this case were said to lie in the fact that through the activities of the salesmen in the state, the company had built up a large intrastate business.

Justice Black wrote a separate opinion, in which he declared that the rule on which the Court upheld the power of the state to tax in this case was such that "tomorrow's judgment may strike down a State or Federal enactment on the ground that it does not conform to this court's idea of natural justice." [151] With regard to the application of due process in this case, Justice Black continued: "And the due process clause is not brought in issue any more by the appellant's further conceptualistic contention that

[147] *Ibid.*, p. 316.   [148] *Ibid.*, p. 321.
[149] 301 U.S. 495 (1937).   [150] 326 U.S. 310, 321 (1945).
[151] *Ibid.*, p. 326. This same conflict appears in other fields of due process, especially in that of criminal proceedings.

Washington could not levy a tax . . . because it did not honor
that state with its mystical 'presence.' For it is unthinkable that
the vague due process clause was ever intended to prohibit a State
from regulating or taxing a business carried on within its boundaries simply because this is done by agents of a corporation organized and having its headquarters elsewhere." [152] Looking at
the situation from the point of view of the citizens of the state,
Justice Black thought that to read such a limitation into the due
process clause "would in fact result in depriving a state's citizens
of due process by taking away from the state the power to protect
them in their dealings within its boundaries with representatives
of a foreign corporation." [153]

The criterion by which the Court will decide the question of
the state's jurisdiction to impose a franchise tax seems to be, not
the presence of the corporation within the state, but whether there
is an activity or transaction carried on or executed within its
borders in behalf of the corporation wherever located. The subjects of such tax are practically unlimited.

Sales and Use Taxes. While the validity of state sales- and use-
tax laws has been challenged before the Supreme Court in many
instances, only a few of the decisions have been concerned with
the due process of law clause.[154] The few which have been decided
on this basis are relatively recent. In Nelson *v.* Sears, Roebuck &
Co.,[155] Justice Douglas, for the Court, upheld a state sales-tax law
which made mail-order houses collectors of the tax for the state.[156]

---

[152] *Ibid.*, p. 323.

[153] *Ibid.*, p. 325. As to the basis of the majority's opinion, Justice Black declared: "There is a strong emotional appeal in the words 'fair play,' 'justice,' and
'reasonableness.' But they were not chosen by those who wrote the original constitution or the Fourteenth Amendment as a measuring rod for the court to use in
invalidating State or Federal laws passed by elected legislative representatives."
The fact that specific constitutional prohibitions require interpretation "is no
reason for reading them into the due process clause so as to restrict the state's
power to tax and sue those whose activities affect persons and businesses within
the state, provided proper services can be had." *Ibid.*

[154] For instance, Stewart Dry Goods Co. *v.* Lewis, 294 U.S. 550 (1935), was
decided on the question of equal protection of the law. Magnano Co. *v.* Hamilton, 292 U.S. 40 (1934), concerned due process as related to the rate of a sales
tax rather than as to jurisdiction. See p. 387.

[155] 312 U.S. 359 (1941).

[156] Monamotor Oil Co. *v.* Johnson, 292 U.S. 86 (1934), was cited as authority
for this decision. In that case due process of law was not discussed with reference

The statute was challenged on the ground that it placed a tax on transactions beyond the jurisdiction of the state and was therefore in violation of the due process of law clause. To this contention, Justice Douglas answered: "The fact that under the Iowa law the sale is made outside the State does not mean that the power of Iowa has nothing on which to operate." [157] If the company did not conduct a business—take orders for goods—in the state, Iowa could not impose such a tax on it. Since the state had extended to the company the privilege of doing business within its borders, it could exact a tax "as the price of enjoying the full benefits flowing from its Iowa business." [158]

Although the case of McLeod v. Dilworth [159] did not turn primarily on the due process issue, it is of sufficient importance in a discussion of the state's jurisdiction to tax sales within the limitations of that clause to warrant mention here. A Tennessee corporation which was not qualified to do business in Arkansas and which had no sales office nor any other place of business in that state made sales of goods in Tennessee for delivery by common carrier in Arkansas. The company sent two traveling men into Arkansas to represent the company and publicize its products. These representatives, residents of Memphis, accepted requests for purchases, but the sales were not consummated until these requests were approved at the home offices in Memphis. Merchandise was shipped F.O.B. from Memphis, title being relinquished upon delivery to the common carrier. Arkansas placed a sales tax on these transactions on the ground that in reality the company's representatives in Arkansas made sales, and the purchases were delivered to persons in the state. The corporation contended that by so doing that state extended the operation of its

---

to the collection of the tax. However, the Court decided on other grounds against the appellant, who contended that due process had been denied by the method of collection.

[157] 312 U.S. 359, 363 (1941). The State Supreme Court had held the law invalid because it taxed sales which were consummated outside the state. See Justice Roberts' dissent, *ibid.*, p. 371.

[158] *Ibid.*, p. 364.

[159] 322 U.S. 327 (1944). For a discussion of this and the two companion cases, see Ralph G. Crandell, "Overlapping Jurisdiction of the State with Respect to the Taxation of Commerce," *National Tax Association: Proceedings* (Lancaster, Pa., 1944), pp. 240–59.

tax laws to events wholly outside its jurisdiction and so violated the due process clause.

In invalidating the application of the tax to such sales, the Court held that the tax was actually upon sales completed beyond the state bounds and hence was violative of the due process guaranteed by the Fourteenth Amendment.[160] Justice Frankfurter, who wrote the opinion for the majority, did not reply to the suggestion that Arkansas might have obtained the same results constitutionally by making its tax a use tax rather than a sales tax.[161]

The Indiana gross-income tax was challenged before the Court in International Harvester Co. v. Department of the Treasury of Indiana.[162] The state imposed a tax on receipts from several different classes of sales. International Harvester Company was authorized to do business in Indiana. It maintained two manufacturing establishments in the state, one at Richmond and the other at Fort Wayne. It had branch sales offices in five leading cities of the state. In some instances a district which covered territory in Indiana had its sales office in an adjoining state. The tax law classified sales such as those made by International Harvester into several groups. Class A consists of sales made by branch offices outside the state to dealers and users within Indiana. Such sales are based upon orders solicited in Indiana by representatives of the out-of-state branches or upon mail orders from Indiana to the out-of-state offices. The goods are shipped directly to the purchaser. Class C sales are those made by the out-of-state branches to Indiana purchasers, the goods being shipped to the factories to save time and expense of shipping. Class D sales are those made by sales offices

---

[160] 322 U.S. 327, 330 (1944).

[161] *Ibid.* Almost identical facts were presented in General Trading Co. v. State Tax Commission of Iowa, 322 U.S. 335 (1944). This case, however, involved a use tax on all retail sales delivered in Iowa in the course of interstate commerce. The tax was upheld as not in violation of the commerce clause. The due process issue was not brought before the Court. It is significant that this tax was intended to reach the same sales which had been taxed by Arkansas and had been held a denial of due process in the Dilworth case. In the General Trading Co. case the Court found that the "tax is what it professes to be—a nondiscriminatory excise laid on all personal property consumed in Iowa. The property is enjoyed by an Iowa resident partly because the opportunity is given by Iowa to enjoy the property no matter where acquired. The exaction is made against the ultimate consumer—the Iowa resident who is paying taxes to sustain his own state government." *Ibid.*, p. 338.

[162] 322 U.S. 340 (1944).

in Indiana to dealers and users outside the state. The purchasers come into Indiana and accept delivery of the goods to themselves in the state. Class E consists of sales in Indiana to purchasers in Indiana, the goods being shipped from points outside the state to the in-state customer. The company alleged a deprivation of property without due process on the ground that some of the sales would be subject to taxation under the Illinois Retailer's Occupation Tax. Justice Douglas, for the Court, disposed of this contention with "it will be time to cross that bridge when we come to it." [163] With regard to the state's jurisdiction to tax the sales Justice Douglas said that "The fact that the sales in Class C are made by an out-of-state seller and that the contracts were made outside the state is not controlling." [164] Delivery of the goods in the state is sufficient to give Indiana jurisdiction to tax. The Court found, in the case of Class D sales, that "Both the agreement to sell and the delivery took place in Indiana." It was not considered material that the goods were shipped out of the state immediately.[165] As to the sales of Class E it was said that there was the "same equivalence" regardless of whether the tax is on the selling or the buying phase of the transaction. "Each is in substance an imposition of a tax on the transfer of property." [166]

Taken with the Dilworth case, this decision would seem to indicate that the name of tax was the significant thing, for in each case the tax was imposed on sales completed outside the state. In either case the taxable event was the bringing into, or the use in, the state of articles bought elsewhere. The important feature of the decisions seems to be the attempt on the part of the Court to uphold the state's power to tax but at the same time not to commit the Court to a policy which appeared to condone an accumulation of taxes on an interstate transaction.[167] The Court was not con-

[163] *Ibid.*, p. 348.

[164] *Ibid.*, p. 345. This is following the decision in South Pacific Co. *v.* Gallagher, 306 U.S. 167 (1939), which upheld the California Use Tax imposed on tangible personal property bought outside the state and used as a part of the interstate transportation equipment. The same tax was upheld as applied to property bought outside the state and later brought into California for use. Felt & Terrant Co. *v.* Gallagher, 306 U.S. 62 (1939). In these cases the decision rested on the fact that the "taxable event is the exercise of the property right in California."

[165] 322 U.S. 340, 345 (1944).   [166] *Ibid.*, p. 348.

[167] In this case, *ibid.*, p. 344, the Court cited Department of the Treasury of

cerned about double taxation simply because it burdened the tax-payer. As the decisions now stand, the same economic interest may be reached by two or more taxes imposed in different jurisdictions under different classifications.[168]

Justice Rutledge, filing a single opinion to cover the three cases, concurred in the decision in the International Harvester Company case and dissented from the results in the Dilworth case. He felt that the Court had allowed a very minor technicality to obscure the realities of the situation involved. For, in his opinion, "Whether a tax is levied on the 'sale' or the 'use' by one state or the other, it is in fact and effect a tax levied on an interstate transaction. Nothing in due process requirements prohibits either state from levying either sort of tax on such transaction. That Tennessee may tax this transaction by a sales tax does not, in any proper conception of due process, deprive Arkansas of the same power." [169] "Due process" and "commerce" conceptions are not always distinguishable and frequently overlap. And therefore he found that

> The great difficulty in allocating taxing power as a matter of due process between the state of origin and the state of market arises from the fact that each state, considered without reference to the other, always has sufficiently substantial relation in fact and in tax benefit conferred on the interstate transaction to sustain an exertion of its taxing power, a fact not always recognized. And from this failure, as well as from the terms in which statutes . . . are phrased, comes the search for some "taxable incident taking place within the state's boundaries" as a hook for hanging the constitutionality under due process of law.[170]

Indiana v. Wood Preserving Corp., 313 U.S. 62 (1941), to the effect that "the Fourteenth Amendment does not prevent the imposition of the tax on receipts from an interstate transaction even though the total activities from which the local transaction derives may have incidental interstate attributes."

[168] See Richard C. Beckett, "Significant New Decisions of Courts—State and Local Taxes," *National Tax Association: Proceedings* (Lancaster, Pa., 1944), p. 14.

[169] 322 U.S. 340, 357 (1944).

[170] *Ibid.* The Court upheld a Texas tax on the production of oil, the amount of the tax to be divided among lessor and lessee according to their respective interests. The law was said not to be unreasonable or arbitrary, because the lessor, who challenged it, had a "definite economic interest in the venture." Barwise v. Sheppard, 299 U.S. 33, 38–39 (1936).

Due process requirements, he said, are met if there are sufficient "factual connections with economic and legal effects, between the transaction and the taxing state. . . ." [171] Justice Rutledge thought that these requirements were met in the Dilworth case equally as well as in the International Harvester Company case.

BENEFITS AND DOUBLE TAXATION

With regard to the jurisdiction of the state to impose a tax, the Court has, within the past two decades, completed a cycle. It has gone all the way from the interpretation of due process of law as placing no limitations on the power to tax intangibles to quite the reverse, holding that double taxation per se violates due process. At the present time, due process is interpreted as not prohibiting two states from taxing simultaneously the same subject or different legal and economic interests of the same taxable event or subject. Intangible property is taxable at the domicile of the owner as well as at its situs if situated outside the domiciliary state. Tangible personal property may be taxed by any state which affords the property protection or benefit sufficient to give it some legal or economic relation to the taxing state.

And what is "benefit" for tax purposes? It may be almost anything. The fact that the state has laws for the protection of the owner, the beneficiary, the property, or the trustee of an out-of-state trust itself confers tax jurisdiction. The owner or the beneficiary may constitutionally be called upon to pay a tax on a specific piece of property because he is allowed to live in an "organized society," made possible by the existence of the state government. The benefit may be the privilege of carrying on a business, employing labor, selling goods or buying them, or just bringing them into the state for use there or reshipment to another state, where the purchaser may be assessed another tax for the privilege of using the article. The benefit may be something which the recipient recognizes as beneficial or it may consist of something which only the state thinks will be good for him; it may be a benefit to the taxpayer personally or individually, or to another group or individual. In other words, "benefit" has come to be a term used by

[171] 322 U.S. 340, 356 (1944).

the Court to cover a multitude of relations which it thinks makes the tax legitimate within the requirements of due process of law. On the other hand, a benefit is not essential to a valid tax, for the Court has held that a tax is not an assessment of benefits.

FEDERAL JURISDICTION TO TAX

In very few cases have federal tax statutes been challenged as being contrary to the due process of law guaranteed by the Fifth Amendment. In some instances the Court has declared that the restraints placed upon the respective governments by the due process clause of the Fifth and Fourteenth amendments are the same.[172] However, by the nature of the two governmental units there would not be comparable territorial restrictions, and whatever limitations have been read into the "due process" of the Fourteenth Amendment as regards double taxation have never been held to apply to the same clause of the Fifth Amendment with regard to state and federal taxation of a single subject.[173]

In the case of a conclusive presumption created by federal statute, the Court held in Heiner v. Donnan [174] that the due process of the Fifth Amendment restricts the national government in the same manner that the Fourteenth Amendment limits the power of the states. Here the Court declared that a federal statute which created the presumption that an *inter vivos* gift made within two years prior to the donor's death was made in contemplation of death and subject to the federal inheritance tax "is so arbitrary and unreasonable" that it cannot stand under the requirements of the due process of law guaranteed by the Fifth Amendment.[175] A conclusive presumption was said to be a statute imposing a tax

[172] Heiner v. Donnan, 285 U.S. 312, 326 (1932); Handy v. Delaware, 285 U.S. 352, 355 (1932); Magnano Co. v. Hamilton, 292 U.S. 40, 44 (1934); Curry v. McCanless, 307 U.S. 357, 369–70 (1939). See Charles L. B. Lowndes, "Spurious Concepts of the Constitutional Law of Taxation," *Harvard Law Review*, XLVII (1934), 628, 658.
[173] See Haglund, "Double Taxation," *loc. cit.*, p. 113.
[174] 285 U.S. 312 (1932).
[175] *Ibid.*, p. 329. See Felix Frankfurter, "Social Issues Before the Supreme Court," *Yale Review*, New Series, XXII (1933), 490–92. Mr. Frankfurter felt that the duty of the Court toward a balanced budget should prevent its sanctifying such gross tax evasion.

upon an assumption of fact which the taxpayer is forbidden to controvert.[176]

The fact that the value of the gift was to be fixed as of the date of the donor's death rather than at the time it was made was thought to be "so obviously arbitrary and capricious as, by itself, to condemn the tax, viewed as a gift tax, as violative of due process of law." [177]

The due process clause of the Fifth Amendment cannot be invoked as a defense against a federal income-tax statute which imposes a tax on a corporation's undistributed profits, on the ground that a state law forbids the corporation to distribute dividends for the year because of a previously existing deficit.[178] Justice Black said that the federal tax was levied on the net income of the corporation, and the fact that the income would have been less had the corporation been allowed under state law to distribute dividends was not material. Nor may a federal tax statute be challenged successfully on the ground that the classification is unreasonable or discriminatory. The Court has held that since there is no equal-protection clause in the Fifth Amendment, inequality in the incidence of the tax is not a legitimate objection.[179] Impliedly equal protection has not been read into the due process guaranteed by the Fifth Amendment. The Court, however, has held that a tax law which embodies a discrimination gross enough to amount to confiscation would be a violation of due process.

The Court found that a congressional tax statute providing that the income from a revocable trust,[180] or from an irrevocable trust when the income is designated to pay premiums on life-insurance policies of the creator of the trust,[181] should be included in the calculation of the gross income for income-tax purposes was not

[176] See Helvering v. Rankin, 295 U.S. 123, 126 (1935), which involved a conclusive presumption on the basis of "first bought—first sold" in regard to profits on the sale of stocks. It was held not violative of due process, for if the owner had any proof of the identity of the shares of stock sold he was free to offer it.
[177] 285 U.S. 312, 332 (1932). Cf. Central Hanover Bank and Trust Co. v. Kelly, 319 U.S. 94 (1943). See p. 370, supra.
[178] Helvering v. New Steel Co., 311 U.S. 46, 51-52 (1940).
[179] Steward Machine Co. v. Davis, 301 U.S. 548, 584 (1937). See Sunshine Anthracite Coal Co. v. Adkins, 310 U.S. 381, 401 (1940).
[180] Reinecke v. Smith, 289 U.S. 172 (1933).
[181] Burnet v. Wells, 289 U.S. 670 (1933).

a denial of the due process guaranteed by the Fifth Amendment. In the case of the first the Court, speaking through Justice Roberts, said that the question of due process would depend on whether the income from the trust actually belonged to the creator. It was said that when a settler retained the power to repossess the corpus of the trust and to enjoy the income, he had enough control to justify the imposition of the tax.[182] In the second case the tax was upheld because the creator of the trust retained control over the way the income was to be spent. Therefore, the transfer of the property came at his death rather than at the time the trusts were created.[183]

In two recent cases the Supreme Court held that the federal government could, consistently with due process of law, assess an inheritance tax upon the value of the property of both husband and wife in the event of the death of either in those states whose law provides for community of property. Chief Justice Stone wrote the Court's opinion in Fernandez v. Wiener [184] and United States v. Rompel,[185] in which appellants contended that upon the death of the husband only one half of the community of property should be taxed as the husband's share of the estate. In upholding the tax, the Chief Justice said:

> the death of the husband of the Louisiana marital com-
> munity of property not only operates to transfer his rights
> in his share of the community to his heirs or those taking
> under his will. It terminates his expansive and sometimes
> profitable control over the wife's share, and for the first time
> brings her half of the property into her full and exclusive
> possession, control and enjoyment. The cessation of these
> extensive powers of the husband, even though they were
> powers over property which he never "owned" and the
> establishment in the wife of new powers of control over
> her share though it was always hers, furnish appropriate oc-
> casions for the imposition of an excise tax.[186]

[182] 289 U.S. 172, 177 (1933).   [183] 289 U.S. 670, 680 (1933).
[184] 326 U.S. 340 (1945).   [185] 326 U.S. 367 (1945).
[186] 326 U.S. 340, 355 (1945). See United States v. Jacobs, 306 U.S. 363, 371 (1939), in which the Court held that upon the death of a cotenant the wife became possessed of the entire estate, and the transfer tax measured by the full value of the property comprising the joint tenancy did not violate due process of law.

And if the wife had died first, her death, it was said, would bring into being a new set of relationships and make it possible for the husband to exercise new and greater powers over his share of the community of property as well as to acquire rights over hers. These would be proper subjects for an excise tax measured by the value of the entire estate.[187]

Since the tax was on the privilege of acquiring new rights in the property, both in that already owned by the wife and that inherited through the husband's will, the Court did not find that it required the taking of the survivor's property to pay the decedent's tax. The Chief Justice explained: "As the tax is upon the surrender of old incidents of property by the decedent and the acquisition of new by the survivor, it is appropriately measured by the value of the property to which these incidents attach." [188] United States v. Rompel [189] involved a similar set of facts, and the Court held that the death of either husband or wife under the Texas community-property laws "effects sufficient alteration in the spouse's possession and enjoyment and reciprocal powers of control and disposition of the community property as to warrant the imposition of an excise tax measured by the value of the entire community." [190] The Court said that the due process clause of the Fifth Amendment restricts the taxing power of the federal government only in rare and special instances. Such instances were said to include tax statutes which were of such a nature as to compel the conclusion that they were not tax measures but rather enactments intended to accomplish some forbidden power.[191] But when the taxing provisions of the second Bituminous Coal Conservation Act [192] were challenged on the ground that they imposed a penalty rather than a tax and were therefore a violation of the due process of law of the Fifth Amendment, Justice Douglas said that "Clearly the tax was not designed merely for revenue purposes." The power of Congress to fix prices in the coal industry had been upheld as a valid exercise of the commerce power, and the tax power had been used as a sanction to enforce

---

[187] Fernandez v. Wiener, 326 U.S. 340, 355 (1945).
[188] Ibid., p. 358.   [189] 326 U.S. 367 (1945).   [190] Ibid., p. 370.
[191] Magnano Co. v. Hamilton, 292 U.S. 40, 44 (1934).
[192] 50 Stat. 72.

these price regulations. But the Court held that "Congress may impose penalties in aid of the exercise of any of its enumerated powers." The taxing power granted to Congress, Justice Douglas said, could, consistently with due process of law, be utilized as a sanction for the exercise of any of the other powers granted to it.[193] In Magnano Co. v. Hamilton [194] the Court implied, at least, that it would hold such a measure invalid as a denial of due process if enacted by a state legislature.

In the case of Burnet v. Brooks [195] the Court was called upon to pass on the validity of a tax imposed on securities deposited in New York and owned by the decedent, subject of Great Britain and resident of Cuba at the time of his death. The tax was challenged on the basis of the rules of jurisdiction laid down by the Court as applying to state taxing power. Justice Hughes, speaking for the Court, declared: "Due process requires that the limits of jurisdiction shall not be transgressed. That requirement leaves the limits of jurisdiction to be ascertained in each case with appropriate regard to the distinct sphere of activity of State and nation. The limits of State power are defined in view of the relation of the States to each other in the Federal Union. . . . These decisions established that proper regard for the relation of the States in our system required that the property under consideration should be taxed by one state only." [196]

But the Court held that none of these restrictions as to jurisdiction applied to the federal government in the exercise of its sovereignty.[197] In this case there was no question of arbitrariness or discrimination, and therefore the Court expressly limited its discussion to territorial jurisdiction.

Thus while the Court has on occasions held that the restrictions on the respective governments under the due process clauses of the Fifth Amendment and the Fourteenth are the same, this would apply only with regard to a relatively few of the instances in which a tax law might be challenged. The Supreme Court has

[193] Sunshine Anthracite Coal Co. v. Adkins, 310 U.S. 381, 393 (1940).
[194] 292 U.S. 40 (1934).   [195] 288 U.S. 378 (1933).
[196] Ibid., p. 401.
[197] Ibid., p. 405. It was said that the criterion of the state's tax power by virtue of the relation of the states to each other "is not the criterion of the taxing power of the United States by virtue of its sovereignty in relation to the property of a nonresident."

expressly held that in relation to the property of nonresidents the United States is not bound by the territorial limitations which, under the Fourteenth Amendment, are binding on the states. Any property situated in the United States is subject to taxation by the federal government, irrespective of the owner's residence or citizenship. Apparently the Court will hold a tax statute invalid under the due process clause of the Fifth Amendment if it is found to be grossly unreasonable, arbitrary, or discriminatory.

RATE AND MEASURE IN TAXATION

In Magnano Co. *v.* Hamilton [198] the Supreme Court declared: "Except in special instances the due process clause of the Fifth Amendment is not a limitation upon the taxing power of the Federal Government. . . . And no reason exists for applying a different rule against a state in the case of the Fourteenth Amendment." [199] Here the appellant company alleged that the flat tax of fifteen cents per pound on all oleomargarine sold in the state violated the due process of law clause of the Fourteenth Amendment because, if enforced, it would destroy its business. Justice Sutherland, for a unanimous Court, stated that the due process clause could be invoked in such cases only if "the act be so arbitrary as to compel the conclusion that it does not involve an exertion of the taxing power, but the direct exertion of some other and forbidden power. . . ." [200] The Court refused to look into the motives which had prompted the legislature to enact such a law and held that the tax would not be stricken down under the due process clause "simply because its enforcement may or will result in restricting or even destroying particular businesses." [201]

It was said that if the measure were plainly not a tax but merely a disguise for a regulatory measure forbidden by the Constitution, the Court would hold it void as a violation of due process of law.[202]

[198] 292 U.S. 40 (1934). [199] *Ibid.,* p. 44.
[200] *Ibid.*

[201] *Ibid.* In Fox *v.* Standard Oil Co., 294 U.S. 87, 100 (1935), it was expressly stated that the state might make the tax heavy enough to discourage the multiplication of the units and by the incidence of the tax burden to foster new forms of industry.

[202] 292 U.S. 40, 46 (1934). See Robert C. Brown, "When is a Tax Not a Tax," *Indiana Law Journal,* XI (1936), 399–428. In Sunshine Anthracite Coal Co. *v.*

In the present case, however, it was found that the statute "is in form plainly a taxing act, with nothing in its terms to suggest that it was intended to be anything else." [203] The Court avoided the appellant's main contention that the rate of the tax was so oppressive that it resulted in a deprivation of property without due process of law. Justice Sutherland argued: "If the tax had been five cents instead of fifteen cents per pound, no one, probably, would have thought of challenging its constitutionality or of suggesting that under the guise of imposing a tax another and different power had in fact been exercised." [204] Yet the whole basis of the contention that there had been a deprivation of property without due process was the very fact that the tax was fifteen cents instead of five. Though the reasoning by which the decision was reached is unconvincing, Justice Sutherland, speaking the final word for the Court, declared that a tax would not be voided as violative of due process merely on the ground that the rate was excessive, regardless of how burdensome such tax might be. [205]

It is impossible to reconcile the holding in the Magnano Company case with that of the case of Great Northern Railway v. Weeks, [206] in which Justice Butler, speaking for the Court, held invalid a tax imposed upon the company, because he thought the valuation of the company's property was excessive. The tax law permitted the imposition of a tax on the full value of the company's property. "Full value," the Court said, meant the amount to which the owner would be entitled as just compensation if the property were taken by the government under the power of eminent domain. [207] The company did not allege that there had been any discrimination in the valuation or assessment of its property. Its sole complaint was that the valuation was excessive. The

---

Adkins, 310 U.S. 381, 393 (1940), the Court said that Congress might impose penalties in aid of the exercise of any of the powers granted it under the Constitution. It was said that the tax power might be used as a sanction for the exercise of another power.

[203] 292 U.S. 40, 47 (1934). But the Court said that "From the beginning of our government, the courts have sustained taxes, although imposed with the collateral intent of effecting ulterior ends which, considered apart, were beyond the constitutional power of the lawmakers to realize by legislation directly addressed to their accomplishment."

[204] Ibid.

[206] 297 U.S. 135 (1936).

[205] Ibid., pp. 46–47.

[207] Ibid., p. 139.

Court found this to be true and invalidated the law, as applied to this company, as a denial of due process guaranteed by the Fourteenth Amendment.[208]

Justice Stone dissented, stating that it was a matter of concern for the Court to set aside a tax as a violation of the Fourteenth Amendment on the ground that the assessment on which it is computed is too high.[209] He, joined by Justices Brandeis and Cardozo, was of the opinion that unless the valuation was discriminatory, it did not place any unequal burden on the taxpayer and could not be said to be arbitrary or oppressive in the constitutional sense. For, said he:

> Even if the valuation of the board be erroneous, the errors of a state judicial officer, however gross, whether of law or fact, are not violations of the Constitution and are not open to review in the federal courts merely because they are errors. If over-valuation, even though gross or intentional, without more, were held to infringe the Fourteenth Amendment, every taxpayer would be at liberty to ask the federal courts to review a state tax assessment upon the bare allegation that it is grossly excessive, and without showing that it does more than subject him to taxation on the same basis as every other taxpayer.[210]

The decision in this case was discredited in the case of Nashville, C. & St. L. Ry. Co. v. Browning,[211] in which the Court held that "even assuming that there was an over-assessment, constitutional invalidity would not follow. If the needs of the state require higher taxes, the Fourteenth Amendment certainly does not bar their imposition. The maintenance of a higher assessment in the face of a declining value is merely another way of achieving the

[208] *Ibid.*, p. 152. Cf. Fox *v.* Standard Oil, 294 U.S. 87, 99 (1935), where the Court said that "When the power to tax exists, the extent of the burden is a matter for the discretion of the lawmakers." Cf. Roberts *v.* New York City, 295 U.S. 264, 277 (1935), where the Court held that the due process clause of the Fourteenth Amendment did not protect against errors of judgment. The fact that appraisal of the property had been erroneous raised no substantial issue under the due process clause. Here the Court said: "Due process is a growth too sturdy to succumb to the infection of the least ingredient of error."

[209] 297 U.S. 135, 154 (1936). Cf. the rate cases in which the rate order was set aside because the valuation was too low.

[210] *Ibid.*, pp. 154–55.   [211] 310 U.S. 362 (1940).

same result." [212] And so it was concluded that an overassessment of property did not constitute a deprivation of property in derogation of any right guaranteed by the Fourteenth Amendment.[213]

Each of the foregoing cases concerned an alleged deprivation of property because of an excessive rate or the application of a flat rate to a piece of property which for tax purposes had been valued at what was said to be an excessive amount. The decision in the Great Northern Railway case seems to be a deviation from the general rule followed by the Court prior to that decision and since then, namely, that a court will not invalidate a tax statute merely because the rate or valuation is too high.

However, in the cases where the complaint is that the rate was determined by reference to particular classes of property or was imposed on only one of several kinds of property, the Court will find that statute invalid as a violation of due process unless there is some distinguishing characteristic which makes the classification reasonable. The mere fact, however, that one class of property is taxed at a rate different from other classes is not adequate basis for the complaint of a deprivation of property contrary to due process.[214] Thus the Court found no basis for complaint, under the due process clause, against a statute which imposed upon residents a tax of ten cents per hundred on deposits in banks within the state but fifty cents per hundred on deposits in out-of-state banks. It was said that the distinction was warranted by the difference in the difficulty of collection.[215]

In 1931 the Court, for the first time, was called upon to pass on the validity of a chain-store tax, the rate to be graduated according to the number of stores in the chain located in the taxing

[212] *Ibid.*, p. 370. Speaking of the decision in Great Northern Railway *v.* Weeks, 297 U.S. 135 (1936), the Court said that it was the only case embodying such a rule and that it was decided by a sharply divided Court; therefore, it would not bar the affirmance of the present tax assessment.

[213] 310 U.S. 362, 371 (1940).

[214] For instance, the Court found that the classification which subjected oleomargarine to a tax of fifteen cents per pound was warranted by the fact that this product differed from butter in food content. Magnano Co. *v.* Hamilton, 292 U.S. 40 (1934). But in the case of the Florida Chain Store Tax Law, which imposed a tax graduated according to the number of stores in the chain, the tax being reduced if the stores were all in one county in the state, the Court found that there was no basis for such a classification and therefore the tax was a violation of due process of law. Liggett *v.* Lee, 288 U.S. 517 (1933).

[215] Madden *v.* Kentucky, 309 U.S. 83, 89–90 (1940).

state. In the case of Tax Commissioner of Indiana *v.* Jackson [216] the Court held that the classification and basis for rate determination was not a violation of due process, because the "economic advantages of the chain store made such classification admissible." [217] Since that time nearly half of the states have enacted this type of tax law. The law of Florida which imposed a tax on the stores belonging to chains and determined the rate by reference to the number of stores operating in a single county was found to be arbitrary and contrary to due process. The Court found no basis for such grouping for tax-rate purposes.[218]

The validity of a chain-store tax of Louisiana was before the Court in the case of Great Atlantic and Pacific Tea Co. *v.* Grosjean.[219] The statute provided that the rate of the tax would be graduated according to the number of stores in the entire chain whether in the state of Louisiana or not. The Court found this a reasonable basis for determining the rate, for "If the competitive advantages of a chain increase with the number of its component links, it is hard to see how these advantages cease at the state boundary. Under the findings, a store belonging to a chain of one hundred, all located in Louisiana, has not the same competitive advantages as one of a hundred Louisiana stores belonging to a national chain of one thousand." [220] The Court held that the tax was a valid exercise of the state's police power and that a "proper and reasonable discrimination between classes to promote fair competitive conditions and to equalize economic advantages is therefore lawful." [221]

In this case, however, a distinction was made between the measurement of the tax rate and the measure of the tax itself. The

[216] 283 U.S. 527 (1931). See Hugh E. Willis, "Chain Store Taxation," *Indiana Law Journal,* VII (1931), 179–87.

[217] 283 U.S. 527, 541–42 (1931).

[218] Liggett *v.* Lee, 288 U.S. 517 (1933).

[219] 301 U.S. 412 (1937). See Beckman and Nolen, *The Chain Store Problem: A Critical Analysis,* pp. 256–58.

[220] 301 U.S. 412, 420 (1937). In 1948 the following states had similar laws: Alabama, Colorado, Delaware, Florida, Georgia, Idaho, Indiana, Iowa, Louisiana, Maryland, Michigan, Mississippi, Montana, North Carolina, South Carolina, South Dakota, Tennessee, Texas, and West Virginia. William M. Lester, *A Summary Comparison of State Revenue Systems,* Tax Revision Committee, State of Georgia (Atlanta, 1948), pp. 197–200.

[221] 301 U.S. 412, 426 (1937).

rate may, consistently with due process of law, be determined on the basis of all the economic resources of the subject of taxation.[222] The rate so determined may be applied only to property within the jurisdiction of the state.[223] In the present case the Court found that "in legal contemplation the State does not lay a tax upon property lying beyond her borders, nor does she tax any privilege exercised or enjoyed by the taxpayer in any other State. The law rates the nature and extent of that privilege in Louisiana in the light of the advantages, the capacity, and the competitive ability of the chain's stores in Louisiana. . . . in their setting as integral parts of a much larger organization." [224]

The rule that the tax rate as fixed by the state may not, within the requirements of due process, be applied to property outside its borders does not seem to have been followed consistently. The Texas franchise-tax statute imposed a tax on all "corporations chartered or authorized to do business in Texas . . ." and provided that the tax would be measured "by a graduated charge upon such proportion of the outstanding capital stock, surplus, and individual profits of the corporation, plus its long term obligations, as the gross receipts of its Texas business bear to the total gross receipts from its entire business." In Ford Motor Co. v. Beauchamp [225] the company contended that the tax deprived it of property without due process in that assets outside the state were taken into consideration in the measurement of the tax. But, as in the Great Atlantic and Pacific Tea Company case, the Court reasoned: "In a unitary enterprise, property outside the state, when correlated in use with property within the state, necessarily affects the worth of the privilege within the state. Financial power inherent in the possession of assets may be applied, with flexibility, at whatever points within or without the state the managers of the business may determine. . . . The weight, in determining the value of the intrastate privilege, given the property beyond

[222] Charles L. B. Lowndes, "Rate and Measure in Jurisdiction to Tax— Aftermath of Maxwell v. Bugee," *Harvard Law Review*, XLIX (1936), 756–83.

[223] In Union Refrigerator Transit v. Kentucky, 199 U.S. 194 (1905), the Court had stated that extraterritorial property could not be considered in the measure of a domiciliary tax. The rule was restated in Frick v. Pennsylvania, 268 U.S. 473 (1925).

[224] 301 U.S. 412, 425 (1937).   [225] 308 U.S. 331 (1939).

the boundaries is but a recognition of the very real effect its existence has upon the value of the privilege granted within the taxing state." [226] Thus, the Court held that a state does not necessarily deny due process of law by applying its tax laws to subjects beyond its jurisdiction.

A much stricter standard under the due process clause is applied when a tax touches upon one of the rights protected by the First Amendment. For instance the Court has found that a tax imposed upon newspapers having a circulation of a given number deprived the American Press Corporation, not of its property, but of freedom of press, which is within the protection of the due process clause of the Fourteenth Amendment.[227] "The tax here involved is bad not because it takes money from the pockets of the appellee. . . . It is bad because, in the light of its history and its present setting, it is seen to be a deliberate and calculated device in the guise of a tax to limit the circulation of information to which the public is entitled in virtue of the constitutional guarantees." [228] There was no complaint that the rate or the measure of the tax had been made by reference to subjects beyond the borders of the state. However, the basis of the measurement was found to violate due process of law because it imposed a previous restraint upon the company's freedom of press.[229]

On the basis of the decisions to the present, it may be assumed that it is a "settled" doctrine of the Court that an excessive tax rate is not ground for invalidating a tax statute under the due process clause. The state is free, so far as due process is concerned, to raise its tax rate and/or its assessed values so as to obtain the revenue needed. Unless the Court finds that the tax discriminates against one class or individual arbitrarily or that it is reasonable to infer that the statute was not intended as a tax measure but rather one to accomplish ends constitutionally forbidden, it will

---

[226] *Ibid.*, p. 336. Cf. Butler Bros. *v.* McColgan, 315 U.S. 501 (1942), in which the Court upheld the California Privilege Tax assessed on the net income of the corporation, although according to the corporation's record, the California branch store did not make a profit for the year.

[227] Grosjean *v.* American Press Corp., 297 U.S. 233, 248, 250 (1936). Snyder, "Freedom of Press: Personal Liberty or Property Right," *loc. cit.*, pp. 1–22, argues that freedom to publish involves only property rights and that that fact should have been recognized in this case.

[228] 297 U.S. 233, 250 (1937).   [229] See p. 10, *supra.*

not hold it invalid as contrary to due process so far as the measurement of the rate is concerned.

The state may be allowed to accomplish some degree of regulation by the exercise of its tax power. It cannot be stated as a rule of the Court that it will not look behind the act to the motives of the legislature and on the basis of the motives hold the law in violation of due process of law. In some instances, however, the Court has not chosen to inquire into the motives of the lawmakers. In recent years the justices have more readily considered legislative motives to invalidate regulations infringing personal liberties than those acts which impinge upon the property rights of individuals or corporations.

Thus as the tax jurisdiction of the state has been extended to subjects beyond the territorial limits of the state in the case of tangible as well as intangible property, the jurisdictional limitations on the basis of the measurement or the rate of the tax have practically disappeared.

Jurisdiction to Tax

The Court has become increasingly more interested in upholding the state's power to tax than in protecting the individual's property. In the early thirties the Fourteenth Amendment was invoked to protect the taxpayer from being burdened with two taxes on the same economic interest. If the subject was taxable in one state, for that reason it was held not to be taxable elsewhere because due process of law did not permit double taxation. This "new" interpretation of due process had acquired importance at a time of economic upswing when many states were not hard pressed for additional sources of revenue. Before the new theory of taxation had time to become a well-established doctrine of the Court, the states found themselves in a very difficult position with regard to revenues. It is possible that the Court did not give "logical application" to the "one thing, one tax" doctrine because it did not feel justified in withdrawing from the states the traditional sources of revenue at a time when state expenditures were steadily mounting and revenues decreasing. Whatever reason may be ascribed, the Court did not see fit to extend its limits of taxation of intangibles by one state only to fields of taxation other than that of transfer taxes.

The restriction of taxation to one state was not applied by the Court except for a short period of time. On January 4, 1932, the Court handed down its decision in the case of First National Bank of Boston v. Maine,[230] in which it was declared that the due process of law concept prohibited double taxation of intangibles. Less than six months later in the case of Lawrence v. Mississippi [231] it was held that Mississippi as the state of domicile might, consistently with the due process of law clause, assess a tax against one of its citizens on the basis of income derived wholly from without the state. Though this case did not involve double taxation of the income, the implication of the opinion was that both states might have imposed a tax. What the decision of the Court would have been had a case concerning the double taxation of the transfer of intangibles come before it soon after this decision must remain a matter of conjecture, for such case was not brought. However, the doctrine of no double taxation of intangibles completely disappeared with the decision in the Curry v. McCanless [232] case. Here each state, in its own right, was found to have the power to impose the challenged tax, and the Court did not limit this power on the ground that on part of the property two taxes would be imposed.

In the matter of tangible personal property the holding of Johnson Oil Refining Co. v. Oklahoma [233] was completely overthrown by the decision in Northwest Airlines v. Minnesota.[234] In the former case the Fourteenth Amendment had been invoked successfully to save the company-taxpayer from what was thought to be an unreasonable tax burden resulting from the particular formula used in computing the amount of the tax. In the latter case the same defense was not successful as against exactly the same tax situation. The home state was said to have jurisdiction to tax the full value of the fleet. Only the question of the home state's jurisdiction to tax was at issue; therefore, the matter of double taxation was not before the Court. Recently the Court up-

[230] 284 U.S. 312 (1932).
[232] 307 U.S. 357 (1939).
[234] 322 U.S. 292 (1944).

[231] 286 U.S. 276 (1932).
[233] 290 U.S. 158 (1933).

held an ad valorem property tax on the out-of-state trustee's "proportionate share" of interest in the corpus of a trust. Here the Court departed most noticeably from previous rulings by confirming the state's jurisdiction to assess against a resident trustee an ad valorem property tax upon a trust situated in another state.

Not since the decision in Connecticut General Life Insurance Co. *v.* Johnson [235] in 1938 has the Court, on jurisdictional grounds, held a state tax statute invalid as depriving the taxpayer of his property without due process of law. The rule in this case has not been cited in invalidating other state statutes, though there have been several cases the facts of which logically might have been interpreted as falling within the prohibition of the decision. It was specifically held not to apply in several such cases. For instance in Wisconsin *v.* J. C. Penney Co.[236] the Court made a distinction on the basis of the facts, though four of the justices dissented, arguing that the tax questioned should have been invalidated on the basis of that decision. It appears that the Court has been more concerned with placing as few impediments as possible in the path of the states' taxing power than with the protection of the individual from a burdensome tax.

The Court has reversed itself with regard to the theories on which the imposition of a tax may be justified. In the early thirties it was held that multiple taxation was bad in its economic effects. The system of double taxation was said to be undesirable, for it disturbed the good relations between the states and placed an unreasonable burden on the taxpayer. This was said to be "unjust" and was held to be prohibited by the due process of law concept. Regardless of the relation of the tax subject to the taxing state, the power or jurisdiction of the state to tax was said to depend on the power of another state to tax the same subject. Whichever state was held to have the prior right to tax was said to have jurisdiction to tax. *Ipso facto* the second state was denied jurisdiction.

In Lawrence *v.* Mississippi,[237] 1932, however, the injustice which might have befallen the individual were a second tax assessed against his income derived from work in Tennessee received no attention. The Court may have considered the fact that at that

---

[235] 303 U.S. 77 (1938).   [236] 311 U.S. 435 (1940).
[237] 286 U.S. 276 (1932).

time Tennessee did not have an income tax. Nevertheless, the basis on which the out-of-state income was held to be taxable in the state of domocile was that the individual pays for the privilege of receiving and enjoying the income there and for the benefits derived from the laws of the state. The theory that if the state offers protection and benefits it may impose a tax was revived. This left the Court free to determine whether such benefits were bestowed by the taxing state. The criterion was held to be applicable to any type of tax on any kind of property. In the case of real property, only the state in which the property is located is in a position to afford protection necessary to confer jurisdiction to tax. In the case of tangible personal property a formula intended to measure adequately the benefits in relation to the property permanently within the state was held to be the proper method of determining the extent of the state's taxing power. This rule was completely upset by the recent Northwest Airlines Corporation case, in which it was held that the home state could tax the entire fleet in spite of the fact that other states may have bestowed protection and benefits. The decision in that case, however, turned on the assumption that regardless of the benefits bestowed by other states, the home state afforded "unique" benefits in return for which it could demand a property tax measured by reference to the full value of the corporation's movable property which was within the state during the year. The state which gives validity to the paper evidences of an obligation or to property rights or has made possible the invocation of its laws to enforce such right is said to have jurisdiction to tax. This would mean that in the field of intangibles the possibility of double taxation is always present.

The theory that protection and benefit to his property placed the individual within the jurisdiction of the state for purposes of taxation was dovetailed with the theory that control over the person of the owner gave the state jurisdiction to tax. By a rather gradual extension of these two theories to enable the state to take jurisdiction when there appeared to be a reasonable relation between the subject of taxation and the benefits and control, the jurisdiction of the state has become almost unlimited; for, in short, the Court holds that the test is whether the state has given something for which it can ask a return or whether it is in a position to give something, if requested, for which it may exact a return.

The rule that the state may not, within the meaning of the due process of law clause, tax an object or event beyond its jurisdiction holds today. But the change in the Court's interpretation of the term "jurisdiction" seems to have rendered that limitation almost meaningless. The Court has held that the state's tax jurisdiction is not limited to objects or events within its borders. The domiciliary state may tax the income of a citizen even though it is derived from sources wholly outside the state. It may tax its residents on the basis of the transfer of intangibles located in another state as well as the transfer of intangibles situated within the state but belonging to residents of another state. The implication in the decision in Pearson v. McGraw [238] is that this same rule would apply in the case of the transfer of tangible property as well. The Court has not, however, followed up that particular part of the Pearson case, and so it is impossible to say what the ruling would be if the issue were actually presented.

In several recent cases the Court has extended the tax jurisdiction to subjects actually bearing a very slight relation to the state but which might serve as a basis for taxation. Wisconsin was upheld in levying a tax on the "privilege of declaring and receiving dividends" from earnings made possible by the state. The tax was ultimately one on the out-of-state stockholder, as the corporation was allowed to deduct the amount of the tax from the funds set aside to pay dividends. In a later case the Court expressly said that it found no objection to the state's passing the burden of the tax to shareholders domiciled in other states, since the shareholders would be the ultimate beneficiaries of the company's business in the state. Rhode Island was said to be "ready, willing, and capable" of conferring benefits, if asked to do so.

The state may, consistently with due process, tax sales completed outside its territorial bounds. Delivery within the state was said to confer jurisdiction regardless of where the sale was actually made. With the application of this theory double taxation per se can no longer be held in violation of due process of law. The Court has expressly declared that the due process clause of the Four-

[238] 308 U.S. 313 (1939).

teenth Amendment no more forbids double taxation than the doubling of the tax in one state.

With regard to the rate of the tax to be imposed, it seems to be the accepted doctrine of the Court at present that a tax statute will not be held to violate due process merely because the rate is thought excessive. As long as the Court was of the opinion that double taxation itself violated the concept of due process, it held that the rate determined by reference to all economic resources of the subject of taxation could not be applied to property outside the borders of the taxing state. Such a method of rate determination did not involve the taxation of the same thing by two states. With the great extension of tax jurisdiction came an abandonment of this rule. At present, in the case of taxes other than those on real estate the rate may be applied to property bearing a legal or economic relation to the taxing state. The Supreme Court has assumed the task of determining whether a sufficient relation exists.

In effect the Court has held that it may look behind the taxing act and discover motives of the legislature which would compel it to overthrow the law as the exercise of a power forbidden to the state by the Constitution. On the other hand, it has expressly stated that it will not consider itself bound to consider such motives. If it is deemed desirable, the Court may overlook very obvious indications of the exercise of a regulatory power which the state would not be allowed to exercise through direct legislation. It appears that the Court has two distinct rules which it may follow. The choice will depend in large part upon the advisability of allowing the taxing statute to stand.

A tax statute is not a denial of due process merely because it is retroactive. Unless the taxpayer can prove to the satisfaction of the Court that his financial situation was altered in reliance upon the tax law as it stood prior to the passage of the retroactive statute, he will not obtain relief on the ground that due process was denied. Only once, in Welch v. Henry,[239] has the Court upheld a tax levy applied retroactively more than one year. The length of the time of retroactivity was stressed in United States v. Hudson.[240]

[239] 305 U.S. 134 (1938).   [240] 299 U.S. 498 (1937).

Due process of law imposes few restrictions upon the national taxing power. The Court has held that there are no restrictions with regard to the rate by which the tax is measured. So far as due process is concerned, it may be imposed upon any person or property situated in the United States. Congress may use the taxing power as a sanction for the enforcement of any of its enumerated powers. The fact that the tax is actually a penalty does not necessarily make it a violation of due process.

VI

Due Process of Law, 1949

A chronological listing of the due process of law cases shows several significant developments in the growth of constitutional law of the past two decades. The shift from the more restrictive to the less restrictive application of due process to economic regulations began, not in 1937, but five years earlier in 1932. It was definitely stated in the fall of 1932 by one of the so-called arch conservatives—Justice Sutherland—that the Court would not override the legislative judgment of the necessity of a given economic policy.[1] While Justice Sutherland failed to follow his theory consistently, other members of the Court supported it; and in 1934 came the momentous decision in the Nebbia case, in which Justice Roberts declared that so far as due process of law was concerned, the state was free to regulate business in any of its aspects.[2] The 1932 Term marks an important change also in the application of due process of law to the conduct of criminal proceedings in state courts. For the first time the Court approved an approach to such cases which would require it to look behind the records of state criminal trials and make an independent determination of the facts as well as of the law applicable.[3] In the case at bar the right concerned was that to assistance of counsel and the standard fixed was that of a "fair trial." The same approach and the same standard, however, has permitted the Court to guarantee many of the procedural rights of the Bill of Rights as an essential part of a fair trial under the due process clause. And thirdly, just before the Court adjourned for the summer in 1932, it put its stamp of

[1] Stephenson v. Binford, 287 U.S. 251 (1932).
[2] Nebbia v. New York, 291 U.S. 502 (1934).
[3] Powell v. Alabama, 287 U.S. 45 (1932).

approval upon the state's attempt to levy a tax upon its citizens on the basis of income derived from work in another state.[4] Responsibility for a part of the cost of government was said to stem from the privilege of residing in the state and the right to invoke the protection of that state's law. And in 1934 the Court ruled that due process of law acted as a limitation upon the power to tax in exceptional cases only. Under no circumstances did it restrict the rate of the tax.[5] Within the decade these decisions became the accepted rules of the Court. The benefit theory of taxation became as fruitful as the fair-trial rule or the rational-basis doctrine with reference to other types of legislation. The freedom of speech and press had been specifically read into the "liberty" of the Fourteenth Amendment by 1931. The Court had very little to say about these rights in the early thirties, for most of its attention was commanded by the economic crisis.

From the Court's opinions between 1932 and 1946 there resulted two distinct substantive due process of law concepts, one applicable to property rights and the other to private rights of individuals specifically guaranteed by the First Amendment and read into the meaning of the Fourteenth. Generally speaking, a majority of the justices during this period have held that our constitutional system does not require judicial protection of a free-enterprise, laissez-faire economic system. That same majority has, with few exceptions, indicated no acceptance of the idea that protection of those freedoms written into the First Amendment might be entrusted to legislative preferences. These two attitudes have led to a "new" constitutionalism which admits of a presumption of validity almost conclusive in favor of legislative action challenged as infringing individual property rights. At the same time, it holds that the mere existence on the statute books of a law which may be applied in such manner as to interfere with freedom of speech and press, of assembly, or of religion embodies a "pervasive threat" to their free exercise and so violates due process of law. Since 1947 a distinct shift has been noticeable. Though the change appeared first in the cases concerning state criminal trials, the deference to state proceedings and legislative

---

[4] Lawrence v. Mississippi, 286 U.S. 276 (1932).
[5] Magnano Co. v. Hamilton, 292 U.S. 40 (1934).

policies has carried into the fields of free speech and press and assembly.[6]

How has the Court explained this dual due process of law concept? The Court as such has not felt compelled to explain. However, in several instances individual justices have set forth the philosophical presuppositions upon which they make the choices necessary to the application of due process of law. For instance, Justice Douglas, speaking before the Association of the Bar of the City of New York in April, 1949, expressed the view that so long as the people are left to manage the social and political problems of the state and nation, there is likely to be long-run stability. "It is when the judiciary with life tenure seeks to write its social and economic creed into the Charter that instability is created, for then the nation lacks the adaptability to master the sudden storms of an era." [7] On the other hand, thought Justice Douglas, the rights of freedom of speech and press and religion are in a preferred position, for these are essential to a democratic society.[8] Therefore, the Court must make decisions as to the validity of particular laws which strike at the substance of these rights.[9] But the use of speech in such a manner as to exercise economic power is something more than the right protected by the First Amendment; therefore, the Court must reserve its power to determine when the permissible line has been crossed.[10] And again, with respect to the procedural rights guaranteed by the Bill of Rights, "due process of law" is a summation of the "standards of fairness and decency that the English-speaking world evolved to protect the essential liberties of the people. . . ." Due process is the "warp and woof" of the rules of the game of law enforcement. It is the distinguishing mark of our civilization.[11]

[6] See dissent in Winters v. New York, 333 U.S. 507 (1948); Justice Jackson's dissent in Terminiello v. City of Chicago, 337 U.S. 1 (1949); Craig v. Harney, 331 U.S. 367 (1947); Justice Frankfurter's dissent and his concurring opinion in Lincoln Federal Labor Union v. Northwestern Iron and Metal Company, 335 U.S. 525 (1949); and Kovacs v. Cooper, 336 U.S. 77 (1949).

[7] William O. Douglas, "Stare Decisis," Columbia Law Review, XLIX (1949), 735, 754. Quoted by permission.

[8] West Virginia Board of Education v. Barnette, 319 U.S. 624, 643-44 (1943).

[9] Ibid., pp. 624, 644.

[10] William O. Douglas, On Being An American (New York, 1948), quoting his address at the National Police Academy, Washington, D.C., October, 1944.

[11] United States v. Carolene Products Co., 304 U.S. 144, n. 4 (1938).

And Justice Stone said, as if it were common knowledge, that the presumption of constitutionality operates in more restricted limits when the legislation challenged touches specific provisions, as those of the First Amendment, than when it merely touches due process in general, as in the Fourteenth Amendment. This is confusing due process with what is protected by it. So far as being specific is concerned, there is not much difference between the quality of the provision which would read, according to Justice Stone, that freedom of speech must not be infringed without due process of law and one saying that property must not be taken without due process. But perhaps he meant what Justice Sutherland said in the case of Associated Press Co. v. National Labor Relations Board [12]—that the rights protected by the Fourteenth Amendment alone are qualified by "without due process of law," while those guaranteed by the First Amendment and read into the Fourteenth are not so qualified. Later, in the flag-salute cases, Justice Stone, now Chief Justice Stone, implied that justice and wisdom must be the test of due process in cases where the issue concerns freedoms named in the First Amendment, for these have been given a preferred status as fundamental to a democratic society.[13]

In 1924, Felix Frankfurter, editorializing upon the Coolidge and Davis opposition toward the La Follette proposal that Congress be permitted to override a Supreme Court decision by a two-thirds vote, declared that judicial applications of due process of law are inevitably determined "by the experience, the environment, the fears, the imaginations of the different Justices." He pointed to the Court's decision invalidating the state regulation of the weight of a loaf of bread as indication of the irresponsibility of the Court. And he continued:

> An informed study of the work of the Supreme Court of the United States will probably lead to the conclusion that no nine men are wise enough and good enough to be entrusted with the power which the unlimited provisions of the due process clause confers. We have had fifty years of experiment with the Fourteenth Amendment and the centralizing

[12] Associated Press Co. v. National Labor Relations Board, 301 U.S. 103 (1937).
[13] Minersville School Board v. Gobitis, 310 U.S. 586, 597 (1940).

authority lodged with the Supreme Court over the domestic affairs of forty-eight widely different states is an authority which it simply cannot discharge with safety either to itself or to the states. The due process clause ought to go.[14]

But fifteen years later when Felix Frankfurter became Justice Frankfurter, he found the due process clauses still intact in large areas of governmental action. True, he came onto a Court which used due process of law less restrictively in fields of economic legislation other than rate regulation [15] but with much greater potency in the fields of personal liberties. One can hardly avoid the conclusion that his decisions in due process cases have for the most part been directed by his own philosophies stated as early as 1924. Whether school children are required to salute the American flag in spite of religious scruples,[16] whether loud-speaking devices shall be permitted on the streets,[17] whether union members shall be protected in their demands for a closed shop [18]—all of these things are matters for the legislature to determine. Whether there are existing conditions which necessitate the extension of a mortgage-moratorium law must be decided by the legislature.[19] At times the question of the fairness of a given trial procedure is within the legislative domain.[20] But here, as with speech and press cases, Justice Frankfurter has left the door wide for judicial determination of the issue when he deems it appropriate. In his judgment the due process of law clause "postulates the authority of the state to translate into local law policies to promote the health, safety, morals and general welfare of the people." [21] He does not believe that the term "due process of law" implies a choice

[14] Unsigned editorial in *New Republic*, XLIV (1924), quoted in *Law and Politics: Occasional Papers of Felix Frankfurter*, eds. Archibald MacLeish and E. F. Prichard, Jr. (New York, 1939), p. 16. The *New Republic* is quoted by permission.

[15] The shift in rate cases possibly began with the case of Driscoll *v.* Edison Light and Power Co., 307 U.S. 104 (1939).

[16] Minersville School Board *v.* Gobitis, 310 U.S. 586, 597 (1940).

[17] Kovacs *v.* Cooper, 336 U.S. 77 (1949).

[18] Lincoln Federal Labor Union *v.* Northwestern Iron & Metal Co., 335 U.S. 525 (1949).

[19] East New York Savings Bank *v.* Haln, 326 U.S. 230 (1945).

[20] See Haley *v.* Ohio, 332 U.S. 596, 604 (1948); and Adamson *v.* California, 332 U.S. 46, 61 (1947).

[21] Carpenters' and Joiners' Union *v.* Ritter's Cafe, 315 U.S. 722, 726 (1942).

among the rights of the Bill of Rights.[22] Rather, every right guaranteed by the Constitution is a fundamental right,[23] and the power of the Court does not vary in intensity with the particular right involved. He has shown great concern over the maintenance of a federal system in which the rights of the states must be respected. However, he has not made federalism or states' rights an exclusive test of his decisions. He did not believe, for example, that the common-law policy of the state could, without violating due process of law, be interpreted to proscribe the right of labor to use peaceful picketing as a weapon in a labor dispute not involving the picketers' own employer. Picketing as a form of free speech was said to be basic to our society and the public benefit produced by it to outweigh private injury to employers. The state, however, might restrict the use of picketing to a narrow scope and might even enjoin all picketing within a context of violence which would endanger the public. "Freedom of speech" was said to protect "rational modes" of communication and "utterances in a context of violence can lose their significance as an appeal to reason"; so also, their constitutional protection.

Justice Rutledge maintained that freedom of speech, press, peaceful assembly, and the others named in the First Amendment had to be granted more diligent protection because they are indispensable freedoms in a democracy. A rational basis will suffice as defense of economic legislation challenged under the due process clause, but only a clear and immediately present danger to the state will justify a restriction of these basic freedoms.[24] He expressed the distinction between the two substantive due process concepts forcefully in the rent-control case, where he explained that though the results of the legislation may be serious, it does not require the scrutiny of the Court as if it were a restriction upon personal liberties. Property rights are protected by rules of procedure less rigid and exacting than are civil liberties.[25] The Court will pay great respect to legislative policy when it strikes at property rights alone. However, Justice Rutledge assumed that the due process clause of the Fourteenth Amendment incorpo-

[22] West Virginia Board of Education v. Barnette, 319 U.S. 624, 648 (1943).
[23] Craig v. Harney, 331 U.S. 367, 394-95 (1947).
[24] Thomas v. Collins, 323 U.S. 516, 530 (1944).
[25] Bowles v. Willingham, 321 U.S. 503 (1944).

rated all of the rights of the first nine amendments.[26] But such interpretation was not thought to have withdrawn from the state all authority to regulate the exercise of speech, press, and other personal freedoms. In the loud-speaker case,[27] he concluded that the municipality could regulate the time, place, and manner of the use of loud-speaking devices but could not ban all use of such devices.

And Justice Black has held rather consistently that the due process of law clause of the Fourteenth Amendment was never intended to protect corporations.[28] Likewise, he has not assumed that due process authorized the Court to judge of the wisdom or reasonableness of legislative policies which are alleged to have deprived persons of their property without due process of law. On the other hand,[29] Justice Black has frequently expressed the opinion that by the due process clause the entire Bill of Rights, including Amendment Nine, was made applicable to the states. There has arisen no case requiring him to defend or refuse to defend such procedures as indictment by a grand jury or trial by petit jury in state courts. He does recognize this as a weakness of his theory, but he has managed to avoid a definite statement on the subject. He seems to have admitted to himself that there may be instances when protection of such rights could not be defended.[30] This concept of due process has certain advantages from the point of view of the judge's desire for objectivity. Most economic and social legislation is ruled out of the purview of due process, and Justice Black has suggested that it would be better for the Court to refuse to take jurisdiction in such cases.[31] It gives the five freedoms of the First Amendment a preferred status, for these are qualified only by the judicially attached clear and present danger test. Justice Black reads Amendment One as applying to

[26] See Adamson v. California, 332 U.S. 46, 71–72 (1947); and Wolf v. Colorado, 338 U.S. 25, 47 (1949).

[27] Kovacs v. Cooper, 336 U.S. 77 (1949).

[28] See Justice Black's dissent in Connecticut General Life Insurance Co. v. Johnson, 303 U.S. 77 (1938); and McCart v. Indianapolis Water Co., 302 U.S. 419 (1938).

[29] Federal Power Commission v. Natural Gas Pipeline Co., 315 U.S. 575 (1942), Justice Black concurring. See his dissent in Polk Co. v. Glover, 305 U.S. 5 (1938).

[30] See Adamson v. California, 332 U.S. 46, 75 (1947).

[31] Polk Company v. Glover, 305 U.S. 5 (1938).

the states rather than supplanting "liberty" of the Fourteenth by whichever of the five rights may be involved.[32] Thus greater protection is afforded these. Thirdly, Justice Black's interpretation of due process makes it possible to guarantee a minimum standard of justice in state criminal trials without reducing judicial protection to these only. It does not force the justice into a position where he must be ready to guarantee only those rights named in the Bill of Rights, for the Ninth Amendment anticipates the protection of rights other than these.[33]

These all too brief and sketchy statements of the seemingly underlying doctrines of only a few of the justices who helped make "due process of law" during the past twenty years are intended to indicate just two things. First of all, that judges, like other people, have preconceived notions of what they want in the way of a government and a society. They are frequently in a position to break down barriers which stand in the way of the development and maintenance of such a government and such a society. Fortunately the justices of the past two decades have held in common the desirability of a democratic society in which individuals are treated as individuals and personal freedoms are respected. Their differences have not been as to the ends but as to the means for obtaining the ends. Secondly, in putting their theories into practice through judicial opinions, they have been forced into positions equally as illogical as those of previous Courts.

The post-1932 judges have come no closer to an objective standard for the application of due process than did the many justices before them. They have replaced the old standards with new ones and thus have thrown the weight of the Court's sanction on the side of a different set of interests and values. As early as 1932, in the Texas relative-minimum-rate case may be found the beginning of a new approach to due process cases involving social and economic legislation.[34] Since that time the Court has read "due process of law" of the Fifth and Fourteenth amendments to embody the same restrictions pertaining to legislation dealing with

---

[32] See Bridges v. California, 314 U.S. 252 (1941); and Marsh v. Alabama, 326 U.S. 501 (1946).

[33] The Ninth Amendment says that the enumeration of certain rights shall not be construed to deny or disparage other rights retained by the people.

[34] Stephenson v. Binford, 287 U.S. 251 (1932).

property rights only. Underlying the vast number of decisions sustaining such legislation is the principle that not only are legislative bodies in a better position to determine the need for regulatory legislation but also that democracy demands that nine judges, appointed and with life tenure, not attempt to supplant the peoples' elected representatives. But in putting this principle in operation the Court has, firstly, appeared to withdraw as reviewing agent, and, secondly, substituted for former major premises a set of new ones even more vague and flexible than the old. Their flexibility has enhanced their values as tools in the hands of the Court. Freedom of contract, the doctrine of businesses affected with a public interest, jurisdiction as a territorial concept in the exercise of tax power, the fair-value theory in rate making—these have for practical purposes been abandoned. These concepts, each of which was propounded to prevent legislatures from tinkering with values dear to the hearts of a majority of the justices at a given time, have met with scant favor from justices who assume that if the people, acting through their elected representatives, want to protect different values, there is nothing in the Constitution to stop them. One cannot escape the conclusion that the values protected by legislatures during the period under consideration coincided with those of the judges.

Since Munn v. Illinois [35] the justices had held fast the "constitutional principle" that a legislature could regulate only businesses affected with a public interest. Depending upon the personnel of the Court, businesses were classified as "public" or "private," hence subject to regulation or protected by due process of law against it. When in 1932 the regulation of a private enterprise—private-contract motor carriers—entailed a distinct advantage to the railroads of Texas, Justice Sutherland led his conservatives, who before and after refused to vote in favor of legislative price fixing, to the defense of the regulatory legislation.[36] Justice Sutherland was as assuredly making policy here as the legislature which passed the law. The validity of the statement becomes more obvious when we place the Texas decision alongside the minority

[35] 94 U.S. 113 (1877).
[36] See Tyson and Bros. United Theatre Ticket Office, Inc. v. Banton, 273 U.S. 418 (1927); Williams v. Standard Oil Co., 278 U.S. 235 (1929); and Nebbia v. New York, 291 U.S. 502 (1934), dissenting opinion.

opinion in the Nebbia case. However, this was the beginning of the end of the affected with a public interest doctrine. That "principle," fifty-odd years old, was supplanted by the general-welfare rule or the rational-basis doctrine, which could be as easily manipulated as their predecessor but usable in a different direction. It is easier to find a reasonable explanation that regulatory legislation is for the best interests of the state than that a private business has suddenly ceased to be private and has become a matter of public interest. By such an interpretation state legislative power has been extended to the regulation of many economic interests heretofore beyond its authority.

For many years the doctrine of "freedom of contract" as read into due process of law had been an effective barrier against legislation regulating labor relations—employer as well as employee— or commodity prices. In spite of the high-flung "liberty" supposedly attached to such a concept, its application invariably worked in favor of the economic interests most capable of protecting themselves—the employer-owner group. The employer had great latitude in the wage he would pay, but jobs were not plentiful and the employee was not in a position to bargain for his own wage. In 1932 the Court permitted a slight inroad upon freedom of contract by sustaining a state law proscribing sales contracts which bound the farmer to the purchase of heavy farm machinery before he had opportunity to try to use the machines on his own farm.[37] But the encroachment upon the fallacious theory of "liberty to contract" was not significant until 1937, when Chief Justice Hughes defined the real situation which resulted from such a doctrine and for five members of the Court sustained the Washington minimum-wage law.[38] Freedom of contract was put on the defensive, and only then was the due process clause capable of protecting realistic freedom.

The theory that due process of law prohibited the double taxation of economic interests went hand in hand with the notion that jurisdiction must be located at some one specific spot and that therefore the tax subject could not possibly be within the jurisdiction of two states at once. A state cannot tax a subject which is

[37] Advance-Rumley Thresher Co. v. Jackson, 287 U.S. 283 (1932).
[38] West Coast Hotel Co. v. Parrish, 300 U.S. 379 (1937).

not within its jurisdiction, for such a tax is a violation of due process of law. That was and is the rule. The post-1932 Court has not changed the rule—it has made it inapplicable by changing the meaning of "jurisdiction." Jurisdiction no longer implies territorial limitations. It refers to a legal relationship which entails some benefit or the possibility of benefit from the state to the taxpayer.[39] Such an interpretation of jurisdiction has enabled the Court to pass favorably upon tax statutes without inflicting any direct injury upon due process of law.

In fields of economic legislation other than taxation, the territorial concept of jurisdiction was replaced by the governmental-interest doctrine. The earlier rule prohibited the state from regulating any extrastate activity, regardless of its effect upon intrastate affairs. The present governmental-interest theory withdraws from the purview of the due process of law restriction regulations touching out-of-state activities in which the regulating state has a substantial interest.[40]

In speech cases the clear and present danger test was expressly revived in 1937.[41] It was said, as if the Court really meant it, that the state was free to restrict freedom of speech, press, religion, peaceful assembly, and petition only when it could justify such restriction by a clear and present danger to the public which could legally be avoided by the challenged regulation. The trick is that the rule does not always apply.[42] Logically it would not be applicable to all forms of "speech" as the right is now interpreted by the Court. It can be applied to picketing as speech because of the tinge of economic coercion involved. It can be made applicable to the content of speech if accompanied by other actions tending toward violence. But it has not, nor could it reasonably be, applied to the distribution of printed matter or the use of loud-speaking

[39] Lawrence v. Mississippi, 286 U.S. 276 (1932); Whitney v. Tax Commissioner, 309 U.S. 530 (1940); Carmichael v. Southern Coal and Coke Co., 301 U.S. 495 (1937); and International Shoe Co. v. State of Washington, 326 U.S. 310 (1945).

[40] Osborn v. Ozlin, 310 U.S. 53 (1940); and Hoopeston Canning Co. v. Cullen, 318 U.S. 313 (1943).

[41] See De Jonge v. Oregon, 299 U.S. 353 (1937); and Herndon v. Lowry, 301 U.S. 242 (1937).

[42] Valentine v. Chrestensen, 316 U.S. 52 (1942), in which the right could be restricted because the leaflets were commercial. See Kovacs v. Cooper, 336 U.S. 77 (1949).

devices. At times the test applied seems to be "public convenience" or perhaps, as Chief Justice Stone advocated, "justice and wisdom" as seen by the judges. The clear and present danger test is frequently read to permit the restriction of speech or press or assembly "likely to create" a danger to the public. This may be a very dangerous criterion upon which to hang constitutional protection of free speech and press. Any protection of these rights embodied in the concept of liberty can be bypassed by such a standard.

At no time during the past two decades has the Court settled upon an objective standard for determining what procedures are guaranteed by due process of law.[43] The clause is said to guarantee a fair trial to one accused of crime. A trial, however, may be unfair for a number of reasons, and under some circumstances one procedure will be fair which in other situations would be quite unjust. But thus far not even a minimum standard has been agreed upon. Justice Sutherland in 1932 practically revolutionized the Court's approach to due process cases from state courts by assuming that the due process clause required the Court to go behind the state record and make an independent finding on the fairness of the proceeding. While on the record appeared the fact that counsel was assigned, extrarecord evidence showed that the assignment was ineffective. Though Justice Sutherland certainly did not say as much, a reading of the opinion leaves the impression that any person accused of a capital crime would need legal advice. Perhaps he and his colleagues felt that a gradual construction of due process protection in this field was desirable. He, therefore, cautiously and in the author's opinion, unfortunately, made the existence of the right depend upon the circumstances of the case at bar.[44] Two years later when the Court was faced with the question of whether due process required that the accused be present when the jury viewed the scene of the crime, Justice Cardozo built upon the 1932 fair-trial rule and held that the accused could not have profited by being present and, therefore,

[43] See George S. Braden, "The Search for Objectivity in Constitutional Law," *Yale Law Journal*, LVII (1948), 571; and especially the opinions written in Palko v. Connecticut, 302 U.S. 319 (1937); Adamson v. California, 332 U.S. 46 (1947); and Bute v. Illinois, 333 U.S. 640 (1948).
[44] Powell v. Alabama, 287 U.S. 45 (1932).

due process did not guarantee him such a right.[45] Justice, in the opinion of the Court, was done without his presence at the view, and nothing more than justice is guaranteed by due process. In 1935 the Court was called upon to decide if due process proscribed the use of perjured testimony in a criminal trial. In a *per curiam* opinion the Court held that the use of perjured testimony was detrimental to the orderly procedure which due process requires.[46]

In Brown *v.* Mississippi,[47] Chief Justice Hughes drew protection against coerced testimony under the wing of due process of law—not as a part of the Bill of Rights' guarantee against self-incrimination but as a newly conceived right. The Fourteenth Amendment was said not to comprehend the specific provision against self-incrimination. But due process requires that the state guarantee the "fundamental principles of liberty and justice which lie at the base of our civil and political institutions." Among these is the right to a fair trial, with guilt or innocence based upon reliable evidence. Such a trial would not be possible when conviction was based upon a confession forced from the defendant by physical torture. This meant that the Court must undertake to determine in each instance if the confession was voluntary or coerced. Thus by 1936 the Court had announced that the due process clause of the Fourteenth Amendment did restrict the state in the enforcement of its criminal law, not because that clause made the Bill of Rights applicable to the state, but because due process of law independently required that the state furnish every accused person a fair hearing.

Any assumption that a more definite standard would be propounded by the Court was forcefully set aside by Justice Cardozo's opinion in Palko *v.* Connecticut,[48] which is a masterpiece of verbalism. Here more clearly than in any previous opinion the Court sets forth the subjective standard which it will follow in the application of due process of law. The issue, that of whether the states were precluded by due process of law from subjecting an accused to double jeopardy, should not have caused any great

[45] Snyder *v.* Massachusetts, 291 U.S. 97 (1934).
[46] Mooney *v.* Holohan, 294 U.S. 103 (1935).
[47] 297 U.S. 278 (1936).
[48] 302 U.S. 319 (1937).

amount of debate. Justice Cardozo chose, however, to place due process on the very precarious ground of comprehending only those protections and rights which are of "the essence of ordered justice" and which are so deeply rooted in the "traditions and conscience" of the American people as to be ranked "fundamental." Even by this test, why was double jeopardy not forbidden by due process of law? Because Justice Cardozo decided that double jeopardy, at least as permitted by Connecticut, was "not so shocking that our polity will not endure it." Such a selection, thought the Court, evidences a keen appreciation of the real nature and implications of liberty. But it is within the prerogative of the Court to describe a guarantee as fundamental or not so fundamental. A right may be fundamental under "the circumstances" of the case but not worthy of protection under different circumstances in another, even though the facts appear to be comparable. It is almost inconceivable that in a civilized society the highest court in the land would go on record as saying that protection against double jeopardy is not a fundamental right of one accused of crime. Regardless of whether the procedure provided by the state law in question actually constituted double jeopardy, the Court was called upon to answer a much broader question and it chose to avoid the issue. So long as the opinion in this case remains an "authoritative" statement to be followed by the Court, there can be no effective protection guaranteed.

Whatever was left in the way of an objective standard for the selection of the meaning of due process of law was depleted to nothingness by Justice Roberts' opinion in Betts v. Brady [49] involving the right to assistance of counsel. In that case it was said that due process of law did not incorporate any of the specific provisions of the Bill of Rights. The protection guaranteed by that clause is a much more fluid one—a much less rigid rule than that of the Bill of Rights. Due process cannot be called in on the case until there has been a denial of fundamental fairness "shocking to the universal sense of justice," whatever that may be at the moment. Justice Roberts found that the "considered judgment of the people" was that the appointment of counsel is not essential to a fair trial in every case. In which cases could it be claimed?

[49] 316 U.S. 455 (1942).

Apparently only when the judges find that it should be. Justice
Black opposed any such interpretation of the Court's discretionary
power. Due process of law guarantees, he thought, the right to
legal assistance whatever the facts of the case.

The fair-trial rule reared an uneasy head in the Malinski case [50]
in 1945. Justice Frankfurter, in a concurring opinion, found that
the question was not whether the Bill of Rights had been violated
but whether Malinski had been given a fair trial. Did the offense
complained of infringe upon "those canons of decency and fairness which express the notions of justice of English-speaking
peoples" toward persons accused of crime? Such was the test he
would apply. Two years later he declared that due process represented the "consensus of society's opinion" concerning justice.
The clause forbids, he says, the states to permit a process which
is "repugnant to the conscience of mankind." [51] Although due
process, according to Justice Frankfurter, did not limit the states
in the formulation or administration of their criminal law, it did
withdraw from them the right "to act in ways that are offensive
to a decent respect for the dignity of man and heedless of his freedom." Later, he explained that due process does not reach the
specific provisions of the Bill of Rights and that it is not at all restricted to those provisions. It is broad enough to protect "ultimate
decency in a civilized society." Justices Black, Murphy, Reed, and
Rutledge disagreed with this broad statement of the content of
due process of law. Justice Black opposed what he called a "natural law" justice rule.

The Court seems to be drifting further away from any objective
yardstick for the measurement of procedural due process. In
Haley v. Ohio,[52] involving a coerced confession, Justice Frankfurter held that the due process clause comprehends all of the
rights which comprise the "fundamental notions of fairness and
justice embedded in the feelings of the American people." The
application of the law depends, says he, upon "an evaluation of
psychological factors, or upon the persuasive feelings of society

[50] Malinski v. New York, 324 U.S. 401 (1945).
[51] See Braden, "The Search for Objectivity in Constitutional Law," loc. cit.,
pp. 571, 585–87, in which the author points to some possible interpretations of
"consensus" as used by Justice Frankfurter.
[52] 332 U.S. 596 (1948).

regarding such psychological factors." Procedures followed must be compatible with the "deeply rooted feelings of the community." And Justice Burton added "the immutable principles of justice which inhere in the idea of a free government." Such principles are those essential to the scheme of ordered liberty. Recently due process was said to comprehend those rights "implicit in the concept of ordered liberty" and to be a "compendious expression of all the rights which are basic to a free society." [53]

By 1946 it seems that the Court had reached the epitome of indefiniteness in its standards of due process. The term had come to comprehend just those things which at least five members of the Court thought should be protected against governmental action. And, too, there had been just enough exceptions to the 1932 approach to these cases to leave the Court free to make the all-important turn back to the pre-1932 acceptance of the state's record of the happenings. The full import of this shift may be seen in Carter v. Illinois, 1946, [54] where Justice Frankfurter states that "There is . . . nothing in the statement of the Illinois Supreme Court alone from which we can infer that the normal requirements of Illinois law prejudiced this defendant or made their observance in this case incongruous with his constitutional rights." In spite of the many sources from which the Court might have learned about this defendant the facts upon which its previous decisions had turned, Justice Frankfurter did not know "what manner of man he was" from the common-law record. The Court held that so long as an accused was free to pursue his rights under the Constitution, "it is for the state and not this Court to define the mode by which they may be indicated." [55] This is certainly bordering upon the interpretation of due process in Hurtado v. California to the effect that the phrase refers to "the law of the land in each state. . . ." And further that any legal procedure which "regards and preserves those principles of liberty and justice [which lie at the base of our civil and political institutions] must be held to be due process." [56] But the Court is not willing to fol-

---

[53] Wolf v. People of the State of Colorado, 338 U.S. 25, 27 (1949).
[54] Carter v. Illinois, 329 U.S. 173 (1946), by a five to four vote.
[55] Ibid., 175.
[56] 110 U.S. 516, 537 (1884). See Tompkins v. Missouri, 323 U.S. 485 (1945); and Williams v. Kaiser, 323 U.S. 471 (1945).

low this theory in all cases. In Foster *v*. Illinois [57] it returned to the fair-trial rule and found that "under the circumstances of the case" due process required the state to furnish counsel.

Under such a reading of due process of law, the Court selects its rule from among a number of alternatives, all equally vague and general. It applies the rule to the indefinite phrase "due process of law," and the result can be protection or no protection without contradictions.

What then is due process of law? It is nothing tangible or concrete or specific. It is an "idea" or "concept," a legal fiction, if you please, which is the Court's most potent weapon in its exercise of judicial review. Its visible bases are to be found in identical phrases in the Fifth and Fourteenth amendments which place protection against deprivation of life, liberty, and property on a par. But the foundations of its present scope and meaning must be sought in the social, economic, and political philosophies of the nine men who sit on the Court at a given time. In the minds of the justices the term "due process" has somehow become an all-inclusive phrase comprehending notions of reasonableness and fairness. It has come to comprise the elements of social justice and liberty—liberty to do and have those things which the justices deem essential to the kind of society they wish to preserve or promote.

This, however, does not represent any drastic change in the meaning of the phrase. "Due process" has always meant these things so far as the Court has been concerned. The significant shift has been in the use of the due process of law instrument to support a set of policies different from those defended by the Court at previous times. The legislatures have been permitted to regulate minimum and maximum commodity prices, and rate making has been brought within the price-fixing camp. "Price" may be used to promote social interests, to protect what the states wish to protect, to make or eliminate competition when deemed necessary. The states are not hindered in their legislative attempts to help labor groups, to regulate employer-employee relations and likewise union members in their relations with nonunion members.

[57] 332 U.S. 134, 139 (1947). Chief Justice Vinson and Justices Frankfurter, Burton, Jackson, and Reed were in the majority.

The legislatures have not been hampered in their attempts to reach new sources of revenue, so that the state is relatively free to tax anything with which it has contact. For many years it appeared that these same legislatures would be unsuccessful in their attempts to curb free speech, press, religion, and assembly. By 1949 one hesitates to state any such rule, for there appears a slight hint of a new approach to these cases as well as to those pertaining to criminal proceedings in state courts.

There is no reason to assume that the due process of law clause will be less useful or less potent in the future than it has been in the past. The standards according to which the Court applies due process are no more precise or explicit than those used by other Courts. They are easily manipulated to suit the needs of society as those needs are interpreted by the justices on the Court.

SUPREME COURT PERSONNEL, 1932–50

		TERM OF SERVICE																		
	DATE OF APPOINTMENT	1932	1933	1934	1935	1936	1937	1938	1939	1940	1941	1942	1943	1944	1945	1946	1947	1948	1949	1950
Hughes	1930	*	*	*	*	*	*	*	*	*	7/41									
Van Devanter	1910	*	*	*	*	*	6/37													
McReynolds	1914	*	*	*	*	*	*	*	*	*	2/41									
Brandeis	1916	*	*	*	*	*	*	*	2/39											
Sutherland	1922	*	*	*	*	*	*	1/38												
Butler [1]	1922	*	*	*	*	*	*	*	11/39											
Stone [2]	1925	*	*	*	*	*	*	*	*	*	*	*	*	*	*	4/46				
Roberts	1930	*	*	*	*	*	*	*	*	*	*	*	*	*	5/45					
Cardozo [3]	1932	*	*	*	*	*	*	7/38												
Black	1937						8/37	*	*	*	*	*	*	*	*	*	*	*	*	*
Reed	1938							1/38	*	*	*	*	*	*	*	*	*	*	*	*
Frankfurter	1939								1/39	*	*	*	*	*	*	*	*	*	*	*
Douglas	1939								4/39	*	*	*	*	*	*	*	*	*	*	*
Murphy	1940									2/40	*	*	*	*	*	*	*	*	6/49	
Byrnes	1941										6/41	10/42								
Jackson [4]	1941										6/41	*	*	*			*	*	*	*
Rutledge	1943												2/43	*	*	*	*	*	9/49	
Burton	1945														6/45	*	*	*	*	*
Vinson [5]	1946															4/46	*	*	*	*
Clarke	1949																		10/49	*
Minton	1949																		10/49	*

* Justice named was a member of the Court for this term.
[1] Did not sit on the Court after October, 1939.
[2] Became Chief Justice in July, 1941.
[3] Did not sit on the Court after December, 1937.
[4] Did not serve on the Court during the 1945–46 term.
[5] Became Chief Justice in April, 1946.

TABLE OF CASES

The figures after the parentheses indicate the pages in the text on which the case will be found.

INDEX

Absolute rights, and coerced confessions, 270; and First Amendment, 95n.; not in property, 137. *See also individual justices*

Administrative actions, and due process, 273-339; and procedural due process, 321; and substantive due process, 320-21; valid for maximum weights, 168. *See also*, Administrative procedures

Administrative agencies, increase of, 274n.; and jurisdictional facts, 276; number of, 274; and provision for judicial review of findings, 335; status of, Frankfurter on, 330-31

Administrative findings, in civil liberties cases, 333-36; facts necessary for support of, 328; of good character, 334; and judicial review, 335; for licenses for solicitations, 335; presumption of validity of, Black on, 306; reasonable-relation test, 329; substantial-evidence test, 293n.; when conclusive, 293; on workmen's compensation, 275

Administrative procedures, affecting time of hearing, 323; arguments and evidence in, 314, 316, 323; Hughes on, 315; oral argument part of, 324, 325; regularity of, 325; require that trier must hear evidence, 315-16; use of tentative report, 315, 317-18

Ad valorem property tax, 352-72

Agricultural production, marketing, 123; quotas for, 122; retroactive quotas for, 123

Aliens, due process extends to, 178; and priority of nationals, 178

Assembly, right of, and closed-shop agreements, 56; and Communist Party, 19; Hughes on, 19; non-unionists and, 57

Assessments, excessive for tax measure, 388-90. *See also* Jurisdiction to tax

Beard, Charles A., on need for social legislation, 101

Benefit test, 366, 371-72, 374n., 397-98; and double taxation, 381-82; Frankfurter on, 349, 357-58, 359-60, 369; Holmes on, 342, 343n.; incidence of tax and, 373; Jackson on, 369-70; and jurisdiction to tax, 346-47; Murphy on, 366n.; and privilege of earning income, 398; and protection of laws, 397-98; Roberts on, 355; Rutledge on, 360; Stone on, 343, 344, 345, 346, 354, 362-63, 367

Bill of Rights, Black on, 407; Douglas on, 212; and Fourteenth Amendment, 210-11; Rutledge on, 260, 406-407. *See also*, Fundamental rights *and individual justices*

Black, Hugo, on Bill of Rights, 220-21, 225, 241-42, 407; in criminal trials, 261; and Court, 220; on due process administrative procedures, 329; on fair trial, 208-209, 241-42, 415; on expertness of administrative agencies, 333; on free press, 67n.; on free speech, 29-31, 51, 56, 80; on freedom of religion, 67, 70-71; on legislative supremacy, 169; on natural law and due process, 241, 415; on "persons" in Fourteenth Amendment, 373n.; on picketing, in restraint of trade, 52; on rate-making, 296, 306-307, 313; on right to public trial, 259; on right to work, 57; on separation of church and state, 82-84, 86-88; on state jurisdiction over foreign corporations, 376; on unreasonable searches and seizures, 266; on legislative determination, 407. *See also*, Legislative supremacy

Blackstone, William, on constructive contempt, 28; on free speech, 7

Brandeis, Louis D., on administrative findings, 329; on conservation meas-